The Woman's Part

The Woman's Part

Feminist Criticism of Shakespeare

Edited by
Carolyn Ruth Swift Lenz
Gayle Greene
and
Carol Thomas Neely

UNIVERSITY OF ILLINOIS PRESS
Urbana   Chicago   London

LIBRARY OF CONGRESS CATALOGING IN PUBLICATION DATA

Main entry under title:

The Woman's part.

    Bibliography: p.
    Includes index.
    1. Shakespeare, William, 1564–1616—Characters—
Women—Addresses, essays, lectures. 2. Women in
literature—Addresses, essays, lectures. I. Lenz,
Carolyn Ruth Swift, 1928–   II. Greene, Gayle, 1943–
III. Neely, Carol Thomas, 1939–   IV. Feminist
criticism of Shakespeare.
PR2991.W6   822.3'3   79-26896
ISBN 0-252-00751-4

To the memory of C. L. Barber

with gratitude for his nurturing, demanding support of us,
of other women, and of feminist criticism

Contents

Preface

In the early seventies, teachers and students began asking new questions about Shakespeare. Is Kate actually tamed? Should we join Cassio and Iago in mockery of Bianca? Why did Romeo leave Juliet behind when he fled Verona? Why do the strong articulate women in the comedies disappear from the tragedies? The traditional answers—that the author was bound by his sources or by the demands of genre or by the customs of his age—had begun to seem inadequate; yet most criticism offered no other responses.

Feminist scholars, working independently of one another, were addressing such questions, but only a few—Germaine Greer, Clara Claiborne Park, and Phyllis Rackin, for example—had done so in published essays. The women's movement was creating a new perspective on literature; yet at professional meetings, Shakespeareans were addressing feminist issues in informal conversations between sessions, but rarely in the sessions themselves. To encourage public discussion of these issues, Carolyn Lenz organized the Modern Language Association Special Session on Feminist Criticism of Shakespeare in 1976 and at the same time began soliciting essays for an anthology of feminist criticism of Shakespeare through notices in *PMLA* and in *Concerns*, the publication of the MLA Women's Caucus. Carol Neely, whose essay on *Othello* had already been accepted for publication in *Shakespeare Studies*, was among the first of the approximately one hundred scholars who submitted essays for consideration. Independently, Gayle Greene, who had been planning to edit an issue of feminist criticism of Shakespeare for *Women's Studies: An Interdisciplinary Journal*, became aware, after attending the 1976 *MLA* Special Session, of how much work was being done in this area and decided that a book-length anthology would reach a wider audience; she too began collecting essays. When she contacted Lenz and Neely in the spring of 1977, the three agreed to cooperate as coeditors of *The Woman's Part*.

Preface

Since then, the anthology, with the help of many people, has gradually acquired its present shape. In marathon correspondence, the three of us debated the merits of essays, criticized each other's drafts of the introduction, and discussed everything from the nature of feminist criticism to the use of commas. Communication with authors about their submissions and discussion with many others about the introduction, the essays, and the bibliography have educated us and improved the book. Our contributors, burdened with three demanding editors, willingly and skillfully wrote and rewrote their papers, revised and rerevised their footnotes, checked and rechecked their quotations. We are grateful for their patience and hard work. We are likewise indebted to Richard Wentworth, our editor at the University of Illinois Press, who showed confidence in the project from the start and who has generously and knowledgeably assisted us with it throughout. The appreciative, thorough, and tough-minded reports of the Press's two readers, C. L. Barber and Norman Rabkin, likewise strengthened the anthology as did the expert copy editing of Carole S. Appel. We owe a great debt to these people and to our contributors, colleagues, friends, and family, who have suffered and labored gladly with us throughout the long gestation of *The Woman's Part*. We especially wish to thank Martha Andresen, Norman S. Cohen, Jack Greenberg, Agnes P. Greene, Bill Greene, Jan Hinely, Ann Howells, David Kay, Jane King, John W. Lenz, Peter S. Lenz, Thomas M. Lenz, Wendy Martin, Frances McConnel, Wright Neely, Cary Nelson, Phyllis Rackin, Richard N. Swift, Paula Treichler, Margaret Dickie Uroff, Cheryl Walker, Joanne Wheeler, and Richard P. Wheeler.

C.R.S.L., G.G., C.T.N.

The
Woman's
Part

Introduction

CAROLYN RUTH SWIFT LENZ, GAYLE GREENE, and
CAROL THOMAS NEELY

It is as difficult to define feminist criticism as it is to define feminism itself. Our own understanding of the enterprise is pragmatic
and provisional, arrived at in the process of considering essays for
inclusion in this anthology. The essays included and the many
necessarily omitted have transformed our conception of Shakespeare and have taught us what feminist criticism can do. This
criticism pays acute attention to the woman's part in literature.
But it is not only and not always feminocentric, for it examines
both men and women and the social structures that shape them.
Such criticism may be written by men; female critics, even when
focusing on women characters, are not necessarily feminist nor
should we demand that they be so. Feminist criticism is more a
matter of perspective than of subject matter or gender. Feminists
assume that women are equal to men but that their roles, more
often than men's and in different ways, have been restricted, stereotyped, and minimized; their aim is to free women from oppressive constraints: "the struggle for women is to be human in a
world which declares them only female."[1] Feminist critics are
profoundly concerned with understanding the parts women have
played, do play, and might play in literature as well as in culture.
Looking at Shakespeare from this perspective, our contributors
see and celebrate his works afresh.

Feminist criticism of Shakespeare begins with an individual reader, usually, although not necessarily, a female reader—a
student, teacher, actor—who brings to the plays her own experience, concerns, questions. Such readers trust their responses to
Shakespeare even when they raise questions that challenge pre-
vailing critical assumptions. Conclusions derived from these
questions are then tested rigorously against the text, its myriad
contexts, and the explorations of other critics. One influence en-

gendering this critical process has been the feminist analysis of such cultural phenomena as women's subordination and marginality, sex-role stereotyping, female bonding, and patriarchal structures by Simone de Beauvoir, Shulamith Firestone, Eva Figes, Germaine Greer, Elizabeth Janeway, Juliet Mitchell, Sheila Rowbotham, Dorothy Dinnerstein, and others.[2] Feminist critics often draw implicitly or explicitly on such writers, and they owe an additional debt to pioneering works of feminist literary criticism: Mary Ellmann's *Thinking about Women*, Kate Millett's *Sexual Politics*, Carolyn G. Heilbrun's *Toward a Recognition of Androgyny*, Ellen Moers's *Literary Women*.[3]

Much of this current analysis and criticism, however, has focused on contemporary society and on nineteenth- and twentieth-century authors, mostly female, mostly novelists and essayists. Feminist critics of Shakespeare must use the strategies and insights of this new criticism selectively, for they examine a male dramatist of extraordinary range writing in a remote period when women's position was in obvious ways more restricted and less disputed than in our own. Acknowledging this, feminist critics also recognize that the greatest artists do not necessarily duplicate in their art the orthodoxies of their culture; they may exploit them to create character or intensify conflict; they may struggle with, criticize, or transcend them. Shakespeare, it would seem, encompasses more and preaches less than most authors; hence the centuries-old controversy over his religious affiliation, political views, and sexual preferences. His attitudes toward women are equally complex and demand examination.

As feminist critics begin to attend to female characters, compensating for the bias in a critical tradition that has tended to emphasize male characters, male themes, and male fantasies, four motifs are prominent. The critics in this volume liberate Shakespeare's women from the stereotypes to which they have too often been confined; they examine women's relations to each other; they analyze the nature and effects of patriarchal structures; and they explore the influence of genre on the portrayal of women. They may note, for example, that Gertrude and Ophelia are characters who have an existence and importance beyond Hamlet's perceptions of them. They notice how Desdemona, Emilia, and Bianca significantly shape the plot, themes, conflicts, and movement of *Othello*. They show that characters such as

Desdemona, Lady Macbeth, and Cressida are hardly the saints, monsters, or whores their critics have often perceived them to be. Like the male characters the women are complex and flawed, like them capable of passion and pain, growth and decay. Feminist critics also explore how productions, necessitating interpretations that limit the text, may stereotype or minimize women characters even more thoroughly than criticism does. Most contemporary films of *Hamlet*, for example, present a lascivious Gertrude, taking their cue from Hamlet's fantasies of her, instead of from an analysis of her decorous, bewildered lines. Productions often cut Desdemona's and Emilia's pivotal willow scene; Morgan's and Garrick's eighteenth-century adaptations of *The Winter's Tale* truncated women's parts more drastically by eliminating the play's first three acts and with them the powerful roles of Hermione and Paulina.

Restoring women to the plays, feminist critics call attention to the importance and intensity of female friendship in Shakespeare. They find that women's shared conversation, mutual affection, and extraordinary intimacy create a kind of female subculture apart from the man's world. In plays as diverse as *Richard III*, *Much Ado about Nothing*, *All's Well That Ends Well*, *Othello*, and *The Winter's Tale*, they delineate a female "counter-universe" that is a repository for styles, attitudes, and values sharply contrasting with those of the dominant male order.[4] But despite the presence of matriarchal subtexts, patriarchy seems to prevail throughout the canon of Shakespeare's plays. Examining its influence, feminist critics share some common ground with Marxist critics who likewise analyze the economic and social causes of women's oppression.

Critics in this anthology find that patriarchal order takes different forms and is portrayed with varying degrees of emphasis throughout the Shakespearean canon. In some comedies it weighs lightly: the power of the father or ruler can be evaded in a green world retreat or countered by the activities of the heroines. Yet at the conclusions of the comedies, the assertiveness of Kate, Rosalind, and others is muted as they declare or imply their submission to their husbands. Elsewhere patriarchy is more oppressive. Its lethal flaws are made manifest in the presentation of rape and attempted rape, in the aggressive, death-dealing feud of *Romeo and Juliet*, in the spurious manliness and empty honor that generate the tragedy of *Othello*, in the militaristic and mercantile values of the Greeks in *Troilus and Cressida* and of the Romans in *Antony and Cleopatra*. Many other plays as well reveal the high cost of patriarchal values; the men who uphold them atrophy, and the women, whether resistant or acquiescent, die. Although women may strive to resist or to correct the perversions of patriarchy, they do not succeed in altering that order nor do they withdraw their allegiance from it. Cordelia, perhaps Shakespeare's strongest woman, stands up to her father's coercion out of love for him and leads an army on behalf of his "right"; she dies a victim of a chain of brutal assertions of manhood—Lear's, Edmund's, the Captain's. In *King Lear* and elsewhere the extent to which Shakespeare aligns himself with patriarchy, merely portrays it, or deliberately criticizes it remains a complex and open question, one that feminist criticism is aptly suited to address.

Shakespeare's relation to patriarchal order is further complicated by the very different roles that women play in the different genres, another topic that repeatedly engages the attention of feminist critics of Shakespeare. In the comedies women are most often nurturing and powerful; as their values educate the men, mutuality between the sexes may be achieved. Critics wonder how much the male disguise of the heroines makes possible their efficacy, freeing them from social restrictions while subduing the threat posed by their sexuality. They note that in tragedy, where women are without benefit of disguise, their roles are at once more varied, more constricted, and more precarious. While in comedy, the heroines achieve their ends gracefully by playing a part, in tragedy they are condemned for acting, accused of being deceitful even when they are not, or relegated to the position of audience to male acting. Good women are often powerless, and powerful women are always threatening and often, in fact, destructive. And, as has been noted, the women in the tragedies almost invariably are destroyed, or are absent from the new order consolidated at the conclusions. Looking beyond the tragedy to the romances, feminist critics celebrate the power and fertility of the later women—daughters, mothers, wives, friends—who transform men, enabling them ultimately to incorporate feminine values. In post-romance *Henry VIII* and *Two Noble Kinsmen*, female sexuality is downplayed, and chastity becomes once again, as it was in the romantic comedies, a source of strength.

While most of the critics in this volume participate in some of the activities discussed—humanizing female characters, challenging stereotypes, analyzing patriarchal structures, exploring genre distinctions—they come from diverse critical traditions and employ varying critical approaches. Whether they explore the plays as historical documents, aesthetic creations, or psychological revelations, they find they must reassess not only the text but also the critical language and procedures they use and the traditions they have absorbed: the historical context, the sources and analogues, Freudian and post-Freudian psychological models, and New Critical methods and assumptions. They find that they must, in a sense, create a tradition for themselves. The selective bibliography, "Women and Men in Shakespeare," which we have compiled for inclusion in this anthology, is one contribution to this effort.

Historical critics, seeking to relate the status of women in the plays to that of women in the period, must struggle with the problems of how to measure the position of women in life and how to conceive the relationship between life and art. The proliferation of contradictory material on women in the Renaissance increases their difficulties. The recent research of family historians like Lawrence Stone and Peter Laslett examines the social, cultural, and demographic structure of marriage and the family in the sixteenth and seventeenth centuries; feminist historians like Joan Kelly-Gadol, Kathleen Casey, and Natalie Zemon Davis explore the relative position of the sexes in the period; a historical critic, Juliet Dusinberre, looks at the drama in relation to the prescriptive literature.[5] Such writers agree that women's position and attitudes toward it were changing in the Renaissance, but they disagree about the extent and direction of that change.

In *Shakespeare and the Nature of Women*, Dusinberre contends that as humanism encouraged improved education of women, and as Puritanism advocated marriage for companionship, opposed the double standard, and allowed women equal participation in its sects, women gained greater authority and freedom. Increased interest in women's roles and improved status is reflected, she argues, in the drama of Shakespeare and his contemporaries, which is "feminist in sympathy" (p. 5). These contentions about the period and the drama have been challenged, as has her claim that Queen Elizabeth's personality, power, and successful reign must have influenced the period's conceptions of women's roles and potential.

Feminist historians doubt whether the presence of isolated "women worthies" has much effect on the overall position of women or on attitudes toward them.[6] They argue that in the Renaissance, as in other progressive periods, women actually suffered a loss in status relative to men—that, for example, the humanist commitment to education for women was a profoundly qualified one.[7] Lawrence Stone's massive and much-debated contributions suggest gains and losses: from the Renaissance on, a gradual increase in affective bonding between husband and wife was accompanied by a decrease in the wife's autonomy, especially noticeable in the "restricted patriarchal family" characteristic of Puritanism.

Feminist critics of Shakespeare, assessing these preliminary, controversial, and conflicting findings and looking to the plays for corroboration or refutation, are forced to recognize the highly problematic relationship between life and art. The plays are aesthetic creations as well as social documents; historical data cannot simply be imported into them or derived from them. Demographic historians, for example, postulate a late age of menarche and a very late average marriage age for women (24) and men (28) during the Renaissance. But *Romeo and Juliet* and other plays imply much earlier puberty and marriageability. Shakespeare does not prove the historians' figures wrong, but his plays suggest how averages distort by rendering invisible the spread at both ends of the statistical distribution. Nor do the figures prove that Shakespeare consciously knew and altered the facts to achieve specific artistic ends. Literature, especially literature about love, is unlikely to trade in or to yield the mean.

Because the plays are literary texts, they must be seen within a literary as well as a historical context. Feminist critics find that comparison of the plays with their sources and analogues can illuminate what is traditional and what unique in Shakespeare's portrayals of women. Some female characters are humanized beyond the limits of the conventions from which they spring. In *The Taming of the Shrew*, Kate is liberated simultaneously from the rigidities of farce and from the narrowly stereotyped role of the analogous figure in conventional shrew-taming literature of the period. Gertrude in *Hamlet* is more opaque than the parallel characters in the sources, who are explicitly guilty— of marriage to the husband's known murderer in *Historiae Danicae*, of adultery during marriage in *Histoires Tragiques*. In Shakespeare's *Hamlet*, the precise nature of Gertrude's faults and the extent of her recognition of them are ambiguous. This ambiguity is not only consistent with the problematic nature of the whole play, but contributes to her characterization as a dependent, solicitous woman. It also emphasizes the stereotypical and fantasized aspects of Hamlet's misogyny as Kate's humanization exaggerates the farcical, conventional, antifeminist elements in Petruchio's shrew-taming.

As they explore the psychosexual dynamics that underlie the aesthetic, historical, and genre contexts, feminist critics find themselves in an increasingly close alliance with psychoanalytic critics. While many feminist critics do not find Freudian models of female sexual and psychological development entirely adequate, they make extensive use of psychoanalytic insights into male ambivalence toward female sexuality. Throughout the canon these critics trace a persistent theme—men's inability to reconcile tender affection with sexual desire and their consequent vacillation between idealization and degradation of women. They suggest how structures of male dominance grow out of and mask fears of female power and of male feminization and powerlessness. Critics differ in their estimate of how much conscious control is apparent in Shakespeare's depiction of relations between the sexes. Some claim that Shakespeare, at least in certain plays, exploits the disjunction between the male characters' fantasies about women and the portrayed nature of the female characters in order to question or explode sexist attitudes toward women. Others think it unlikely that Shakespeare's own attitudes can be so clearly separated from those of his gender, his male characters, his period; they see the profound fears of female sexuality and the desperate attempts to control it in the plays as reflections of male ambivalence rather than criticisms of it. No psychological models, no amount of data from the historical or aesthetic contexts, and no reading of the plays, however careful, can resolve the general issue of what relationship the man, Shakespeare, has to the texts that bear his name, or the narrower issue of whether these

texts prove Shakespeare a feminist, a sexist, or something in between. While feminist critics do not rule out such speculations,
they are implicit rather than explicit in their essays.

All of the writers in this anthology, of whatever critical
persuasion, owe a substantial debt to New Criticism. All use
techniques of close textual analysis to search out the woman's
part in Shakespeare. But the indispensable method is used in the
service of a goal other than, larger than, the discovery of unity in
the text. These writers challenge New Criticism's separation of
author from text, text from audience. The approach fostered a loss
of identity in authors, texts, and readers alike by isolating and val-
orizing the text; by underestimating the subjective perspective of
the individual reader and the importance of the social and historical context; and by minimizing the personal and political
implications of literature and criticism. Feminist critics now
employ New Critical methods while trying to restore female
identity to the texts of the plays. In this enterprise feminist criticism finds itself part of a growing body of revisionist contemporary thought—in evidence in literary, Marxist, and psychoanalytic theory, in history, sociology, anthropology, and elsewhere—
which brings into theory and practice content that has traditionally been excluded or minimized: the necessarily subjective
responses of individual readers to texts that are themselves richly
unstable; the interaction between text and reader, ego and world,
individual and institution, the psychosexual dynamics that lie beneath literature, criticism, history, culture. Like other revisionist
enterprises, feminist criticism struggles to free itself from the assumptions, the dichotomies, the styles of traditional criticism
and thought; and this effort itself, if it cannot entirely succeed,
can generate new illuminations.

Feminist critics of Shakespeare restructure their critical
heritage as they discover in earlier critics sensitive to the woman's part a tradition to which they may ally themselves. In particular, by becoming aware of the forgotten strengths and culturally induced limitations of some female predecessors, they
achieve insight into their own work. Anna Jameson, in *Characteristics of Women, Moral, Poetical, and Historical* (1832; in
some later editions entitled *Shakespeare's Female Characters* or
Shakespeare's Heroines), fluctuates in her attitudes toward her
subject. She decries the stifling education given to the women of

her day and admires the depth of passion and intellect in Shake-speare's women; yet she assumes female subordination and is un-easy when heroines behave in ways she regards as unwomanly. Mary Cowden Clarke, in *The Girlhood of Shakespeare's Heroines* (1850–55), creates for Beatrice an adventuresome childhood and enthusiastically depicts her courage, loyalty, and witty outspo-kenness, while Mrs. M. Leigh Elliott, in *Shakespeare's Garden of Girls* (1885), admires women characters for their passionate strong-mindedness. But as their titles suggest, both works praise girlish sweetness and modesty in a style that today appears effu-sive. Helena Faucit Martin, in *On Some of Shakespeare's Female Characters* (1885), affirms Desdemona's strength, courage, "war-rior spirit" (p. 72). Her own portrayal, presenting a strong, pas-sionate Desdemona, broke with the contemporary acting tradi-tion of a compliant, simple heroine. A fellow actor asserted that she "restored the balance of the play by giving her character its due weight in the action" (p. 61). But she has fewer reservations about Desdemona's dying forgiveness of Othello than would most contemporary feminist readers.

A more recent critic, Agnes Mure MacKenzie, in the pref-ace to her *Women in Shakespeare's Plays* (1924), announces a new and distinctly feminist approach to the topic (which is no longer "heroines" or "girls" or "female characters," but "women") by noting that her predecessors had the "disadvantage" of writing in a period when "the opinions of women upon themselves were derived not from direct observation of the subject but from atti-tudes toward it of the opposite and more articulate sex, which whether colouring their minds by insidious influence of sugges-tion or the more overt but more turbid one of contra-suggestion, was not altogether adapted to produce the dry light, nor always the sweet reasonableness, that best informs the truly discriminat-ing critique."[8] MacKenzie's preface expresses other assumptions shared by contemporary feminist critics: that women are a dis-tinct category in the plays and require more ample treatment from a new perspective; that they are "one of the main determi-nants in men's affairs" (p. xiii); that their function varies through-out the canon. Yet MacKenzie's harsh criticism of Helena in *All's Well That Ends Well* for her participation in the dialogue on vir-ginity and the bed-trick suggests the influence of her culture's prescriptions for appropriate female behavior. On the other hand,

some contemporary feminist critics influenced by their own desire to liberate women from such prescriptions may too much admire the boldness of the bed-trick while ignoring its demeaning
aspects. Reading their predecessors, feminist critics are made
acutely aware of how difficult it is to resist substituting new bias
for old, replacing one set of stereotypes with another, reestablish-
ing different but equally rigid gender distinctions.

Fortunately, feminist criticism of Shakespeare is still too
new to have established any orthodoxies; the essays in this anthology show great diversity of tone, style, attitude, approach,
and interpretation. They are alike only in that they avoid sexist
rhetoric, reject sexist prescriptive behavioral norms in the evaluation of dramatic characters, and explore stereotypes without simply transmitting them unawares. As they undertake this large en-
deavor, feminist critics strive to remain open to its complexities.
They must play—or read—the woman's part in their lives while
examining it in the plays and redefining it.

The multiple implications of the phrase "the woman's
part," which gives this anthology its title and theme, suggest the
manifold aspects of the enterprise of feminist criticism of Shakespeare. The phrase contains the assumption that women play a
distinct, gender-determined part in Shakespeare's plays as they do
outside them. The bawdy meaning of "part," exploited by Shakespeare, implies the importance of women's sexuality. Women's
parts are social as well as sexual, and they may be false—roles
adopted to deceive or inflicted by the dominant patriarchal culture. They make up but one portion of a whole and must be understood in relation to that whole. Although examining that
larger picture, feminist criticism is avowedly partisan; it takes
the woman's part. Ultimately, the woman's part eludes definition, since feminine characteristics, like masculine ones, are
changing cultural constructs and are not limited to females.

Both Shakespearean sources of the phrase "the woman's
part" serve to break down boundaries between male and female.
The first occurrence, spoken in an early comedy by a woman disguised as a man, manifests the complex, indirect ways by which
women must define and express their identity, and suggests how
male disguise can both impede and facilitate the expression of
this identity. The second use, by a man in a late romance, rever-
berates through the most extreme statement of misogyny in the

Shakespearean canon and suggests how profoundly male identity is bound up with attitudes toward and relations with women.

In *The Two Gentlemen of Verona*, Julia, disguised as a page, invents for her rival, Silvia (now pursued by Julia's fiancé, Proteus), a story that describes her apparent male self playing "the woman's part" in the clothes of her real female self. The layers insulating this story from reality enable her to reveal herself through her disguise, to express her deep grief at being abandoned, and to engender a sympathetic response from her onstage and offstage audience.

> JULIA.   at Pentecost,
>   When all our pageants of delight were played,
>   Our youth got me to play the woman's part,
>   And I was trimmed in Madam Julia's gown,
>   Which servèd me as fit, by all men's judgments,
>   As if the garment had been made for me.
>   Therefore I know she is about my height
>   And at that time I made her weep agood,
>   For I did play a lamentable part.
>   Madam, 'twas Ariadne passioning
>   For Theseus' perjury and unjust flight,
>   Which I so lively acted with my tears
>   That my poor mistress, movèd therewithal,
>   Wept bitterly; and would I might be dead
>   If I in thought felt not her very sorrow!
>
> SILVIA. She is beholding to thee, gentle youth.
>   Alas, poor lady, desolate and left!
>   I weep myself to think upon thy words.[9]   (IV.iv.158–75)

Julia, by playing male and female, actor and audience, herself and not herself, shares with Silvia grief at male betrayal and female abandonment.

In the second source of the phrase, Posthumus, in *Cymbeline*, is falsely persuaded that he has been betrayed, that his wife, Imogen, has been unfaithful. He defines "the woman's part" in order to eradicate it from himself and recover a fixed autonomous identity apart from women.

> Could I find out
> The woman's part in me! For there's no motion

That tends to vice in man but I affirm
It is the woman's part. Be it lying, note it,
The woman's; flattering, hers; deceiving, hers;
Lust and rank thoughts, hers, hers; revenges, hers;
Ambitions, covetings, change of prides, disdain,
Nice longing, slanders, mutability,
All faults that have a name, nay, that hell knows,
Why, hers, in part or all, but rather all.
For even to vice
They are not constant, but are changing still
One vice but of a minute old for one
Not half so old as that. I'll write against them,
Detest them, curse them.   (II.v.19–33)

This vehement, doctrinaire, terrified misogyny painfully degrades women, but it degrades Posthumus more. The vices he attributes to women are, of course, his own. Later in the play, recognizing this, he recovers his faith in Imogen and hence in himself. She, disguised as the boy, Fidele, has had to come to terms with masculine faithlessness. At their reunion she fiercely declares her steadfastness: "Why did you throw your wedded lady from you? / Think that you are upon a rock, and now / Throw me again." In response, Posthumus affirms a new, but perhaps still limited conception of the generative part she plays for him and within him: "Hang there like fruit, my soul, / Till the tree die!" (v.v.261–64). Similarly, feminist critics of Shakespeare seek to recover a truer sense of women's parts and of men's. Enlarging our conception of relations between men and women in Shakespeare, we enlarge our conceptions of the plays, of ourselves, and of others.

NOTES

1. Juliet Dusinberre, *Shakespeare and the Nature of Women* (New York: Barnes & Noble, 1975), p. 93.
2. Simone de Beauvoir, *The Second Sex*, trans. and ed. H. M. Parshley (New York: Bantam, 1961); Shulamith Firestone, *The Dialectic of Sex: The Case for Feminist Revolution* (New York: Morrow, 1970); Eva Figes, *Patriarchal Attitudes* (London: Faber and Faber, 1970); Germaine Greer, *The Female Eunuch* (New York: McGraw-Hill, 1971); Elizabeth Janeway, *Man's World, Women's Place* (New York: Morrow, 1971); Juliet Mitchell, *Women's Estate* (New York: Pantheon,

1972) and *Psychoanalysis and Feminism* (New York: Pantheon, 1974); Sheila Rowbotham, *Woman's Consciousness, Man's World* (Baltimore: Penguin, 1974); Dorothy Dinnerstein, *The Mermaid and the Minotaur: Sexual Arrangements and Human Malaise* (New York: Harper & Row, 1976).

3. Mary Ellmann, *Thinking about Women* (New York: Harcourt Brace Jovanovich, 1968); Kate Millett, *Sexual Politics* (New York: Doubleday, 1970); Carolyn Heilbrun, *Toward a Recognition of Androgyny* (New York: Knopf, 1973); Ellen Moers, *Literary Women* (New York: Doubleday, 1976).

4. The term "counter-universe" is de Beauvoir's in *The Second Sex* (p. 511). The female communities in Shakespeare have interesting affinities with those explored in nineteenth- and twentieth-century novels by Nina Auerbach, *Communities of Women: An Idea in Fiction* (Cambridge, Mass.: Harvard University Press, 1978), and with those being delineated by feminist historians. See for example Carroll Smith-Rosenberg, "The Female World of Love and Ritual: Relations between Women in Nineteenth-Century America," *Signs*, 1 (1975–76), 1–29.

5. Lawrence Stone, *The Crisis of the Aristocracy, 1558–1641* (Oxford: Clarendon, 1965); Stone, "The Rise of the Nuclear Family in Early Modern England: The Patriarchal Stage," in *The Family in History*, ed. Charles E. Rosenberg (Philadelphia: University of Pennsylvania Press, 1975); Stone, *The Family, Sex, and Marriage in England, 1500–1800* (New York: Harper & Row, 1977); Peter Laslett, *The World We Have Lost*, 2d ed. (London: Harper & Row, 1977); Joan Kelly-Gadol, "The Social Relation of the Sexes: Methodological Implications of Women's History," *Signs*, 1 (1975–76), 809–23; Kelly-Gadol, "Did Women Have a Renaissance?" in *Becoming Visible: Women in European History*, ed. Renate Bridenthal and Claudia Koonz (Boston: Houghton Mifflin, 1977); Kelly-Gadol, "Notes on Women in the Renaissance and Renaissance Historiography," in *Conceptual Frameworks in Women's History* (Bronxville, N.Y.: Sarah Lawrence Publications, 1976); Kathleen Casey, "The Cheshire Cat: Reconstructing the Experience of Medieval Woman," in *Liberating Women's History*, ed. Berenice A. Carroll (Urbana: University of Illinois Press, 1976); Natalie Zemon Davis, "Women on Top" and "City Women and Religious Change," in *Society and Culture in Early Modern France: Eight Essays* (Stanford, Calif.: Stanford University Press, 1975).

6. The question of the influence of "women worthies" is explored by Gerda Lerner in her contribution to *Conceptual Frameworks in Women's History*. She takes the term from Natalie Zemon Davis's review article, "'Women's History' in Transition: The European Case," *Feminist Studies*, 3, Nos. 3–4 (1976), 83–103.

7. Susan Groag Bell, "Christine de Pizan (1364–1430): Humanism and the Problem of a Studious Woman," *Feminist Studies*, 3, Nos. 3–4 (1976), 173–84; Margaret L. King, "The Religious Retreat of Isotta

Nogarola (1418–1466): Sexism and Its Consequences in the Fifteenth Century," and Gloria Kaufman, "Juan Luis Vives on the Education of Women," both in *Signs*, 3 (1977–78), 807–22, 891–96.

8. Anna Jameson, *Characteristics of Women* (London: Saunders & Otley, 1832), 2 vols.; Mary Cowden Clarke, *Girlhood of Shakespeare's Heroines*, 3 vols. (London: W. H. Smith and Son, 1850–55); M. Leigh Elliott, *Shakespeare's Garden of Girls* (London: Remington, 1885); Helena Faucit Martin, *On Some of Shakespeare's Female Characters* (London: Blackwood, 1885); Agnes MacKenzie, *Women in Shakespeare's Plays* (London: Heinemann, 1924), p. xii. See the bibliography for recent reprints of Jameson, Clarke, Martin, and MacKenzie.

9. All citations are from *The Complete Signet Classic Shakespeare*, gen. ed. Sylvan Barnet (New York: Harcourt Brace Jovanovich, 1972).

The Woman's Part

Female Sexuality as Power in Shakespeare's Plays

PAULA S. BERGGREN

Despite all the ink spilled on inventing fanciful histories for Falstaff with Mowbray, Hamlet at Wittenberg, and the like, it is Shakespeare's women, rather than his men, who have most consistently moved his readers to a peculiarly cloying, gossipy condescension. No one, after all, has written a book on the boyhood of Shakespeare's heroes, complete with illustrations, nor have critics ritually agonized over who deserves to be hailed as the manliest of Shakespeare's men. Even worse, the contagion spreads from contemplation of his female characters to fatuous musings on their creator himself: we are invited to ponder not only Rosalind's happy hours in her forest of Arden, but Shakespeare's in his. A positively unwholesome curiosity about the author's erotic predilections springs naturally, it would appear, from a study of his women: we read of his "feminine" imagination, his bisexual tastes, his relations with his mother, his wife, his daughter, his mistress.[1]

In the wake of these deplorable critical fallacies, it takes some temerity to reopen the question of Shakespeare's characterization of women. Yet in the past few years a number of scholars have returned from the blameless consideration of rhetorical and

A shorter version of this paper was presented at a Special Session on Feminist Criticism of Shakespeare at the 1976 MLA convention.

structural elements in Shakespeare's dramatic poetry to a newly sophisticated investigation of his dramatic characters. While the time has happily passed when such a study must wallow in an evocation of the "real lives" of what J. Leeds Barroll has called "artificial persons," microscopic examinations of individual personalities may still profitably be undertaken.[2] It is not my purpose to do so, however, but, risking some broad generalizations, I propose to take a synoptic view of feminine character development through Shakespeare's plays, arguing that underlying his detailed, idiosyncratic portraits of women is one constant that unites them all: the central element in Shakespeare's treatment of women is always their sex, not as a focus for cultural observation or social criticism (though these may be discerned),[3] but primarily as a mythic source of power, an archetypal symbol that arouses both love and loathing in the male.

To begin, certain facts seem clear: although Shakespeare's women "live" on stage as the women of his immediate predecessors do not, they never achieve the grand and tragic dominion of the seventeenth century's heroines, French as well as English. In Shakespearean comedy, it is true, the heroine dominates; in Shakespearean tragedy, she most emphatically does not. Moreover, the women in tragedy seem to split into two basic types: victims or monsters, "good" or "evil." While Shakespeare drew on conventional sources for almost all of his characters, male and female, we need a fuller range of categories to group the men adequately: not just heroes and villains, but warriors, princes, courtiers; Machiavels and Vices; braggart soldiers, clowns, fools. Despite the fertility of local, imaginative touches that beggar our attempts to delimit, we can nevertheless perceive a fundamental distinction along sexual lines. The women in Shakespeare remain the Other; there are fewer of them, certainly, and they seem more regularly than the fuller array of male characters to bear heavy symbolic burdens. Furthermore, I would suggest, they become more or less crucial to the dramatic proceedings by virtue of the one act of which women alone are capable. The comic world requires childbearers to perpetuate the race, to ensure community and continuity; the tragic world, which abhors such reassurance, consequently shrinks from a female protagonist.[4] Such women as exist in tragedy must make their mark by rejecting their womanliness, by sublime sacrifice, or as midwives to the passion of the hero. We wonder how many children Lady Macbeth had only because she has dismissed them as an irrelevance in her life. The curse of the tragic world is to be barren; the salvation of the comic is fecundity.

It is a paradox, therefore, that the romantic heroines so frequently disguise themselves as boys, thus denying the procreative function that makes them undisputed rulers of their terrain; but like all paradoxes, upon examination this one reveals more than it obscures. At first glance, the male disguise acknowledges the shortcomings of the female: in virtually every instance in Shakespeare, the heroine changes clothes because she needs to present herself in circumstances where a woman would be rebuffed or, more typically, subjected to injury. Traditional female fashions are designed to hamper movement as traditional female roles hamper mobility; only an exceptionally gifted woman will dare cross the boundaries defined by both fashion and role. The disregard for these limitations underscored by the change in costume might suggest a radical criticism of society, but while the wearing of pants allows expression of a talent otherwise dampened by convention, it does not, in Shakespeare, lead to a direct challenge of the masculine order. Portia does not take the bar exam and Viola does not organize a search party; they are content to reassume their womanly duties (but we must ask neither how their husbands coped with them nor how many children they had).[5]

Yet it would be foolish to see the male disguise merely as an indication of the female's infirmity; clearly derived from the romance tradition, the assumption of masculine garb creates no lady knights in Shakespeare's scheme of things, but rather celebrates a flexibility and responsiveness that few men, in comedy or tragedy, can match.[6] Shakespeare's boy-heroines move effortlessly through their impersonations, despite—and because of—the encumbrance imposed by an actual change of costume. The disguises taken up by Shakespeare's men, on the other hand, are more often psychic than physical, demanding relentless concentration if they are to be sustained. The heroine, who can rely on her outfit to shroud her true identity, dresses up with amused nonchalance, innocent of the calculation typical of the masterdisguiser, the Machiavel. Disguise remains incidental, though useful, for Shakespeare's women; for his men, it is the very core of experience.

So extensive a topic as disguise in Shakespeare cannot, of course, be adequately dealt with simply as a sex-linked phenomenon, yet I think one can see easily enough that the woman's disguise alters her far less than that undertaken, for very different reasons, by either the plotting villain or the alienated hero. Richard of Gloucester sets the pattern of the Shakespearean villain's reliance on disguise. Like the chameleon, like Proteus, he cannot exist without it: when he is finally stripped of disguise, the Machiavel has no form and disintegrates, deflated, silenced, insubstantial. The tragic hero, who rarely initiates his "disguise," must yet endure the profoundest crisis on its account. At once self-revelation and self-betrayal, his false identity goes deeper than the consciously contrived dissimulations of the heroine or the villain, yet the full achievement of tragic stature depends on his return to the original heroic self, leaving the audience to wonder whether the insight gained through the tragic disguise continues to inform the mind restored to greatness.[7] Only the heroine seems to emerge from disguise enriched, however momentary our final view of her as woman once again may be.

The aimless and impromptu nature of the heroine's transformation confirms her identity instead of shattering it. Bent on neither devious manipulation of others nor frenzied interrogation of self, she simply activates the masculine resources within the normal feminine personality without negating her essential femininity. Thus she manages to absorb and retain what she has learned about being another sort of creature, for the female self in Shakespeare's plays rests on a foundation of purposes understood and accepted, a feature I would attribute to the sexual nature that gives her both roots and limits. The heroines are personally vulnerable, as are any of the non-villains who take up disguises, but they have a kind of faith—in time, in themselves, in biology—that anchors them, making the existential plunge into the self a short one. Where the tragic hero discovers quicksand, the comic heroine finds solid rock instead.

In the painful pursuit of self, Shakespeare's heroes may dress in borrowed robes, but they never assume a woman's garments. We can deduce a certain insecurity in this fear of seeming feminized; significantly, Antony, sexually the most mature of Shakespeare's men, is alone among them in having worn woman's dress. Still we never see him so attired, but learn from Cleopatra's recollection of their love games that she once decked him in her "tires and mantles" (II.v.22).[8] Nor can we explain the general failure of Shakespeare's men to dress themselves like women by citing their tragic seriousness, for a man in woman's clothes need not be embarked on mere frivolity. Euripides' Pentheus demonstrates how devastating an avenue for self-examination such costume provides. For Anglo-Saxon audiences, however, a man in travesty, as the term suggests, remains an instrument of farce. In a society where men are ashamed to weep, to appear womanly can only be a humiliation, but in avoiding any semblance of the opposite sex, Shakespeare's men cut themselves off from an understanding of the fullest range of human experience. Thus, while women have the power to confound men, the masculine world holds little sway over a female who has walked around in trousers (or doublet and hose) unchallenged.[9]

Whether they have dressed like men or not, Shakespeare's women as a rule maintain a remarkably disinterested view of the masculine physique. In private his women may laugh at the expense of ungainly men, as Portia does, leaving no doubt in the reader's mind that they will choose good-looking husbands, but Shakespeare rarely writes a scene that explicitly delineates female sexual longing. The awkwardness of charging a boy actor with material of this sort has often been cited, but, as usual, Shakespeare capitalizes on a technical stricture. The heroine in disguise is more likely to admire herself in her boy's costume than she is to praise her lover's bodily attributes. In this complacency, she wittily remarks the superficiality of physical attractiveness. Similarly, when a Phebe or Olivia makes a sonneteer's inventory of the beloved's attractions, the joke lies in her misapprehension of externals: the man she admires is a woman. No woman in Shakespeare, not even Cleopatra, thirstily catalogues a lover's parts as Romeo and Troilus do in their poetry of frustration, the last gasp of Petrarchan worship of the unattainable.[10] Shakespeare's women have it within their means eventually to fulfill their sensual needs and act rather than moon over rejection. As early as *The Two Gentlemen of Verona*, Julia, the first of the heroines in pants, deflates the pomposity of phallic show. If she must wear a codpiece to guarantee her disguise, it is no more absurd a sartorial note for her than for the up-to-date males who affect the style in order to stick pins on it (II.vii.56). She settles for what is "most mannerly" (58) in a pun that reminds us how often Shakespeare's women prove more "manly" than their lovers.

By obscuring their own sex, the heroines gain extraordinary access to the men they love, with the result that friendship validates marriage in Shakespeare's comedies. Consequently, when his heroines cease to adopt men's clothes, they forgo the rewards of friendship as well, and the comic world darkens. Helena's disguise as a female pilgrim rather than an adventurous boy signals a momentous shift in Shakespeare's treatment of women: "realistic" psychological development takes second place to a determined reification of gender. Because intellectual compatibility in sexual relationships becomes a luxury they can dispense with, the heroines of *All's Well That Ends Well* and *Measure for Measure* shock some sensibilities. Shakespeare does not impede their already tortuous route toward consummation by dressing Helena, Isabella, and Mariana in masculine garments, but seems perversely to force a showdown between holiness and lust by clothing them instead in pilgrim's gown and nun's habit, cloistering them (like Mariana in her moated grange) from physical contact. This apparent perversity, however, brilliantly exposes the shallow religiosity that presumes chastity can be achieved simply by hiding all evidence of sexuality: both *All's Well That Ends Well* and *Measure for Measure* insist that body as well as spirit may serve the divine plan.

The early comedies generally culminate in the ceremony of marriage or its promise; with *All's Well* and *Measure for Measure*, the ceremony itself does not suffice, for it threatens to become an empty legalism.[11] Helena and Bertram, like Angelo and Mariana, are not truly married, while Claudio and Juliet, anticipating their rites, assuredly are. The problematic nature of these plays can be sensed in their demand for physical confirmation of relationships to which they fail to lend psychological credence. Helena finds that she must draw on her womanhood where the earlier heroines are free to release their boyishness; the image of ideal love enshrined in the universally appealing Ganymede and Cesario[12] yields to the proof of physical encounter that only childbirth can give.

Like Helena, Rosalind boasts the twin advantages of disguise and an undefined personal magic, a source of power she must tap if a satisfactory conclusion to the riddles of *As You Like It*'s antepenultimate scene is to be found (v.ii.82–125). Even in this most confidently artful of the great comedies, an increasing sense of strain begins to tell. On her wedding day, as Rosalind conjures Hymen's presence to bless a series of unions arranged on an ascending scale of mutual devotion, a new physical urgency bids farewell to games. The intensity of Celia's and Oliver's passion for each other compounds Orlando's despairing inability to live by thinking: Ganymede the artificer must vanish so that Rosalind the woman can supply the fleshly solution the lovers long for.

As You Like It alerts us to the supernatural admixture that strengthens the Shakespearean heroine, but neither Ganymede's glib invention of an old magician friend nor the last-minute introduction of an actual god should deceive us into thinking that she needs outside assistance. Rosalind's sexuality endows her automatically with the magic she requires: Hymen does not condescend to save an impossible situation, but merely enhances a foregone conclusion. If anything, Rosalind uses him to cover her tracks, manipulating a minor deity as skillfully as she has everyone else. While the men with magic power in Shakespeare need external aids, the women need only be themselves to become conduits of extraordinary forces. In reaffirming their sexual natures they exercise the most potent magic of all: Ganymede must become Rosalind; Cesario, Viola; the Pilgrim, Helena. Disguise provides the opportunity for, but not the substance of, their authority.

After Helena, disguise rarely aids Shakespeare's women, since the creative sexuality it fosters no longer enchants, but repels, the masculine protagonist. A man who doubts the very value of existence cannot spare the energy required to appreciate delicate ambivalence. The loathing of the flesh variously spat out by a Lear, Hamlet, Timon, or Posthumus represents a coarsened sexual sensibility that blames life's ills on a force outside oneself and beyond male comprehension. The same drive toward procreation that enriches female personality in the comedies expunges it in the tragedies: "Down from the waist they are Centaurs, / Though women all above" (*Lear*, IV.vi.126–27). Precisely their lack of clear motivation points to the importance of these woman-hating speeches of disgust. In a malign world, the perceived source of life best deserves to be attacked.

The climate of masculine prudery which seeks to deny male complicity in the "act of darkness" is inhospitable to nubile women, accounting in large measure for the powerlessness of the female in Shakespearean tragedy. As Barroll points out, even romantic heroines like Juliet and Desdemona are really "well-behaved ingenues";[13] young women in these plays must be desexualized. Cordelia (whom one might call the ultimate "ingenue" of Shakespeare's middle period) is never allowed the seductiveness that leads Ophelia to an equivocal madness and Desdemona to the double entendre of death between her wedding sheets. In a way, Desdemona's progress through *Othello* is a more leisurely and explicit version of Cordelia's virtual canonization. The full-blooded, courageous bride of Act I, the witty yet reserved Venetian lady of Act II, flowers into the womanly warrior who greets Othello after the storm but then must slough off her joyous sensuality to become the naïve innocent who counters Emilia's worldly venality in Act IV: rather than temper her husband's fury with a sexual invitation in Act V, Desdemona prays. Cordelia's womanliness, totally stylized, finds its only expression in her disembodied voice, "soft, / Gentle and low" (v.iii.272–73).

Lear's three daughters in effect sum up the Manichaean view of female sensuality in Shakespeare's high tragic world: if not Cordelia, then Goneril and Regan. After blessing them at first with the natural abundance embodied in "plenteous rivers and wide-skirted meads" (i.i.65), King Lear reverses his promise to Goneril and Regan, bidding Nature instead "dry up [their] organs of increase" (i.iv.288). They consequently manifest that depraved and nonprocreative lasciviousness that the sonnets attribute to the Dark Lady; indeed, evil in Shakespearean women seems to grow from a sexuality so out of tune with its procreative potential that it breeds villainy rather than children. When female lechery is not actually sterile, its progeny is malignant: from Tamora to Cymbeline's Queen, the impulse to destroy passes inevitably from dissatisfied mother to dissatisfied son. Even the complex women of the major tragic phase suffer from an excess of libidinal energies that neither marriage nor motherhood can channel. Purgative transvestism might have done wonders for Goneril, Lady

Macbeth, and Volumnia, but no outlets for safety-valve experimentation of this sort exist in the rigid masculine world of Shakespearean tragedy.[14]

Only Cleopatra relaxes this rigidity, symbolized in *Antony and Cleopatra* by the cold calculation of Rome, because she can put on Antony's sword, experience the trials of the masculine ruler, and renew her femininity at the last—the formula for the comic heroine restated in grander terms. Like the comic heroines, she enters a maternal phase in her final moments. Antony's botched suicide, his suggestive inaccuracy in the placing of his sword, is redeemed as Cleopatra takes the asp to her breast, mothering it like the stupendous vision of Antony to which she gives birth in her dialogue with Dolabella. She augments the imaginative generosity of the Desdemonas and Cordelias who, cherishing a vision of the men they love at their best, have died to perpetuate it; the "ingenue" tragic heroines spur on the men who survive them to a glory of self-delivery (Hamlet leaping into Ophelia's grave, Othello pulling out his weapon, Lear with his looking glass), while Cleopatra encompasses both the ultimate death and the glorification. In an important anticipation of the matriarchal final romances, Antony's fourth-act death leaves to Cleopatra the heretofore masculine prerogatives of the fifth.

In his last moments, the flawed Shakespearean protagonist converts himself into the tragic redeemer by sheer will; whether we call it self-realization or cheering oneself up, his transformation remains solipsistic, its price being death. The final plays enlarge this movement toward salvation by removing the sting: in place of the tragic sacrifice that leaves the world as much impoverished as redeemed, they substitute a promise of cosmic regeneration. Like Rosalind (and all the disguised heroines) a forerunner of the openly magical conciliators led by Prospero, Cleopatra, the first of Shakespeare's characters to be freed from the restraints imposed by the material world, prefigures a great aesthetic shift.[15] Nursing the asp, voluptuous even as she prepares to die, Cleopatra assumes a posture that apparently was a medieval emblem of the dull earth.[16] Yet at the last this enchanting queen triumphs over physical nature, readjusts the elements themselves, and sublimates herself into fire and air (v.ii.288–89).

Although Cleopatra sits grandly in maternal posture as she dies, performing a rite of translation to a higher realm, a ritual rebirth like that of her gods, this rebirth remains metaphor. Rebirth as miracle and as physical accomplishment becomes the frank subject matter of the last plays, which reinstate maternity as the primal fact that justifies the ways of God to men.[17] The late plays confront again the misogynistic fears that cloud the tragedies, but resolve them with their paired mothers and daughters. The victim's death endured by Cordelia and Desdemona is here undergone by Thaisa and Hermione, but only provisionally, while their daughters clarify the merits of the mothers and prepare the repentant husbands and fathers for their return.

Incest, which haunts the fathers in the last plays, is the obverse of misogyny: it reveals the narcissism underlying the vilification of the female that Shakespeare's tragic heroes so arbitrarily indulge in.[18] When men revile women, they cry out against their own failures, hating themselves for what women "tempt" them to; women, by contrast, curse men for external, verifiable wrongs against them. Women resent men for oppressing them, while men despise women for reminding them that they are creatures of the flesh. If a man can accept himself in this state, the false reassurance of personal worth that incest seems to promise holds no power over him. Thus, in refraining from the incestuous coupling with his own child, the Shakespearean father reestablishes his own sense of dignity and restraint, so that he once again deserves the company of his wife. This chastening process makes possible in turn the refreshing of the species by the next generation and weds the comic insistence on sheer physical continuity to the tragic achievement of self-purification.

In the tragic heroes, often uneasy about their sexual appetites, there is occasionally an anticipation of the riddle of incest which Pericles dares to understand. Thus the Fool castigates Lear for the obscene reversal of his relationship with his daughters; Hamlet, of course, transfixed by his mother, copes more directly with a confusion of idealism and desire. The women in the tragedies seem often to excite illicit responses, yet even the most treacherous among them do not nourish incestuous longings of their own, perhaps because even the troubled women in Shakespeare accept their bodies' limits and claims more easily than do men. As the heroines in disguise are never physically aggressive, so Lady Macbeth and Volumnia, who might profit from disguise and chafe against the constraints of their womanly roles, personify them in their final appearances. In her nightgown, with her hair loose, Lady Macbeth resembles not only an undisciplined madwoman, but a frightened innocent child, or a seductive unsatisfied wife; she is caught in the web that cripples women in a paternalistic society and is doomed to frustration in any case, for the husband who is neither father nor lover is beyond helping her. More secure in her social niche, more massive in her presence, Volumnia may want her son's opportunities, but not (at least consciously) his body. Indeed, she throws her motherhood up to him almost savagely, equating herself with Mother Rome in an exaltation of the womb to which the bewildered boy-hero can only yield.

The mature heroines of the last plays, on the other hand, represent an ideal, curative maternity. Loved by fathers, husbands, and friends till a great crisis deprives them of all three, in serene self-knowledge they survive, ultimately to be "resurrected," not merely by reproducing themselves, but also by enduring tragic disharmony to emerge the more beautiful for having undergone it. The quasi-religious retirement they enter into does not disqualify them from returning to the living world of bodies. While this movement back into family life recalls the prophetic frame of *The Comedy of Errors*, only the final romances give us this expansive view of married women. Domesticity in Shakespeare's earlier plays bears out Millamant's sad recognition in *The Way of the World* that witty ladies dwindle into wives. One thinks, for example, of Kate Percy's carefully rationed outings with a husband she can still charm if only she gets the chance. The full equation of wifehood with heroism begins with *All's Well*; unfortunately, the Shakespearean husband seems the last to know it.

If Helena in her mysteriously sanctified determination looks forward to the fruition of the maternal type represented by Hermione, Imogen's career explicates the transition from the comedies' resourceful virgins to the romances' beatified mothers. The nineteenth century preferred Imogen to the earlier heroines because her male disguise discomfited her, but if she lacks their high spirits, she has good cause. Even before Posthumus casts her off, in the simple act of marrying him she has set herself within a framework none of the boy-women had to cope with. The tomboy vivacity of the unmarried woman does not become the wife, who has already narrowed her choice of the options that a Rosalind is free to explore. Nevertheless, Imogen's change in clothes prompts her to the insight implicit in Rosalind's and Viola's bemused appreciation of their androgynous powers, as all three learn that being a man is not as easy as it looks. When the disguises donned for protection expose them instead to unexpected danger, the heroines stand their ground as males despite the onrush of that stereotyped "feminine" apprehension with which Shakespeare seems to signal their forthcoming return to their true selves. More sorely tried than Viola faced with a duel or Rosalind with a bloody handkerchief, Imogen more generously expresses the sympathy for men that all gain through imposture: "I see a man's life is a tedious one" (*Cymbeline*, III.vi.1).

Posthumus, thinking himself betrayed, has sought to eradicate "the woman's part" from his being; Imogen, knowing herself wished dead, worries not only for herself but for the male reputation for honor as well. Throughout these last plays, the tragic predicament afflicts male and female protagonists equally, but the men remain more comfortably self-indulgent in their pain. Here too Shakespeare's works ask more resilience of women, and the women are able to supply it. Thus with marvelously egotistical humility, Posthumus suggests that "every villain / Be call'd Posthumus Leonatus," and keens: "O Imogen! / My queen, my life, my wife, O Imogen, / Imogen, Imogen!" When the disguised Imogen makes so bold as to answer his cry by identifying herself, the hero turns on this impudent "page," furious at the interruption of his showstopping theatrics, and strikes her: "Shall's have a play of this? Thou scornful page, / There lie thy part" (v.v.223–29). This heroine in boy's clothing lacks the power to fascinate a lover that the earlier androgynes enjoy. In his colossal self-absorption, Posthumus typifies the tragic hero, who demands compliant fidelity from women and little more. An extension of her husband rather than an autonomous object of desire, Imogen has chosen her disguise name wisely—Fidele.

As sole heroine of *Cymbeline*, Imogen combines the roles taken separately by mother and daughter in *Pericles* and *The Winter's Tale*. In her supposed death and apparent resurrection, she participates in the miracle experienced by Thaisa and Hermione, but their agony and rebirth more directly exemplify the woman's role as savior of the race through childbirth. Similarly, in the catalog of flowers strewn over her grave, Imogen's correspondence to the filial heroines of the other romances may be remarked. Less assertive than her younger counterparts, Imogen is appropriately the recipient, not the donor, of the bouquet; Marina and Perdita gather their own blossoms. In each case, however, the flowers themselves differ significantly from those connected with women in the tragedies—though events perplex Imogen more than Marina and Perdita, she never lets them defeat her. Thus floral passages in the tragedies are emblems of death and chaos, inventories of willows, nettles, and weeds. The romances offer visions of life-in-death: Marina, the unplucked flower, carpets her nurse's grave with brightly colored blooms; Arviragus sweetens his sister's rest with delicate primroses, antidotes to the wicked Queen's flower-based poisons. The culmination comes in the long fourth act of *The Winter's Tale*, which reminds us that spring returns to earth. Tragic soil breeds weeping willows, while tragicomedy regathers the flowers that Proserpina let fall.

The Tempest's island, though fertile with life, is not a horticulturist's dream. Caliban sings of brine pits and bogs; Miranda and Ferdinand play chess rather than dally in gardens. That elusive form, tragicomedy, admits of complication here: critics have long noted the distinction between *Pericles*, *Cymbeline*, and *The Winter's Tale*, tragicomedies, however divergent, that share a similar outlook, and *The Tempest*. For me, the contrast between the first three and the last of the late romances demonstrates succinctly the differences between masculine and feminine in Shakespeare. In telling opposition to the ripe overflow of *The Winter's Tale*, *The Tempest* is presided over by a magician adept at careful pruning. *The Tempest* itself has been similarly cut back. Its confines admit only one female character, Miranda, in whom femininity has been refined to the point of attenuation; herself a wonderer, she is more to be wondered at than understood. *The Winter's Tale*, in its greater abundance, has room not only for a mother and a daughter, but for a third heroine as well, Paulina, who seals the image of feminine power in the late plays. Like Cerimon, she preserves the maternal heroine, but without recourse to potions and infusions. Though her magic cannot be identified with her fertility, she has been introduced to us as the mother of three girls, sufficient recommendation in a world where boy children die of shock while infant girls survive far worse. Paulina's management remains so mysterious that even the audience wonders at her means, whereas Prospero's plans are engineered in our full view.[19] *The Tempest* seems an anomaly among the romances, a masculine stronghold where masques break off abruptly and no statues come to life. Rebirth here seems more a matter of sleight of hand than a dramatic embodiment of humanity's marriage with time. The taboo on premarital sex, an undercurrent throughout these explorations of sensuality's consequences and rewards, becomes the morbid preoccupation of a man who has known temptation, who speaks of contracts and warns of weeds.

Paulina as priestess arranges for Leontes' love to reincarnate his wife, yet she has made no provision for herself. Celia's generous support of the love-elated Rosalind deserves the praise it frequently wins for her, but Paulina seems to me the most selfless of all Shakespeare's women, ruthless in a cause that offers no personal profit whatsoever. In his fury at her persistence, Leontes calls Paulina a "mankind witch" (II.iii.67); the adjective perfectly encapsulates the spirit of *The Winter's Tale*, which exorcises the violence of masculine jealousy and redeems it through the kind of patience Penelope achieved. The tragic actor finds correction not in action but in passivity: Leontes has to learn the woman's part, by unknowingly emulating Hermione as if he had tried on a woman's robes, before he can find her again. In fact, the chastened Leontes learns his lesson so well that he works what may be the play's ultimate miracle. Excluded from the marriage circle that traditionally consummates Shakespearean comedy, Paulina prepares like "an old turtle" to fly to "some wither'd bough" (v.iii.132–33) and mourn her widowed state. But in *The Winter's Tale* turtledoves come in pairs: Leontes gives Paulina's hand to Camillo and bids the young yield pride of place to their elders. Thus fittingly Paulina once more leads the way, ushering the group out of her chapel back into a world of flux where even withered boughs may bloom anew.

Though another husband can be found for Paulina, no second wife could possibly warm Prospero's remaining years. Weddings in *The Tempest* rid fathers of fear for their daughters, but discord prevails despite them. The malignity of the flesh evades Prospero's intellectual solutions and spiritual lessons: the matriarchal figure in *The Tempest* is Sycorax, whose demonic powers and appetites bedevil Prospero in the shape of Caliban, who cannot be reformed. As *Pericles* and *The Winter's Tale* expatiate on the romance elements in *The Comedy of Errors*, *The Tempest* reaches back to the interlocking politics and witchcraft of the *Henry VI* trilogy. Female sexuality corrupts in this final statement as in the first; natural impulses must be straitened and rationalized. "Earth's increase" takes the form of a harvest prudently stored in barns and garners. Cupid breaks his arrows as Prospero his staff; masculine potency has limits no fourteen-year-old daughter can restore.[20] Prospero's magic exhausts itself: like the tragic hero, he uses himself up. In Shakespeare's world, only the woman, sometimes witch, sometimes saint, sometimes mother, commands the innate energy that renews and revives.

NOTES

1. The studies of Shakespeare's women by women, like Anna Jameson's *Heroines of Shakespeare* (New York: Wiley and Putnam, 1848) or Mary Cowden Clarke's *The Girlhood of Shakespeare's Heroines*, 2 vols. (New York: G. P. Putnam, 1851), rhapsodize over the heroines. Those by men, and of more recent vintage, prefer the "biographical" approach. See Frank Harris, *The Women of Shakespeare* (London: Methuen, 1911); Wyndham Lewis, *The Lion and the Fox* (1927; rpt. London: Methuen, 1951), especially on *Antony and Cleopatra*; Leslie Fiedler, *The Stranger in Shakespeare* (New York: Stein and Day, 1972).

2. The most complete recent study is J. Leeds Barroll's *Artificial Persons: The Formation of Character in the Tragedies of Shakespeare* (Columbia: University of South Carolina Press, 1974), which deals almost exclusively with Shakespeare's men. Not surprisingly, writers who discuss the comedies have more to say about the women. I would cite particularly the character analyses resulting from Ralph Berry's assumption that "the behavior of the dramatis personae is, or ought to be, explicable in terms of naturalistic psychology," in *Shakespeare's Comedies* (Princeton, N.J.: Princeton University Press, 1972), p. 18, and Hugh M. Richmond's emphasis throughout *Shakespeare's Sexual Comedy* (Indianapolis: Bobbs-Merrill, 1971).

3. See Juliet Dusinberre, *Shakespeare and the Nature of Women* (London: Macmillan, 1975), which stresses the importance of the Puritan, bourgeois background in the formation of the heroines of Shakespeare and his contemporaries.

4. This is true of Shakespearean tragedy, but not of the Jacobeans in general, as Webster's *Duchess of Malfi* emphasizes. But while the later

drama uses tragic women, it never allows them the introspective scope of the Shakespearean tragic hero. My general debt to Northrop Frye's treatment of Shakespearean comedy and romance in *Anatomy of Criticism: Four Essays* (Princeton, N.J.: Princeton University Press, 1957) and *A Natural Perspective* (New York: Columbia University Press, 1965) will be obvious here. See too Dusinberre's comments on women's sense of "the physical process of birth and death," pp. 169–71.

5. Dusinberre, *Shakespeare and the Nature of Women*, however, insists on the "insubordination" implicit in the male disguise in the plays, because she connects it to the seventeenth-century attacks (memorialized by the *Hic Mulier-Haec Vir* debate) on women who wore men's clothing. See especially pp. 231–44.

6. Cf. the concluding paragraphs of Thomas Greene's "The Flexibility of the Self in Renaissance Literature," in *The Disciplines of Criticism*, ed. Peter Demetz, Thomas Greene, and Lowry Nelson, Jr. (New Haven, Conn.: Yale University Press, 1968). To prove that Shakespeare's plays lack the earlier Humanistic confidence in man's ability to shape himself as he will, Greene distinguishes between "the adroit improviser," including the disguised women and Petruchio, Puck, and Prince Hal in this category, and the tragic heroes, "too stiff to adjust, obstinately and massively embedded in roles which no longer fit," p. 263. I would see a further distinction: disguise is no spontaneous self-extension but a shrewd political tactic for the not-quite-tragic characters like Hal and Edgar. Their early soliloquies announcing disguise unnervingly recall the Machiavel's confidences to the audience, and, again somewhat like the villains (see text below), they seem lesser figures in reaffirming their official selves, Edgar oddly oblivious to the astonishing inner journeys that produced Poor Tom, Hal sadly diminished by his retrenchment into a king.

7. See Maynard Mack's discussion of the hero's "cycle of change" in "The Jacobean Shakespeare," in *Jacobean Theatre*, ed. John Russell Brown and Bernard Harris (1960; rpt. New York: Capricorn, 1967), particularly the treatment of madness and the contrast between change in comedy and in tragedy, pp. 33–40.

8. Shakespeare is cited throughout in the Arden texts, as follows: *Antony and Cleopatra*, ed. M. R. Ridley, rev. ed. (London: Methuen, 1954); *The Two Gentlemen of Verona*, ed. Clifford Leech (London: Methuen, 1969); *King Lear*, ed. Kenneth Muir, rev. ed. (London: Methuen, 1957); *Cymbeline*, ed. J. M. Nosworthy (London: Methuen, 1955); *The Winter's Tale*, ed. J. H. P. Pafford (London: Methuen, 1955); *As You Like It*, ed. Agnes Latham (London: Methuen, 1975).

9. Thomas Kelly says that one reason for the heroines' disguise "is to dramatize the rigidly circumscribed perception of the young men with whom they are paired," in "Shakespeare's Romantic Heroes: Orlando Reconsidered," *Shakespeare Quarterly*, 24 (1973), 13. The male

disguise is in this view a deliberate tactic for keeping the man secondary in comedy.

10. See Rosalie Colie, *Shakespeare's Living Art* (Princeton, N.J.: Princeton University Press, 1974) for a discussion of the use of Petrarchan rhetoric in the plays, especially pp. 135–67.

11. In *Shakespeare and the Traditions of Comedy* (Cambridge: Cambridge University Press, 1974), Leo Salingar postulates the existence in the problem plays, among others, of what he calls "the complex of the judge and the nun," a formula whereby a man will be saved from death if a woman is released from a convent, suggestive of a "conflict in [Shakespeare's] mind over the claims of love and the claims of law in Elizabethan society," pp. 311–12. I would stress the importance of the childbearing function: unless women get out of the convent, man will die.

12. See Jan Kott's discussion of androgyny as an image of the vanished Golden Age in "Shakespeare's Bitter Arcadia," in *Shakespeare our Contemporary*, trans. Boleslaw Taborski (Garden City, N.Y.: Doubleday/Anchor, 1966), pp. 287–342.

13. Barroll, *Artificial Persons*, p. 184.

14. Cf. Richmond's discussion of sexual imbalance in Shakespeare's heroines, passim. Perhaps the first full-scale analyses of the relationship between masculine and feminine in Shakespeare, G. Wilson Knight's essays on *Antony and Cleopatra* and *Macbeth* in *The Imperial Theme* (1931; rpt. London: Methuen, 1965) still seem to me among the best. His study of *All's Well That Ends Well*, "The Third Eye," in *The Sovereign Flower* (London: Methuen, 1958), pp. 93–160, is also worth considering.

15. Harold C. Goddard speaks of Cleopatra as participating in an "alchemic effect," in *The Meaning of Shakespeare*, 2 vols. (1951; rpt. Chicago: University of Chicago Press, 1960), II, 203; while Phyllis Rackin, in "Shakespeare's Boy Cleopatra, the Decorum of Nature and the Golden World of Poetry," *PMLA*, 87 (1972), 201–12, sees her as an artist figure. Many have noted, too, the resemblance between Prospero and the powerful comic heroines; see, for example, Bertrand Evans, *Shakespeare's Comedies* (Oxford: Clarendon, 1960), p. 149 and elsewhere.

16. I am thinking in particular of a set of metalwork figures representing the Four Elements owned by the Bayerisches Nationalmuseum in Munich and displayed in New York in 1970. *Terra* is a woman with a serpent pressed to her breast. See Konrad Hoffmann, *The Year 1200: A Centennial Exhibition at the Metropolitan Museum of Art*, The Cloisters Studies in Medieval Art (New York: The Metropolitan Museum of Art, 1970), I, 85–87. The serpent at Cleopatra's breast links her as well with the ancient images in which snakes draped around female bodies represent the interrelationship of the male and female principles. See Erich Neumann, *The Great Mother*, trans. Ralph Man-

heim, 2d ed., Bollingen Series, 47 (Princeton, N.J.: Princeton University Press, 1963), pp. 185–89, also 153 and plates 55–59.

17. Cf. Neumann, *The Great Mother*, p. 59: "Whenever we encounter the symbol of rebirth, we have to do with a matriarchal transformation mystery, and this is true even when its symbolism or interpretation bears a patriarchal disguise."

18. As Milton knew when he had Sin recall her incestuous mating with Satan, who first recoiled from her until he saw his "perfect image" in her and conceived Death upon her (*Paradise Lost*, II, 759–67).

19. See Evans, *Shakespeare's Comedies*, pp. 325 ff.

20. Cf. R. E. Gajdusek, "Death, Incest and the Triple Bond in the Later Plays of Shakespeare," *American Imago*, 31 (1974), 156. This essay, which treats incest as a manifestation of the feminine world that the masculine heroes of the last plays must conquer, notes the phallic symbolism in Prospero's gesture.

"Neither mother, wife, nor England's queen"

The Roles of Women in Richard III

MADONNE M. MINER

> Richard sufficiently dominates the play so that analyses of
> his personality virtually exhaust the play's possibilities.
> *Psychoanalysis and Shakespeare*

Although Norman Holland[1] speaks here primarily with reference
to psychoanalytic interpretations of Shakespeare's *Richard III*,
his comment actually serves as indication of the initial assumption behind almost all critical readings of the play; literary critics
generally indulge in an a priori and unacknowledged Forsterian
division of characters into round (Richard) and flat (everyone
else), focus upon the former, and then weave their own particular
analytic threads according to patterns perceived in the character
of Richard.[2] Such threads comprise the traditional web of literary
criticism—and deservedly so—but, because of the initial division
of character and limitation of focus, certain questions raised by
Richard III tend to fall outside the critical web. Why does one figure appear to assume a roundness of dimension while others,
suffering from advanced anorexia, appear to atrophy? What is the
nature of the interaction *among* "atrophied" figures as well as *between* such figures and the other, more "substantial" figure? This
essay, organized into three sections, considers such questions

with respect to one group of formerly ignored "flat characters": the women of *Richard III*. Section I studies the interaction between Richard and women, an interaction characterized by his determination to cast women in unattractive roles: as scapegoat for men, currency of exchange between men, and cipher without men. Section II suggests that interaction occurs among the women of the play, and Section III further substantiates the integrity of female figures with an analysis of the way in which metaphors of birth and pregnancy are used and abused throughout the play.

I

Richard III opens with a soliloquy, in which Richard, Duke of Gloucester, distinguishes time past, time present, and what he perceives to be time future:

> Grim-visaged War hath smoothed his wrinkled front,
> And now, instead of mounting barbèd steeds
> To fright the souls of fearful adversaries,
> He capers nimbly in a lady's chamber
> To the lascivious pleasing of a lute.
> . . . .
> Why, I, in this weak piping time of peace,
> Have no delight to pass away the time.
> . . . .
> And therefore, since I cannot prove a lover
> To entertain these fair well-spoken days,
> I am determinèd to prove a villain.
>
> (I.i.9–13, 24–25, 28–30)[3]

Out of step with his time, Richard determines to force it into closer conformity with his own nature. Implicitly, the quality of the present which Richard finds so onerous is its femininity; present days belong to "wanton ambling nymphs," not to marching warriors, not to hunchbacked younger brothers.[4] The opposition between war and peace is expressed as opposition between male and female; "male" is associated with "bruisèd arms," "stern alarums," and "barbèd steeds," and "female" with "merry meetings," "delightful measures," and "sportive tricks."[5] It makes no difference whether we agree or disagree with Richard's sexual collocations; what is of importance is Richard's exclusive identification with one side of the antithesis and his determination to obliterate those who represent the opposite—those who, according to the imagery of Richard's soliloquy, are women.

In addition to introducing the poles of opposition in *Richard III*, Gloucester's opening soliloquy also introduces a tactic that Richard employs throughout: an allocation of guilt along sexual lines so that women are invariably at fault. Within the soliloquy it is apparent that women are to blame for effacing the countenance of "Grim-visaged War" and, immediately following the soliloquy, Richard explains to brother Clarence that women are to blame for other things as well. Even though Richard has just told us that he has spun "inductions dangerous" so as to set Clarence and Edward "in deadly hate the one against the other," when Clarence enters, under guard, Richard maintains that women are at the root of his woes:

> Why, this it is when men are ruled by women.
> 'Tis not the king that sends you to the Tower.
> My Lady Grey his wife, Clarence, 'tis she
> That tempers him to this extremity.   (I.i.62–65)

Richard's allegation not only deflects suspicion from himself and onto Elizabeth, but also tends to unite the two brothers against an intruder (the sister-in-law, the "Other"). While challenging bonds of marriage, Richard appears to be reaffirming bonds of consanguinity. Clarence catches the impulse of Richard's comment and carries it yet further, naming Mistress Shore as another female force undermining the throne; if one woman is not to blame, another may be found. Clarence cites Shore's intervention in favor of Hastings and Richard agrees: "Humbly complaining to her deity / Got my Lord Chamberlain his liberty" (I.i.76–77). Obviously, according to Richard, when prostitutes capture the ear of kings, when wives wield more power than brothers, the time is out of joint.[6]

In the subsequent exchange with Anne, who follows the corpse of her father-in-law Henry to Chertsey, as in that with Clarence, Richard directs culpability from himself and onto the female figure.[7] He greets the recently widowed woman as "sweet saint" (I.ii.49), and bolsters this greeting with a string of compliments, to which she responds with curses. When Anne charges him with the slaughter of her father-in-law, Henry VI, and her husband, Edward, Richard initially scrambles for a surrogate (blaming Edward IV and Margaret) but then hits upon a far more effective line, accusing Anne as the primary "causer" of the deaths:

> Your beauty was the cause of that effect;
> Your beauty, that did haunt me in my sleep
> To undertake the death of all the world,
> So I might live one hour in your sweet bosom.
>
> (1.ii.121–24)

Thus, Anne is responsible; her beauty serves as incentive for murder. Richard, of course, lies; he kills Edward and Henry so as to come closer to the throne, and he woos Anne for the same reason. By the end of the scene, however, this hunchbacked Machiavellian is able to acknowledge his role in the murders of Edward and Henry, to offer Anne his sword to use against him, and to smile in the knowledge of his victory as she refuses to take vengeance.

> Nay, do not pause, for I did kill King Henry,
> But 'twas thy beauty that provokèd me.
> Nay, now dispatch; 'twas I that stabbed young Edward,
> But 'twas thy heavenly face that set me on.
> Take up the sword again, or take up me.   (1.ii.179–83)

By focusing on her beauty, Richard insists that Anne fit the very flat definition of "womankind" he articulated in his opening soliloquy—a definition that divides the world into male and female provinces, denying the latter any possibility of communion with emblems (such as swords) of the former. Focusing upon Anne's guilt, Richard deflects responsibility from himself, and constructs a bond of alliance between Anne and himself, against the House of Lancaster, rendering her powerless.

While the exchange between Richard and Anne may be the most dramatic example of Richard's aptitude with respect to sexual dynamics and the allocation of guilt, it is by no means a final example. Another variation occurs in Act III, scene iv, when Richard determines to weed out the ranks of those in opposition to his coronation. Because Hastings is involved with Mistress Shore, all Richard need do is accuse Shore, implicate Hastings (guilt by association) and be rid of him. Thus, in the midst of an assembly meeting, Richard draws forth his withered arm and announces: "And this is Edward's wife, that monstrous witch, / Consorted with that harlot strumpet Shore, / That by their witchcraft thus have markèd me" (III.iv.69–71). Hastings's reply, "If they have done this deed, my noble lord" (72), is twisted by an enraged Richard into unimpeachable evidence of guilt: "If! Thou protector of this damnèd strumpet, / Talk'st thou to me of ifs? Thou art a traitor. / Off with his head!" (73–75). In spite of the incredible and illogical nature of Richard's accusation (his arm has always been withered; the association of Elizabeth and Mistress Shore as conspirators is extremely unlikely), it holds: Hastings loses his head on the basis of his involvement with a woman. Although the dynamics in the three examples cited above vary considerably, in each instance Richard blames women in order to benefit himself and, in so doing, he creates or destroys associational bonds between men.

If, in the scenes above, Richard is able to manipulate women and blame so as to cut or spin associational threads, his tailoring skills appear yet more impressive when he sets himself to matchmaking—an activity which appears to encourage the reduction of female status from "person" to "thing exchanged." As Lévi-Strauss observes in *Structural Anthropology*, marriage functions as the lowest common denominator of society; based as it has been on the exchange of a woman between two men, marriage brings together two formerly independent groups of men into a kinship system.[8] Richard takes advantage of these associational possibilities, but, interestingly enough, the impulse behind his marital connections most often appears to be one of destruction rather than creation; society is wrenched apart rather than drawn together. We see Richard play the role of suitor twice, with Lady Anne and with Queen Elizabeth (whom he approaches to request the hand of her daughter Elizabeth). To be sure, in formulating his marital plans, Richard approaches women—an eligible widow and a widowed mother—but in both cases, Richard actually focuses on men behind the women. Before meeting Anne en route to Chertsey, he reveals his designs on her:

> For then I'll marry Warwick's youngest daughter.
> What though I killed her husband and her father?

The readiest way to make the wench amends
Is to become her husband and her father.   (i.i.153–56)

"To make the wench amends"? Such, of course, is not the actual motivation behind Richard's system of substitution; he realizes that in order to substantiate his claims to the position previously held by Henry VI, it is politic to align himself with Henry's daughter-in-law. Further, maneuvering himself into Anne's bed-chamber, Richard moves closer to replacing Edward, former occupant thereof, and former heir to the throne. Thus, after killing Anne's "husband and father," Richard can assume their sexual and political roles.[9] Finally, Richard's speech clarifies the function of women in the marital game: whether the game be one of exchange or one of substitution, the female serves as a piece to be moved *by others*, and a piece having value only *in relation* to others.

Political values, however, like those of the stock market, fluctuate wildly, and by Act IV, Richard (now king) recognizes that Anne has outlived her usefulness to him. After instructing Catesby to rumor it abroad that Anne is "very grievous sick," Richard ruminates alone: "I must be married to my brother's daughter, / Or else my kingdom stands on brittle glass. / Murder her brothers and then marry her!" (iv.ii.58–60). As in his earlier choice of bride, Richard here pursues a woman from whom he has taken all male relatives; although not fully responsible for the death of Elizabeth's father, Richard conspires to lessen the natural term of Edward's life, and he employs more direct measures with respect to Clarence (Elizabeth's uncle) and the two princes (Elizabeth's brothers). However, not all possible rivals have been obliterated: Richmond also seeks the hand of Edward's daughter, and Richard's awareness of a living male rival sharpens his desire to legitimize his claim:

Now, for I know the Britain Richmond aims
At young Elizabeth, my brother's daughter,
And by that knot looks proudly on the crown,
To her go I, a jolly thriving wooer.   (iv.iii.40–43)

Elizabeth, of course, has been a loose end; with the young princes dead ("cut off") she remains the only legitimate possibility of access to the throne. By tying his own knots, Richard plans to exclude Richmond from making any claims to the kingdom. In sum, Richard woos both Anne and Elizabeth because of the position they occupy with respect to men. However, in proposing marriage (which might lead to a bonding of male to male through female), Richard does not seek a union *with* other men but rather *replaces* them by assuming their roles with respect to women.

In considerations of the way Richard employs women as scapegoats and currency, younger female figures have received most attention. However, when we consider how Richard uses women as ciphers, three older women—Queen Elizabeth, Margaret, and the Duchess of York—step, reluctantly, into the foreground. All of these women suffer, on one level, a loss of definition at the hand of Richard. Caught in a society that conceives of women strictly in relational terms (that is, as wives to husbands, mothers to children, queens to kings), the women are subject to loss of title, position, and identity, as Richard destroys those by whom women are defined: husbands, children, kings.[10] Early in the play, Queen Elizabeth perceives the precarious nature of *her* position as her husband, King Edward, grows weaker and weaker. "The loss of such a lord includes all harms" (1.iii.8), she tells her son Grey. Elizabeth's words find verification not only in later scenes, but also, here, before Edward's death, in the figure of Margaret, England's former queen. Margaret, hiding in the wings, listens as Richard taunts Elizabeth and accuses her of promoting her favorites. When Elizabeth replies, "Small joy have I in being England's Queen" (109), Margaret can barely restrain herself; she says in an aside: "As little joy enjoys the queen thereof; / For I am she, and altogether joyless" (154–55). Margaret's aside pinpoints the confusion that results when women must depend upon men for identity and when Richard persists in removing these men. Is a woman to be considered "queen" after her "king" has been killed? Does one's title apply only as long as one's husband is alive? And, after her husband's death, what does the "queen" become? Margaret serves, of course, as model for the women of *Richard III*; she enters in Act I and shows Elizabeth and the Duchess of York what they have to expect from the future; like her, they are destined to years of sterile widowhood. But the women of York do not yet perceive Margaret's function; with Richard, they mock her and force her from the stage. Before leaving, however, Margaret further clarifies her relationship to Elizabeth by underlining the similarity of their woes:

> Thyself a queen, for me that was a queen,
> Outlive thy glory like my wretched self!
> Long mayst thou live to wail thy children's death;
> . . . .
> Long die thy happy days before thy death,
> And, after many length'ned hours of grief,
> Die neither mother, wife, nor England's Queen!
>
> (I.iii.201–3, 206–8)

Alive—but neither mother, wife, nor England's queen: the description may apply to Margaret, Elizabeth, and the Duchess. Only a very short time elapses between the day of Margaret's curse and the day Elizabeth suffers the death of her lord. Addressing the Duchess, the twice-widowed woman cries: "Edward, my lord, thy son, our king, is dead! / Why grow the branches when the root is gone? / Why wither not the leaves that want their sap?" (II.ii.40–42). Elizabeth's questions forecast her upcoming tragedy.

Not only does Richard subvert the role of queen, he also undermines roles of mother and wife. For example, while the death of Edward robs Elizabeth of a husband, it robs the Duchess of York of a son. Having lost son Clarence earlier, the Duchess's "stock" suffers a depletion of two-thirds. She turns to Elizabeth, commenting that years ago she lost a worthy husband,

> And lived with looking on his images;
> But now two mirrors of his princely semblance
> Are cracked in pieces by malignant death,
> And I for comfort have but one false glass
> That grieves me when I see my shame in him.
> Thou art a widow, yet thou art a mother
> And hast the comfort of thy children left. (II.ii.50–56)

Stressing Elizabeth's yet-current claim to motherhood, the Duchess appears to abjure her own; it is as if she no longer wants to assume the title of mother if Richard is the son who grants her this right; accepting "motherhood" means accepting responsibility for "all these griefs," for the losses sustained by Elizabeth and by Clarence's children.

It is not enough for one mother to abandon her claim to the title of mother; Richard pursues a course of action that eventually forces Elizabeth to relinquish her claim also (note that as the play proceeds, Elizabeth comes to bear a closer resemblance to Margaret). The process leading to Elizabeth's forfeiture of her title is more complicated than that of the Duchess and is accomplished in a series of steps: Buckingham and Richard override maternal authority and, parenthetically, the right of sanctuary, by "plucking" the Duke of York from the sheltering arms of his mother; Brakenbury, under order from Richard, denies Elizabeth entrance to the Tower, thereby denying her right to see her children; Richard casts doubt on the legitimacy of Edward's marriage to Elizabeth, and hence, on the legitimacy of her children; Richard preys upon Elizabeth to grant him her daughter in marriage while Elizabeth knows that to do so would be to sentence her daughter to a living death.

As this process is set in motion, the "Protector" refuses to grant Elizabeth her status as mother; as it comes to a close, Elizabeth freely abjures her motherhood in an attempt to protect her remaining child. Up until the murder of her sons, Elizabeth insists, often futilely, upon her maternal rights. When, for example, Brakenbury refuses to admit her to the Tower, she protests violently upon the grounds of familial relation: "Hath he set bounds between their love and me? / I am their mother; who shall bar me from them?" (IV.i.20–21). Almost as if she were determined actively to dispute Richard's allegations that her children are illegitimate, Elizabeth reiterates, time and time again, the status of her relationship and that of her children to Edward. After the deaths of young Edward and Richard, however, Elizabeth is forced to perform an about-face. Because of Richard's manipulations, a "mother's name is ominous to children"; hence, she must deny her title of mother in order to express her genuine identity as a mother concerned for her children's welfare. She dispatches her son Dorset to France—"O Dorset, speak not to me, get thee gone!" (IV.i.38)—and expresses her willingness to deny the legitimacy of young Elizabeth's birth to save her from marriage to Richard.

> And must she die for this? O, let her live,
> And I'll corrupt her manners, stain her beauty,

Slander myself as false to Edward's bed,
Throw over her the veil of infamy;
So she may live unscarred of bleeding slaughter,
I will confess she was not Edward's daughter.

(IV.iv.206—11)

It is the love of a mother for her daughter which prompts Elizabeth's offer; she willingly renounces her titles both of wife and legitimate mother.

In the examples cited above, Richard's general course of action is such to encourage women to abandon traditional titles, to de-identify themselves. Richard more specifically encourages this cipherization by confounding the integrity of titular markers: that is, by juggling titles without regard for the human beings behind these titles (although Richard does not restrict himself to female markers, females suffer more grievously from these verbal acrobatics than do males, who may draw upon a wider range of options with respect to identifying roles). Richard's changing choice of title for his sister-in-law Elizabeth most clearly exemplifies his policy of confoundment. Richard's first reference to Elizabeth occurs in a conversation with Clarence, in which Richard promises that he will employ any means to procure his brother's freedom: "And whatsoe'er you will employ me in, / Were it to call King Edward's widow sister, / I will perform it to enfranchise you" (I.i.108—10). Several things are happening here. First, as the wife of Edward, Richard's brother, Elizabeth *is* Richard's sister (sister-in-law); she need not solicit the title from Richard, although Richard certainly implies that it is his prerogative to grant or withhold the title at will. Second, the title Richard actually bestows on Elizabeth is "King Edward's widow," an equivocation of marvelous subtlety; Elizabeth *is* the widow of Grey but Richard's phrasing makes it possible to read this description as a prediction: Elizabeth will wear weeds again. And finally, when Richard and Elizabeth meet in the following scene, it is Elizabeth who twice addresses Richard as "Brother Gloucester"; Richard refuses to call her anything, because, at this time, he has nothing to gain by doing so. Later, in Act II, following the convenient demise of Edward IV, Richard, as if to ensure a smooth transference of power, attempts to placate Elizabeth: he calls her "sister." In Act IV, however, after Richard has approached Elizabeth for the hand of young Elizabeth, he calls her "mother": "Therefore, dear mother—I must call you so— / Be the attorney of my love to her" (IV.iv.412–13). The exchange between Richard and Elizabeth also supplies a rather startling example of Richard's indifference to the human beings who actually give substance to the titles he juggles with such apparent ease. Richard insists that he will provide substitutes for the children Elizabeth has lost at his hand:

> To quicken your increase I will beget
> Mine issue of your blood upon your daughter.
> A grandam's name is little less in love
> Than is the doting title of a mother.   (IV.iv.297–300)

Focusing exclusively upon a "grandam's *name*" and the "*title* of a mother," Richard attempts to obscure the very real difference between these two positions; he attempts to confound all meaning attached to female position markers—a policy in keeping with his determination to confound women altogether.

II

Given Richard's perception of woman as enemy, as "Other," we should not be surprised that the action of the play depends upon a systematic denial of the human identity of women. Richard's apparently successful attempts to obscure Elizabeth's titular "sense of self" and Elizabeth's rejection of both her own identity and that of her daughter exemplify, on one level, the progression of women in *Richard III*: from mother to nonmother, wife to widow, queen to crone. However, this "progression" does not take into account a less obvious and more positive progression of women from a condition of bickering rivalry to a condition of sympathetic camaraderie. In the midst of loss, the women turn to each other. Thus, an interesting, but generally ignored, countermotion of interaction *among* women is introduced; having been reduced to the condition of nothing, Margaret, Elizabeth, and the Duchess evidence a new humanity, a humanity apparent nowhere else in the play. We need only explore the progression in the four scenes in *Richard III* in which women confront each other (I.iii; II.ii; IV.i;

IV.iv) to see this countermotion. Act I, scene iii, opens with Elizabeth and Richard at each other's throat; with the entrance of Margaret, however, Richard is able to direct all hostility toward her. Even Elizabeth joins with crook-backed Gloucester in condemning the widow of Lancaster; angry words fly across the stage. When Elizabeth applauds Richard for turning Margaret's curse back on herself, Margaret chides the "poor-painted queen":

> Why strew'st thou sugar on that bottled spider
> Whose deadly web ensnareth thee about?
> Fool, fool, thou whet'st a knife to kill thyself.
> The day will come that thou shalt wish for me
> To help thee curse this poisonous bunch-backed toad.
>
> (I.iii.241–45)

Margaret's prediction proves true, but the women must suffer first.

If the preceding scene depicts the hostility between women of different Houses, Act II, scene ii, depicts hostility between women of the same House. Instead of coming together in sympathy upon learning of the deaths of Clarence and Edward, the women of York and the children of Clarence engage in a chorus of moans, each claiming the greater loss. An appalling absence of empathy characterizes this meeting. A few lines may serve to indicate the mood of the entire scene:

> DUCH. O, what cause have I,
>   Thine being but a moi'ty of my moan,
>   To overgo thy woes and drown thy cries!
> BOY. Ah, aunt, you wept not for our father's death.
>   How can we aid you with our kindred tears?
> DAUGHTER. Our fatherless distress was left unmoaned;
>   Your widow-dolor likewise be unwept!
> ELIZABETH. Give me no help in lamentation;
>   I am not barren to bring forth complaints.   (II.ii.59–67)

Obviously, the tendency here is away from commiseration and toward a selfish indulgence. It is not until Act IV, scene i, that a reversal of this tendency begins to make itself felt, the result of the women's sympathy as their position continues to erode. Elizabeth, the Duchess of York, Anne, and Clarence's daughter meet en route to the Tower to greet the young princes. When Elizabeth is denied visitation privileges, the Duchess and Anne support her maternal rights. Even when Stanley announces that Anne is to be crowned queen, the bond of sympathy between Anne and Elizabeth is not destroyed. Given her history of suffering, Elizabeth can respond now with feeling to Anne as Margaret could not when she was replaced by Elizabeth. When the new queen expresses her wish that the "inclusive verge of golden metal" were "red-hot steel to sear me to the brains," Elizabeth attempts to console her: "Go, go, poor soul! I envy not thy glory. / To feed my humor wish thyself no harm" (IV.i.63–64). The Duchess of York adds her blessing also: "Go thou to Richard, and good angels tend thee!" (92). How different from the feeling of Act II, scene ii! Even though this union of sympathy may not generate any practical power (Richard continues to confound the women) it does prompt a revision in our responses to them: they attain a tragic dignity.

The most moving example of women-aiding-women, however, occurs in Act IV, scene iv, where the women of York join Margaret of Lancaster in cursing Richard. This union is achieved only gradually. Old Queen Margaret enters alone and withdraws to eavesdrop on Elizabeth and the Duchess of York, who sit down together to lament the death of the princes and lament their uselessness: "Ah that thou wouldst as soon afford a grave / As thou canst yield a melancholy seat" (IV.iv.31–32). When Margaret comes forward and joins the two women on the ground, she first claims that her griefs "frown on the upper hand" and it seems the scene will be a reiteration of the earlier contest.

> If sorrow can admit society,
> Tell o'er your woes again by viewing mine.
> I had an Edward, till a Richard killed him;
> I had a husband, till a Richard killed him.
> Thou hadst an Edward, till a Richard killed him;
> Thou hadst a Richard, till a Richard killed him.
>
> (IV.iv.38–43)

The Duchess, catching the rhythm of Margaret's refrain, interrupts in order to wail a few lines of her own. Margaret, however, regains voice, reminding the Duchess that it is her womb that has bred the cause of all their sorrows: "From forth the kennel of thy

womb hath crept / A hellhound that doth hunt us all to death"
(iv.iv.47–48). These words signal a reversal in the dynamics of the
scene; no longer willing to recognize the legal ties to men which
prohibit a communion between women of different parties, these
women join together in sorrow, in suffering; it is easy enough to
imagine the three of them, seated on the earth, hand in hand. The
Duchess abandons her competition with Margaret for the title of
most grief-stricken, and turns, in commiseration, to her: "O
Harry's wife, triumph not in my woes! / God witness with me I
have wept for thine" (59–60). Elizabeth, too, moves toward Margaret, admitting that the prophesied time has come for her to request Margaret's help in cursing the "foul bunch-backed toad"
(81) Richard. Thus, the exchange among the women leads to the
decision to arm themselves (to assume a male prerogative) with
words; Margaret provides lessons in cursing and the Duchess suggests that they smother Richard in "the breath of bitter words"
(133); no more wasted or feeble words—instead, the women now
use words as weapons. Accordingly, when Richard enters a short
while after Margaret's departure, Elizabeth and the Duchess verbally accost and accuse him. Unaccustomed to such noise, an in-
dignant Richard commands: "Either be patient and entreat me
fair,/ Or with the clamorous report of war / Thus will I drown your
exclamations" (152–54). Richard's response to these insistent
female voices is worthy of note as it reiterates the alliance of
Richard with war and against women, and as it serves as summary statement of Richard's policy with respect to women—they
must be silenced. The Duchess, however, finds voice, and her
final words to Richard take the form of a curse; she turns against
her own House, prays for the adverse party, and damns her son
Richard to a death of shame. Her ability to do so with such
strength is surely a result of the communion of sympathy shared
by the three women. If, in previous scenes, a meeting of women
merely leads to angry words and altercation, the meeting of Act
IV, scene iv, leads to the formation of bonds among the women
against a single foe.[11] When the progression of female characters
is charted on this level, it becomes apparent that they do not de-
serve the a priori dismissal they too frequently receive. Although
attenuated by Richard, women take on an emotional solidity, a
roundness of true humanity.

III

A consideration of birth metaphor clarifies, yet further, the paradoxically double presentation of women in *Richard III*; specifically, perversion of birth metaphors suggests the negative condition of women articulated in Section I (from mother to nonmother, etc.), while the persistence and importance of these metaphors suggest the very positive condition of women articulated in Section II (as individuals having considerable power and human value). Although examples of the birth metaphor are so numerous as to render selection a problem, three categories may be arbitrarily distinguished: metaphor as descriptive of the condition of the times; as descriptive of Richard's activities and of Richard himself from the perspective of other characters; and as descriptive of Richard's mind as revealed in his own comments.

As mentioned previously, Richard "declares war" on the present time in his opening soliloquy; the extent to which he realizes this declaration may be felt in comments made by other characters throughout the play about the changed condition of the times—comments which most often work through a distortion of imagery usually associated with birth. When a group of citizens gathers to discuss the recent death of Edward and the probable confusion that will result, one compares his apprehension of ensuing danger to the swelling of water before a boisterous storm (II.iii.42–45). Although "swelling" is not, by any means, a term associated exclusively with pregnancy, it almost always conveys a feeling of pregnant expectation. Here, and at all other times throughout *Richard III*, that which is expected, that which swells the body, is something ominous, something negative. This consistently pejorative use of the term "swelling" stands in contrast to a possible positive application of the word: that is, swelling as indicative of a generous fertility.[12] A similarly pejorative application of usually positive terms occurs in the speech of Elizabeth when she, like the citizens, is informed of Edward's death. Refusing all offers of sympathy from others, she cries: "I am not barren to bring forth complaints. / All springs reduce their currents to mine eyes, / That I . . . / May send forth plenteous tears to drown the world" (II.ii.67–68, 70). Two aspects of Elizabeth's choice of metaphor are worthy of note. First, the widow asserts her fertility, but a fertility that gives birth to complaints, instead of children. Second, the "children" that Elizabeth does produce assume the shape of tears, tears which, under normal conditions, might function as springs of life. Given the corruption of conditions under Richard, however, Elizabeth sends forth her tears to destroy life, "to drown the world."

Examination of Richard's specific activities reveals more explicitly his perversion of regenerative processes. When the thugs employed to murder Clarence attempt to convince him that Richard is the father of this deed, Clarence shakes his head in disbelief: "It cannot be, for he bewept my fortune / And hugged me in his arms and swore with sobs / That he would labor my delivery" (I.iv.247–49). While Clarence assumes that Richard will "deliver" him from prison, to freedom, Richard intends to deliver Clarence from prison to death. Thus, Richard reverses the normal delivery process; instead of drawing Clarence forth from the womb, two midwives push him back into a yet darker womb (specifically, into a butt of malmsey). The speech of Tyrrel, another murderer employed by Richard, provides a second commentary on Richard's activities. Having commissioned the execution of the young princes, he tells the king: "If to have done the thing you gave in charge / Beget your happiness, be happy then, / For it is done" (IV.iii.25–27). "The thing" given in charge is the murder of two children; once more, begetting and killing are conjoined. The comments of Margaret and the Duchess affirm this unnatural conjunction, transferring it to the literal level: Richard's unnatural birth. Margaret attacks Richard as "Thou slander of thy heavy mother's womb! / Thou loathèd issue of thy father's loins!" (I.iii.230–31). Similarly, because of son Richard, the Duchess of York cries out against her own womb, revealing an extreme of female debasement and acceptance of guilt: "O my accursèd womb, the bed of death! / A cockatrice hast thou hatched to the world, / Whose unavoided eye is murderous" (IV.i.53–55). Richard, forcing an association of the womb with "the bed of death," succeeds, at least *partially*, in debasing the value of women, these creatures with wombs.

One final category of defective birth imagery is that employed by Richard in describing his own activities. After the general altercation of Act I, scene iii, for example, Richard steps off alone and comments: "I do the wrong, and first begin to brawl. / The secret mischiefs that I *set abroach* / I lay unto the grievous charge of others" (I.iii.323–25, emphasis added). Or, just a short time later, when Edward, unaware of Richard's expeditious execution of Clarence, informs his court that peace has been made "between these swelling wrong-incensèd peers," Richard replies: "A blessèd *labor* my most sovereign lord" (II.i.52–53, emphasis added). But undoubtedly the most graphic of the many examples of debasement of the language of birth occurs in Act IV, scene iv, as Richard encourages Elizabeth to allow him to right previous wrongs by marrying her daughter. When Elizabeth protests, "Yet thou didst kill my children," Richard counters: "But in your daughter's womb I'll bury them, / Where in that nest of spicery they will breed / Selves of themselves, to your recomforture" (IV.iv.423–25). Richard will bury old Elizabeth's children in young Elizabeth's womb? Could Richard hit upon a line of argument any more perversely unnatural? Up to this point, most birth metaphors have been constructed so as to suggest that the womb breeds no good (as, for example, that the Duchess's womb breeds a cockatrice); here, Richard forces the metaphor to work in reverse as well: the womb serves as tomb, functioning as both sprouting ground and burial plot. In forcing this perverse alliance of terms, Richard reaffirms, on a linguistic level, the impulse behind all of his activities with respect to women—the impulse to silence, to negate. Yet, paradoxically, the persistence with which Richard acts upon this impulse gives the lie to the possibility of its fulfillment: Richard's *need* to debase birth imagery implies that women (those capable of giving birth) have a power which finally cannot be devalued or eliminated; further, his repeated attempts, on a larger level, to rob women of their identity as mothers, wives, or queens, are doomed to frustration in that he cannot rob women of their identity as creative, regenerative human beings.

    Richard III opens with a series of complaints directed, implicitly, against women. It is women who tame "Grim-visaged War," who caper to lutes, who play Love's games—and who govern the times. *Richard III* ends with a series of scenes on the battlefield; men engage in combat with men, and women are nowhere to be found (the last female on stage appears in Act IV). On one level, the process of the play is one of denial and deflation; as Richard destroys husbands, kings, and children, as he confounds traditionally stable sources of identity and subjects women to an unnatural association with the forces of death, he suggests that women are without value—or, even worse, that they are destructive of value. But a reading of *Richard III* on just this one level does an injustice to the play; running parallel to the process described above is a counterprocess, one that insists upon the inherently positive value of women. We see evidence of this counterprocess in the progression of women from a condition of rivalry, battling amongst themselves, to a condition of camaraderie, sympathizing with each other, and in the persistence of the attack that Richard feels compelled to wage, both in life and in language, against these powerful foes. Even Richmond's final speech contributes to our sense of the invincibility of these females; after describing the bloody hatred between brothers which has divided England, Richmond proposes a reunification through his conjunction with the young woman Elizabeth. Hence, the argument of *Richard III* moves in two directions. The first insists that women are purely media of exchange and have no value in themselves; the second, overriding the first, insists that even when used as currency, women's value cannot be completely destroyed.

NOTES

1. Norman Holland, *Psychoanalysis and Shakespeare* (New York: McGraw-Hill, 1966), p. 261.
2. Just to cite a few of the major examples: see Wolfgang H. Clemen, *A Commentary on Shakespeare's "Richard III,"* trans. Jean Bonheim (London: Methuen and Co., 1968), and E. M. W. Tillyard, *Shakespeare's History Plays* (New York: Macmillan, 1946); as representative of historical-political interpretations, see John Palmer, *Political Characters of Shakespeare* (London: Macmillan, 1961) or M. M. Reese, *The Cease of Majesty* (New York: St. Martin's Press, 1961); for psychoanalytic interpretations, see essays in M. D. Faber, *The Design Within* (New York: Science House, 1970), or Holland, *Psychoanalysis and Shakespeare*; as representative of "type criticism" see Bernard Spivack, *Shakespeare and the Allegory of Evil* (New York: Columbia University Press, 1958). All of these works offer something to the his-

tory of criticism of *Richard III*, but all, initially, take their cue from the star performer-cum-director, Richard. The exception to this generalization is Leslie Fiedler. In *The Stranger in Shakespeare* (New York: Stein and Day, 1972), he shows his sensitivity to the "problem of woman" in Shakespeare: "Obviously, the beginning for Shakespeare is the problem of woman, or more exactly perhaps, his problem with women. Certainly, in his first plays, members of that sex are likely to be portrayed as utter strangers" (p. 43). The only other critic from the list above who makes any more than cursory mention of the women is Reese.

3. All citations are from *The Complete Signet Classic Shakespeare*, gen. ed. Sylvan Barnet (New York: Harcourt Brace Jovanovich, 1963, 1972).

4. Although this soliloquy has elicited comment from a wide range of critics, most of them appear oblivious to its misogynic thrust. Focusing upon Richard's statement that he is "determined to prove a villain," they ignore the motivation behind his determination. William B. Toole, for example, insists that we should *not* "seek a modern psychological explanation for Richard's behaviour on the basis of this passage. The main purpose of this part of the soliloquy [1.i.1–30] is to indicate that the protagonist has freely chosen to be a villain" ("The Motif of Psychic Division in *Richard III*," *Shakespeare Survey*, 27 [1974], p. 25). A more interesting reading that appears closer to the text than Toole's, is Sigmund Freud's in "Some Character-Types Met with in Psycho-Analytic Work," included in Faber, *The Design Within*. Freud explains that we accept Richard's articulation of his disadvantages in the soliloquy because we identify with him: "And now we feel that we ourselves might become like Richard . . . Richard is an enormous magnification of something we find in ourselves as well. We all think we have reason to reproach Nature and our destiny for congenital and infantile disadvantages" (p. 345). Remaining true to both Freud and Richard, we might emend Freud's comment: "We all think we have reason to reproach women (the "Great Mothers") for our disadvantages."

5. See also Richard's soliloquy in *Henry VI*, Part 3, III.ii.124–95, in which the sexual opposition is more explicit.

6. Interestingly enough, although Shore may have a hand in Hastings's release, the evidence against Elizabeth's involvement in Clarence's imprisonment is such that we must dismiss all charges against her— but the probable guilt of one and the certain innocence of the other make no difference; when Richard requires a scapegoat, any woman will serve.

7. Again, although critical response to this scene has been abundant, it has also been very narrow in focus. Palmer, *Political Characters*, p. 81, maintains that the prime purpose of Richard's wooing "is to show Richard's insolent virtuosity in persuasion, his delight in the exercise of his mind and will, his pride in attempting the impossible and his

triumph in its achievement." Palmer does not choose to see the sexual ramifications of the *contents* of Richard's virtuosity, delight, pride, and triumph. Similarly, Reese, *The Cease of Majesty*, pp. 217–18, notes that Shakespeare invents most of the first act in order to "show off [Richard's] powers," but does not comment on the fact that these powers are directed against women.

8. Claude Lévi-Strauss, *Structural Anthropology*, trans. Claire Jacobson and Brooke Grandfest Schoepf (New York: Basic Books, 1976), I, 46: "a man obtains a woman from another man who gives him a daughter or a sister."

9. See Otto Rank, *Das Inzest Motiv in Dichtung und Sage* (Leipzig: Franz Deuticke, 1926), pp. 211–12, for a more complete analysis of incest motifs in *Richard III*. Also see Charles A. Adler, "*Richard III*— His Significance as a Study in Criminal Life-Style," *International Journal of Individual Psychology*, 2, No. 3 (1936), 55–60, for a brief, and rather crude, commentary on the way Richard attempts to conquer his murdered opponents by "possessing their ladies" (p. 59).

10. Although guilty of several murders throughout the play, Richard never raises his sword against a woman; he does not need to; instead, he effectively disposes of women by disposing of the "primary terms" according to which they identify themselves. (Richard's wife Anne is the possible exception; it is questionable whether her death should be attributed to poison from the hand of Richard or to the equally lethal experience of marriage to him.)

11. Very few critics pay much attention to this scene. Fiedler provides an especially sympathetic reading of the way in which Margaret, "squatting on the ground with Queen Elizabeth and the Duchess of York . . . has helped project the image of the Triple Goddess in darkest form" (*The Stranger in Shakespeare*, p. 50). As Fiedler explains a while later, this Triple Goddess is comprised of "Hera, Aphrodite, Persephone: mother, mistress and queen of the underworld," but in Shakespeare, "the first two functions blur into the third [which is why] . . . in that terrible scene of *Richard III* in which Queen Margaret, Queen Elizabeth, and the Duchess of York gather together, the second two are portrayed as mere shadows of the first, who, we suspect, will disappear when she leaves the land which has never really been hers" (p. 73). Richard Wheeler, in "History, Character, and Conscience in *Richard III*," *Comparative Drama*, 5 (1971–72), 314, also takes note of the scene, observing that although Richard virtually makes a career out of killing men, "the real suffering of the play comes to be focused in the voices of widowed mothers." Reese, on the other hand, is completely unsympathetic. Although he believes scenes with the women are important ones—"They provide a formal setting for Richard's crimes and epitomise the Elizabethan reading of history" (*The Cease of Majesty*, p. 209), he insists that the women's indifference to Richard's immortal soul "shows how low these women themselves have fallen. Except in an emptily rhetorical way, they are not touched

by the finer issues" (p. 223). Finer issues?! Must such issues revolve around the eternal salvation of the male figure?

12. Shakespeare consistently chooses to use the terms "swell" and "swelling" in a pejorative fashion. Cf. *The Winter's Tale,* ii.i.62; *Timon of Athens,* iii.v.102; *Troilus and Cressida,* i.ii.276; *Othello,* ii.iii.57. In each case, swelling promises something undesirable in the future or is evidence of ugliness in the past.

Shakespeare and the Soil of Rape

CATHARINE R. STIMPSON

Shakespeare's sympathy toward women helps to create an attitude toward rape that is more generous and less foolish than that of many of our contemporaries. He never sniggers and assumes that women, consciously or unconsciously, seek the rapist out and then enjoy the deed: brutal, enforced sex; the ghastly tmesis of the flesh. He never gives "proud lords" the right to "Make weak-made women tenants to their shame."[1] Nor does the act dominate his imagination, as it might that of a lesser writer as concerned with violence, war, and sexuality as Shakespeare is. In the complete works, the word "rape" occurs only seventeen times; "rapes" three; and various forms of "ravish" thirty-eight.[2] "Ravish" is perhaps like a poetic gloss that both hints at and denies rape's brutal force.

When rape occurs, it is terrible in itself. Like murder, it displays an aggressor in action. Shakespeare and his rapists use stridently masculine metaphors of war and of the hunt to capture that flagrant energy. Tarquin

> . . . shakes aloft his Roman blade,
> Which, like a falcon tow'ring in the skies,
> Coucheth the fowl below with his wings' shade, . . .
>
> *(Lucrece,* lines 505–7)

An earlier version of this essay was presented at the International Shakespeare Association Congress, April 20, 1976, Washington, D.C. The author is grateful to Allison Heisch and Carol T. Neely for their helpful comments.

Like murder, rape also pictures a helpless victim, powerless vulnerability. Because rape's violence is sexual, an audience watching it can live out voyeuristic fantasies. Moreover, Shakespearean rape signifies vast conflicts: between unnatural disorder and natural order; raw, polluting lust and its purification through chastity or celibacy; the dishonorable and the honorable exercise of power; "hot-burning will" and "frozen conscience" (*Lucrece*, line 247); and the sinful and righteous begetting of children. A chaste wife, a "clean" marriage bed, guarantee that property rights will pass to a man's blood heirs. For a man to rape a woman, then, is to take sides; to make a series of choices. Rape tempts and tests him, physically and morally.

The structure of Shakespearean rape scenes itself embodies a conflict. The language in which rapes are imagined and then enacted is vivid, immediate, extended, garish, sometimes hallucinatory: "Night-wand'ring weasels shriek" (*Lucrece*, line 307); Lucrece's breasts are "like ivory globes circled with blue" (line 407). The breast, at once erotic and maternal, swells to symbolize the body that will be overcome. However, the setting of the rape scenes in the plays is remote in time or place or both, usually near Italy, if not actually within it. The result is a dramatic sexuality that has the simultaneous detail and distance of a dream/nightmare. The dream/nightmare also contains frequent references to past rapes, to the Trojan War, to the legend of Philomel. Shakespeare compares Lucrece to "lamenting Philomele" (line 1079), a bitterly poignant allusion she herself will make. In *Titus Andronicus*, both Aaron and Marcus will join Philomel and Lavinia in a female community of suffering (II.iii.43; II.iv.26). Aaron judges Lavinia as pure as Lucrece. (II.ii.108.) Such reminders give the dream/nightmare the repetitive weight of myth and history, of experiences that have occurred before and will occur again.

When a man pursues, besieges, and batters a woman's body, he assaults a total world. The female flesh is a passive microcosm. Lucrece is a world, a "sweet city" (line 469). In *Coriolanus*, Cominius says to Menenius:

> You have holp to ravish your own daughters and
> To melt the city leads upon your pates,
> To see your wives dishonour'd to your noses—
> . . . .

Your temples burned in their cement, and
Your franchises, whereon you stood, confin'd
Into an auger's bore.   (IV.vi.81–83, 85–87)

In *Titus Andronicus*, "Lavinia and Tamora may be seen as symbolic personifications of female Rome."[3] The question then becomes, "To whom does the world belong?" The order of Cominius's clauses, as well as his pronouns, provides an answer. The world belongs to men: fathers, husbands, lovers, brothers. Because in Shakespeare only well-born women are raped, their violation becomes one of property, status, and symbolic worth as well. The greater those values, the greater the sense of power their conquest confers upon the rapist.

Because men rape what other men possess, rape becomes in part a disastrous element of male rivalry. The woman's body is a prize in a zero-sum game that men play. Collatine's boasting about Lucrece, an act of excess that is a rhetorical analogue to Tarquin's sexual will, helps to provoke the ruler's desire to conquer the pride of his subordinate. In *Titus Andronicus*, the vicious competition of Demetrius and Chiron parallels the sibling hostilities between Saturninus and Bassianus. However, Demetrius and Chiron stop fighting over Lavinia when it comes time to rape, mutilate, and humiliate her. The joys of controlling a woman together subsume the difficulties of deciding which one will control her independently. Their horrible, giggling plan—to use Bassianus's "dead trunk" as "pillow to our lust" (II.iii.130)—deflects and satisfies their need to defeat other men, to deprive them of their rights and gratifications. When their mother gives birth to Aaron's child, their half-brother, Demetrius and Chiron also unite in their disgust, an emotion that yokes Oedipal jealousy, racist revulsion at miscegenation, and fear of the Roman political consequences of their mother's adultery.

Such rivalry can occur within a man as well as between men. Tarquin, in his long internal debates, struggles between the good self, who argues against rape, and the bad self, who demands sexual triumph. Tarquin is unable to use the common justifications for rape: political or familial revenge. He is equally unable to forget that Collatine is a principal man in his army, a kinsman, and a friend; these are male bonds that invert and undermine male rivalries. Tarquin mourns:

Had Collatinus kill'd my son or sire,
Or lain in ambush to betray my life,
Or were he not my dear friend, this desire
Might have excuse to work upon his wife,
As in revenge or quittal of such strife;
But as he is my kinsman, my dear friend,
The shame and fault finds no excuse nor end.

(lines 232–38)

In psychoanalytical terms, Tarquin's ego is torn between the demands of a libido and a superego whose appeals Lucrece vainly tries to reinforce. After the rape, the superego takes its belated revenge. Guilt immediately deprives Tarquin of any sense of sexual pleasure. In *Measure for Measure*, Angelo will later act out Tarquin's struggle. He will put Isabella in the position of a potential rape victim, for the "choice" he offers her—submit to me sexually or commit your brother to death—is a version of the "choice" Tarquin presents to Lucrece—submit to me sexually or commit yourself to death.[4]

For women, rape means both submission, death, and more. Shakespeare never falters, never hedges, as he shows how defenseless women are before sexual violence and the large destructiveness it entails. Forced sexual submission enforces female death. For the loss of chastity, "a dearer thing than life" (*Lucrece*, line 687) stains women irrevocably. Lavinia knows that being murdered is better than being subjected to a "worse than killing lust" (*Titus*, ii.iii.175) that will deprive her of her reason for living. Women are unwillingly responsible for a "cureless crime" (*Lucrece*, line 772). Lucrece, her act at once sacrificial, redemptive, and flamboyant enough to make her husband's friends wish to revenge her, must kill herself. Because "the girl should not survive her shame" (v.iii.41), Titus stabs Lavinia. Their deaths purge the lives and honor of the men whom they have ornamented: Lucrece's husband and father, whose mournings mingle over her corpse; Lavinia's father alone, her husband being dead.[5]

Few of Shakespeare's dramas about traumatic injustice are as clear, or as severe, as those about the raped woman who must be punished because she endured an aggression she never sought and against which she fought. Shakespeare deploys the voice of moderate men to comment on such unfair expiations. In *The*

Rape of Lucrece, Brutus thinks Lucrece's suicide a final act of excess in a Rome Tarquin and his family have ruled. Discarding the mask of silliness he has expediently worn to now reveal an authentic self, he tells Collatine not to "steep thy heart / In such relenting dew of lamentations . . ." (lines 1828–29). He urges Collatine to abandon private grief for political action and rid Rome of Tarquin. In a sense, Brutus uses Lucrece's anguish as a weapon in a struggle between men for power. In *Titus Andronicus*, Marcus asks for compassion for his niece and shows her how to publicize her plight. The reasonableness of a Brutus or Marcus contrasts to the despicable excesses of will of the rapist and the dangerous excesses of rhetoric of husbands who brag about their wives' chaste fidelity. Oddly, moderate women (like Paulina) who play prominent, articulate roles defending the victimized woman in Shakespeare's explorations of sexual jealousy, are missing from the examinations of rape.[6] Their absence starkly points to women's inability to control and to influence in benign ways the public structures that judge rape and the psychosexual needs that generate it.

Indeed, women assist in the rapes that attack other women. In *Lucrece*, night is allegorically female, a sable "mother of dread and fear" (line 117). In *Titus Andronicus*, Tamora wants to destroy Lavinia. Like Clytemnestra, she seeks revenge for the sacrifice of her children. She is also annoyed and threatened because Bassianus and Lavinia have discovered her sporting with Aaron in the woods. However, Tamora's encouragement of her sons to rape not simply Lavinia but any Roman woman has a lascivious quality that flows beyond these motives. Letting her boys "satisfy their lust" (II.iii.180) expresses her enjoyment of her sons' potency, which veers toward and approaches a sublimated incest.

Tempting such taboos, Tamora deliberately turns away from Lavinia. She ignores the plaintive cry, "O Tamora! thou bearest a woman's face—" (II.iii.136) and denies, as Lady Macbeth will do, her own femaleness. This is but one act in a series that will end when she eats her dead children; when she incorporates them back into her body it is an inversion of the release of a living child that marks natural maternity. The forest setting of Lavinia's rape increases the play's sense of distorted, squalid sexuality. The soil is soiled in a perversion of nature comparable to the perversion of domesticity Tarquin creates in Collatine's and Lucrece's marriage bed. The pit that becomes Bassianus's grave, "unhallowed and blood-stained" (II.iii.210), symbolizes the violated female genitalia and womb as well.

Self-reflexive Shakespeare, ever rewriting his materials, also offers a darkly comic study of imagined rape. In *Cymbeline*, Posthumus flaunts Imogen's virtue before Iachimo and dares him to assail it. Iachimo does not physically rape Imogen, but his theft of her good reputation, like his penetration of her bedchamber, is a psychic equivalent. He admits this when he compares himself to Tarquin. Learning that Posthumus thinks her a strumpet and her sex a regiment of strumpets, Imogen begins to imitate Lucrece by stabbing herself in the heart. In addition, clod Cloten sees Posthumus as his rival. Cloten's fantasies parody a conflict between men in which victory means the right to assume the identity of the vanquished, to wear his clothes, to have his wife. Cloten also desires to revenge himself upon the woman who, defending herself against his advances, has offended him. With the encouragement of his mother, he imagines his sexuality as a vehicle of punishment. So he mutters:

> . . . With that suit [Posthumus's] upon my back will I ravish her; first kill him, and in her eyes. There shall she see my valour, which will then be a torment to her contempt. He on the ground, my speech of insultment ended on his dead body, and when my lust hath dined (which, as I say, to vex her I will execute in the clothes that she so prais'd), to the court I'll knock her back, foot her home again. She hath despis'd me rejoicingly, and I'll be merry in my revenge.
>
> (III.v.140–50)

However, crude Cloten cannot transform fantasy into act. Such inadequacies become a grossly comic figure. In *Cymbeline*, comedy blunts the force of Shakespeare's analysis of male enmity and the reunion of Posthumus and Imogen mitigates the force of his brief against the wagers, literal and figurative, that men place on women's virtue.

The fact of having been raped obliterates all of a woman's previous claims to virtue. One *sexual* experience hereafter will define her. Such a strict interpretation of rape may be an index to a shift in the position of women during Shakespeare's time. One historian has suggested: "What the Reformation era witnessed was the changing delineation of women's roles. As this period drew to a close, women's roles became defined increasingly by sex—to the detriment of all women—rather than by class."[7] Other historians have postulated that the more controlled female sexuality is in particular societies, the less power women have. Shakespeare warns his audience about breakdowns in the boundaries on male sexuality, showing rapists as vicious and out of control. However, he also reminds his audience about the boundaries that marriage places on female sexuality. His protest is not against such confinements, but against assaults upon them. If Shakespearean rape does indeed signify such a double retraction—of female identity to sexual identity, of female sexual expressiveness to marital fidelity—it might illustrate the intricate development, between 1580 and 1640, of what Lawrence Stone has named the Restricted Patriarchal Nuclear Family. Stone writes: ". . . both state and Church, for their own reasons, actively reinforced the pre-existent patriarchy within the family, and there are signs that the power of the husband and father over the wife and the children was positively strengthened, making him a legalized petty tyrant within the home."[8] Coppélia Kahn then correctly reads *The Rape of Lucrece* as the poetic version of an ideology that justifies this male power through imputing "a sort of natural inevitability to the relationship between men and women as the relationship between the strong and the weak. . . ."[9] In brief, the rape victim may be painfully emblematic of the plight of women during a period of constriction. Her sexual terror stands for the difficulty of her sex. Men, who have more power than women, abuse it. Women, who have less power than men, must absorb that abuse. In Shakespeare, women also have language and the dignity of stoicism as well as the choral commentary of decent men to provide a sympathetic response to their condition.

Psychologically, Shakespeare's rape sequences shrewdly unravel some of the reasons why men rape and the justifications they offer for such exploitation of their strength. Morally, the sequences compel sympathy for women, though they offer, as an inducement to the audience, some recoiling titillation. Shakespeare acutely shows—through Lucrece's speeches, through Lavinia's amputations—the agony a woman experiences after rape. Yet breeding that agony is the belief that the unwilling betrayal of a man's patriarchal position and pride matters more than the destruction of a woman's body and sense of being. Shakespeare deplores warped patterns of patriarchal authority but not the patterns themselves. I cannot prove that the Judith Shakespeare Virginia Woolf imagined in *A Room of One's Own* would have more skeptically asserted that patriarchy itself, not simply malicious and overweening representatives of it, helps to nurture rape. No fabulist, I cannot manufacture texts for history, a "Lucrece" by Judith Shakespeare. We must attend to what we have: Shakespearean victims to mourn, victimizers to despise, and a hierarchical order to frame them both.

NOTES

1. *The Rape of Lucrece*, lines 1259–60. All quotations are from *The Complete Works of Shakespeare*, ed. by George Lyman Kittredge (Boston: Ginn, 1936).

2. Marvin Spevack, *A Complete and Systematic Concordance to the Works of Shakespeare*, V (Hildesheim: Georg Olms, 1970), 2713–14, 2718.

3. David Wilbern, "Rape and Revenge in *Titus Andronicus*," *English Literary Renaissance*, 8 (1978), 164.

4. In contrast, the deceiving of Angelo in the matter of the bed-trick, though underhanded, is not comparable to rape. Angelo is neither forced into something against his will nor conscious of pain and humiliation during the sexual act.

5. Leo C. Curran, "Rape and Rape Victims in the Metamorphoses," *Arethusa*, 11, Nos. 1/2 (1978), 223, also points out that rape is "perceived primarily as an offense against the property or honor of men." In brief, rape in a shame culture makes women guilty.

6. Because husbands perceive rape as a form of infidelity, their psychic response to the raped wife has similarities to the attitude toward a possibly unfaithful wife: a disruptive suspicion, confusion, anger, and sense of loss, conveyed metaphorically through references to the sheets of the marriage bed that no longer seem white.

7. Sherrin Marshall Wyntjes, "Women in the Reformation Era," *Becoming Visible: Women in European History*, ed. Renate Bridenthal and Claudia Koonz (Boston: Houghton Mifflin, 1977), p. 187. See, too, in the same volume, Joan Kelly-Gadol, "Did Women Have a Renaissance?" pp. 137–64, and Richard T. Vann, "Toward a New Lifestyle: Women in Preindustrial Capitalism," pp. 192–216.

8. Lawrence Stone, *The Family, Sex and Marriage in England, 1500–1800* (New York: Harper & Row, 1977), p. 7. Others have likewise

claimed that the junction of the sixteenth and seventeenth centuries was "an important crisis in the historic development of Englishwomen." I quote from Alice Clark, *Working Life of Women in the Seventeenth Century* (New York: Harcourt, Brace and Howe, 1920), p. 2. Stone, though he realizes that women were important economic assets, denies the view "that the economic contribution of the wife to the family budget necessarily gave her higher status and greater power, and that her progressive removal from the labour force as capitalism spread prosperity slowly downward was the cause of her social degradation" (p. 200). Clark supports such a theory.

9. Coppélia Kahn, "The Rape in Shakespeare's *Lucrece*," *Shakespeare Studies*, 9 (1976), 68. After giving the first version of this paper, I read in manuscript Kahn's essay which explores several of the same issues with admirable depth, subtlety, and persuasiveness.

Comic Structure and the Humanizing of Kate in *The Taming of the Shrew*

JOHN C. BEAN

Much recent criticism of Shakespeare's *The Taming of the Shrew* can be divided into two camps, the revisionists and the anti-revisionists.[1] The revisionists have argued that Kate's notorious last speech is delivered ironically and that Kate, in retaining her psychological independence from the "duped" Petruchio, remains untamed. As seen by the revisionists, *The Taming of the Shrew* is a relatively sophisticated social comedy, the ironic texture of which directs our attention not primarily to Kate's psychological illness but to the social illness of a materialistic patriarchy.[2] The anti-revisionists, on the other hand, insisting on historical accuracy, have argued that Kate is tamed through the reductive procedures of rollicking, old-fashioned farce. In *The Taming of the Shrew*, argues the anti-revisionist Robert B. Heilman, "Kate is conceived of as responding automatically to a certain kind of calculated treatment, as automatically as an animal to the devices of a skilled trainer."[3]

In this essay I wish to object to both camps—to the revi-

An earlier, shorter version of this essay was presented at the Pacific Northwest Renaissance Conference, March 1977, University of British Columbia, Vancouver.

sionists' belief that we should not take Kate's last speech straight-
forwardly and to the anti-revisionists' belief that Kate responds in
an animallike fashion to Petruchio's taming tactics. What we
should emphasize in *The Taming of the Shrew* is the emergence
of a humanized heroine against the background of depersonalizing farce unassimilated from the play's fabliau sources. If we can
appreciate the liberal element in Kate's last speech—the speech
that strikes modern sensibilities as advocating male tyranny—we
can perhaps see that Kate is tamed not in the automatic manner
of behavioral psychology but in the spontaneous manner of the
later romantic comedies where characters lose themselves in
chaos and emerge, as if from a dream, liberated into the bonds of
love. I shall not be arguing that the play fits neatly into the genre
of romance, for the older farcical elements are continually at odds
with the romantic; rather, I shall try to show that the play reveals
a relationship between the sophistication of comic structure and
the liberation of women from medieval notions of male autocracy.[4] Since farce treats persons as if they lacked the sensitivities
of an inward self, that genre is appropriate to a view of marriage in
which the wife is mainly the husband's chattel. But Shakespeare's romantic comedy is concerned with the discovery of the
inward self, with love as personal, and hence with the relationship of lovers who face together the problem of reconciling liberty
and commitment in marriage. Shakespeare's *The Taming of the
Shrew* rises from farce to romantic comedy to the exact extent
that Kate, in discovering love through the discovery of her own
identity, becomes something more than the fabliau stereotype of
the shrew turned household drudge.

Shakespeare's handling of the shrew-taming theme can be
best appreciated by comparing *The Taming of the Shrew* with
other shrew-taming stories. Jan H. Brunvand has discovered a
well-developed medieval and Renaissance oral tradition of folk
tales on the shrew-taming theme.[5] Brunvand has listed dozens of
variations of these tales, a number of which are remarkably similar to Shakespeare's play and include such parallel incidents as a
father with two daughters, one modest, one shrewish; a brash
young wooer who vows to tame the shrew; a clownish wedding
scene; a journey to a country house; altercations about the sun
and the moon (in many of the stories the wife is compelled to call

foxes ravens, or cows sheep, etc.); and a concluding wager about whose wife is most obedient. All versions of the folk tale assume that man unconditionally rules woman, and in most of them the taming proceeds by the husband's reducing the wife psychologically to the status of an animal. Often the husband unmercifully beats a horse, or rips apart a chicken, or wrings the neck of a cat; the wife is tamed when she recognizes that she is next. The first extant printed version of a play on the shrew-taming theme is the anonymous *The Taming of a Shrew* (published in 1594), which closely parallels in many details Shakespeare's *The Taming of the Shrew*. The heated critical debate over which play precedes which need not detain us here.[6] Of the two plays, the anonymous *A Shrew* is clearly the more primitive in its uniformly misogynist treatment of women. The audience's interest is in the farce and slapstick through which Ferando (Petruchio's equivalent) finally breaks the will of shrewish Kate. Although critics all agree that Shakespeare's version of the play is more witty, the taming process more civilized, and the characters more vital and alive, most believe that the attitude toward women and matrimony—an attitude "adopted in cold blood," according to Mark Van Doren[7]—is roughly similar to that of *A Shrew*. Shakespeare's touch, says Geoffrey Bullough, is "one of enrichment and of smoothing; *The Shrew* is as much a social comedy preaching the subjection of women as was *A Shrew*. . . ."[8]

But the similarities which critics have found between *A Shrew* and *The Shrew* disappear under closer examination, for the vision of matrimony in Shakespeare's play differs significantly from that of the fabliau tradition of shrew-taming, the tradition for which the anonymous *A Shrew* is an excellent dramatic example. Since I shall be arguing that Shakespeare's play does *not* preach the subjection of women, the place to begin is with Kate's last speech about the duties of wives, a speech that has embarrassed generations of critics.[9] Far from reiterating old platitudes about the inferiority of women, however, what Kate actually says reflects a number of humanist assumptions about an ideal marriage popularized by Tudor matrimonial reformers. If we wish to see a real vision of subjugated woman, we should turn to the parallel speech of Kate in the anonymous *A Shrew*. When Ferando in that play orders Kate to instruct the other wives on their matrimonial duties, she recites a medieval argument about women's moral inferiority, an argument repeated in misogynist tracts at least to the time of Milton.

> Then to his image he did make a man,
> Olde *Adam* and from his side asleepe,
> A rib was taken, of which the Lord did make,
> The woe of man so termd by *Adam* then,
> Woman for that, by her came sinne to us,
> And for her sin was *Adam* doomd to die. . . .
>
> (*A Shrew*, xviii, 31–36)[10]

Kate simply gives the Genesis account of woman's responsibility for original sin, her speech emphasizing only the sinfulness and abjection of women. There is nothing in the *A Shrew* version about the husband's duties to the wife or about positive feminine powers such as beauty or nurturing softness; the writer's emphasis is solely on feminine sin. In the *The Shrew* version of the speech, however, Shakespeare makes no reference to moral inferiority in women. His emphasis instead is on reciprocity of duties in marriage, based on the complementary natures of man and woman.

> Fie, fie! unknit that threatening unkind brow,
> And dart not scornful glances from those eyes,
> To wound thy lord, thy king, thy governor:
> It blots thy beauty as frosts do bite the meads,
> Confounds thy fame as whirlwinds shake fair buds,
> And in no sense is meet or amiable.
> A woman mov'd is like a fountain troubled,
> Muddy, ill-seeming, thick, bereft of beauty;
> And while it is so, none so dry or thirsty
> Will deign to sip or touch one drop of it.
> Thy husband is thy lord, thy life, thy keeper,
> Thy head, thy sovereign; one that cares for thee,
> And for thy maintenance commits his body
> To painful labour both by sea and land,
>
> . . . .
>
> And craves no other tribute at thy hands
> But love, fair looks, and true obedience;
> Too little payment for so great a debt . . .   (v.ii.137–55)[11]

Here the woman's softness and beauty, in complementing the man's strength, are affirmative and potent virtues associated with warmth, harmony, peace, and refreshment. Because she now appreciates her own powers, Kate is able to envision the family as an ordered kingdom in which the subject's obedience is a response not to the king's will but to the king's love. The husband is "lord," "governor," "king," "sovereign," and the shrewish wife a "foul contending rebel," a "graceless traitor to her loving lord." "Such duty as the subject owes the prince, / Even such a woman oweth to her husband" (v.ii.156–57), says Kate, and Petruchio believes that Kate's acknowledgment of this obedience means "love, and quiet life, / An awful rule and right supremacy" (109–10). In our own age, perhaps, the distinction between matrimonial tyranny and "right supremacy" is difficult to appreciate, and hence Kate's speech has been deprecated as antifeminist dogma. But in the late sixteenth century, an age obsessed with the nature of ideal kingship and the rightful use of power, such a distinction was important.

Beginning with the Catholic humanists Erasmus and Juan Luis Vives and continued by such Protestant reformers as Heinrich Bullinger and Robert Cleaver, numerous sixteenth-century writers of matrimonial literature examined the problem of hierarchy and kingship on the family level.[12] The marriage reformers attacked three medieval notions about women and matrimony which they found particularly abusive. The first was the scholastic contention that the chief purpose of marriage is procreation. The humanists subordinated procreation to companionship so that we find throughout the domestic handbooks the innovative idea that a man's best friend is his wife. The second abuse was the idealized image of women in the chivalric romances, which the marriage writers denounced as depersonalizing fictions, and the third was the converse notion that the wife was somehow a domestic drudge or servant whom the husband could tyrannize. The last of these abuses—male autocracy—the matrimonial writers attacked with special vigor. The husband ought to understand, says Vives, "that matrimonye is the supreme and most excellent part of all amitie, and that it farre differreth from tiranny."[13] Robert Cleaver says virtually the same thing. "Some husbands there bee, that through evill and rough handling, and in threatning of their wives, have and use them not as wives, but as their servants. And yet surely they are but very fooles, that judge and thinke matrimony to bee a dominion."[14] The problem the matrimonial writers faced was how to reconcile the notion of matrimonial friendship, which tended to make husband and wife equals, with the notion of hierarchy, which asserted the husband's supremacy. The reconciliation occurs through analogy to the political concept of loving kingship wherein the prince's love for his people (analogous in turn to Christ's love for his church) converts tyranny to harmonious order. Subjects who would rebel against a tyrant freely serve a loving king. The concept of loving kingship allows hierarchy without tyranny, for both the subject and the ruler are bound by the mutual obligations of love. Thus the model for marriage is ultimately political: the family is a miniature kingdom ruled in benevolence by the husband. If the first duty of wives is to obey their husbands, the first duty of husbands, stressed again and again in the domestic books, is to love their wives; and in so loving them husbands relinquish their claims to tyrannical authority and regard their wives as friends rather than as servants. According to Vives "yf a man (as nature, reason, and holy scripture, do saye unto us) be the head of the woman, and Christ the father, there ought to be betwene them such societe and felowship, as is betwene the father and the sonne, and not such as is betwene the maister and the servaunt."[15] The effect of the husband's love is to raise the wife's status from mere drudge to a position of importance and dignity. "Thou shalt not have [thy wife] as a servant, . . . but . . . as a most faithful secretary of thy cares and thoughts, and in doubtful matters a wise and a hearty counsellor. This is the true society and fellowship of man. . . ."[16]

Kate's final speech in *The Shrew*, then, in its use of political analogies and its emphasis on woman's warmth and beauty rather than on her abject sinfulness, is not a rehearsal of old, medieval ideas about wives but of relatively contemporary ideas growing out of humanist reforms. Male tyranny, which characterizes earlier shrew-taming stories, gives way here to a nontyrannical hierarchy informed by mutual affection. In Kate's speech there are no arguments supporting the husband's right to capricious domination nor any recommendation of the wifely submissiveness we find in, say, the patient Griselda, for Kate's submissiveness depends on Petruchio's "honest will," on his being a "loving lord." Like Cordelia, Kate will love only according to her bond, no more, no less, and the limits of her bond will be reached whenever Petruchio's authority ceases to be loving. Within such a marriage model, the wife becomes her husband's friend and companion rather than his faceless drudge so that Kate's last speech, rather than supporting Heilman's contention that the play is farce, opposes the depersonalizing procedure of that genre.

We are now faced with a new problem: how to interpret Petruchio's taming of Kate in a way consistent with the humanized vision of marriage contained in her last speech. A partial solution is to focus on the fairly consistent pattern of romantic elements in the taming scenes, namely, those elements that show Kate's discovery of her inward self through her discovery first of play and then of love. Such elements look forward to the festive comedies rather than backward to medieval farce, and, although they jar with elements that remain irretrievably farcical, they reveal Shakespeare's conscious attempt to humanize Kate and thereby to achieve a richer comic form.

Let us begin with a reading of Kate's taming that focuses on the romantic elements. If Kate's last speech is not an assertion of male tyranny, as is the equivalent speech in *A Shrew*, there is such an assertion in Shakespeare's play, one as rude as any we find in the medieval misogynist tracts, but it occurs significantly in Act III before Kate is tamed while Petruchio is playing his preposterous role at the first wedding feast.

> Nay, look not big, nor stamp, nor stare, nor fret;
> I will be master of what is mine own.
> She is my goods, my chattels; she is my house,
> My household stuff, my field, my barn,
> My horse, my ox, my ass, my anything. (III.ii.231–35)

Here is the harsh doctrine of male superiority, and it may be said that this view of women governs the whole of the parallel play, *The Taming of a Shrew*. But in Shakespeare's play the movement away from Padua to the country house and back again to Padua takes on a new significance so that the view of women changes as the play progresses. Or, to put it more accurately, the chattel speech is never the play's real view of matrimony but is adopted by Petruchio as part of his outrageous mask at the wedding. The audience's realization that Petruchio is game-playing, that he is posing behind the mask of a disorderly male shrew and is having considerable fun exploiting his role, is the key to a romantic reading of the play. Thus Kate is tamed not by Petruchio's whip but by the discovery of her own imagination, for when she learns to recognize the sun for the moon and the moon for the dazzling sun she is discovering the liberating power of laughter and play. In the later festive comedies, the chaos in the middle acts—brought on by the characters' spontaneous love of play and disguise—proves a generative cauldron for magic changes and sudden discoveries of love. If shrewishness is a kind of rigidity, a behavioral pattern locked into closed, predictable responses, then the chaos of play is a liberating force, and Kate's initial bad temper is directly related to her failure to embrace it. In the country-house scenes in the anonymous *A Shrew*, Kate is depersonalized because she is denied any possibilities of play. At one point Ferando offers the famished Kate some pieces of meat on the tip of a dagger in a parody of animal taming. Ferando's purpose is to break Kate's will through hunger and lack of sleep. In Shakespeare's play, however, Petruchio's madcap antics are meant to reduce Kate not so much to hunger as to bewilderment. She is to be immersed in chaos, in that irrational world where we lose our bearings and our old sense of truth, and she is challenged to respond as Christopher Sly does in the Induction by yielding to the confusion, abandoning her old identity in favor of a new one. After a day and night at the country house we learn that Petruchio so

> rails, and swears, and rates, that she, poor soul,
> Knows not which way to stand, to look, to speak,
> And sits as one new-risen from a dream.   (IV.i.186–89)

In the great comedies to follow, many characters will find themselves, like Kate, "new-risen from a dream," where temporary surrender to the irrational will lead to liberation from former rigidities.

Kate's transformation occurs on the road to Padua. All the details of the scene are in the anonymous *A Shrew*, but in that play the incidents are merely a final testing of how efficiently Ferando has broken Kate's will to resist. When Kate reluctantly agrees that the sun is the moon, Ferando replies:

> I am glad *Kate* your stomack is come downe,
> I know it well thou knowest it is the sun,
> But I did trie to see if thou wouldst speake,
> And crosse me now as thou hast donne before,
> And trust me *Kate* hadst thou not named the moone,
> We had gon back againe as sure as death.
>
> (*A Shrew*, xv.13–18)

There is no laughter on Ferando's part, only a harsh warning that his methods are "as sure as death." Ferando seems as rigid as Kate, and his unyielding authority is nonplayful. In Shakespeare's play, however, Petruchio's method of shrew-taming celebrates life, for Petruchio is playing, and when Kate suddenly joins him, Shakespeare presents her as cured. Kate's sense of fun throughout the road scene becomes increasingly apparent as she begins to make puns on "sun" (meaning both the planet and Petruchio, who is "his mother's son") and as she herself notes the sexual humor in turning the bewildered old Vincentio into a fresh, budding virgin. When Petruchio decides to restore Vincentio to himself, Kate, obviously now enjoying her husband's game, apologizes magnificently:

> Pardon, old father, my mistaking eyes,
> That have been so bedazzled with the sun
> That everything I look on seemeth green.   (iv.v.45–47)

This emphasis on sunshine and greenness is significant because the weather during their previous trip from Padua to the country house was dominated by frost and cold. When Kate discovers laughter, the weather turns springtime, for Shakespeare sees in Kate not a taming but a renewal and rebirth. When she is liberated from shrewishness, she perceives the world with new eyes and everything "seemeth green."

Kate's transformation, associated as it is with the magical powers of imagination, is something quite different from the rough and tumble "taming" she undergoes in *A Shrew*. Her temporary immersion in chaos is renewing and brings her in touch with some deeper creative energy. She is neither intellectually nor morally inferior to her husband, and if she is subordinate to him in the political hierarchy, this difference does not allow for tyranny but requires instead "honest will" and "right supremacy."

In the final happiness of Kate, we have thus discovered comic possibilities beyond the primitive limits of farce.

And yet the play never breaks completely from farce, and an emphasis on its romantic elements will be misleading if we do not see how the romance is at odds with the fabliau. For example, Petruchio's antics at the country house—his beating of servants, his throwing of food and bedding, his railing at the tailor—can be accommodated in a romantic reading if we emphasize, as I have done, the need to create bewilderment and loss of identity in the transforming middle acts of romantic comedy and if we cite passages such as Curtis's on Kate's awakening from a dream. These same antics will seem closer to farce if we cite instead Petruchio's soliloquy beginning "Thus have I politicly begun my reign" (IV.i.191–214), in which Petruchio compares his taming of Kate to the training of a falcon.[17] This uneasy mixing of romance and farce suggests that Shakespeare's own sense of purpose is unclear, that he is discovering possibilities of one kind of comic structure while working within the demands of another.[18] The coincidence of farce and romance is especially evident during the final wager scene, where the farcical elements prevent the kind of festive conclusion that will mark the later comedies. The problem, as we know intuitively, is Kate's last speech. But what should bother us about the speech is not what Kate actually says—the content of the speech, as I have shown, is consistent with Shakespeare's humanized version of shrew-taming—but the way she is forced by Petruchio to say it. Shakespeare has tried to invest Kate with dignity, and yet when she is compelled to come on stage at the end of the play, to stomp obediently on her new hat, and to lecture on cue about the duties of wives, she still has some of the vestiges of a trained bear. The clear distortion here between humanized character and dehumanizing plot suggests that if Shakespeare is to express adequately civilized notions about women he must turn from old fabliau tales that demand an impersonal, even mechanical female. The problem Shakespeare faces in *The Shrew* returns to him later in his career in the two dark comedies, *Measure for Measure* and *All's Well That Ends Well*, whose plots are also taken from sources allied with older, more primitive attitudes toward women. A case in point is the convention of the bedtrick. Helena in *All's Well*, for example, may well be the culmination of Shakespeare's studies of women. She is unquestionably his most erotic heroine, and her femininity is magically potent. Helena creates for us a world in which sexual experience matters, and it matters most because it cannot be separated from the emotional and the personal. Helena is erotic because she is in love. In such a world the bed-trick is jarring because bed-tricks can work only where sex is impersonal, where bodies unite without the complications of spirit, where women are *things*. What shocks us is not the bed-trick itself or any subtle problem of ethics but the collusion of the human and the mechanical.[19] When Helena pretends in the dark of night to be Diana, we feel on a deeper, more disturbing plane what we feel during Kate's last speech—the incoherence that comes from combining old tales and humanized women.

I have mentioned *All's Well* only to clarify further what is already quite clear in *The Taming of the Shrew*, that the emergence of a humanized heroine demands a comic form completely unlike farce. To emphasize the farcical element in *The Shrew*, therefore, is to neglect the romance inherent in Kate's discovery of laughter, for this is the major difference between Shakespeare's play and earlier versions of shrew-taming. And to insist still on a revisionist conclusion, complete with an untamed Kate and a duped Petruchio, is to show again the alliance of our age with those Renaissance villains who seek liberation from all bondage, especially the bonds of love. It is not Kate's submission to her husband that should make us feel that *The Taming of the Shrew* is more primitive than the later comedies; rather it is the unassimilated elements of farce that continue to depersonalize Kate.

NOTES

1. The terms are suggested by Robert B. Heilman's discussion of "revisionist" interpretations of *The Shrew* in "The *Taming* Untamed, or, The Return of the Shrew," *Modern Language Quarterly*, 27 (1966), 147–61.
2. Heilman's survey of the history of "revisionism" emphasizes the commentaries of Nevill Coghill, Harold C. Goddard, and Margaret Webster. (See "The *Taming* Untamed," pp. 149–51.) For a recent article in the revisionist tradition, see Coppélia Kahn's persuasive "The Taming of the Shrew: Shakespeare's Mirror of Marriage," *Modern Language Studies*, 5 (1975), 88–102. See also George Hibbard, "The

Taming of the Shrew: a Social Comedy," *Shakespearean Essays*, ed. Alwin Thaler and Norman Sanders, Special Number 2, *Tennessee Studies in Literature* (Knoxville: University of Tennessee Press, 1964), pp. 15–28. Although Hibbard does not propose an ironic reading for Kate' s last speech, his sensitivity to the social causes of Kate's shrewishness is typical of revisionism. According to Hibbard, Kate's "shrewishness is not bad temper, but the expression of her self-respect" (p. 23).

3. Heilman, "The *Taming* Untamed," p. 155.
4. An early and clear vision of this relationship is suggested by George Meredith, who, in his *An Essay on Comedy and the Uses of the Comic Spirit*, ed. Lane Cooper (New York: Charles Scribner's Sons, 1918), speaks of the development from low to high comedy. "There never will be civilization," says Meredith, "where comedy is not possible; and that comes of some degree of social equality of the sexes." He continues: "Let them [cultivated women] look with their clearest vision abroad and at home. They will see that, where they have no social freedom, comedy is absent; where they are household drudges, the form of comedy is primitive; where they are tolerably independent, but uncultivated, exciting melodrama takes its place, and a sentimental version of them. . . . But where women are on the road to an equal footing with men, in attainments and in liberty—in what they have won for themselves, and what has been granted them by a fair civilization—there, and only waiting to be transplanted from life to the stage, or the novel, or the poem, pure comedy flourishes . . ." (pp. 118–19).
5. Jan H. Brunvand, "The Folktale Origin of *The Taming of the Shrew*," *Shakespeare Quarterly*, 17 (1966), 345–59.
6. For many years scholars believed that *A Shrew* was the source of *The Shrew*, and Geoffrey Bullough includes the complete text of the play in *Narrative and Dramatic Sources of Shakespeare*, I (New York: Columbia University Press, 1957). But Richard Hosley, in "Sources and Analogues of *The Taming of the Shrew*," *Huntington Library Quarterly*, 27 (1964), 289–308, argues that *A Shrew* is neither the source of Shakespeare's play nor a bad quarto of an older "lost shrew play" but simply a bad quarto of *The Shrew* itself. His essay surveys the lengthy debate of scholars on this issue and, as nearly as I can determine, has carried the day against Bullough and others who support the *A Shrew*-as-source theory. But to my mind the troublesome relationship between the plays is still an open question. I seek here to show that the conception of women and marriage in *The Shrew* is influenced by humanist reforms and by Shakespeare's developing romantic ideas about psychological change, while the conception of marriage in *A Shrew* is allied to the fabliaux and the misogynist tracts. If *A Shrew* is simply a bad quarto of *The Shrew* (that is, a "memorial reconstruction," as Hosley argues [p. 289]), it is a bad quarto of the most improb-

able kind, since its perpetrator must have wished consistently to remove the romantic and humanist elements in *The Shrew*. The more logical thesis is Bullough's, namely, that *A Shrew* precedes *The Shrew*, but Hosley's arguments against Bullough cannot be lightly dismissed. I can say at present only that all suggested theories about the relationship between the plays seem unsatisfactory.

7. Mark Van Doren, *Shakespeare* (1939; rpt. New York: Doubleday, 1953), p. 37.

8. Bullough, ed., *Narrative and Dramatic Sources of Shakespeare*, I, 64.

9. "As if Shakespeare could ever have meant it!" exclaims Harold C. Goddard in *The Meaning of Shakespeare*, 2 vols. (Chicago: University of Chicago Press, 1951), I, 71; and George Bernard Shaw, writing in 1897, calls the final speech "altogether disgusting to modern sensibility"; see *Shaw on Shakespeare*, ed. Edwin Wilson (New York: Dutton, 1961), p. 188. Juliet Dusinberre calls it "disconcerting," a "reactionary comment on women's obedience," in *Shakespeare and the Nature of Women* (London: Macmillan, 1975), p. 105, although elsewhere she appreciates the difference between Kate's speech in *The Shrew* and the equivalent speech of *A Shrew* (pp. 78–79). Coppélia Kahn claims that "the contextual irony of Kate's last speech" makes it clear to us "that her husband is deluded." The sentiments of the speech, Kahn says, contain all the "platitudes of male dominance" ("Mirror of Marriage," pp. 98–99). Even the anti-revisionist Robert Heilman seems embarrassed by the speech. He asks us gently to pass over it since it is a "more or less automatic statement . . . of a generally held doctrine" that we no longer believe in, "just as we no longer believe in the divine right of kings" ("The *Taming* Untamed," p. 159). For a view of the speech closer to the one proposed here, see Margaret Loftus Ranald, "The Manning of the Haggard; or *The Taming of the Shrew*," *Essays in Literature*, 1 (1974), 149–65. Ranald sees in the speech not Kate's submission before an authoritarian husband but a celebration of partnership in mutuality.

10. All quotations from *The Taming of a Shrew* are taken from the text in Bullough's *Sources of Shakespeare*.

11. All quotations from Shakespeare are taken from *The Complete Works of Shakespeare*, ed. W. J. Craig (New York: Oxford University Press, 1919).

12. See my essay "Passion versus Friendship in the Tudor Matrimonial Handbooks and Some Shakespearean Implications," *Wascana Review*, 9, No. 1 (1974), 231–40.

13. Lodovicus Vives, *The Office and Duetie of an Husband*, trans. Thomas Paynell (London, 1553), sig. K8^r.

14. Robert Cleaver, *A Godly Form of Householde Governement* (London, 1598), p. 211.

15. Vives, *Office and Duetie of an Husband*, sig. L1^r.

16. Lodovicus Vives, *The Office and Duetie of an Husband*; rpt. in *Vives and the Renascence Education of Woman*, ed. Foster Watson (London: Edward Arnold, 1912), p. 209.

17. Petruchio's comparison of shrew-taming to the training of a falcon has been a stumbling block to critics who try to demonstrate Petruchio's kindness and humanity. "How," E. M. W. Tillyard asks, "can we escape from this soliloquy?" To Tillyard, Petruchio's comparison means that Petruchio will follow "the direct and brutal method by which a man tames a hawk"; see *Shakespeare's Early Comedies* (London: Chatto and Windus, 1966), p. 85. Similarly Coppélia Kahn suggests that Petruchio's "animal metaphor shocks us" and that it was meant "to shock Shakespeare's audience, despite their respect for falconry as an art . . ." ("Mirror of Marriage," p. 95). Other critics, however, have argued that the falcon-taming analogy is not necessarily reductive and dehumanizing. See George Hibbard and Margaret Loftus Ranald.

18. Tillyard expresses the same point of view in *Shakespeare's Early Comedies*; see especially pp. 78–89.

19. My discussion of the bed-trick in *All's Well* is indebted to Barbara Everett's excellent introduction to the New Penguin *All's Well That Ends Well*, ed. B. Everett (Harmondsworth, Eng.: Penguin, 1970), p. 10.

Those "soft and delicate desires"

Much Ado and the Distrust of Women

JANICE HAYS

The Hero-Claudio plot in *Much Ado about Nothing* is one of Shakespeare's earliest treatments of a theme that he was to examine several times: the sexual distrust of woman, and her subsequent testing and vindication.[1] And in *Much Ado*, as in several of the mature comedies and romances, Shakespeare uses a woman to lead the male protagonist away from the individualistic aspiration, assertiveness, and narrow rationality that characterize the male role in Renaissance society—as in patriarchal Western society in general—so that the man may develop the emotional facility, the empathy, that will make it possible for him to relate to others in a genuinely caring way.[2] The establishing of the woman's trustworthiness makes it safe for him to take this step.

In *Much Ado*, Shakespeare brings the traditionally male sphere of war, honors, and triumph into contact with the private and potentially expressive world of Messina, a world whose functioning is communal and cyclical and whose heirs are women—although at the play's beginning it is ruled by a father whose goals appear to be as instrumental as those of the soldiers whom he welcomes. As the play opens, another father-figure, Don Pedro, arrives in Messina, himself and his young soldiers covered with the glory of battle. In particular we hear of young Claudio, who has done "in the figure of a lamb the feats of a lion" (1.i.14–15).[3] That Messina's father is named "Leonato" suggests the male-instrumental function of such deeds. The play's initial section establishes in courtly and ceremonial language the heroism of the young warriors and seems almost to elevate the actions of war to those of a chivalric tournament. Beatrice's ironic comments, however, give us another, probably biased, perspective upon this male enterprise, drawing a picture of Benedick—and, by inference, of the play's other young men—as a self-serving late-adolescent swaggerer whose life is lived principally in the company of a changing cast of comrades who are yet all basically the same and whose emotions are attached to the male world of soldiering and hell-raising, young men similar to Hotspur, Mercutio and Tybalt, and Bertram.

Having heard from the messenger about Claudio's feats of honor, we expect to see a swashbuckling hero assert himself on the scene. Yet during all the initial exchange between Benedick, Beatrice, Don Pedro and Leonato, Claudio utters not a syllable. Apart from the church scene, this is his posture in mixed company throughout the play, and only when he is with men alone does he speak freely. In this first scene, a scene whose playful banter is larded with references to cuckoldry, it is after the larger company has left the stage that Claudio is heard from. Significantly, his first speeches are to ask Benedick for *his* opinion of Hero—and particularly to inquire whether or not Hero seems to him to be "modest" (virtuous, chaste). Although Benedick responds flippantly to his questions (1.i.163–230), Claudio pursues the matter with an earnest importunity that suggests that he both wants and needs to have his perceptions validated by another. His declarations of feeling are tentative and provisional, phrased as questions or in the conditional (183, 197–98, 221–22), or made contingent upon perception (190–91). When Don Pedro states unequivocally that Hero is "very well worthy," Claudio replies, "You speak this to fetch me in, my lord" (225), an indication of his wariness.

Critics have argued over whether or not Claudio in his pursuit of Hero is a fortune-seeker. Prouty has suggested that he behaves in a businesslike way that accords with Elizabethan marriage customs,[4] and a study of these customs partially supports this view. Yet Claudio's behavior, particularly his scathing denunciation of Hero in the church, raises questions that cannot be answered simply by viewing him as a partner in a business enterprise. I believe that Shakespeare's purpose in the Hero-Claudio plot is not just to show us the anti-romantic aspects of an arranged marriage but rather to confront the psychological difficulties of joining the traditional arranged marriage, which takes into account social and economic reality, with romantic and erotic love. If such a merger could be effected, it would lead to a love marriage between equals in which neither partner was idealized nor degraded and would thus constitute a new ideal relationship, one rooted in the reciprocity of mutuality.

Although we cannot read Claudio's character as a rounded psychological portrait, his actions, together with those of the play's other characters, do show us the contours of a psychology common to the period and one that has bearing on Shakespeare's theme: that of the men who aspire for glory and honor as compensation for a deep lack of self-esteem.[5] Claudio's exchanges with Benedick and Don Pedro in Act I, scene i, show us a young man who is either very cautious about committing himself or else very unsure of his own judgment, or both.

He asks Don Pedro to press his suit for him—"My liege, your Highness now may do me good" (1.i.292–93)—an entirely usual way of arranging a marriage,[6] but his phrasing suggests that for him matrimony is primarily an enterprise; "do me good" certainly smacks of getting ahead in the world, and Claudio is careful to ascertain that Hero is Leonato's heir before he proceeds further. Yet his association with the male world, his silence in the presence of women, and his hesitation about affirming his tentative feelings for Hero imply that he is more at home with the actions of war than the emotions of love, and the speech in which he finally declares his feelings suggests the basis for his diffidence:

> Oh, my lord,
> When you went onward on this ended action,
> I looked upon her with a soldier's eye,
> That liked but had a rougher task in hand
> Than to drive liking to the name of love.
> But now I am returned and that war thoughts
> Have left their places vacant, in their rooms

Come thronging soft and delicate desires,
All prompting me how fair young Hero is,
Saying I liked her ere I went to wars.   (1.i.298–307)

On a commonsensical level it is appropriate that a soldier going off to war should subordinate the pursuit of love to the pursuit of the enemy. Yet at a deeper level, Claudio's words suggest that in him "war thoughts" may have substituted for thoughts of love, in fact may have been a defense against them, and that he has embraced the duties of a soldier because he is disinclined, or afraid, to embrace a woman. Significantly, it is only because "war thoughts / Have left their places vacant" that "soft and delicate desires" now come "thronging," desires that "prompt" Claudio to the conclusion that Hero is "fair" (both "beautiful" and "unsullied") and remind him that he "liked her ere [he] went to war" (1.i.306–7).

The speech suggests a disjunction between thinking and feeling. "Thoughts" have to do with "war" and "feelings" with desire; Claudio's attempt to reason his earlier "liking" into present "loving" appears like an effort to structure and control sexual feelings by making them respectable. We may deduce that Claudio is a young man whose energy has been channeled into male pursuits but who now finds himself physically attracted to a gorgeous young woman and is afraid of being overwhelmed by his feelings. He worries that his "liking might too sudden seem" (1.i.316) and suggests that he would "salve it with a longer treatise" (317). The use of the verb "salve"—to apply a healing ointment to a bodily sore—unconsciously suggests the physical origin and troubling nature of this "liking." The sexual component of Claudio's feelings becomes even more evident after the match has been arranged, when he expresses to Leonato his wish to be married "tomorrow, my lord. Time goes on crutches till love have all his rites" (II.i.372–73).

It thus appears that Claudio is trying to defend himself against a sudden surge of sexuality by being very careful to do the right thing, to be certain that the proposed marriage is a safe one in which he dare invest both his sexual and his affectionate feelings. For to love a woman with affection is to respond to her as one has to the ideal, nurturing, "good mother"-figure of early childhood. Also to love her sexually is to mobilize fears about the

"bad mother" who, in the male child's eyes, betrayed and abandoned him.[7] The fact that Renaissance mothers often did "abandon" their children by putting them out to a wet-nurse would
only add to the intensity of these fears, for, according to Lawrence
Stone, most upper-class Renaissance adults had as children rou-
tinely experienced what must have been severe separation anxiety when they were weaned and abruptly taken away from their
original nurturing caretaker, the wet nurse. Stone further states
that the effects of such early childhood deprivation, "an inability
to maintain human relations; psychotic-like attacks of rage; and a
tendency to erect projective defenses against the world, giving a
paranoid colouration to [such people's] character . . . are overwhelmingly obvious in all the documentation of the period,"
these characteristics in turn suggesting the deep dependency
needs that result from early-childhood trauma. From a psychoanalytic viewpoint, it seems clear that in young adults growing up
with such childhood disturbances, the yearning for love would
arouse terrible fears about both the impossibility of having such
needs fulfilled and the unreliability of the person fulfilling them.[8]

Further, for the young adult male to relate to a tenderly regarded woman sexually might seem perilously akin to incest,
since the idealized woman would recall the nurturing figures who
were the objects of the boy's earliest tender feelings, whether
those figures were wet nurse, natural mother, or the sister who, in
Elizabethan upper-class family life, was often the object of the
male child's deepest affections—all these women, in Renaissance
patriarchal society, clearly the property of the father or father-
figure.[9] Although the frequent consequence of such divided perceptions in the male psyche is its splitting of woman into the
part-perceptions already discussed, in the middle comedies
Shakespeare attempts to move his male characters to a more mature level of functioning in which a woman may be loved as a
complete human being.

To understand both Claudio's behavior and the play's subsequent developments, we must look at the young man's relationship to Don Pedro and Don John. While it is reasonable and even
probable in the light of conventional marriage practices that
Claudio should ask Don Pedro, who clearly stands in the role of
father to him, to make the necessary overture to Leonato, it does
not at all follow that Don Pedro should disguise himself as Clau-

dio, approach Hero, and woo her. Stone suggests that Elizabethan marriages were negotiated by the parents; at most, children were given the right of veto.[10] In the Bandello novella that is one source for *Much Ado*, Timbreo (the Claudio character) sends a friend to negotiate with Fenicia's father; there is no face-to-face courtship between the young lovers.[11] Thus Hero's wooing is neither necessary nor in accord with custom, nor does such courtship occur in the play's sources. Consequently, we may suspect that this part of the play contains latent content that is shaping the story's manifest presentation.

If we return to the discussion between Claudio and Don Pedro (1.i.292 ff.), we notice that Claudio almost seems to be asking Don Pedro to protect him from the intensity of his feelings by seconding the young man's tentative suggestion that he ought to exercise restraint. But instead of advising caution and thus assuming the role that strong fathers customarily fill for their adolescent sons,[12] Don Pedro rather urges Claudio to proceed without delay: "What need the bridge much broader than the flood?" (1.i.318). Such permission from a parental authority-figure to follow the promptings of desire, which in any adolescent male might well contain remnants of his feelings toward the original woman or women in his life, could let loose a flood indeed of incestuous fantasies and consequent fears of retaliation from the "father." Further, Don Pedro enters into the surrogate wooing with considerable enthusiasm, avowing that "in her bosom I'll unclasp my heart, / And take her hearing prisoner with the force / And strong encounter of my amorous tale" (1.i.325–27). This male zest would certainly reinforce the adolescent Claudio's unconscious fear that he is in Oedipal competition for his beloved and, further, could expect to be bested in such a contest.

Don John's function in *Much Ado* is similar to Iago's in *Othello*. He plants the seeds of distrust in Claudio's mind, and I would suggest that he does so by externalizing unconscious aspects of Claudio's psyche. As a bastard younger son who has fallen out of favor through his ambition to "stand out" against his older brother, Don John is the negative, or "double," of Claudio's subordination of his strivings to the prince's service.[13] His malice appears to come from his thwarted ambitions. The pattern is characteristic of the Jacobean malcontent and a mode of behavior that Karen Horney suggests is typical for certain character types who, when their strivings fail, retaliate with vindictiveness against those who have thwarted them.[14] Since Claudio has had "the glory of [his] overthrow" (i.iii.69), the younger man is a logical target for Don John's malice. At a deeper psychic level, however, Don John may express Claudio's own punitive conscience, a conscience that expects retaliation as a consequence of wishing to compete against the father-figure repesented by Don Pedro. Certainly there is much in Renaissance social history that suggests a competitive struggle between fathers and sons, with consequent guilt and vindictiveness on both sides.[15]

In the masked-ball episode, Claudio is quick to conclude the worst: that the prince has wooed Hero for himself and thus has "stolen" her from Claudio. During the masque, Claudio stands to one side, watching but not participating, shut out from the interaction between Don Pedro and Hero, his posture suggesting what psychoanalysis terms a "primal scene," in which the child sees (or fantasizes seeing) sexual relations between the parents and feels excluded and thus defeated in the hopes of securing idealized parental love.[16] The rapidity with which Claudio is persuaded of Don Pedro's duplicity and the speed with which he relinquishes his hopes of Hero mirror the depth of his distrust and his lack of self-esteem, for it does not occur to him that he could successfully compete with Don Pedro. Further, his reluctance to compete may reflect not only fear but also love and dependency: ultimately, he does not wish to risk losing Don Pedro's affection and his powerful protection. All these factors suggest that Claudio's allegiance is still invested in the sphere of male bonding and male achievement, perhaps as a defense against the anxieties occasioned by heterosexuality, and that he is not yet ready to take his place in the measured dance that signifies marriage and adult responsibility.

Yet Claudio's fears prove groundless, and the initial episode draws to a close when Don Pedro presents Hero to him. What this first movement accomplishes psychologically is to remove the threat of a retaliatory father from Claudio's psyche. With the restraint of this paternal figure out of the way, Claudio is now forced to confront the incestuous fantasies that have hitherto been held in check.

Shakespeare uses the mock-assignation scene, in which Claudio, Don Pedro, and Don John watch Borachio woo Margaret disguised as Hero, to externalize both Claudio's sexual fantasies about Hero and his inability to accept his sexual impulses. If we assume with psychoanalysis that many slips of the tongue reveal unconscious meaning,[17] there is no other adequate explanation for the parapraxis involved in Borachio's speech outlining the deception plan to Don John:

> Find me a meet hour to draw Don Pedro and the Count Claudio alone. Tell them that you know that Hero loves me. . . . They will scarcely believe this without trial. Offer them instances which shall bear no less likelihood than to see me at her chamber window, hear me call Margaret [who will be disguised as Hero] Hero, hear Margaret term me *Claudio*, and bring them to see this the very night before the intended wedding. (II.ii.33–46; emphasis added)

Since the entire point of the deception is to persuade Claudio that Hero is sexually involved with Borachio, it makes no sense for Margaret to call Borachio "Claudio."[18] Perhaps this slip of Shakespeare's pen is simply an instance of Homer's nodding, but it is axiomatic in psychoanalytic theory that when the ego dozes, id material works its way to the surface, as happens, for example, in dreams and fantasies. Of course, even in dreams, the normally repressed material must be sufficiently disguised to slip past the ego-controls that persist even in the sleeping state.[19]

As Borachio describes it in Act II, scene ii, the episode indeed takes on a delusional and fantastic quality that Shakespeare later augments by having the actual scene, which we never see, reported by a Borachio who by this time (III.iii) is drunk and foulmouthed. What the mock-assignation suggests is a disguised version of Hero being made love to by a Borachio who bears enough resemblance to Claudio so that Shakespeare could inadvertently confuse their names. Its outlines resemble what Freud reported as being certain masturbatory fantasies, common during male adolescence, in which the young man imagines the mother or sister "in sexual situations of the most manifold kind" and in which "the lover with whom the mother commits the act of unfaithfulness almost invariably bears the features of the boy himself."[20] Thus Don John's staging of the apparent rendezvous between Hero and Borachio is a dramatic enactment of Claudio's internal conflict. The incestuous root of Claudio's anxiety is, I feel, fur-

ther suggested in his words to Leonato in the church after the latter suggests that it may be Claudio himself who has "made defeat
of [Hero's] virginity":

> No, Leonato,
> I never tempted her with word too large,
> But, as a brother to his sister, showed
> Bashful sincerity and comely love.　　　　(IV.i.52–55)

His righteous insistence that he has behaved toward Hero "as a
brother to a sister" is precisely the point, for underneath the
"bashful sincerity and comely love" of brother for sister lie unconscious incestuous fantasies,[21] and such feelings would have
been especially likely during Shakespeare's time when brother-
sister relationships were often close and intense.

Claudio's rage in the church scene is an index of his humiliation and his sense of betrayal. The male fear that she who seems
so beautiful, so virtuous, so deserving of tender love will prove to
be a whore and seek out other men to satisfy her supposedly insatiable sexual desires has, apparently, been confirmed. In a patriarchal value system that views woman and her sexuality as a
man's exclusive possession, this infidelity is the ultimate betrayal, a fundamental wound to male self-esteem. To a young man
whose self-esteem is fragile to begin with, who has tried to but-
tress that self-esteem by carefully arranging an honorable and advantageous marriage, such a blow would mobilize a narcissistic
rage that could be appeased only by vindictive punishing of the
guilty party.[22] Hence Claudio's vicious public denunciation of
Hero in the church.

After Hero faints, Leonato continues for a total of some
thirty lines to berate her in the most extravagant terms. In its
staging, this is an excruciating scene, for Hero, in her white gown
and wedding finery, lies as if dead at Leonato's feet while he ha-
rangues her beyond the point of endurance, wishing that she
might die rather than awaken to shame him with her tainted life.
Both men's speeches make it clear that Hero is for them little
more than a pawn on the masculine chessboard. She becomes a
virgin sacrifice, and Leonato's emphasis upon his ownership of
her (IV.i.138–41) makes us question the system of values that
makes a woman's virginity an extension of male pride—particularly when no one has even thought to ask about Claudio's

sexual purity or lack of it. Shakespeare has seen to it that we know how unjust these accusations are, and the emotional force of the scene drives us to a strong identification with and sympathy for Hero.

At this point (IV.i.157) the priest interrupts Leonato's tirade to interpose his own intuitive responses to the situation, to assert that Hero is surely innocent. The solution that he proposes, that Hero pretend to be dead, has little to do with rational schemes and striving after goals. Rather, it opens the play's action to a perception of reality different from that of the instrumental chain of seeming cause-and-effect that has led to Hero's slander. Claudio has vowed (106–9) to defend himself against love, to guard his eyes with "conjecture" (a word whose root suggests an aggressive hurling motion) against the entrance of beauty so that it will never more "be gracious." The priest proposes a reversal of this process, a release of graciousness, or Grace, whereby "the idea of her life shall sweetly creep / Into his study of imagination" (226–27).

In the play's earlier movement, darkness and night have been associated with depravity, sexual sin, soiling. Leonato has taken over Borachio's imagery when he speaks of Hero as "smirchèd thus and mired with infamy" (IV.i.135). But the priest invokes another aspect of night and darkness, the mode of dream and imagination, the creative, expressive dimension of experience, to exonerate Hero, suggesting that "imagination" and "soul" will yield the truth about her. The friar, in speaking of "this strange course" that he "dreams on" (214), says, "But on this travail look for greater birth" (215). The Christian implications of this sacrificial death are obvious, and the friar's subsequent words—"doubt not but success / Will fashion the event in better shape / Than I can lay it down in likelihood" (236–38)—allude to Providence, itself an aspect of the Christian concept of grace.

Structurally, this dying in order to live (see IV.i.255) conveys the psychological rhythm of what David McClelland rather clumsily terms the "Demeter-Persephone life style," a pattern that he considers a distinctively "feminine" experience of power, in part because of its obvious analogy to giving birth but more fundamentally because it suggests the patterns of relating to and coping with experience that women have developed and refined in a society in which they have been, until recently, restricted to the role of caretaker for others and have been denied participation in the society's power structures.[23] As Jean Baker Miller suggests, these historical circumstances have required women to develop sensitivity to the responses of others as well as honestly to confront and accept the facts of individual vulnerability and weakness. Women have become

> the "carriers" for society of certain aspects of the total human experience—those aspects that remain unsolved [aspects having to do with human feelings and relationships]. The result of such a [dichotomizing] process is to keep men from fully integrating these areas into their own lives. . . . That women are better able than men to consciously admit to feelings of weakness or vulnerability may be obvious, but we have not recognized the importance of this ability. That women are truly much more able to tolerate these feelings . . . is a positive strength. Many adolescent boys and young men especially seem to be suffering acutely from the need to flee from these feelings *before* they experience them. In that sense, women, both superficially and deeply, are more closely in touch with basic life experiences—in touch with reality. By being in this closer connection with this central human condition, by having to defend less and deny less, women are in a position to understand weakness more readily and to work productively *with* it.[24]

What both Miller and McClelland are talking about is that area of human functioning that I have termed "expressive," a way of relating to experience that is potentially available to members of either sex, as indeed is the instrumental behavior that is its counterpart. There is nothing innate or "biological" about either of these forms of human psychological functioning even though Western society has rather stringently relegated one to women, the other to men.

As Miller, McClelland, and many others make clear, mature human development requires the integration of these two ways of thinking about and confronting experience, but because Western culture has been skewed on the side of instrumentality, the more pressing need, in Shakespeare's time as in our own, has been for the integration of expressiveness into the human repertoire. For without expressiveness there is no empathy, and empathy is a necessary component of the mutuality that is the condition of mature love, since it is empathy that enables one to be receptive and responsive to the feelings and needs of others, temporarily setting aside one's own aims and desires in order to understand the emotions of another human being. In psychoanalytic terms, mutuality may at times mean the limiting or relinquishing of some of the claims of "self" for the sake of the "other" for whom one cares. The goal of mutuality is not aggrandizement by and enhancement of the self—individual victory—but rather development of a relationship in which both self and other are equally fulfilled and in which the self is enhanced not by triumphing over but by interacting reciprocally with a valued other. This is the dynamic of affiliation, whether at the level of the individual love relationship or of the relationship of the self to its wider community. As McClelland describes the Demeter-Persephone pattern of responding to experience, its central feature is what he terms a "go[ing] down in order to come up"[25]—a choice to surrender a measure of individual autonomy, perhaps even to accept deprivation and suffering, for the sake of a greater future enhancement that includes the reward of a caring relationship with another.

Now all this would seem to be reading Shakespeare with a very modern eye indeed, except that clearly the mature comedies and several of the romances are organized around some such pattern. The structure of Shakespearean comedy differs from the instrumental securing and experiencing of comic triumph that is the pattern of the main body of Western dramatic comedy, a pattern that is organized around a relatively direct rising action that ends with the protagonist's triumph over the environment. The Demeter-Persephone pattern is an expressive action depending more upon the entire context of the play's events than upon the exercise of individual instrumentality upon the world of the play. In Shakespeare, the pattern involves some development of autonomy and assertiveness by the protagonist(s), female as well as male; in *Much Ado*, Hero never becomes assertive or self-directed, but Beatrice does, and certainly Portia, Rosalind, Viola, and Helena demonstrate this phase of the comic action. At some point in the play there is a crisis that brings deprivation or pain and seeming failure. However, suffering or yielding up becomes

an opportunity rather than a defeat, for through voluntary surrender to and acceptance of deprivation, the protagonist achieves
a reward that proves to be of greater value than individual triumph. The action turns upon the protagonist's willingness to be
acted upon rather than to act, to be "seized" by powers higher
than herself or himself.

The forms of and assumptions behind such action are
hardly unique to modern psychology, having a long history in the
religious traditions of both East and West; and indeed, the two
ways of thinking and being that I have called "instrumental" and
"expressive" have been described, in a variety of terms, throughout the history of Western thought. More important for the study
of Shakespeare, however, is the fact that Renaissance Neoplatonism, whose ideas permeate the air of sixteenth- and seventeenth-century thought, advocates something very like "go[ing]
down in order to come up" as the path to a knowledge of truth
that transcends the limits of human reason. Neoplatonism's "circle of grace," a rhythm consisting of *emanatio*, *raptio*, and *re-
meatio*, or "procession, rapture, and return,"[26] suggests just such
a movement, and the Neoplatonists explicitly compared this experience to the union of lovers, which they considered the closest
purely human equivalent to the direct experiencing of God or of
the truth. In this pattern God or the gods (or, by analogy, the
lover) reach out to human beings, a reaching out that involves
some sacrifice of godly power in order to make contact with people. Individuals, in turn, must then respond to that "reaching
out" by opening themselves to receive it and, in Neoplatonism's
terms, to surrender themselves to the "darkness," the Orphic or
Dionysian experience of being possessed by something that transcends the understanding of the rational mind. The result is a return to, a knowing of, the godhead.[27]

When one strips away Neoplatonism's rather fanciful metaphors, what remains is something akin to the dynamics of mutuality: the limiting of the self's claims, the opening of the self to
experience a reality that transcends it—the experience of the
"other"—and the resulting enrichment of union with the other.
In Shakespearean comedy, the "going down in order to come back
up" is usually enacted by a female rather than a male protagonist,
and here Shakespeare follows Western thought's long tradition of
splitting the instrumental and the expressive between male and

female, a dichotomizing also made explicit in many of Neoplatonism's metaphors. The real-life consequence of this splitting, of course, has been to make women always the agents of giving and sacrifice, men the receivers of their sacrificial gift; this fact does not rule out the validity of the psychological pattern but rather suggests that perhaps men ought to try it too. And certainly again and again in the comedies and romances, Shakespeare seems to question the limitations of the male-instrumental experience and to suggest that the more valuable spheres of love and affiliation, the "something of great constancy," the "wonder" that concludes so many of the comedies and romances, require ways of behaving more characteristic of women than of men—since so often it is the play's women who lead the way into this dimension. Whether or not these women often become more than agents of their men's salvation is another question.

In *Much Ado*, Hero does not initiate the plan, but she does voluntarily become its agent; as the spokesman for Christian grace, the priest is an asexual figure associated with expressive functioning, for the theology of Grace predicates a passive reception of unmerited favor rather than the active pursuit of an earned reward.

At a general level, the Demeter-Persephone pattern seems to express the grounding in a reality larger than individual life to which human beings must cede some of their sovereignty for the sake of the greater benefits of mutuality,[28] one of whose preconditions is an ego mature enough to accept its limitations as well as its potentialities. To the immature or poorly structured psyche, this loosening of the self's boundaries feels like the threat of chaos, of psychosis and engulfment. Sexual intercourse is the act in which supremely this giving up of self takes place, particularly for the male, for whom coitus means a loss, a descent into chaos symbolically equivalent to the descent into the earth's darkness that death represents. This fear of loss recapitulates the early childhood struggle between symbiosis and individuation, the fear on the one hand of maternal engulfment and on the other of loss of self-esteem through failure to please, and thus failure to win approval from the all-powerful mother of primitive perception. Hero's "death" deals with these fears through a ritual transformation of darkness into light, death into the new life that such a descent can yield.[29]

However, the play's resolution does not come any more according to the priest's than to Don John's scheming, for it appears that once Hero has "died," Claudio does not give her another thought. Yet ultimately the priest's faith is correct, for it is the Sexton's ability to perceive the substance of reality rather than its forms that unscrambles all the confused signals. *Much Ado*'s Sexton, whose ecclesiastical duties would include the digging of graves,[30] can read and write and is therefore a figure linked both to reason and to receptivity, both to the corporeal and the spiritual. The resolution of the Claudio-Hero plot is thus contingent upon the intervention of a benign Providence that has placed a man who can function with both his head and his heart in the right place at the right time. The return to sanity seems to depend not upon human assertiveness but upon a human willingness to entrust itself to the workings of this Providence, a pattern suggesting the trust of mutuality rather than the assertiveness of narcissistic instrumentality.

Claudio is required to mime something like this pattern before the action can be fully resolved. First he must go through a ritual of atonement that amounts to an act of contrition, penitence, and penance, necessary steps to obtain the forgiveness that makes possible God's extension of Grace.[31] Claudio stands before the tomb in which Hero ostensibly lies and, in the incantation of song, invokes the "goddess of the night," a female lunar deity symbolically linked to the mysterious dimension of the emotions.[32] The song's general intent is the invocation of life out of death, and Claudio's final words, "Now, unto thy bones goodnight! / Yearly will I do this rite" (v.iii.22–23), suggest the cyclical nature of the ritual and relate it both to the passage of time and to a long-term commitment to think of Hero as she really was, not as Claudio has projectively imagined her to be. The scene's actions, which in their staging echo both the Russian Orthodox Easter service and the central ritual of the Eleusinian mysteries,[33] represent a surrender of individual instrumentality to those forces that go beyond the ken of human reason; the scene's invoking of life out of the earth itself appears to undo human attempts to deny corporeal origins.

Claudio's final test comes when he must accept and wed Leonato's fictitious niece sight unseen. Emblematically, his willingness to do so represents a working out of his deep distrust,

both of himself and of others. When he says to Leonato (in response to the latter's injunction to "give her [the 'niece'] the right
you should have given her cousin"—v.i.301), "I do embrace your
offer, and dispose / For henceforth of poor Claudio" (v.i.304–5), I
take it to mean that he is bringing under control the mean-spir-
ited part of himself that has led to his excessive distrust and
hence to Hero's death.[34] During the final scene, when Hero is
brought before him hidden by a veil, he asks to see her face. Leonato replies, "No, that you shall not till you take her hand / Before
this friar and swear to marry her" (v.iv.56–57), and Claudio
agrees—an indication of his willingness, now, to subsume his
self-seeking volition to the good of the wider community.

Thus "one Hero," whom Claudio had suspected of promiscuity, is replaced by another, who is pure; Don Pedro's words,
"The former Hero! Hero that is dead!" and Leonato's reply, "She
died, my lord, but whiles her slander lived" (v.iv.65–67), join
these disparate images into one person—the Hero who died is the
same Hero whose beauty excited Claudio's sexual horror and the
doubts that symbolically killed her. Still beautiful, she can now
be perceived as she is: honorable, chaste, and trustworthy. Her ritual death has been the ransom for Claudio's distrust, demonstrating both the consequences of such distrust and their baselessness.
After Don John has flown (the disposal of "poor Claudio"),
Claudio can take the action that moves him forward toward mutuality. The ritual act at Hero's tomb symbolizes allegiance to the
cyclical forces of generation and acceptance of the fact that the
"death" of the sexual act can, when combined with trust, lead to
new life; this sexual death in turn represents the death of the narcissistic self through union with another. This acceptance of the
cyclical processes of time is an accepting of individual death in
the realization that it leads to renewed life for the larger community. Finally, the revelation that Claudio's new wife and his
"other wife" are the same woman joins the tender and the sensual
in one love object, making it possible for him to entrust himself
to a marriage that combines life in the real social world with love
for a woman who is both sexually desirable and trustworthy.

The resolution of the Hero-Claudio plot leaves us, however, with a good many unanswered questions, the foremost of
which is the genuineness of Claudio's change of heart. But of
course I have considered this portion of *Much Ado* as a separate

entity, divorced from its framing by the Beatrice-Benedick plot, whose machinations I will not go into here. Let me merely suggest that the Hero-Claudio plot is primarily a ritual action, by itself not fully credible and convincing. The Beatrice-Benedick plot works through many of the same fears on a cognitive level that includes psychological change. In the theater, the two work together to make one coherent experience whose resolution is credible and even persuasive.

Notes

1. The theme is central to *The Merry Wives*, *Othello*, *Cymbeline*, and *The Winter's Tale*. The more general issue of woman's trustworthiness or lack of it is raised in the *Henry VI* plays and in *Hamlet*, *Troilus and Cressida*, *King Lear*, and *Antony and Cleopatra*.

2. In his exploration of heterosexual relationships, Shakespeare seems to be considering two differing kinds of human behavior, those that sociologists characterize as "instrumental" and "expressive." Loosely following Talcott Parsons, I would define "instrumentality" as that mode of functioning, linked to abstraction, rationality, and categorization, that enables the individual to behave actively and assertively and to have an impact upon his or her environment, to effect change, solve problems, "get things done," and make a mark in the world. Instrumentality is the vehicle of individual triumph and power, and its development is a necessary part of the maturational process in both sexes. "Expressive" behavior, equally necessary to mature functioning, enables human beings to open themselves to experience as well as to assert themselves upon it, to see totalities as well as their categorizable parts, to be receptive to and to interact with other people in reciprocal and caring ways, to function emotionally and with sensitivity as well as rationally and cognitively; see Talcott Parsons and Robert F. Bales, *Family, Socialization and Interaction Process* (Glencoe, Ill.: Free Press, 1955), pp. 22–24, 45–47, 317–20, 342–44. The behaviors that Parsons and Bales describe as "instrumental" and "expressive" are in many ways similar to those which recent research into bilateral brain functioning has identified as left-hemispheric and right-hemispheric functioning, behaviors that have, in Western culture, been characterized among other things as being masculine and feminine; on the subject of split-brain functioning, see Robert E. Ornstein, *The Psychology of Consciousness* (1972; rpt. Baltimore: Penguin, 1975), pp. 65–89.

   Reporting on research in this area, Jack Fincher, in *Human Intelligence* (New York: Putnam, 1976), writes: ". . . the popular notion that men are naturally more left hemisphere in their thinking—more analytical, logical, and rational if not more verbal—and women more right hemisphere—more intuitive, comparative, holistic—may be nothing more than a socially convenient mass delusion. Men may ordinarily use their left hemisphere more as adults, but there may be nothing natural about it if by natural we mean innate, inborn. It may very well be natural if by natural we mean the inevitable outcome of a social system designed to reward disproportionately certain left hemisphere attributes and those who learn to exercise them best while wielding the levers of power—namely, men. Women, by the same token, may ordinarily use their right hemisphere more as adults, but that too may be only the foregone result of a social system that leaves to them the right hemisphere abilities it deems least important while reserving recognition in the few arts it values to those whose talents in them have been fostered—again, men" (pp. 275–76). Ornstein and Fincher argue that both modes of consciousness—"the intellectual and its complement, the intuitive"—must be cultivated: see "Preface," *The Nature of Human Consciousness: A Book of Readings*, ed. Robert E. Ornstein (New York: Viking, 1974), p. xi.

3. William Shakespeare, *The Complete Works*, ed. G. B. Harrison (New York: Harcourt Brace, 1968 ed.), p. 701. All subsequent Shakespeare references are to this edition unless otherwise noted.

4. Charles T. Prouty, *The Sources of Much Ado about Nothing* (New Haven: Yale University Press, 1950), pp. 43–50.

5. See Anthony Esler, *The Aspiring Mind of the Elizabethan Younger Generation* (Durham, N.C.: Duke University Press, 1966), pp. 235–37; L. C. Knights, *Drama and Society in the Age of Jonson* (London: Chatto & Windus, 1951), pp. 327–30.

6. See Lawrence Stone, *The Crisis of the Aristocracy, 1558–1641* (Oxford: Clarendon, 1965), pp. 594–605.

7. On the split between the sensual and the tender components of love, see Sigmund Freud, "On the Universal Tendency to Debasement in the Sphere of Love (Contributions to the Psychology of Love II)," in *The Standard Edition of the Psychological Works of Sigmund Freud*, 11, trans. and ed. James Strachey (London: Hogarth Press, 1957), pp. 179–90; on the subject of the son's perception that his mother has betrayed him, see "A Special Type of Choice of Object Made by Men (Contributions to the Psychology of Love I), *ibid.*, pp. 165–75; on the conflict surrounding the resolution of the tender and the sensual components of love during adolescence and on the vicissitudes of the adolescent Oedipus complex, see Peter Blos, *On Adolescence: A Psychoanalytic Interpretation* (New York: Free Press, 1962), pp. 101–2, 104–5; on the subject of the infant's splitting of his or her perceptions of the mother into "good" and "bad," see Melanie Klein, "Some Theoretical Conclusions Regarding the Emotional Life of the Infant," in *Envy and Gratitude and Other Works, 1946–1963* (New York: Delacorte Press/Seymour Lawrence, 1975), pp. 62–67; for a more recent discussion of the effect of early childhood splitting of good and bad

objects and the consequent splitting of the sensual and the tender upon the ability to form mature love relationships, see Otto Kernberg, "Barriers to Falling and Remaining in Love," *Journal of the American Psychoanalytic Association*, 22 (1974), 486–511.

8. Lawrence Stone, *The Family, Sex, and Marriage in England, 1500–1800* (New York: Harper & Row, 1977), pp. 99–101; see also Lloyd De-Mause, "The Evolution of Childhood," in *The History of Childhood*, ed. Lloyd DeMause (New York: Psychohistory Press, 1974), pp. 32–36; for a recent discussion of the influence of reliable nurturing figures on a child's development, see Margaret Mahler, Fred Pine, and Anni Bergman, *The Psychological Birth of the Human Infant, Symbiosis and Individuation* (New York: Basic Books, 1975), pp. 48–63.

9. On the subject of the mother as first love-object, see Otto Fenichel, *The Psychoanalytic Theory of Neurosis* (New York: Norton, 1945), pp. 87–88; on the subject of brother-sister relationships in sixteenth- and seventeenth-century England, see Stone, *Family*, pp. 115–16.

10. Stone, *Crisis*, pp. 649–52.

11. "Timbreo and Fenicia," novella 22 of *La Prima Parte de le Novelle del Bandello*, trans. and ed. Geoffrey Bullough, in *Narrative and Dramatic Sources of Shakespeare*, II (London: Routledge & Kegan Paul, 1958), p. 114.

12. The father, or his internalized imago, not only acts as a brake upon the son's sexual impulses but also makes it clear that the "incestuous objects" (mother, sister) are forbidden to him.

13. For a discussion of the literary and psychoanalytic concepts of the "double," see Robert Rogers, *A Psychoanalytic Study of the Double in Literature* (Detroit: Wayne State University Press, 1970), pp. 1–17.

14. Karen Horney, *The Neurotic Personality of Our Time* (1937; rpt. New York: Norton, 1964), pp. 178–87.

15. See Esler, *The Aspiring Mind*, pp. 59–60; Stone, *Crisis*, pp. 591–93.

16. For a discussion of "primal scene," see Fenichel, "Theory of Neurosis," p. 92.

17. See Sigmund Freud, "Slips of the Tongue," in *The Psychopathology of Everyday Life*, SE, 6, pp. 61–64, 68–91; also see pp. 120–21, 125–28, on slips of the pen.

18. I have heard it argued that Margaret is to call Borachio "Claudio" in order to persuade Claudio that his sweetheart is mocking him by addressing another lover by his name. This seems to me a more convoluted piece of reasoning to account for the passage than simply to read it as a meaningful "slip" of Shakespeare's pen. However, the former reading does not rule out the latter, for the conscious rationale could well be a screen for the unconscious meaning and would add to the nightmarish quality of Claudio's delusion.

19. For a discussion of the relationship between conscious and unconscious factors in artistic production, see Ernst Kris, *Psychoanalytic Explorations in Art* (1952; rpt. New York: Schocken, 1964), pp. 31–47, 59–63, 253–59.

20. Freud, "A Special Type of Choice of Object," *SE*, 11, p. 171; like the earlier masked-ball scene, the rendezvous as Shakespeare renders it suggests a fantasy: Claudio stands to one side, watching an enactment of what appears to be Hero's sexual behavior with a young man who resembles Claudio himself, a set of circumstances certainly similar to those of a sexual fantasy. And because such impulses and fantasies would be highly guilt-laden, the psyche would defend against them via projection, the line of defense being, "I'm not sexual—*she* is."

   If we look at the work of art as being in part a system of impulses and defenses against those impulses, we can see the defensive workings of the episode as Shakespeare has constructed it: Hero herself does not take part in it; rather, the Hero who encourages sexual overtures is portrayed by Margaret disguised as Hero—and elsewhere in the play Shakespeare uses Margaret to express female interest in sexuality (see III.iv.29–38, v.ii.9–19), thus articulating a point of view that sees female sexual pleasure as being healthy and normal and at the same time keeping Hero and to some degree Beatrice free of the "taint" of sexual knowledgeableness. The assignation scene is narrated rather than enacted, and so the audience is distanced from it emotionally. Further, the entire ploy has been devised by Don John's sidekick, Borachio, a strategy that guarantees its dissociation from Claudio. I have suggested that Don John and Claudio are psychological doubles and that what Don John dreams up may be unfinished business in Claudio's psyche. Certainly Borachio's only function in the play is to act as Don John's henchman; further, it is Borachio who provides Don John the raw material—the news of Don Pedro's courtship of Hero—for the earlier fantasy represented in the masked-ball scene.

21. Freud writes that "anyone who is to be really free and happy in love must have surmounted his respect for women and have come to terms with the idea of incest with his mother or sister"; see "On the Universal Tendency," *SE*, 11, p. 186.

22. On the relationship between narcissistic rage and "total lack of empathy toward the offender," see Heinz Kohut, "Thoughts on Narcissistic Rage," in *The Psychoanalytic Study of the Child*, 27, ed. Ruth Eissler, et al. (New York: Quadrangle, 1973), pp. 385–87.

23. See David McClelland, *Power: The Inner Experience* (New York: Irvington, 1975), pp. 96–102.

24. Jean Baker Miller, *Toward a New Psychology of Women* (Boston: Beacon, 1977), pp. 22–23, 31–32.

25. McClelland, *Power*, p. 98.

26. See Edgar Wind, *Pagan Mysteries in the Renaissance*, rev. ed. (New York: Norton, 1968), pp. 38, 39.

27. On the subject of the gods' sacrifice, see *ibid.*, pp. 133–35; on the subject of the surrender to darkness, see *ibid.*, 53–54, 156–57.

28. McClelland characterizes such behavior, which he calls a "Stage IV"

orientation, as representing the most mature phase of human development; *Power*, pp. 20–21, 23–24, 69–76.

29. For a Jungian reading of Hero's death as a mimesis of the Persephone myth, see Alex Aronson, *Psyche and Symbol in Shakespeare* (Bloomington: Indiana University Press, 1972), pp. 168–72.

30. See *OED* entry under "sexton"; in *Hamlet*, the First Gravedigger identifies himself as "sexton": "I have been sexton here, man and boy, thirty years" (v.i.176–77).

31. For a full discussion of this doctrine, see Henry H. Adams, *English Domestic or Homilectic Tragedy* (New York: Columbia University Press, 1943).

32.
> Pardon, goddess of the night,
> Those that slew thy virgin knight,
> For the which, with songs of woe,
> Round about her tomb they go.
>> Midnight, assist our moan,
>> Help us to sigh and groan,
>>> Heavily, heavily.
>> Graves, yawn, and yield your dead,
>> Till death be uttered,
>>> Heavily, heavily.   (v.iii.12–21)

The song's words suggest that the mourners carry torches (24) and circle about Hero's tomb (15), and the womb-tomb identity here is evident and seems again to symbolize a surrendering of individual self-will to the ongoing processes of life itself. G. B. Harrison, an exceedingly literal-minded editor, states that lines 19–21 "do not make sense, unless the meaning is that the dead are to come up to listen to the dirge. The 'sad inventions' of Claudio have indeed been 'labored'" (p. 729). But the *Oxford English Dictionary* says that "utter" can mean "to put or thrust forth, shoot or urge out; to discharge, emit, eject, exhale," and cites a Shakespearean example for this usage; see entry under 3b.

33. See Erich Neumann, *The Great Mother* (1963; rpt. Princeton, N.J.: Princeton University Press, 1972), pp. 318–19; McClelland, *Power*, pp. 97–99.

34. See *OED* entry 8a under "dispose" and 5b under "poor."

As We Like It

How a Girl Can Be Smart and Still Popular

CLARA CLAIBORNE PARK

In the major literature there are no useful Bildungsromans for girls. A boy's development into manhood through testing experience is one of the oldest themes in literature; Homer's Telemachus presents the first model of how to grow into the kind of man one's society approves and has need of. From the *Odyssey* to "The Bear," literature affords a long procession of raw youths; almost all manage to become men. Girls, however, had to wait out a twenty-five-hundred-year literary history before anyone made fiction of their growth. When Evelina and Emma did at length appear on the scene, a capable girl—let us imagine, for example, the young Florence Nightingale—might have been pardoned for feeling that whatever else they did, these characters scarcely enlarged her sense of possibility. The scope of their activities was even more restricted than that of the ladies who created them—who did, at least, write books. Only the dearth of images of the possibilities open to a developing girl can explain the immense influence of a novel that most males never read—Louisa May Alcott's *Little Women*.

Yet young females, like young males, create themselves ac-

This essay is reprinted by permission, with revisions, from The American Scholar, *42 (Spring 1973), 262–78;* © *1973 by the United Chapters of Phi Beta Kappa.*

cording to the models their society provides for them; and like young males, those who read look in literature for images of what they could be and what they ought to be. Stories of female trial and initiation are by their nature difficult for male writers to provide, and we should remember that from Sappho—*floruit* 600 B.C.—to Jane Austen, there were hardly any writers who were not male. Male writers, of course, can and do provide models for females, but not very many. A cursory check of the dramatis personae of any Elizabethan play will demonstrate what is still true of modern fiction: female characters are greatly outnumbered. (A London director estimated last year that there are five times as many parts for actors as for actresses.) Still, quantity is not everything. Literate girls could find without difficulty images which, although they lacked the dimension of development, still provided a warm variety of ways of being female. They could—like everybody else—read Shakespeare.

As classics go, Shakespeare isn't bad reading for a girl. The conventions of tragedy and romance offer horizons considerably wider than those available in Fanny Burney and Jane Austen; the courts of Europe and the seacoasts of Bohemia provide backgrounds in which a girl can imagine herself doing far more interesting things than she could at home. It is true that, unlike those paradoxical dramatists of male-chauvinist Athens, Shakespeare never allows a woman a play of her own. He provides neither *Antigones* nor *Medeas*; no feminine name appears in his titles except as the second member of a male-female pair. Yet a girl can read Shakespeare without calling upon the defenses necessary for Milton or Hemingway, or Lawrence or Mailer—writers she must read calloused for survival, a black in Mr. Charlie's land. Shakespeare liked women and respected them; not everybody does. We do not find him, like Milton, luxuriating in the amoebic submissiveness of an Eve in Paradise, and we can surmise that he would have found little interest in the dim Marias and complaisant Catherines whom Hemingway found nonthreatening. He is not afraid of the kind of assertiveness and insistence on her own judgment that Eve displays when she gets busy bringing death into the world and all our woe; the evidence of the plays is that he positively enjoyed it.

From Mrs. Jameson on, critics, male and female, have praised Shakespeare's women. "The dignity of Portia, the energy of Beatrice, the radiant high spirits of Rosalind, the sweetness of Viola"[1]—William Allan Neilson's encomia can stand for thousands of others. Juliet, Cordelia, Rosalind, Beatrice; Cleopatra, Hermione, Emilia, Paulina—Shakespeare's girls and mature women are individualized, realized, fully enjoyed as human beings. His respect for women is evident in all the plays, but it is in the middle comedies that the most dazzling image recurs. It is an image significant for what it can tell us about the extent—and the limits—of acceptable feminine activity in the Shakespearean world, a world which in this as in other things remains, over time and change, disconcertingly like our own.

Limits? What limits? It would seem that no girl need feel herself diminished when she reads *As You Like It*, *The Merchant of Venice* or *Much Ado*. Rather, she is given a glittering sense of possibility. Who would not, if she could, be beautiful, energetic, active, verbally brilliant and still sought after by desirable men, like these Shakespearean heroines? Hebraic and Pauline tradition might subordinate the female; secular codes might make her, like Juliet and Portia, her father's to dispose of as he wished, to a man who, once her husband, could exercise over her the same absolute dominion. Yet Juliet and Portia, like Rosalind and the ladies of *Love's Labour's Lost*, clearly think of themselves as autonomous people. Submissive mildness is not lacking in Shakespare; Bianca and Hero and Mariana would content a Milton and reassure even a Mailer. But such characters are never central to the action—logically enough, because they do not act. Apparent exceptions are seen to prove the rule: beneath Cordelia's gentleness is a strain of iron stubbornness that Milton would probably have welcomed much as Lear did.

Bianca and her like do not interest Shakespeare. When he does bring this kind of woman to full individuality it is, significantly enough, not to present her as an effective human being but to offer her to our sympathies, as he does with Desdemona and Ophelia, as a helpless victim. What catches his imagination in *As You Like It*, *The Merchant of Venice*, and *Much Ado* is a young woman of an entirely different kind: one who, by her energy, wit, and combativeness, successfully demonstrates her ability to control events in the world around her, not excluding the world of men. Perhaps we should not be surprised that the greatest Elizabethan was attracted by the qualities of his sovereign, who told her lords that "though I be a woman, I have as good a courage answerable to my place as ever my father had. . . . I thank God I am endued with such qualities that were I turned out of the realm in my petticoat, I were able to live in any place in christendom."[2] But perhaps we should be surprised; there are no such women in Marlowe or Jonson or the other dramatists who could have been expected to remember the qualities of the Virgin Queen. In drama as elsewhere, men find such women hard to handle, and often hard to take. Shakespeare knew how to manage them—at least on stage. That he could create women who were spunky enough to be fun to be with, and still find ways to mediate their assertiveness so as to render them as nonthreatening as their softer sisters, is one of the secrets of his perennial appeal. His is one of the surer methods of keeping a love story from liquefying prematurely, durable enough to remain serviceable to Yale professors who write best-sellers.

We should note at the outset something that Shakespeare's wide-ranging geography and tapestried history can easily obscure: that whoever and wherever they are, the sphere of action he allows his women is severely limited. As Betty Bandel shows in her fascinating 1951 Columbia dissertation, "Shakespeare's Treatment of the Social Position of Women," Shakespeare never dramatizes, even peripherally, a learned woman (although women may be, even should be "wise").[3] Nor, in so many plays that deal with politics, does he ever present a woman who is active in politics on her own behalf, in spite of the example of the sovereign under whom he spent his formative years. The type of "la très sage Héloïse" interests him no more than Joan of Arc does, and although his women often intervene forcefully in political matters, it is always in the interest of the male to whom they are attached, whether husband, lover or son; and usually—as with Lady Macbeth—their influence is for the worse. Professor Bandel points out that even when a tradition of independent action clearly exists, as with Cleopatra, Shakespeare does not use it; he leaves undeveloped Plutarch's suggestions of the queen's political ability and power. "The play is not the play of a woman ruler; insofar as Cleopatra is concerned, it is the play of one of the sisterhood 'that trade in love.'"[4] Similarly, it would have been easy, in *All's Well That Ends Well*, to give Helena the credit for the skill that cures the king of France; the knowledge of herbs and simples was an acceptable part of the feminine role. Instead, she merely administers the medicine bequeathed her by her father the physician.

But what Shakespeare does not do is far less immediately striking than what he does, and what he does is to glorify as never before the image of the bright young girl. In *Much Ado*, in *As You Like It*, in *The Merchant of Venice*, the image recurs, lovingly differentiated, but the same in its essentials: a young woman who is to delight the audience by her beauty, vigor, self-confidence and wit.

It is Beatrice and Benedick who provide the real interest of *Much Ado*. As we have seen, when Shakespeare himself couples a masculine and a feminine name, the feminine comes last, but although Juliet follows Romeo, and Cleopatra, Antony, in the mouth of both common reader and critic Beatrice precedes Benedick. From the beginning, it is Beatrice who determines the tenor of the relationship: "I wonder that you will still be talking, Signior Benedick. Nobody marks you." Benedick's parry is instant—"What, my dear Lady Disdain! are you yet living?" (I.i.116–20)—but it is a response to her initiative; the lady has taken the offensive, and Beatrice will give as good as she gets. The young woman and the young man are endowed with the same kind of wit and the same enjoyment of verbal competitiveness. The pleasure of watching them lies in the equality of the match.

It is significant that Shakespeare went to the trouble of inventing Beatrice and Benedick; there is no trace of them in the Renaissance originals. It is already clear in *Love's Labour's Lost* that he enjoyed this kind of relationship, and this kind of woman. Born in a merry hour, when a star danced, Beatrice clearly is delightful to her creator. The older men in the play also find her attractive and charming; although her uncle warns her she will never get a husband if she "be so shrewd of her tongue," the tone of the reproof is light and it leads merely to further cheerful repartee. Don Pedro considers her "a pleasant-spirited lady" (II.i.355) and actually makes her a semi-serious proposal, to which she replies that so grand a match would only do for Sundays. Like Benedick, she has a good time making jokes against marriage, and there is no tinge of bitterness in them. Both are good-natured beneath their repartee; they are obviously well-suited, and it's no wonder their friends decide to bring them together.

Beatrice's capacities match Benedick's; so does her cheerful self-assertion. That, it would seem, is the point of what's going on; that is what Shakespeare intends his audience to enjoy. Yet if we examine more closely this apparent glorification of equality between the sexes, we will discover that what it in fact demonstrates is exactly what its glitter obscures: that if the bright young girl is to be made acceptable—to audiences, to readers, perhaps even to her creator—ways must be found to reduce the impact of her self-confidence, to make sure that equality is kept nominal.

There is an undercurrent of uneasiness in the audience's response to Beatrice. Ellen Terry warned that Beatrice's encounters with Benedick "can easily be made to sound vulgar and malicious," and cautioned the actress taking the part to speak with "the lightest raillery with mirth in voice and a charm in manner."[5] Don Pedro may find her charming, her uncle may value her gaiety, but young males are more vulnerable. *Much Ado* is not out to test the limits of our tolerance for feminine assertiveness. Shakespeare's bright young girls are meant to please, not to make us uncomfortable. A way must be found to mitigate this lightest of threats. We need some reassurance that Beatrice cannot hurt us, and Shakespeare will provide it.

Beatrice and Benedick are both scoffers at Cupid, and as their personalities are similar, so the stratagems that are to make them fall in love seem at first glance strictly parallel. Equally matched, male and female apparently are to be treated with strict equality. Their friends arrange for each to overhear a put-up conversation; planted in it is the information that in spite of all appearances, each is hopelessly in love with the other. We might expect that the two conversations, parallel in their effects, also would be parallel in content, but this is by no means so. Benedick merely overhears a circumstantial account of how much Beatrice is in love with him. Beatrice, however, must hear herself accused of scornful carping which "turns . . . every man the wrong side out" (III.i.68), of disdain, of pride, of egoism. "Her wit," says her cousin Hero,

> Values itself so highly that to her
> All matter else seems weak. She cannot love,
> Nor take no shape nor project of affection,
> She is so self-endeared.   (III.i.53–56)

Although she and Benedick have been presented up to this point as two of a kind, Benedick is not thus criticized. Young females are expected to temper their behavior to the vulnerability of the male, and those who fail to do so expose themselves to the censure of their peers. We remember that earlier, although Beatrice bore up well under Benedick's taunt that she got her wit from a joke book, her retort (that he was called "the Prince's jester"—II.i.142) sent him off to complain to his friends that "she speaks poniards, and every word stabs" (II.i.254–55). Merry Beatrice is no Katharine, but she is tainted with shrewishness. Although her cousin's criticism is touched with hyperbole, Beatrice is evidently meant to take it to heart. And so she does. Benedick does not hear her recantation, delivered in soliloquy, but the audience must.

> What fire is in mine ears? Can this be true?
> Stand I condemn'd for pride and scorn so much?
> Contempt, farewell! and maiden pride, adieu!
> No glory lives behind the back of such.
> And, Benedick, love on; I will requite thee,
> Taming my wild heart to thy loving hand. . . .
> (III.i.107–12)

At the end she is still joking; when Benedick tells her that he takes her for pity, she replies that she yields only to save his life. But the audience can feel quite comfortable. The slight ambiguity of her character need never be resolved. We need not decide whether or not there is a bit of the shrew in Beatrice; since we know that she will need no taming, it does not matter.

This is, of course, the ideal: the high-spirited woman who will tame herself. She offers both men and women that most precious of assurances—that they can have it both ways. To women, a girl like Beatrice affirms their bright potentialities, but also the warm safety of their conviction that these should never be displayed in any way that could threaten men. The men in the audience—like the men in the play—can enjoy her company, free from both the threat of insubordination and the necessity of putting her in her place. Only the most flamboyant of Petruchios enjoys playing the tyrant; it is much pleasanter not to have to.

If Beatrice is delightful, Rosalind is even better. Neilson (who, as president of Smith College, occupied a privileged position for girl-watching) describes her as having "the wit of Portia and Beatrice softened by the gentleness of Viola"[6]—exactly as we like it. In *As You Like It*, however, Shakespeare does not hesitate to tip the equal balance that affords the fun of *Much Ado* in favor of the lady; in wit and energy, Rosalind has no male rival. Insofar as any other character is able to match her repartee, it is Celia, who although she is usually remembered as the gentle foil, the "other kind" of girl, turns out to have a surprising number of the snappy lines. Orlando, however, is merely a nice young man.

Rosalind, however, is more than witty. *As You Like It* is her play. This is, of course, unusual in Shakespeare. Heroes act, but heroines commonly do not, which is why, unlike Antigone and Lysistrata, none of them gets a Shakespearean title to herself. Neither does Rosalind—although Thomas Lodge had accorded her one—but nevertheless it is she who moves the play. She is energetic, effective, successful. She has the courage to accept exile; she decides to assume male dress, and, playing brother, she guides her friend to the Forest of Arden. The late comedies no longer present these forceful young women, and the faithful Imogen of *Cymbeline* retroactively exposes the extent of Rosalind's autonomy. It is not Imogen but her husband's servant who originates the idea of male disguise; the necessity for her journey originates not in her own position but in her relation to her husband, and as soon as she lacks a man to guide her, she gets lost. Her complaint at this point measures her distance from Rosalind: "I see a man's life is a tedious one" (III.vi.1). (Her previous remark to Cloten also bears thinking about: "You put me to forget a lady's manners / By being so verbal"—II.iii.110–11.) Through Imogen we can appreciate the unique position of Rosalind in her play. Rosalind's decisions control the progress of *As You Like It*, and it is by her agency that the four couples assemble in the concluding nuptial dance which, as in *The Boke of the Governor*, "betokeneth concord" and embodies for the audience the harmony restored that is the essence of Shakespearean comedy.

Yet Shakespeare arranges for her to do all this without making the ladies censorious or the gentlemen nervous. He has various methods of rendering her wit painless and her initiatives acceptable. The most obvious way is to confine them to love matters, a proper feminine sphere. Rosalind is a political exile, but she shows no disposition to meddle in politics; it is not through her agency that her father is restored to his rightful place. Her wit is not, like Portia's, exercised in the service of sensible men engaged in the serious business of the world, nor are her jokes made at their expense. Her satire is, in fact, narrowly directed at two classes of beings—sighing lovers, and women. In the course of the fun she works her way through most of the accusations already traditional in a large antifeminist literature (inconstancy, contrariness, jealousy, unfaithfulness, etc.)[7] to the point where Celia tells her, "We must have your doublet and hose pluck'd over your head, and show the world what the bird hath done to her own nest" (IV.i.206–8). Add that we know all along that she herself is the butt of her own jokes, being herself both lovesick and female, and it would be a fragile Benedick indeed who could feel himself stabbed by her poniard.

The most useful dramatic device for mediating the initiatives of the female, however, is the male disguise. Male garments immensely broaden the sphere in which female energy can manifest itself. Dressed as a man, a nubile woman can go places and do things she couldn't do otherwise, thus getting the play out of the court and the closet and into interesting places like forests or Welsh mountains. Once Rosalind is disguised as a man, she can be as saucy and self-assertive as she likes. (We can observe a similar change come over sweet Viola of *Twelfth Night* as soon as she begins to play the clever page.) The characters, male and female, will accept her behavior because it does not offend their sense of propriety; the audience, male and female, because they know she's playing a role. With male dress we feel secure. In its absence, feminine assertiveness is viewed with hostility, as with Kate the Shrew, or at best, as with Beatrice, as less than totally positive. Male dress transforms what otherwise could be experienced as aggression into simple high spirits.

The temporary nature of the male disguise is of course essential, since the very nature of Shakespearean comedy is to affirm that disruption is temporary, that what has turned topsy-turvy will be restored. It is evident that Rosalind has enjoyed the flexibility and freedom that come with the assumption of the masculine role, but it is also evident that she will gladly and voluntarily relinquish it. "Down on your knees," she tells the proud shepherdess who scorns her faithful swain, "And thank heaven, fasting, for a good man's love" (III.v.57–58). Rosalind, clearly, is thankful for Orlando's, and although she is twice the person he is, we are willing to believe that they live happily ever after, since that's obviously what she wants.

Portia is another lady who outweighs her man. Bassanio is one of the most firmly nonmemorable of Shakespeare's characters, but Portia is nonetheless delighted with him. It is true that she has more excuse than Rosalind. Bassanio may be no more than a pleasantly affectionate incompetent in need of a rich wife to free him from his debts. But Portia is not free to choose her husband; Shakespearean fathers may dispose of their daughters as they will, and she must marry the fellow who chooses the right casket. Among suitors who include a drunken German, an Englishman who speaks no European language, and an African prince in whose negritude she finds no appeal, Bassanio looks good. She can make up, after all, what he lacks in intelligence and force. His improvidence and poor judgment have put his friend's life in jeopardy, and he lacks the wit to extricate him. It is not he who possesses the resourcefulness to pass himself off as a lawyer, or the brains to find a technicality to win on. Portia sends her newly wed husband off to Venice to bid goodbye to the friend he has ruined, since this is evidently all he is capable of. She herself posts off to assume the male attire that will make possible her triumph over Shylock.

Portia recalls Beatrice and Rosalind, but unlike them, she is allowed to engage her intelligence with matters more serious than the pairing of lovers. The law, the quality of mercy, the survival of a man—alone of Shakespeare's heroines, Portia is allowed to confront a man over matters outside a woman's sphere, and to win. (A somewhat similar confrontation occurs in *Measure for Measure*—not mediated by male dress—but Isabella's opposition to Angelo is swiftly reduced to sexual terms, and she thereafter loses the center of the stage.) Even the male disguise will hardly be enough to render harmless such a formidable lady. We may expect that special means will be necessary to mitigate this unusually serious threat.

One way is to reduce the significance of her male adversary. Shylock is a man, but not one with whom the audience was expected readily to identify. The Elizabethan response to Shylock was far less ambiguous than our own. Shakespeare's audience unquestionably would have found it reassuring that the man Portia confronted and vanquished was not a person of her own status in society, but a misbelieving Jew.

The audience, however, needs more explicit reassurance than this. It is provided. Here, in the only play besides *As You Like It* where Shakespeare allows a woman's action to control the outcome,[8] Shakespeare makes sure that Portia does not have her day in court until she has explicitly affirmed her subordination to her husband-to-be. Portia's betrothal speech to Bassanio rivals in its length, its emphasis, and its poetry even the *locus classicus* where Shakespeare showed the proper attitude of a girl whose assertiveness was unmitigated by charm and good nature toward a husband likewise not notably endowed with either. Katharine's submission to Petruchio is famous:

> Thy husband is thy lord, thy life, thy keeper,
> Thy head, thy sovereign; one that cares for thee.
> . . . .
> Such duty as the subject owes the prince
> Even such a woman oweth to her husband;
> And when she is froward, peevish, sullen, sour,
> And not obedient to his honest will,
> What is she but a foul contending rebel
> And graceless traitor to her loving lord?
> I am asham'd that women are so simple
> To offer war when they should kneel for peace,
> Or seek for rule, supremacy, and sway,
> Where they are bound to serve, love, and obey.
>   (v.ii.146–47, 155–64)

And a great deal more of the same. Katharine's speech, considering what she's just been through, might be considered a bit overwrought. Portia's, however, seems to well up quite spontaneously, and it is just as strongly phrased. She wishes herself "a thousand times more fair, ten thousand times / More rich" just to be good enough for Bassanio. Yet, says this lady who is about to astonish the Venetian courts,

> . . . the full sum of me
> . . . .
> Is an unlesson'd girl, unschool'd, unpractis'd;
> Happy in this, she is not yet so old

> But she may learn; happier than this,
> She is not bred so dull but she can learn;
> Happiest of all is that her gentle spirit
> Commits itself to yours to be directed,
> As from her lord, her governor, her king.
> Myself and what is mine to you and yours
> Is now converted. But now I was the lord
> Of this fair mansion, master of my servants,
> Queen o'er myself; and even now, but now,
> This house, these servants, and this same myself
> Are yours, my lord. . . .   (III.ii.155–71)

"Thy lord, thy life, thy keeper, / Thy head, thy sovereign"—or "Her lord, her governor, her king." But this is not an admission wrung from ill-natured, headstrong Katharine, this is Portia speaking, brilliant Portia, confident Portia, who will soon be off to accomplish what no male Venetian seems able to. She speaks in this vein for twenty-four lines—Katharine's submission takes forty-four. No audience, as far as I know, has complained of the length. It is interesting, then, to compare Shakespeare's treatment of one of the rare occasions when a man submits. In such a case, our patience is assumed to be short. In *The Merry Wives of Windsor* Master Ford makes an apology to his wife for incorrectly suspecting her virtue. He imprudently begins "Pardon me, wife. Henceforth do what thou wilt." This is too much; he scarcely gets out four more lines before Master Page interrupts him:

> 'Tis well, 'tis well; no more.
> Be not as extreme in submission as in offence.
>   (IV.iv.6–11)

Once again we are shown that when the sexes are reversed, parallel situations lose their similarity.

Brilliant and fascinating women are a pleasure to watch, once we can be sure they will accept the control even of the Bassanios and Orlandos of the world—at least this was so in Elizabethan England. That was, however, a long time ago. Shakespeare's feminine models certainly can be seen as significant to the pre-twentieth-century reader. But today's young girls have never heard of Rosalind and Beatrice. To consider that Shakespeare's comic heroines have something to tell us about the twentieth-century feminine image would seem to be academicism gone overboard.

And yet—have you by any chance seen *Love Story*, or read it?[9] Millions have, if you have not; for many, the story of the doomed love of Jenny Cavilleri and Oliver Barrett III stands as an epitome of what the relationship between young male and young female should be. The popularity of *Love Story* is genuine and significant; it expresses what a very large number of people believe. If we scrutinize it we will discover something that we may find encouraging or disconcerting: Professor Segal has demonstrated that the Shakespearean formula is still a winner.

Invent a girl of charm and intellect; allow her ego a brief premarital flourishing; make clear that it is soon to subside into voluntarily assumed subordination; make sure that this is mediated by love. Today, however, the archetypal bright young girl is to be found not in courts or forests, but in the Radcliffe library.

When a likely Harvard jock tries to borrow a book, Jenny, like Beatrice, takes the offensive. "Do you have your own library?" she asks, and the parry and thrust that follow impart a sense of *déjà vu*. It glitters with I.Q., and the heroine wins it. It is only the first of a series; she wins them all. However tricky her Benedick's riposte, she always tops it. She's lovely when she takes off her glasses; she is brilliant, but she is nice too, sweet and warm and young, and the audience cries at the end much as it did when Juliet died some years ago in another successful love story. We who teach college students, especially female ones, had better watch out how we knock *Love Story*; those tears are wet, and as many of our students have told us, they don't care what we say, it's a beautiful story. And if we take the unaccustomed trouble to consider it from a young girl's point of view, we must concede that it is a compelling one: who wouldn't want to be beautiful, clever, and good, like Jenny?

Like Shakespeare, Professor Segal writes for the box office, and like Shakespeare in the romantic comedies, he writes not to disturb, but to reassure. Oliver and Jenny are no more likely to disrupt the social order than are Florizel and Perdita. The Harvard they inhabit is as remote from today's vexed colleges as the Forest of Arden. *Love Story* is built to last—on the hypothesis that demonstrations and demands for relevance are temporary phenomena, but that images of youthful brilliance, generational misunderstanding, love, and early death are likely to retain their traditional interest. So, evidently, is the bright young girl. We may refuse to accept Jenny as an avatar of Rosalind and Beatrice, but we are bound to recognize her, complete with the assertiveness, the charm, and the fundamental acquiescence in traditional sex roles that allow us to have our cake and eat it.

Jenny's verbal one-upmanship must not be allowed to mislead us. Her aggressiveness is only apparent, part of the delightful game that assures us that this prize is worth having. Since Jenny wins each verbal passage, her Benedick has to discover this in bed, the minimal measure of how far the social mores have progressed since Shakespeare. The necessary reassurance comes with the required explicitness: "Our first physical encounter was the polar opposite of our first verbal one. . . . This was the real Jenny—the soft one, whose touch was so light and loving." The real Jenny is as different from the clever one as the "unlesson'd girl" is from the shyster lawyer. The clever Jenny has a scholarship to study in Paris; the real Jenny gives it up without hesitation when Oliver asks, "What about our marriage?" The bright Jenny keeps up the repartee and never loses a set, but the real Jenny has given up all for love. When Oliver is disinherited by a stern father, Jenny teaches music to support him through law school. She gives up participation in music groups. "She came home from Shady Lane exhausted, and there was dinner to cook." Woman's work is never done. Oliver, after all, is making a sacrifice too; he has had to give up football. There is no suggestion that the independent exercise of her highly trained abilities gives her the slightest satisfaction; her work is obviously temporary. When Oliver lands the lucrative job proper to an all-Ivy jock who has graduated third in his class, the only WASP in the top ten, Jenny retires contentedly into an expensive apartment on East Sixty-third Street and assumes the activities proper to a woman whose husband is supporting her. She cooks for him (even later, when she's dying, she fends off his attempts to help because that isn't "man's work"). She goes to work on getting pregnant. And she obediently enters upon the conspicuous consumption that he sees as the blazon of his triumph.

It pleases us to see that, like Rosalind and Portia, she's wiser than her man, and it's made clear that she uses her charge accounts, as she does everything else, only because he wants her to. We are allowed to understand that her own values are less crudely materialistic, but that she is too wise not to indulge her husband's fierce competitiveness in these unimportant matters. For all the verbal victories are kept carefully only verbal. The one matter of substance on which she and Oliver disagree is his implacable refusal to understand his father, and although she is shown to be absolutely right when she calls her husband a heartless bastard, she obediently abandons her attempt to soften him, and the final reconciliation between father and son is brought about only through her death. Jenny, we are given to understand on the last page, is more than a tender memory, she is an enduring influence—but an influence of the traditional womanly kind, whose strength is in its gentleness and willingness to give way.

So Jenny dies, and millions weep for her, including many who will not afterwards admit it. I teach at an extremely unsophisticated college,[10] but unsophisticated students are not without perspicacity. The force with which my students insist on the enduring beauty of *Love Story* is intensified by a certain irritation growing out of their suspicion that their sophisticated teachers are, as usual, trying to put something over on them. They suspect that we are quite simply lying; that either we did cry at *Love Story*, or, that if we did condescend to read it, we would. I suspect they are right. Our need for images of brightness and beauty, fidelity and tenderness, is insatiable. Sophisticated modern literature refuses to give them to us, and rightly; the cleverer we are, the surer it is that we will repudiate in today's fiction the old patterns that free us to weep at *Romeo and Juliet* and smile at *As You Like It*. Yet love stories are hardy, as Segal knew when he chose his title. Stereotypes do not necessarily detract from their durability, for truth, unfortunately for us sophisticates, is an essential component of stereotypes. Women commonly do smooth their assertiveness into acceptability, and it is those who do so who are experienced as charming—by men and by women. Women frequently do exercise a softening influence on the extremes of male competition; they do, like Portia and Isabella and Jenny (and Antigone) speak out for mercy and the relaxation of the lethal rigidities of men. Literature is not unrealistic in representing this as one of the most satisfactory ways in which women interact with men, and Shakespeare may not be unrealistic, either, in bodying forth the repulsion of the race when even women abandon gentleness for ambition and aggression. "Proper deformity shows not in the fiend / So horrid as in woman" (*King Lear*, IV.ii. 60–61). Theodore Roszak has recently called for a liberation of "the compassionate virtues"—in men as well as in women—and warned that the world will not be better if women exercise their indubitable right to be "every bit the brutes and bastards men have been. . . . Courage, daring, decisiveness, resourcefulness are good qualities, in women as much so as in men. So, too, are charity, mercy, tenderness. But ruthlessness, callousness, power, lust, domineering self-assertion . . . these are destructive, whether in man or woman."[11] Literature, however, which is still overwhelmingly produced by males, has not been very helpful in providing the young girl with the Bildungsroman that would show her how to combine the compassionate virtues with the expansion of ego-strength that is her due as a human being. Shakespeare does better than the rest; as accurately as if he had died yesterday, he represents the limits a girl can reach and still be sure of the approval of her society. But it remains true that no major writer since those curious woman-obsessed Athenians has made a woman's active heroism his or her central concern, and that a girl who wants, in George Eliot's words, "to make her life greatly effective" can search the literature of her own civilization and find even in George Eliot only treatments of how to fail in the attempt. The point of the male Bildungsroman, however, is that it deals not with failure but with success. *The Mill on the Floss* and *Middlemarch* come as close to the model as the feminine situation has allowed, yet Maggie is destroyed by her surging emotions, and Dorothea Brooke is explicitly presented as an Antigone with no brother to bury, a Saint Theresa with no convents to found. George Eliot wrote *Middlemarch* to show the forces that prevent a woman from being a hero. Unless or until these forces lose their strength, the best a girl can hope for is to be a heroine, while waiting for the new literature that will render *Love Story*— but not, we hope, Shakespeare—hopelessly out of date.

NOTES

1. William Allan Neilson and Charles Jarvis Hill, eds., *The Complete Plays and Poems of William Shakespeare* (Boston: Houghton Mifflin,

1942), p. 457. All subsequent Shakespeare citations are to this edition.

2. Quoted in G. M. Trevelyan, *History of England* (New York: Longmans, Green, 1926), p. 327.

3. Betty Bandel, *Shakespeare's Treatment of the Social Position of Women* (Ann Arbor, Mich.: University Microfilms, 1975), Dissertation Ser. No. 2793, pp. 174–97.

4. Bandel, *Social Position of Women*, p. 189.

5. Thomas Marc Parrott, *Shakespearean Comedy* (New York: Oxford University Press, 1949), p. 160.

6. Neilson and Hill, *Complete Plays*, p. 212.

7. The survey of this tradition is one of the most valuable contributions of Professor Bandel's dissertation, which reviews the position of women in English literature from Anglo-Saxon times to Shakespeare.

8. If *Macbeth* and *Antony and Cleopatra* present themselves as exceptions, we should reflect both that the actions of Lady Macbeth and Cleopatra do not uniquely determine the outcome—and that the outcome is catastrophe. As much can be said of Volumnia in *Coriolanus*.

9. Erich Segal, *Love Story* (New York: New American Library, 1970).

10. The reader will note that many things have changed since 1972, when this was written, among them where I teach.

11. Theodore Roszak, "The Hard and the Soft: The Force of Feminism in Modern Times," in *Masculine/Feminine: Readings in Sexual Mythology and the Liberation of Women*, ed. Betty and Theodore Roszak (New York: Harper Colophon Books, 1969), pp. 102–3.

Counsels of Gall and Grace

Intimate Conversations between Women in Shakespeare's Plays

CAROLE MCKEWIN

Juliet Dusinberre has observed that Shakespeare's theater offers a "consistent probing of the reactions of women to isolation in a society which has never allowed them independence from men either physically or spiritually."[1] The sense of both dependence and probing awareness is perhaps nowhere more evident than in those scenes where women can consider the relationship between the feminine decorum espoused by their society and their own impulses to break free, scenes in which women talk to each other apart from men. The sheer theatrical pleasures of these exchanges, from Adriana and Luciana's argument about wifely virtue in *The Comedy of Errors* to the sly conference about sex and power between Anne Bullen and the Old Lady in *Henry VIII*, attest to Shakespeare's enduring mimetic skill in creating the sound of women's voices placing themselves in a man's world, voices that vibrate with a special meaning in our own time:

> . . . wench, how will the world repute me
> For undertaking so unstaid a journey?

I fear me it will make me scandalized.
> (Julia to Lucetta, *The Two Gentlemen of Verona*,
> II.vii.59–61)[2]

Why should [men's] liberty than ours be more?
> (Adriana to Luciana, *The Comedy of Errors*, II.i.10)

I had rather be a giantess and lie under Mount Pelion.
> (Mistress Page to Mistress Ford, *The Merry Wives
> of Windsor*, II.i.71–72)

Dost thou think, though I am caparisoned like a man,
I have a doublet and hose in my disposition?
> (Rosalind to Celia, *As You Like It*, III.ii.185–87)

. . . I have within my mind
A thousand raw tricks of these bragging Jacks,
Which I will practice.
> (Portia to Nerissa, *The Merchant of Venice*, III.iv.76–78)

. . . O, these men, these men!
Dost thou in conscience think—tell me, Emilia—
That there be women do abuse their husbands
In such gross kind?
> (Desdemona to Emilia, *Othello*, IV.iii.58–61)

In faith, for little England
You'ld venture an emballing.
> (Old Lady to Anne, *Henry VIII*, II.iii.46–47)

Why, we have galls; and though we have some grace,
Yet have we some revenge.
> (Emilia to Desdemona, *Othello*, IV.iii.91–92)

The scenes from which these lines come, as different as they are from one another in mood, share a common quality of invoking the atmosphere of feminine companionship set apart from the world of men. Whether we want to call that woman's world the private as opposed to the public, or following Lévi-Strauss's and Sherry B. Ortner's social structuralism (the inner as opposed to the outer sphere),[3] these scenes of women's exclusive company in Shakespeare's plays are akin to what Simone de Beauvoir defines as a "counter-universe."[4] They provide space in which women together can express their own perceptions and identities, comment on masculine society, and gather strength and engage in reconnaissance to act in it. An exploration of these scenes reveals the freedoms and constraints of women in the patriarchal society of Shakespeare's plays.

Nineteen of the plays include scenes of private talks between women, in which the dialogue, according to the text, is conducted apart from the speaking or silent presence of male characters.[5] These private talks share some general characteristics. First, privacy seems to be more emphasized in women's conferences than in men's. The conversation is often set in an interior, such as the bedrooms or dressing rooms of *Much Ado* and *Othello*, or the specific exclusion of society is evident through dialogue or stage directions. Celia banishes Touchstone when she wants a private word with Rosalind (III.ii.153), and, according to the stage directions of both folio and quarto, the exchange between Regan and Goneril at the end of the first scene of *Lear* is conducted in a space emptied of family, members of the court, and attendants. In contrast, despite a feeling of surveillance, Hamlet and Horatio share confidences in the midst of an active court; and in the first scene of *The Merchant of Venice*, Antonio and his friends talk openly on the Rialto in intimate tones about a nameless melancholy: "In sooth I know not why I am so sad. / It wearies me, you say it wearies you" (I.i.1–2). As Luciana instructs her sister, men's business is "out o' door" (*Comedy of Errors*, II.i.11), whereas women's business is interior, secret, and, hence often to the male society outside, vaguely mysterious, or threatening. The Chamberlain in *Henry VIII*, wondering about the fate of the kingdom, interrupts the dialogue of Anne Bullen and the Old Lady with an earnest wish to know "the secret of your conference" (II.iii.50).[6] And, in one of Othello's most terrifying gestures of murderous intent, he banishes Emilia from Desdemona's bedroom (IV.iii.13).

The intimate talk between men is less enclosed in another way because its themes move easily between public and private concerns. Antonio and his friends speak of romance and financial speculations in the same breath. Their talk inevitably drifts from the personal problems at hand to the venue of public power and change. Solanio and Salerio sympathize with Antonio's malaise, but we feel the pull of their attention toward the business of the day. So too, Valentine confirms his love and friendship for Proteus at the beginning of *Two Gentlemen of Verona*, but their closeness is strained by Valentine's urge to be off on his journey. Private moments between men include the centrifugal force of the public world, which eventually spins away intimacy and melts the line between interior and exterior realities.

Talk between women often prepares for action too, but more intimately and indirectly. Some feminine conversations in Shakespeare's plays circle around estates of mood or feeling (romance, unease, despair, frustration, anger). As such, these scenes seem like walled cities cut off from the metropolis. They are talk for talk's sake, and not the talk which gets things done. But such conversations can reveal a vital private truth and the springs of identity. Julia, in *Two Gentlemen of Verona*, tells her maid, Lucetta, "[You] art the table wherein all my thoughts / Are visibly charactered and engraved" (II.vii.3–4). In such talk, self is not only mirrored but released as public strictures are relaxed. The wise Countess in *All's Well* invokes Helena's reluctant confidence by saying as much: "Come, come, disclose / The state of your affection, for your passions / Have to the full appeached" (I.iii.182–84). Helena, for once, gains the relief of pouring the waters of her love not in that "captious and intenible sieve" (195) of class boundaries and Bertram's disaffection, but in the empathetic ears of a woman who calls her daughter. In a similar manner, the counsel among the grieving queens of *Richard III* may also be seen as catharsis, here on a choric scale. Although they feel futile in the midst of tyranny, the women suggest that speech is an avenue of self-expression in a world that kills their babies and denies them the means of political reform. If words, says Queen Elizabeth, "Help nothing else, yet do they ease the heart" (IV.iv.130–31).

At the other extreme, female conversations are sometimes, like men's, direct preparation for action. The private exchange between Regan and Goneril after the appropriation of the kingdom has, in contrast to other Shakespearean feminine conferences, an uncharacteristic expediency. Only twenty-two lines long, and therefore one of the shortest scenes of women talking alone together, the close dialogue between the sisters about the conduct of their father ends with Goneril's fiercely insistent: "We must *do something*, and i' th' heat" (I.i.306, emphasis added). And Helena, before the bed-trick, uses talk chiefly as a vehicle toward effecting some decisive move in her pursuit of Bertram. Her first private conference with the Countess, in which she admits her love for the Count, concludes with her intentions to go to Paris, and her confidence with the widow of Florence is less a sharing of minds and hearts than the penultimate stage in the execution of the bed-trick: once she has convinced the older woman that all will be well, talk is temporarily done. Helena's comment concluding the scene signals the boundary between words and action: "But let's about it" (III.vii.48).

But most of these scenes are neither sheer talk nor mere preparation for action. Instead they explore the possibilities and limits of women's action, often leading indirectly to it. In the early *Two Gentlemen of Verona*, Julia, in conversation with Lucetta, can weigh the dangers of scandal against the loss of the heart's desire. Shall I take the journey to find Proteus? she asks, or shall I stay home, as modest maids do? Lucetta helps to tip the delicate balance: ". . . never dream on infamy, but go" (II.vii.64). Thus, the private peace of women provides a chance for them to consider the options of conformity or self-assertion. In other plays, the dialectic between the "is" and the "ought" of a woman's experience is resolved less peacefully. In *The Comedy of Errors*, Adriana punches holes in her maiden sister Luciana's theory of the patient wife. Having suffered through the practice of a wandering husband, Adriana mocks the woman who knows only the clichés of the code (II.i.10–41). Here conversation becomes an acceptable form of protest that ultimately socializes the two women: Adriana releases much of her anger within the boundaries of the counter-universe; Luciana learns a lesson that prepares her for a future role.

Even Portia, that most fortunate of Shakespearean heroines, gifted with intelligence, money, and luck, protests against and adjusts to those restrictions which circumscribe her will—the wishes of her dead father that she marry only the winner of the lottery. Her first words in *The Merchant of Venice*, the private ones to Nerissa, compose a physical metaphor for bearing up under the pressures of the patriarchal plan: "my little body is aweary of this great world" (I.ii.1). Spiritually, she feels her will "curbed"; her situation—however materially luxurious—"hard." Nerissa, the voice of the status quo, assures Portia (rather illogically) that because her father was virtuous, fate will be kind in choosing the right husband, but Nerissa also offers a more effective comfort to Portia in the invitation to express her feelings: "But what warmth is there in your affection towards any of these princely suitors . . . ?" (I.ii.31–33). Uncurbing her tongue in the ensuing character assassinations of the men who sue for her hand, Portia unpacks her heart with satire and vents her spleen with wit. The nervous energy of this litany moves toward the slower, more formal rhythm of the final line in the interview, when Nerissa invokes Bassanio's name and Portia replies, "I remember him well, and I remember him worthy of thy praise" (I.ii.111). The mention of Bassanio has no doubt soothed her spirits, but the verbal attack against the men who might claim her has also played its part in reconciling Portia to her fate. Brilliant conservative that she is, the lady of Belmont demonstrates the therapeutic value of woman's verbal misanthropy in a world of men. The Princess of *Love's Labour's Lost* expresses this fugitive comfort to be found in women's conversations when she remarks, "We are wise girls to mock our lovers so" (v.ii.58).

The counter-universe is not totally cut off from the male society around it; the enclosed space of feminine intimacy is often shaped by the larger world of the play. Women's private talk offers an important commentary on the public reality, and it reflects changes in dramatic context. We can see this most clearly in the contrasted settings of *As You Like It*, where women converse under constraint, and in freedom.

At the court of Duke Frederick, Rosalind and Celia are surrounded by a cankered society in which feminine friendship, like brotherly love, is threatened by envy and a rampant self-regard. The Duke advises Celia concerning Rosalind, "Thou art a fool. She robs thee of thy name, / And thou wilt show more bright and seem more virtuous / When she is gone" (I.iii.76–78). In this context, not only is a woman's identity based on the will of a father, who in this case is *not* virtuous, but also, the counter-universe of feminine friendships is curtailed. It is no wonder, then, that Rosalind and Celia's private conversation at court turns to topics which they can do nothing about—Fortune and Nature.[7]

ROSALIND. What shall be our sport then?
CELIA. Let us sit and mock the good housewife Fortune

from her wheel, that her gifts may henceforth be be-
stowed equally.

ROSALIND. I would we could do so, for her benefits are
mightily misplaced, and the bountiful blind woman doth
most mistake in her gifts to women.   (I.ii.28–34)

Rosalind and Celia express in allegory what is their true condition. Nature has made them women, Fortune has disenfran-
chised Rosalind, and by extension, Celia and all women. Observing themselves as victims of cosmic forces, their talk, however
elegant, is enervated, a flaccid exercise in diversion. This little dialogue, graceful, and yet full of gall, is utterly innocent of the vec-
tors of action, or the issues of conformity and self-assertion. Like
the helpless Queen of *Richard II*, these women talk to each other
in order to distract themselves.[8]

It is not until they move out of the court, and into the less
structured world of Arden, that their energies are renewed. Although the green world is no paradise, it is, by nature, a counter-
universe that reverses social codes and hierarchies, and so invites
feminine liberty.[9] What had been crucial at court for Celia and
Rosalind—the subject of fathers, their literal and metaphoric inheritance—here becomes a matter of casual regard. In Arden,
Rosalind merely remarks in passing that she has met her own
banished father, but the encounter hardly affects her course of action, and she does not reveal her true identity: "I met the Duke
yesterday and had much question with him. He asked me of what
parentage I was. I told him, of as good as he; so he laughed and let
me go. But what talk we of fathers when there is such a man as
Orlando?" (III.iv.31–35). And so Arden fairly bellows out with
their talk. In this open air, far from court, where fathers laugh and
let daughters go, Ganymede and Aliena shape women's talk into a
dynamic art form. They celebrate their bodies, themselves; engage in literary criticism; consider the follies of lovers and love;
wonder about the unfaithfulness of men; and laugh at the inan-
ities of women. Thoughtful, irreverent, affectionate, compan-
ionable, bawdy, woman's personality resonates and expands,
pushing the boundaries of the counter-universe outward to suit
herself. Sweet are the conversational uses of letting go in Arden,
especially for the queen of feminine conversationalists, Celia,

who demonstrates the way a good friend can weave amidst our moods, affirm and qualify them, yet remain herself. More exuberant than Antonio, and as giving; more articulate than Horatio, and as true, Celia is perhaps too good, even for the dazzling Rosalind.

The conversations of Arden show the facets of womanly friendship through verbal exchanges which are, generally, the happiest and most liberated in Shakespeare's canon. Even the shadows have their pleasures. Rosalind's concerns dominate the talk, yet through her insistent regard for Orlando, we have a chance to see the patience, compassion, and astringent humor of Celia. And while the conversations themselves have a giddy freedom that we know cannot last, both women manage to take from Arden a permanent reminder of their spree, when talk was not only a pleasure, but also a means of creating their own worlds. It is Rosalind, after all, who conducts the marriages at the end of the play.[10] Whatever we may think of their choices in husbands, we must admit that Rosalind and Celia have had more than romantic pleasures in a setting where fathers, unwittingly or not, let daughters choose their own mates. In the patriarchal world where most of Shakespeare's women live, that is a step in the right direction.

The heady conversations of Rosalind and Celia in the forest have no equal in Shakespeare's other plays. In *Much Ado about Nothing*, for example, the private exchanges between women have more the lassitude of Duke Frederick's court than the vibrancy of Arden. The scene in which Hero, Margaret, and Beatrice converse in Hero's dressing room before the wedding has a curious unease about it, an unease not completely accounted for by Shakespeare's more obvious dramatic purposes of separating from the group Margaret, the trouble-maker, and showing Beatrice's preoccupation with Benedick. What is most frequent in Shakespeare's feminine conversations—the atmosphere of shared experience and understanding—is strikingly absent from this long scene. The women's communication, their very moods, are radically out of kilter. Hero's heart is heavy with prenuptial fears, with premonition; but she will not invite the others into her confidence, and her generally compliant character flares with nasty impatience over the choice of a certain rabato. When Margaret presses, Hero snaps, "My cousin's a fool and thou art another. I'll wear none but this" (III.iv.11). Beatrice is also unlike herself.

Carole McKewin

Suffering from a cold, the brightest wit of Shakespeare's heroines either doesn't get the broad sallies of the maid, or doesn't feel like countering the bawdy allusions that Margaret is strenuously injecting into the queasy atmosphere. The maid chatters on, ignoring the other women's malaise of heart and body. Celia and Rosalind had at least tried to cheer each other at court through wit-games, but these female conversationalists hardly communicate at all. The sense of immanent complicity which we have come to expect among women in the comedies is painfully absent from this conference, yet the scene suggests significance in its length of eighty-four lines—longer than that of the parallel scene between Conrade and Borachio preceding—and in its positioning, in Act III, scene iv, just right of center in the play. What is the point of this lingering look into the private world of women in a bad mood?

The clue may be found in the other conversations of the play, all of which, in one way or another, suffer a violation of privacy or meaning by being overheard. Antonio, overhearing the Count speak to Claudio about wooing Hero, misconstrues the Count's words. Benedick, overhearing Don Pedro and Claudio, assumes that they are speaking candidly about Beatrice's unrequited love for Benedick; Beatrice, overhearing Ursula and Hero, likewise thinks that they are sincere about her cold character and Benedick's languishing passion. The world of this play is one where intimate conversations are not intimate at all, where the value of such counsels—candor and the privacy to speak one's heart—is falsified, ignored, or obliterated by both talkers and eavesdroppers. Personal utterances become public property and in that transfer are misshapen. Of course, some of these violations in privacy are benign or positive in their ultimate effect. By overhearing their friends' fake private conversations, Benedick and Beatrice realize the potential of love between them. And the Watch's eavesdropping on Conrade and Borachio's conference eventually saves the day. Through the alchemy of comedy, Shakespeare transforms the violations of privacy into the unmasking of evil and the revelations of love. But in Act III, scene iv, and the colloquy of the women in Hero's dressing room, we are still under the spell of error, before that transformation has taken place.

The counter-universe of women in *Much Ado about Nothing* is neither a place where women can ease their hearts in frank and open exchange, nor a healthy island of self-expression in a patriarchal world. It is instead an uncomfortable landscape where good friends will, with whatever mixed intentions, deceive one another (II.i.334), and where waiting women, impatient with keeping below stairs (v.ii.9), are not allies of their mistresses, but treacherous, if unwitting, imposters at midnight windows. The conversation among the women in Hero's bedroom is not overheard: its corruption of privacy comes not from without, but from within. The solidarity of the women is fissured, and the opportunity for honest, open exchange is lost. The physical and psychological discomfort of the women in the bedroom scene of *Much Ado* is not only a most appropriate emotional prelude to the disaster of the wedding, but also an emblem of the social atmosphere that breeds the crisis.

The world of Hero and Beatrice is, unlike that of Rosalind and Celia, a smaller and more crowded world with no escape hatch, a world where privacy is infected or disaffected by other people.[11] And with no Arden to run to, women must cope with restraint in the best way they know how. Ironically, talk does help the individual woman: Beatrice wins a considerable measure of freedom from the social codes of Messina by her sharp tongue, yet Shakespeare shows us little comfort for Beatrice from her conversations with other women. All the more admirable is her loyalty to Hero—a friend so different in temperament—and, in the speech with Benedick in Act IV, her furious outburst against the victimization of her sex. In *Much Ado*, woman must vent her spleen in unlikely places—in the first intimate conversation with her lover. Here, receiving the quiet offer of Benedick's devotion, "Come, bid me do anything for thee," Beatrice responds with lashing fury against the masculine code which destroyed Hero: "Kill Claudio" (IV.i.283–84). With no relief from the counter-universe, and with the world of effective action closed off to her, Beatrice's rage against feminine impotence rises dazzlingly, shockingly, in this strange love scene, like a geyser in the midst of a quiet dawn.

Although Shakespeare's comedies offer the richest variety of women's private scenes, the development of those conversations from the early to the later comedies shows a diminishing of the counter-universe. After the early comedies, and except for the bright expanses of *As You Like It*, the atmosphere darkens, as in *Much Ado*; or it is strained and minimal, as in *All's Well*; or it disappears altogether. Viola has no confidante in *Twelfth Night*, and we are not invited into Isabella's crucial conversation with Mariana at the end of *Measure for Measure*. And, in the late romances, in some ways extensions of comic form, Shakespeare apparently finds little use for such scenes. But it is difficult to read this evidence. The lack of dramatized communication between women may mean a darker comedy, or it may indicate that intimate conversation is no longer necessary for a woman's psychic and social ease. Or, it may point to other ways Shakespeare chooses to reveal female character (soliloquy, for example).

In the tragedies, where the patriarchal world is more oppressive, women are sometimes able to do more, but they talk less to each other. In Shakespeare's tragic world, this important means of self-expression for women is almost invariably imperfectly realized, perverted, or blocked. Juliet, seeking advice from her old counselor, the Nurse, is deprived of communication by the older woman's acceptance of the status quo: "Speak'st thou from thy heart?" she says, when the Nurse degrades Romeo for Paris. Then, "Thou and my bosom henceforth shall be twain" (III.v.228–42).[12] Ophelia and Gertrude, despite their similarities in temperament, are estranged from one another by a setting of corrupt politics, as well as by their own self-absorption. Regan and Goneril's comradely interchange after the disposal of the kingdom shows the intimacy between two women who can almost read each other's thoughts, but their relationship becomes a grotesque parody of sisterly understanding in the fatal rivalry over Edmund. Lady Macbeth and Cordelia have no female confidantes at all. Cleopatra may seem to be an exception to this pattern, for her relationships with Charmian and Iras prove upon their part a devotion beyond slavery. But her talks with them, only briefly "private" in the hectic pace of the play, are never allowed adequate time to unfold in a mutual sharing of thought and feeling. And Cleopatra, for all her brilliance, cannot go beyond the unilateral attitude of jealousy for Octavia. We might wish for a conversation between the two queens, as did Virginia Woolf, who admired Shakespeare above all, but who lamented the lack of complexity in Cleopatra's attitude toward the other woman.[13]

Only in *Othello*, with Emilia and Desdemona, are we allowed a feminine friendship of considerable dimension, and a dramatic moment long enough to reveal that relationship.

The willow-song scene in *Othello*, one of Shakespeare's last, and perhaps his greatest, intimate dialogue between women reflects both the increased oppression of the outside world and the effect, however limited, the counter-universe can have on its opposite. It recalls some aspects of the bedroom scene in *Much Ado*. Hero, like Desdemona, is also found ill at ease in her chambers with a more energetic waiting maid, and in both comedy and tragedy, small talk of fashion and a bit of gossip nestle us into the atmosphere.[14] But Hero prepares for a wedding that ends in the "death" of her reputation; Desdemona prepares for bed in the wedding sheets that shall be her winding sheets. In both scenes, women are threatened by the slander that kills: in the dressing room in Messina and in the bedroom at Cyprus, we hear the premonitory rumble of disaster.

But it is imminent in *Othello*. With no family or friends, Desdemona and Emilia are alone in a military camp, where masculine conceptions of honor define what a woman is,[15] and no bungling, well-meaning watches come to save the day. The conversation between Emilia and Desdemona reflects the texture of that oppression. Their language is imbued with frustration and evasion. The conditional mood pervades their syntax: "*Wouldst* thou do such a deed . . . I *might* do't . . . I *should* venture . . . *If* wives do fall . . ." (IV.iii.65–87, emphasis added). Emilia entertains a dream of power in which women, for a small labor, would own the world and remake the laws. Desdemona turns away from the present to sing of a woman abandoned in the past. What they *would* do, what *had been*, is the subject of their talk, not what they *will* do in the face of a terrifying reality. Yet, at the same time, Desdemona and Emilia reveal a feminine friendship that is affectionate and frank, generous and nurturing. Whatever their weakness or blindness in coping with the world of men, their relationship remains intact to affect that world ultimately.[16]

This relationship is central to the play in a number of ways. The women's friendship is an implied rebuke to the masculine relationships of Iago/Othello, Iago/Roderigo, and Othello/Cassio, and the willow-song scene, ". . . sandwiched between two exchanges of Iago and Roderigo, sharply contrasts the genuine intimacy of the women with the hypocritical friendship of the men. . . ."[17] The counter-universe of women provides us with an alternative reality, one which finally has a profound impact on the larger world of the play. The friendship between women—explicated so movingly in this scene—does at last speak the truth of Desdemona's innocence in a world that has declared her otherwise. Emilia's loyalty to her friend, enlightened by her egalitarian view of man and woman in marriage, is what remains whole in the debacle of *Othello*.[18] Her controlled vehemence in the speech at the end of her conversation with Desdemona—"Why we have galls; and though we have some grace, / Yet have we some revenge" (IV.iii.91–92)—is the preparation and warning for her cleansing fury in the final act. Women's friendship will not finally be contained in the counter-universe, but will emerge to reveal what woman is, and to reshape the chimeras of slander. With the grace of her friendship, with the gall of her indignation, Emilia makes bearable the horrifying waste of innocence and love in *Othello*. Within her courage, her anger, and her revelation is a measure of hope.

Private conversations between women in Shakespeare's plays provide opportunities for self-expression, adjustment to social codes, release, relief, rebellion, and transformation. We surely need to ask more questions about these scenes and their functions. What is the connection between women's conversations and characterization, between women's talk and genre? And what do these conferences tell us about women's responsibility in the tragic world? In the sororal atmosphere of feminism, when the dialogue of women has been emphasized as a vital part of our collective and individual self-realization, we should especially appreciate Shakespeare's art of overhearing the voices of women in an oppressive context, or the voices of women who are free, or discovering how to be free.

Notes

1. Juliet Dusinberre, *Shakespeare and the Nature of Women* (New York: Barnes & Noble, 1975), p. 92.
2. All Shakespeare quotations are from *William Shakespeare: The Complete Works*, gen. ed. Alfred Harbage (Baltimore: Penguin Books, 1969).

3. Sherry B. Ortner, following Lévi-Strauss's structural model, sees the family unit (female and babies) in opposition to the extrafamilial domain of society and culture; the male, however, stands "outside" this unit (for the father has no "natural role"). But because of this outsider status, men have gained "all of society as their world." See her essays, "Is Female to Male as Nature Is to Culture?" *Feminist Studies*, 1 (1972), 5–31, and "Oedipal Father, Mother's Brother, and the Penis: A Review of Juliet Mitchell's *Psychoanalysis and Feminism*," in *Feminist Studies*, 2 (1975), 167–82, esp. 174–75.

4. Simone de Beauvoir, *The Second Sex*, trans. and ed. H. M. Parshley (New York: Knopf, 1952), pp. 542–43.

5. In the comedies these scenes are: *Comedy of Errors*, II.i.1–43, 86–115; *Taming of the Shrew*, II.i.1–21; *Two Gentlemen of Verona*, I.ii.1–49, 66–104, 131–40; II.vii.1–90; *Love's Labour's Lost*, v.ii.1–78; *Merchant of Venice*, I.ii.1–111; III.iv.57–85; *As You Like It*, I.ii.1–40, iii.1–33, 86–134; III.ii.157–237, iv.1–42; IV.iii.1–5; *Much Ado*, III.i.1–103, iv.1–84; *Merry Wives*, II.i.30–96; IV.ii.173–95; *All's Well*, I.iii.121–249; III.v.1–27, vii.1–48; IV.iv.1–36. (I have excluded the scene between Helena and Hermia in *Midsummer Night's Dream*, III.ii.195–242, because there is no mutual tone of intimacy: Hermia does not respond to Helena's reminder of the "counsel that we two have shared." Also, Lysander and Demetrius are near enough to interrupt, if not overhear, the dialogue. Despite, or because of, the ambiguity of the text, some productions act and stage this as a private talk between the women.) In the history plays they are: *Richard III*, IV.i.1–11, iv.9–135; *Richard II*, III.iv.1–23; *Henry V*, III.iv.1–57; *Henry VIII*, II.iii.1–49, 81–107. In the tragedies they are: *Romeo and Juliet*, I.iii.1–99; II.v.21–79; III.ii.36–143, v.65–126, 197–236; *Othello*, III.iv.21–34, 97–106, 140–164; IV.ii.95–106, iii.10–104; *Lear*, I.i.284–306; *Antony and Cleopatra*, IV.xv.1–5, 63–94; v.ii.191–96, 207–32, 280–316; *Coriolanus*, I.iii.1–45. (I have excluded the exchanges of the weird sisters in *Macbeth* because of their questionable human nature. As I see it, the counter-universe involves "real" women in imaginary gardens.) The single romance that includes such a scene is *Winter's Tale*, II.ii.21–68.

6. F. David Hoeniger, in the introduction to his edition of *Henry VIII* (*Works*, ed. Harbage, p. 781), includes the conversation between Anne and the Old Lady among scenes that have been generally accepted as Shakespeare's. The echoes in this scene of an earlier intimate conversation help confirm this judgment. Anne's intuition about the dangers inherent in high places, "I would not be a queen / For all the world," recalls Desdemona's wonder about women who commit adultery "for all the world." The Old Lady's response, ". . . for little England / You'ld venture an emballing" (II.iii.46–47) suggests Emilia's rejoinder that the woman who gains the world for her sin could change the morals of that world to suit herself.

7. Gail Kern Paster, seminar lecture and discussion, "Women and Literature," George Washington University, Spring, 1973.

8. Act III, scene iv, which begins with the Queen's words to her women, "What sport shall we devise here in this garden / To drive away the heavy thought of care?" shows how Shakespeare uses the counteruniverse as a frame for a comment on the larger world of the play. The lack of vigor in the Queen's opening lines and the futility of her curses at the end of the scene provide the setting for the gardener's comparison of the state to an untended garden. The simile is not spoken by the Queen, but it is her fruitless talk which establishes the appropriate atmosphere for the description of decay and disorder.

9. See Northrop Frye's allusion to the distinctly female energies of the green world in *Anatomy of Criticism: Four Essays* (Princeton, N.J.: Princeton University Press, 1957), p. 183.

10. For a discussion of Rosalind's power in the play, and a balanced appraisal of Shakespeare's qualifications on women's freedom, see Clara Claiborne Park, "As We Like It: How a Girl Can Be Smart and Still Popular," *American Scholar*, 42 (1973), 269–71, reprinted in this anthology.

11. Sherman Hawkins, "The Two Worlds of Shakespearean Comedy," *Shakespeare Studies*, 3 (1967), 62–80, has described the closed worlds of *Love's Labour's Lost* and *Much Ado*, which reverse the outward movement of the green-world comedies by dramatizing the intrusion of outsiders.

12. My thanks to Coppélia Kahn for letting me read, while still unpublished, her "Coming of Age in Verona," which first appeared in *Modern Language Studies*, 8 (1977–78), 5–22 and is reprinted in this anthology. Kahn discusses the conversations between the Nurse and Juliet and shows how, in opposition to the orthodox view of woman's roles espoused by the Nurse and Lady Capulet, is Juliet's "unconventional, fully conscious and willed giving of herself to Romeo" (p. 183). Juliet's gradual estrangement from the Nurse is a measure of her development toward adulthood and her growing independence.

13. Virginia Woolf, *A Room of One's Own* (New York: Harcourt, Brace & World, Inc. 1957), p. 86.

14. S. N. Garner reviews the critical commentary on Desdemona's problematic line in this scene, "This Lodovico is a proper man" (IV.iii.35), in "Shakespeare's Desdemona," *Shakespeare Studies*, 9 (1976), 233–52. Garner shows how misinterpretation of the line, in light of the complex nature of Desdemona's character, may foster a view of the heroine which is close to Iago's.

15. Jean Klene, in "Othello: 'A fixed figure for the time of scorn,'" *Shakespeare Quarterly*, 26 (1975), 139–50, sees the tragic characters' naïve approaches to the Renaissance code of honor. All the characters, but especially the men, are enslaved by notions of reputation and opinion in the public world.

16. Carol Thomas Neely, "Women and Men in *Othello*: 'What should such a fool / Do with so good a woman,'" offers an essentially positive reading of the female characters and of female friendship, but notes that both sexes share in tragic responsibility: the men "misconceive" the women; the women "overestimate" the men (this volume, p. 228). I am grateful to Carol Neely for allowing me to read this essay before its original publication.

17. Neely, "Women and Men," p. 225.

18. See Betty Bandel's defense of Emilia in *Shakespeare's Treatment of the Social Position of Women*, (Ann Arbor, Mich.: University Microfilms, 1975, Dissertation Ser. No. 2793), p. 167.

Shakespeare's Cressida
"A kind of self"

GAYLE GREENE

"Let it not be believ'd for womanhood!"

That human nature is not "natural," but is, rather, shaped by social forces and values, is an understanding we have long had in
relation to men but one which has been more difficult to grasp
with regard to women. *Troilus and Cressida* may seem the last
place to look for such insights, informed as it is with a loathing of
humanity, an aversion to sex and the physical, and more misogyny than is usual with Shakespeare. Cressida is the clearest representative of woman's "frailty" in his plays, the "frailty" that
Hamlet says is woman's "name." Whereas Hero, Desdemona,
Hermione, and Imogen redeem woman from the general curse,
Cressida is a type of Eve whose error will "soil our mothers" and
"square the general sex."[1] Proverbial in literary tradition as a
source, standard, and symbol of faithlessness, Cressida's inconstancy fulfills what Leslie Fiedler calls the "male nightmare of
unmerited betrayal."[2] But even in this least sympathetic of portraits, Shakespeare provides a context that exonerates Cressida.
Shown in relation to men who value her little yet insist that she
be as she "is valued" (II.ii.52), she is portrayed in a relation to her
society that demonstrates the principle feminists have come to
understand, that (in Simone de Beauvoir's terms) "one is not born,
but rather becomes a woman . . . it is civilization as a whole that
produces this creature."[3]

In Cressida's character and fate we see epitomized the values of both Trojan and Greek societies, the working out of Troilus's position that a woman is as she "is valued." The worth of an individual, object, or event, rather than being inherent and objective, is subjective and relative to "will" (II.ii.53, 62, 66) and "opinion"—conferred by the "prizer," not in the "prize" (II.ii.55–56).[4] Daughter to a traitor in a world at war, Cressida has had to understand her society clearly and unsentimentally in order to survive, and the values she has grasped on a personal level are the same that motivate her world politically and philosophically—relativistic and mercantile standards which commit all the characters in the play to appearance and make them "subjects all / To . . . Time" (III.i.173–74). Though these principles apply to both men and women, they do not apply equally. Without positive, assertive ways of defining selfhood—lacking even, as Cressida says, "men's privilege / Of speaking first" (III.ii.128–29)—women are more dependent than men on external supports for identity, more vulnerable to "opinion":[5] they are "formed in th' applause" (III.iii.119) of others, "in the glass" of others' "praise" (I.ii.285), "but by reflection" (III.iii.99).

The stereotypical antifemale slanders are there, of course, and on one level we are encouraged to respond to them. In an ugly, calumniating play in which all come under "the common curse of mankind" (II.iii.28) pronounced by Thersites, Cressida is "the very crown of falsehood" (IV.ii.100), her betrayal earning her Troilus's malediction, "Let all untruths stand by thy stained name, / And they'll seem glorious" (v.ii.178–79). She herself pronounces judgment on "our sex," as she turns from Troilus to Diomedes, in terms that generalize her "error":

Ah, poor our sex! this fault in us I find,
The error of our eye directs our mind.
What error leads must err; O then conclude
Minds sway'd by eyes are full of turpitude.   (v.ii.109–12)

Thersites moralizes this, saying, "A proof of strength she could not publish more, / Unless she said, 'My mind is now turn'd whore" (113–14). Her representativeness is stressed by her analogue in the war plot with another faithless woman whose "contaminated carrion weight" (IV.i.72) has dragged the war on through the years. And critics have been content generally to accept the worst of these terms as adequate to her character; taking their cues from the men in the play, their responses to Cressida have been overwhelmingly negative.[6]

As disturbing as her inconstancy is her inconsistency, and we must account not merely for the stereotypical in her character, but for Shakespeare's handling of her defection so that it occurs within a few lines of these vows to Troilus—

> Time, force, and death,
> Do to this body what extremes you can;
> But the strong base and building of my love
> Is as the very centre of the earth,
> Drawing all things to it.   (IV.ii.101–5)

The next time we see her, she is being "kiss'd in general" (IV.v.21) by the Greek camp. This sudden and complete violation of declared intentions damages her coherence in "realistic" terms and indicates the presence of some principle of characterization other than the realistic. One critic accounts for her as an amalgam of four character types: romantic, modest maid; satiric, forward maid; satiric shrew; and pathetic penitent—"all four stereotypes are amalgamated into one, the eclectic Cressida"—a combination which he claims creates complexity.[7] But while it is useful to note this variety of traits, it is questionable whether a collection of stereotypes makes for a more complex character than a single stereotype, unless they are combined according to some meaningful principle; nor does it explain the conspicuous disjunction between Cressida's words and actions. We are left with a character who makes so little connection between the vows of one scene and the deeds of the next that she seems to have, morally as well as artistically—as she herself says—"a kind of self" (III.ii.148). Her instability is emphasized when Troilus's response to her betrayal seems to split her in two: "This she? . . . this is not she; . . . This is, and is not, Cressid!" (v.ii.137–38, 146).

But Cressida is merely complying with "opinion," with the assumption of her society that the worth of an individual is in the eye of the beholder: and, as opinion changes, so does she. "Valued" first as love object, then as "daughter of the game" (IV.v.63), the swiftness of her "turn" (v.ii.114) indicates how far her price has fallen. Her characterization thus demonstrates several principles we have come to understand as crucial to women's psychology—the tendency of a woman to define herself in "relational" capacities, to derive self-esteem from the esteem of others, and to "objectify" herself. As Judith Bardwick and Elizabeth Douvan have written, "In the absence of independent and objective achievements, girls and women know their worth only from others' responses, know their identities only from their relationships as daughters, girl friends, wives, or mothers. . . . Women use interpersonal success as a route to self-esteem. . . . In general, they have continued, even as adults, to esteem themselves as they are valued by others."[8] It follows that, in de Beauvoir's terms, "woman sees herself and makes her choices not in accordance with her nature in itself, but as man defines her."[9]

The "self" Cressida fashions is an "object" for the "present eye['s] praise" (III.iii.180). She herself senses the consequences of this, expressing fear of accepting love in terms that indicate awareness of her potential:

> I have a kind of self resides with you;
> But an unkind self, that itself will leave
> To be another's fool. (III.ii.148–50)

Defined in relation to "you" or "another," she is left with two alternatives: at worst, with an "unkind self"—unkind in the sense of cruel and "unnatural"; but at best, with a "kind of self"—one that is partial, unreliable, and not her own. Her fate is the working out of a character that lacks integrity or autonomy, and her terms prefigure the "turning" that will split her so insanely and irrevocably for Troilus, and for herself.

To some extent, of course, Shakespeare accepted a conception of the individual in "relational" capacities; such an idea of selfhood was implied by belief in a hierarchical order, and only characters like Edmund, Iago, and Richard III are so benighted as to claim autonomy and self-sufficiency. But with the breakdown of hierarchy that is the subject of this play, the consequences predicted by Ulysses—"This chaos, when degree is suffocate" (I.iii.125)—are exactly fulfilled: the traditional bonds that once defined human relations are replaced by "appetite . . . will and power" (119–22). Proper relationship is destroyed, and the ethics of the marketplace—what Marx calls the cash nexus—govern men's and women's dealings with one another, as Ulysses' terms for Ajax indicate: "Let us like merchants first show foul wares, /

And think perchance they'll sell" (358–59). The disturbance of the hierarchical order leaves the individual not autonomous and free, but bound to definition by relation of a different, more destructive sort. Deprived of the legitimate sanctions of hierarchy, the individual must create his or her own value, an appearance to please the beholding eye, in what is essentially a selling of the self.

The society from which Cressida's nature takes its shape is thus modern and familiar, a society that reduces people to terms of appetite and trade. This is a world informed with the "spirit of capitalism," in Raymond Southall's terms, "busily reducing life to the demands of the belly" and "making merchandise of mens soules."[10] Our first introduction to Cressida, "in the glass" of the "praise" of Troilus and Pandarus (1.ii.285)—a glass that reflects more of their characters than hers—reveals their conceptions of woman as something to be bought and sold, and to be devoured. Cressida is discussed as a "cake" to be leavened, kneaded, baked, and made (1.i.15–26); is praised as a "pearl" for which Troilus is the "merchant" (100–104); and is the object, as throughout, of Pandarus's attempts to sell her. But their "mercenary-mindedness" and "appetitiveness" is, as Southall notes, "but an abstract of the corruptive spirit" that characterizes the society as a whole;[11] and Cressida, as the obliging object of these attitudes, illustrates their effects in extreme form. This society prompts a powerful indictment of the mercantilism of the age, and Cressida reminds us of the effects of capitalism on woman.

Troilus's predatory attitudes are masked by his exalted idealism but emerge inadvertently through his language and imagery. Cressida is distantly and conventionally adored as "stubborn-chaste against all suit" (1.i.97), and Troilus, complaining in the language of the sonnets, is enjoying his role of unrequited lover, indulging in an idealized self-image and an image of Cressida which are of far more interest to him than the realities.[12] His Petrarchan terms seem incongruous with Cressida as "cake," but his praise, too—"Her eyes, her hair, her cheek, her gait, her voice . . . her hand . . . to whose soft seizure / The cygnet's down is harsh" (54–58)—reveals a conception of her which is primarily sensual and self-centered. His self-consciously elaborated analogy—"O, that her hand, / In whose comparison all whites are ink" (55–56)—reveals more interest in his own poetic invention than in his supposed subject, Cressida. To his own question, "What Cressid is, what Pandar, and what we" (99), he offers an answer in lines which combine the conventional and unintentional:

> Her bed is India, there she lies, a pearl;
> Between our Ilium and where she resides,
> Let it be call'd the wild and wand'ring flood,
> Ourself the merchant, and this sailing Pandar
> Our doubtful hope, our convoy, and our bark. (I.i.100–105)

The too-precise naming of her "bed" as his goal and himself as "the merchant" impugns his lofty idealism, but the contradiction revealed is a familiar one; exalting woman as goddess, reducing her to object, what he omits is the person. Predatory on the one hand and in love with his own illusions on the other, Troilus's failure to see Cressida whole anticipates, and in part accounts for, the division both of them later experience. The irony with which Shakespeare invests his delusions is consistent with an attitude that Juliet Dusinberre has noticed in other Elizabethan authors who, writing for a bourgeois and Puritan-influenced audience, rejected the deifying stereotypes of courtly love.[13]

Nor is Troilus's view of woman reserved for Cressida: it forms the basis of his argument for continuing the war, as he describes Helen, too, in the Trojan council scene, as "a pearl, / Whose price hath launch'd above a thousand ships, / And turn'd crown'd kings to merchants" (II.ii.81–83). His terms, again just slightly sour, reduce value to "price" and the Marlovian allusion to an echo from a world gone by. In fact, his every attempt at defense of Helen demeans her:

> We turn not back the silks upon the merchant
> When we have soil'd them, nor the remainder viands
> We do not throw in unrespective sieve,
> Because we now are full.   (II.ii.69–72)

Once more, terms of trade and appetite taint his praise, only now in the form of scraps and soiled merchandise. His view of woman as no more than the qualities and attributes he projects onto her finds philosophical sanction in the idea of value he states here— "what's aught but as 'tis valued" (II.ii.52). (It is significant, also, that though Troilus mentions "wife" in this argument (61), it is a word and idea conspicuously absent from his references to Cressida; preferring a safely distanced love object, he is content with a mistress.) And his is no private delusion; it is persuasive as argument in the public realm because it speaks to the values of his society as a whole.

The discrepancy between the idealized creature of Troilus's imagination and the Cressida we meet in the second scene is startling, and the juxtaposition of fantasy and reality casts some doubt, at this early stage, on the validity of his versions of reality. In her bantering with Pandarus, we see Cressida as a cynical coquette who acts in full understanding of the rules of the game, aware of the "wiles," "lies," "wards," and "watches" (II.ii.260–64) that are necessary to defend herself. The terms demonstrate a conception of love as combat which is consistent with so defensive a posture. Left alone, Cressida reveals herself in soliloquy as a deliberate exploiter of Troilus's illusions, as exploitative of him as he is of her, though more conscious than he of the nature of their transaction:

> Yet hold I off. Women are angels, wooing:
> Things won are done, joy's soul lies in the doing.
> That she belov'd knows nought that knows not this:
> Men prize the thing ungain'd more than it is.
> That she was never yet that ever knew
> Love got so sweet as when desire did sue.   (I.ii.286–89)

Aware of herself as a commodity whose value varies with supply and demand, a "thing ungained" which "won" is "done," she creates an appearance of scarcity in what is essentially an attempt to sell herself. But she is merely complying with Troilus's desires and with the expectations of an entire society that values appearance and treats people as objects; she differs from the rest of her world only in the degree of self-awareness with which she plays. Simultaneously victim and critic of these processes, she is a commentator on values with which she nevertheless conforms, in that peculiar relation to her society described by de Beauvoir in which "woman knows that the masculine code is not hers" and so "feels daily the ambiguity of her position" and can "put in question . . . ready-made values, hypocritical . . . morality."[14] Cressida is, paradoxically, in a better position than the men to understand the principles that motivate her world, though she is helpless to act on what she knows. Her role as commentator is consistent with the function of women in a number of Shake-speare's other plays.[15]

The rest of their relationship demonstrates the working out of these conscious and unconscious strategies of deception. At their meeting—their first and only love scene—Troilus's "imaginary relish" (III.ii.19) reveals the same combination of appetite and idealization apparent earlier. Again, a kind of jaded epicureanism informs his "expectation," as "sense," "wat'ry palates," and "thrice-repured nectar" (18, 20–22) undermine his vaunt of "purity" (167). More interested in the style and idea of love than in Cressida, he cuts off her unusually sincere remonstrances with his rapturous protestations—"O that I thought it could be in a woman— / As, if it can, I will presume in you— / To feed for aye her lamp and flames of love" (158–60)—in a statement which is rather chillingly impersonal in its implications that it is "a woman," not Cressida, he cares for.

Cressida's behavior in this scene is a curious blend of her customary calculation and an uncustomary loss of control. She confesses that she was "hard to seem won; but I was won" (III.ii. 117), and expresses reluctance to relax her guard and "speak / The thing I shall repent" (130–31); yet she does, and "blabs" (124) revealingly, offering some astute observations. She expresses a poignant awareness of the necessity of illusion in love—"for to be wise and love / Exceeds man's might; that dwells with gods above" (156–57)—and a sense of the value of vows that indicates more understanding of Troilus than he has of her: "They that have the voice of lions and the act of hares, are they not monsters?" (88–89). Her awareness of her "kind" and "unkind" selves indicates that she has more self-knowledge than Troilus has, but, frightened by the implications of these perceptions, she retracts— "Perchance, my lord, I show more craft than love, / And fell so roundly to a large confession, / To angle for your thoughts" (153– 55). Struggling both to maintain and to relinquish the defenses she has so carefully constructed, she combines roles of coquette and commentator in this scene; but, reducing herself to "angler," she forfeits claim to our feelings. Whatever involvement we still feel is further diminished by the stylized gesture at the end of the scene, in which all three characters, reducing themselves to caricatures, swear in terms that foreshadow the fulfillment of their literary destinies: "Let all constant men be Troiluses, all false women Cressids, and all brokers-between Pandars!" (202–4).

These stylized, simplistic definitions are not, however, the last word, and should not be taken out of context—as they frequently are—as identifying tags for their characters. Though Cressida is false, her inconstancy is qualified by the world of the play; and though Troilus is loyal, his "truth" is similarly qualified by context. The "simplicity" he protests is, for one thing, comically undercut by his tortuous language, his "Few words to fair faith" belied by his elaboration, "Troilus shall be such to Cressid as what envy can say worst shall be a mock for his truth, and what truth can speak truest not truer than Troilus" (III.ii.95–98). Moreover, his definition of himself as "truth" and a touchstone of truth (169–70, 172–83) is suspect, both psychologically and philosophically: he is, as we have seen, incapable of truth to himself, and truth defined as loyalty to a woman who traffics in appearances is unsound in its own terms. He may be "truth's authentic author" (181) in a sense he does not intend—its "author" not as a touchstone, but as of a fictional construct, of a Cressida created of desire and words, though his faith is an illusion which cannot survive her falseness.

The illusion on which their love is based has been partially dispelled with Cressida's yielding: "Come, draw this curtain, and let's see your picture" (III.ii.46–47)—a detail that associates her, emblematically, with the veiled daughter of time. Now, the veil lifted, the reality revealed (in the scene where they part) is bleak and unlovely, its bleakness intensified by the evocation of poetic convention:

> O Cressida! but that the busy day,
> Wak'd by the lark, hath rous'd the ribald crows,
> And dreaming night will hide our joys no longer,
> I would not from thee.   (IV.ii.8–11)

Again, Troilus's words work at odds with intentions, and, in parody of the aubade, which functions (as does the Marlovian allusion) like an echo of a vanished ideal, he evokes ribald crows for nightingales, to end with, "you will catch cold and curse me" (IV.ii.14). A worried tone of nagging informs Cressida's lines— "are you a'weary of me?" (7). This worry is a bit premature, one would think, but explicable in terms of her understanding that "won," she is "done": "You men will never tarry . . . I might still have held off, / And then you would have tarried" (16–18). He in his idealization of "woman" and she in her suspicion of men are yet strangely similar in their conceptions of one another, each reducing the other to a class or category.

Between the night of their meeting and the morning of their parting, there has intervened Ulysses' great speech on the power of time, and by the end of the scene, Cressida has learned that she must leave Troy. The contraction of their affair to the duration of one night stresses the vulnerability of a love "no sooner got but lost" (IV.ii.74). Time now becomes, in the central metaphor of the play, the devourer, and they, "food for fortune's tooth" (IV.v.293). Cressida's protestations—"the strong base and building of my love / Is as the very centre of the earth" (IV.ii.103–4)— are vows that are, in Ulysses' terms, "devour'd / As fast as they are made, forgot as soon / As done" (III.iii.148–50). Ironic in context, thay are also ironic in their own terms:

> I'll go in and weep.
> . . . .
> Tear my bright hair, and scratch my praised cheeks,
> Crack my clear voice with sobs, and break my heart
> With sounding Troilus. (IV.ii.105–8)

Even in the deepest anguish of which she is capable, Cressida can never lose sense of herself as an object, as an appearance for an appraising eye. Perhaps, too, knowing that "won," she is "done," she senses that she can no longer be characterized by these Petrarchan terms, and she imagines disfiguring herself literally as she feels herself to have been despoiled figuratively.

At their parting, Troilus's interest is again in the ideal and in language. He is less concerned with the fact of their parting than that they have no time for proper farewells, that "injury of chance . . . rudely beguiles our lips / Of all rejoindure, . . . strangles our dear vows" (IV.ii.33–37). His lines on time are more convincing than any on his love, his words working, for once, together with intentions:

> Injurious time now with a robber's haste
> Crams his rich thiev'ry up, he knows not how.

As many farewells as be stars in heaven,
With distinct breath and consign'd kisses to them,
He fumbles up into a loose adieu;
And scants us with a single famish'd kiss,
Distasted with the salt of broken tears.   (IV.ii.42–48)

Though the power of time is movingly and compellingly evoked,
it does not intensify our sense of tragic significance, as in *Romeo
and Juliet* and the Sonnets, but simply destroys and defaces; the
"quick bright things" that "come to confusion" (*Midsummer
Night's Dream*, I.i.149) are rather more tarnished than bright, and
even without the intervention of circumstance, these two, untrue
in themselves, create nothing of substance that might endure.
Troilus, who has identified himself so staunchly with truth, becomes obsessed now with the idea of Cressida's untruth:

Be thou but true of heart—
. . . .
I speak not 'be thou true' as fearing thee,
. . . .
But 'be thou true' say I to fashion in
My sequent protestation: be thou true,
And I will see thee.
. . . .
But yet be true.   (IV.iv.58, 62, 65–67, 73)

Cressida finds the reiteration remarkable (IV.iv.74), but we may
understand it as "protesting" too much. It may be Troilus's
awareness of his own inauthenticity that accounts for his obsession with hers: his view of her is, again, determined by projection,
though not now of desire, but fear.

Seen by the Greeks as "daughter of the game" (IV.v.63) and
"sluttish spoil of opportunity" (62), Cressida is quick to live down
to their view of her, allowing herself to be "kiss'd in general" (21).
From here, it is but a short distance to complying with the opinion of Diomedes, who values her so little that he wastes few
words on her, prizing her, simply, "To her own worth" (IV.iv.133).
He is the most taciturn of Shakespeare's wooers—"Fo, fo, come,
tell a pin" (v.ii.22)—and his taciturnity is remarkable in view of
Thersites' characterization of him as one who "will spend his
mouth and promise, like Brabbler the hound" (v.i.90–1); appar-

ently, Cressida is not worth his "spending." But we have heard him describe Helen—as "the lees and dregs of a flat tamed piece" (IV.i.63) and "contaminated carrion weight" (72)—in terms which reflect inevitably on Cressida. In the dialogue of their first meeting, Cressida's vacillation is, as with Troilus, partly sincere, partly "fooling"; but whereas Troilus praised her for "speak[ing] so wisely" (III.ii.152), Diomedes does "not like this fooling" (v.ii. 101), and she is unable to "hold off" because he is willing, simply, to let her go. Deprived of her customary means of creating her value, Cressida knows that her price has fallen. But she does not yield to Diomedes from feeling, or, as Thersites would have it, from "lechery" (56), but rather, from fear; in a position of danger, bereft, as she says, of "consanguinity . . . kin . . . love . . . blood" (IV.ii.97–98), she grasps what support she can, knowing, with her characteristic clarity, that she leaves "one that lov'd me better than you will" (v.ii.89). "Turning," she consigns Troilus to oblivion—"'tis done, 'tis past" (97)—in what is perhaps the most loveless encounter between lovers in Shakespeare.

Observing the scene, Troilus's first instinct is to cling to his earlier image of Cressida, declaring that this is "not she" (v.ii.142). Then, intellectual argument takes the place of Petrarchan poetry as a means of transforming the reality before him: "Instance, O instance" (153). If we try to imagine Antony or Othello responding to betrayal in this way, we realize the extent to which words mediate Troilus's responses to Cressida. But, as his opinion of her diverges from her actual behavior, he has no way of reconciling the division: "This is, and is not, Cressid!" (146). The consequence of his assumption that a woman is as she "is valued" is the fragmentation which she, too, experiences— "Troilus, farewell! one eye yet looks on thee, / But with my heart the other eye doth see" (107–8). And he is as responsible as she for the split, having made no attempt to see her whole and having facilitated her duplicity with his own self-deception; neither of them is capable of love because neither is authentic. Accepting her words and appearance, he is left, finally, with only her words —"Words, words, mere words, no matter from the heart"—as she "edifies another with her deeds" (v.iii.107, 112).

Defined as food (I.i.15–26), Cressida has rotted fast, and Troilus's final designation of her as "fragments, scraps . . . bits and greasy relics" (v.ii.159), though the antithesis of his Petrarchan idealization, follows from his conception of her as "cake." Whereas the discrepant versions of Helen—the "theme of honor and renown" (ii.ii.199) and the "lees and dregs of a flat tamed piece"—varied, not with the passing of time, but with different perspectives, Cressida's value has altered in time. The "truth" revealed by time in this play, the daughter to which time gives birth, is a "withered truth" (v.ii.46). But Shakespeare's depiction of this world makes this less a portrayal of a universal human condition than a comment on a society that creates nothing of enduring substance. Even the best of them, Hector himself, succumbs to base motives, and the "putrefied core" (v.viii.1) revealed within the "fair" outside he has so ignominiously "hunt[ed]" (v.vi.31) is emblematic of his destruction by time. We leave Troilus and Troy bound for "sure destruction" (v.x.9), in fulfillment of Ulysses' prediction of the "universal prey" (i.iii.123) of self-devouring appetite—a prey fed by Cressida's "o'er-eaten faith" (v.ii.160).

"Turning" from one man to the next, Cressida generalizes her "turpitude" in terms of "our sex" (v.ii.109–12). But Shakespeare's depiction of woman in this play is more sympathetic than these terms indicate. By showing Cressida in relation to the men and society who make her what she is, he provides a context that qualifies the apparently misogynist elements of her characterization, and far from presenting a simple character type or even a complex of types, the stereotypical in her character occurs in a context that constitutes a critique of stereotyping. Basing her identity on male desires and definitions, Cressida is the sum total of "opinions" of men whose opinions are in themselves societally determined, and she is thus only representative of her world.[16] Obliging expectations that require the worst of her, she has made herself an object whose worth depends on appearance, varies with supply and demand, and is enhanced by the excitement of the chase. Her feelings for Troilus prompt a brief struggle to escape these modes of self-presentation; but even her best self, which is Troilus's, is guarded and calculating, a "kind of self" that derives existence from "the present eye's praise." Deft as she is at obliging, she becomes "daughter of the game," victim of a strategy that costs no less than her self, though remaining clear-eyed throughout.[17] Astute but helpless commentator, able to calculate her losses but not to prevent them, she relinquishes claim to a loyalty from others of which she is incapable herself: "Who shall be true to us, / When we are so unsecret to ourselves?" (III.ii.124–25).

The effect of this society on the individual life is purely destructive, its influence on character, crushing and irresistible. The destinies of all in this play are shaped by values that turn them strategic and predatory. The play is thus marked by a fatalism uncustomary to Shakespeare, who usually grants his characters more control of their lives, or at least more complicity in their destructions. Whereas Romeo and Juliet and Antony and Cleopatra win a kind of triumph over their world, retaining their integrity and our admiration, the lovers in *Troilus and Cressida* are of their world, tainted by the corruption that makes "the whole world kin" (III.iii.175). In its strange, disorienting combination of comedy and tragedy, of classical and medieval, and in its scathing cynicism, the play seems unique in the canon. Yet in his portrayal of this doomed, pagan world Shakespeare expresses his sense of the worst potentials of his age—potentials which were to be fulfilled by subsequent ages. Shaw said that with *Troilus and Cressida*, Shakespeare seemed ready to begin the twentieth century.[18] He was referring to the play's cynicism; but there is nothing more timely than this portrayal of character in relation to society—of woman as a being who, basing her survival on the "opinions" of men, assures her destruction. In the "game" she is "daughter of," no one can win.

NOTES

1. *Troilus and Cressida*, v.ii.134, 132, *The Riverside Shakespeare*, ed. G. Blakemore Evans (Boston: Houghton Mifflin, 1974). All textual references are to this edition.
2. Leslie Fiedler, *The Stranger in Shakespeare* (New York: Stein and Day, 1972), p. 148.
3. Simone de Beauvoir, *The Second Sex*, trans. and ed. H. M. Parshley (New York: Random House, 1974), p. 301.
4. Though various conceptions of value are expressed and debated, it is the relativistic assumptions stated by Troilus in the Trojan council scene (II.ii.61–68) and elaborated in the exchange between Ulysses and Achilles (III.iii.74–190) that determine, consistently, the action of the play. The opposing views, presented by Ulysses to the Greek council (I.iii.83–137) and by Hector to the Trojan council (II.ii.172–89), are both based on a view of value as absolute and reality as or-

dered and objective, and are stated only to be contradicted. (Ulysses bases his argument for unity and reason on the principle of "degree," but then acts according to a plan which depends on faction and irrationality; Hector argues to return Helen on the basis of the "laws / Of nature and of nations," II.ii.184–85, but he immediately reverses his position, inexplicably joining his brothers in the pursuit of an irrational honor; indeed, he reveals at the end of the scene that he has already sent a challenge to the Greeks that renders the entire argument irrelevant.) Thus the view of value as subjective and relative is, for practical purposes, unchallenged, and the play is less a dialectic, as Norman Rabkin suggests in *Shakespeare and the Common Understanding* (New York: Free Press, 1967), pp. 30–53, than it is an exploration of the implications—psychological, social, linguistic—of the breakdown of an ordered, hierarchical notion of reality. The whole problem reflects the transition in conceptions of value that was occurring in the Renaissance: whereas Aquinas defined value as inherent and absolute, to Hobbes, it was relative to "opinion." See William R. Elton, "Shakespeare's Ulysses and the Problem of Value," *Shakespeare Studies*, 2 (1966), 95–111.

5. The word is recurrent (as, for example, in the dialogue between Ulysses and Nestor, I.iii.336, 353, 372, 382) and points to the dichotomy between "opinion" and "truth" that is central to *Troilus and Cressida*. In the world of the play, "opinion," associated with external standards of valuation, has undermined "truth" and absolute standards. See Winifred Nowottny, "'Opinion' and 'Value' in *Troilus and Cressida*," *Essays in Criticism*, 4 (1954), 282–96; and Frank Kermode, "Opinion, Truth and Value," *Essays in Criticism*, 5 (1955) 181–87. For this theme elsewhere in Renaissance literature, see Peter Ure, "A Note on 'Opinion' in Daniel, Greville, and Chapman," *Modern Language Review*, 46 (1951), 331–38.

6. Judgments such as E. M. W. Tillyard's and L. C. Knights's are typical. Tillyard calls Cressida "shallow, hard, and lascivious," in *Shakespeare's Problem Plays* (Toronto: University of Toronto Press, 1949), p. 90. To Knights, she is "the wanton of tradition," in "*Troilus and Cressida* Again," *Scrutiny*, 18 (1951–52), 154. For a survey of negative critical opinions regarding Cressida, see Grant L. Voth and Oliver H. Evans, "Cressida and the World of the Play," *Shakespeare Studies*, 8 (1975), 237, notes 1 and 2. In a sympathetic interpretation they account for the "unattractive" and "calculating" aspects of her nature in relation to her world (p. 234), but their reading differs from mine in attributing to her a development of awareness (see my note 17). Robert Ornstein also places her in context—"She is a daughter of the game which men would have her play and for which they despise her"—and is astute about men's "brutal casualness" toward her and "the larger commentary which Shakespeare makes upon the masculine ego"; but he rather disconcertingly falls back on words like "wanton" and "slut" in describing her; see *The Moral Vision of Jaco-*

bean Tragedy (Madison: University of Wisconsin Press, 1965), p. 245. In "'Sons and Daughers of the Game': An Essay on Shakespeare's *Troilus and Cressida*," *Shakespeare Survey*, 25 (1972), 11–25 (esp. 21–23), R. A. Yoder interprets her character in relation to her world. Other sympathetic readings include Carolyn Asp, "'Th' Expense of Spirit in a Waste of Shame,'" *Shakespeare Quarterly*, 22 (1971), 345–57, and Camille Slights, "The Parallel Structure of *Troilus and Cressida*," *Shakespeare Quarterly*, 25 (1974), 42–51.

7. William W. Main, "Character Amalgams in Shakespeare's *Troilus and Cressida*," *Studies in Philology*, 58 (1961), 170–78.

8. Judith M. Bardwick and Elizabeth Douvan, "Ambivalence: The Socialization of Women," in *Woman in Sexist Society: Studies in Power and Powerlessness*, ed. Vivian Gornick and Barbara K. Moran (New York: Basic Books, 1971), pp. 231–32 and 236. This principle has, of course, become so widely recognized as to be commonplace; but see also Dana Densmore, "On the Temptation to Be a Beautiful Object," in *Toward a Sociology of Women*, ed. Constantina Safilios-Rothschild (Lexington, Mass.: Xerox, 1972), pp. 96–99.

9. de Beauvoir, *The Second Sex*, p. 155.

10. Raymond Southall, "*Troilus and Cressida* and the Spirit of Capitalism," in *Shakespeare in a Changing World*, ed. Arnold Kettle (New York: International Publishers, 1964), p. 226. For "merchandise of mens soules," see John Wheeler, *A Treatise of Commerce* (1601), pp. 6, 7; quoted by Southall, p. 218.

11. Southall, "*Troilus and Cressida*," p. 228.

12. For elements of sickness and sensuality in Troilus's language, see D. A. Traversi, *An Approach to Shakespeare*, 2d ed. (Garden City, N.Y.: Doubleday, 1956), pp. 66–74; and Rosalie Colie, "Forms and their Meaning: 'Monumental Mock'ry,'" in *Shakespeare's Living Art* (Princeton, N.J.: Princeton University Press, 1974), p. 330. Colie also discusses Troilus's use of Petrarchan imagery, pp. 329–30.

13. Juliet Dusinberre, *Shakespeare and the Nature of Women* (New York: Barnes & Noble, 1975), pp. 6–7. Dusinberre also observes the increasing interest, in late Elizabethan drama, in "the struggle for women . . . to be human in a world which declares them only female," in the "interplay between breaking free and submitting to the male world's view of women" (pp. 92–93)—a struggle which takes place, though feebly, in Cressida.

14. de Beauvoir, *The Second Sex*, pp. 605, 403.

15. Dusinberre, in *Shakespeare and the Nature of Women*, describes the role of women in the comedies as "spectators of the idolatry directed towards them" (p. 156) and, in the histories, as commentators on the "sound and fury" of the political world (p. 297).

16. Cressida's closest analogue in this is, surprisingly, Portia. Though at first sight the stoic Brutus and his wife seem the antithesis of the decadent Trojans, there are some significant similarities which point to Shakespeare's interest in these problems of character and society in a

play written about three years earlier. Brutus also defines himself by reference to externals—by reputation and the "opinion" of Rome—and sees himself "by reflection, by some other things" (I.ii.53). Portia, who twice calls herself Brutus's "self"—"yourself, your half" (II.i.274, 282)—represents the extreme of the process implicit in him, basing her claim to worth on relationships with father and husband: "I grant I am a woman; but withal / A woman that Lord Brutus took to wife. / I grant I am a woman; but withal / A woman well reputed, Cato's daughter. / Think you I am no stronger than my sex, / Being so father'd and so husbanded?" (292–97). Despite her protestations, Portia is not the strongest of her sex, and her weakness may be accounted for, in part, in terms of a conception of selfhood which is precarious at best.

17. Voth and Evans, "Cressida and the World of Play," describe her as progressing "from awareness to self-deception and back to awareness again" (p. 231): "Against what she knows to be the reality of the world of the play. . . . Full of false hope and true regret, she . . . closes her eyes to the grim reality of her world, and yields to her lover" (p. 235). But Cressida does not deceive herself; she yields in full awareness, and maintains awareness throughout.

18. In *Troilus and Cressida* "we find him ready and willing to start at the twentieth century if the seventeenth would only let him." George Bernard Shaw, 1898 Preface, *Plays Pleasant and Unpleasant* (London: Constable, 1931), I, xix.

"I wooed thee with my sword"
Shakespeare's Tragic Paradigms

M ADELON G OHLKE

> Traditional textual interpretation founds itself on this par-
> ticular understanding of metaphor: a detour to truth. Not
> only individual metaphors or systems of metaphors, but
> fiction in general is seen as a detour to a truth that the
> critic can deliver through her interpretation.
>
> Gayatri Chakravorty Spivak,
translator's preface, Of Grammatology

Much of what I have to say about Shakespeare and about the possibility of a feminist psychoanalytic interpretation of literature,
or, for that matter, of culture, depends on a reading of metaphor. It
is metaphor that allows us to sub-read, to read on the margins of
discourse, to analyze what is latent or implicit in the structures of
consciousness or of a text. A serious feminist critic, moreover,
cannot proceed very far without becoming paranoid, unless she
abandons a strictly intentionalist position. To argue sexism as a
conscious conspiracy becomes both foolish and absurd. To pursue
the implications of metaphor, on the other hand, in terms of plot,
character, and possibly even genre, is to adopt a psychoanalytic

*An earlier version of this essay was presented at a Division Meet-
ing on Psychoanalytic Criticism and Women at the MLA Annual Convention, December 1977, Chicago, Illinois.*

strategy that deepens the context of feminist interpretation and reveals the possibility at least of a feminist psychohistory.

Metaphor provides a convenient entrance into a text, as it provides a point of departure for psychoanalytic interpretation because of the way in which vehicle consistently outdistances tenor. The following two lines, from *A Midsummer Night's Dream*, for instance, "Hippolyta, I wooed thee with my sword, / And won thy love, doing thee injuries" (1.i.16–17), convey far more than the simple prose explanation offered in my text: "Theseus had captured Hippolyta when he conquered the Amazons."[1] These lines, in which the sword may be the metaphoric equivalent of the phallus, in which love may be either generated or secured by hostility, and in which the two partners take up sadistic and masochistic postures in relation to one another, are not irrelevant to the concerns of the play. They may be seen to reverberate in the exaggerated submission of Helena to Demetrius, in the humiliation of Titania by Oberon, in the penetration by violence of the language of love. They even bear an oblique relation to the "lamentable comedy" of *Pyramis and Thisbe*, the failed marriage plot contained within the larger structure of successful heterosexual union celebrated at the end of the play.

Metaphor may also elucidate character, as in the case of *Much Ado about Nothing*'s Claudio, whose speech is relatively poor in imagery until it erupts into his condemnation of Hero in the middle of the play, where among other things he claims "But you are more intemperate in your blood / Than Venus, or those pamp'red animals / That rage in savage sensuality" (IV.i.58–60). It is Claudio's suspicious predisposition which composes this violent and disproportioned outburst. It is no accident that the "solution" to this conflict hinges on the fiction that Claudio has killed Hero through his slander. In this sense the conventional marriage plot of Shakespeare's comedy may also be read metaphorically. The prospect of heterosexual union arouses emotional conflicts which give shape to the plot, unleashing a kind of violence which in the comedies remains symbolic, imagined rather than enacted.

I shall, in the following pages, be considering the uses of metaphor in several related ways. In some instances, I will refer to the function of metaphor in individual discourse, assuming that it is this kind of highly charged imagistic expression that offers the most immediate clues to unconscious awareness. I am assuming furthermore that metaphor may be seen to structure action, so that some features of plot may be regarded as expanded metaphors. Moving outward from this premise, I then want to consider the possibility that certain cultural fictions may be read metaphorically, that is, as expressions of unconsciously held cultural beliefs. I am particularly interested in Shakespeare's tragedies, in what seem to me to be shared fictions on the part of the heroes about femininity and about their own vulnerability in relation to women, fictions interweaving women with violence, generating a particular kind of heterosexual dilemma.

The primacy of metaphor in the structures of individual consciousness, as in the collective fiction of the plot, appears in an early tragedy, *Romeo and Juliet*, where the failure of the play to achieve the generic status of comedy may be read as the result of the way in which heterosexual relations are imagined. In the conversation between the servants Sampson and Gregory, sexual intercourse, through a punning reference to the word "maidenhead," comes to be described as a kind of murder.[2]

> SAMPSON. 'Tis all one. I will show myself a tyrant. When I
> have fought with the men, I will be civil with the maids—
> I will cut off their heads.
> GREGORY. The heads of the maids?
> SAMPSON. Ay, the heads of the maids or their maidenheads.
> Take it in what sense thou wilt. (1.i.23–28)

To participate in the masculine ethic of this play is to participate in the feud, which defines relations among men as intensely competitive, and relations with women as controlling and violent, so that women in Sampson's language "being the weaker vessels, are ever thrust to the wall" (1.i.17–18). That Romeo initially rejects this ethic would seem to redefine the nature and structure of male/female relationships. What is striking about the relationship between Romeo and Juliet, however, is the extent to which it anticipates and ultimately incorporates violence.

Both lovers have a lively imagination of disaster. While Romeo ponders "some vile forfeit of untimely death" (1.iv.111), Juliet speculates "If he is married, / My grave is like to be my wedding bed" (1.v.136–37). Premonition, for both, has the force of self-fulfilling prophecy. While Romeo seeks danger by courting Juliet, and death by threatening suicide in the wake of Tybalt's death,

Juliet, under pressure, exclaims: "I'll to my wedding bed; / And death, not Romeo, take my maidenhead!" (III.ii.136–37). Read metaphorically, the plot validates the perception expressed variously in the play that love kills.

The paradigm offered by *Romeo and Juliet*, with some modifications, may be read in the major tragedies as well. Here, the structures of male dominance, involving various strategies of control, expressed in the language of prostitution, rape, and murder, conceal deeper structures of fear, in which women are perceived as powerful, and the heterosexual relation one which is either mutually violent or at least deeply threatening to the man.

Murder in the Bedroom: *Hamlet* and *Othello*

Hamlet's violent behavior in his mother's bedroom expresses some of the violence of his impulses toward her. Obsessed as he is with sexual betrayal, the problem of revenge for him is less a matter of killing Claudius than one of not killing his mother.[3] Hamlet's anger against women, based on his perception of his mother's conduct, finds expression in the language of prostitution in his violent outburst against Ophelia: "I have heard of your paintings, well enough. God hath given you one face, and you make yourselves another. You jig and amble, and you lisp; you nickname God's creatures and make your wantonness your ignorance. Go to, I'll no more on't; it hath made me mad" (III.i.143–48). It is painting which makes women two-faced, which allows them to deceive, to wear the mask of chastity, while lust "Will sate itself in a celestial bed / And prey on garbage" (I.v.56–57). Like whores, all women cannot be trusted.

The paradox of prostitution in the tragedies is based on the masculine perception of the prostitute as not so much the victim as the agent of exploitation. If women are classed as prostitutes and treated as sexual objects, it is because they are deeply feared as sexually untrustworthy, as creatures whose intentions and desires are fundamentally unreadable. Thus, while Helen in *Troilus and Cressida* is verbally degraded, as the Trojans discuss her in terms of soiled goods and contaminated meat, she is, through her infidelity to Menelaus, the source of the sexual pride and humiliation that animate the entire conflict between the two warring nations. Honor among men in this play, though it takes the form of combat, is ultimately a sexual matter, depending largely on the fidelity or infidelity of women. For a man to be betrayed by a woman is to be humiliated or dishonored. To recover his honor he must destroy the man or woman who is responsible for his humiliation, for placing him in a position of vulnerability.

In *Hamlet*, it is the player queen who most clearly articulates the significance attributed to feminine betrayal. "A second time I kill my husband dead / When second husband kisses me in bed" (III.ii.188–89). It hardly matters whether Gertrude was implicated in the actual death of the elder Hamlet. Adultery is itself a form of violence and as great a crime. Hamlet, who reacts as an injured husband in seeking revenge against Claudius, also seeks retribution against his mother. Not having any sanction to kill his mother, however, he must remind himself to "speak daggers to her, but use none" (404). That his manner suggests physical violence is confirmed by Gertrude's response: "What wilt thou do? Thou wilt not murder me? / Help, ho!" (III.iv.22–23). It is at this point that the violence that Hamlet seeks to contain in his attitude toward his mother is deflected onto another object presumed to be appropriate.

This single act of displaced violence, moreover, has further ramifications in terms of Hamlet's relation to Ophelia, whose conflicted responses to the killing of her father by her lover increase the burden of double messages she has already received from the men in the play and culminate in her madness and death. It is not his mother whom Hamlet kills (Claudius takes care of that) but Ophelia. Only when she is dead, moreover, is he clearly free to say that he loved her. Othello, in whom are more specifically and vividly portrayed the pathology of jealousy, the humiliation and rage that plague a man supposedly dishonored by the woman he loves, will say of Desdemona late in the play "I will kill thee, / And love thee after" (v.ii.18–19).

If I seem to be arguing that the tragedies are largely about the degeneration of heterosexual relationships, or marriages that fail, it is because I am reading the development from the comedies through the problem plays and the major tragedies in terms of an explosion of the sexual tensions that threaten without rupturing the surface of the earlier plays. Throughout, a woman's power is less social or political (though it may have social and political ramifications) than emotional, expressed in her capacity to give or to withhold love. In a figure like Isabella the capacity to withhold arouses lust and a will to power in someone like Angelo, whose enforcing tactics amount to rape. In Portia, the threat of infidelity, however jokingly presented, is a weapon in her struggle with Antonio for Bassanio's allegiance. Male resistance, comic and exaggerated in Benedick, sullen and resentful in Bertram, stems from fears of occupying a position of weakness, taking in essence a "feminine" posture in relation to a powerful woman.

The feminine posture for a male character is that of the betrayed, and it is the man in this position who portrays women as whores. Since Iago occupies this position in relation to Othello, it makes sense that he seeks to destroy him, in the same way that Othello seeks to destroy the agent of his imagined betrayal, Desdemona. There is no reason to suppose, moreover, that Iago's consistently degraded view of women conceals any less hostile attitude in his actual relations with women. He, after all, like Othello, kills his wife. The difference between the two men lies not in their fear and mistrust of women but in the degree to which they are able to accept an emotional involvement. It is Othello, not Iago, who wears his heart on his sleeve, "for daws to peck at" (I.i.62). Were it not for Othello's initial vulnerability to Desdemona he would not be susceptible to Iago's machinations. Having made himself vulnerable, moreover, he attaches an extraordinary significance to the relation. "And when I love thee not, / Chaos is come again" (III.iii.91–92). "But there where I have garnered up my heart, / Where either I must live or bear no life, / The fountain from the which my current runs / Or else dries up" (IV.ii.56–59).

Once Othello is convinced of Desdemona's infidelity (much like Claudio, on the flimsiest of evidence), he regards her, not as a woman who has committed a single transgression, but as a whore, one whose entire behavior may be explained in terms of lust. As such, he may humiliate her in public, offer her services to the Venetian ambassadors, pass judgment on her, and condemn her to death. Murder, in this light, is a desperate attempt to control. It is Desdemona's power to hurt which Othello seeks to eliminate by ending her life. While legal and social sanctions may be invoked against the prostitute, the seemingly virtuous woman suspected of adultery may be punished by death. In either case it is the fear or pain of victimization on the part of the man that leads to his victimization of women. It is those who perceive themselves to be powerless who may be incited to the acts of greatest violence.

The paradox of violence in *Othello*, not unlike that in *Macbeth*, is that the exercise of power turns against the hero. In this case the murder of a woman leads to self-murder, and the hero dies attesting to the erotic destructiveness at the heart of his relation with Desdemona. "I kissed thee ere I killed thee. No way but this, / Killing myself, to die upon a kiss" (v.ii.357–58). If murder may be a loving act, love may be a murdering act, and consummation of such a love possible only through the death of both parties.

"Of Woman Born": *Lear* and *Macbeth*

The fantasy of feminine betrayal that animates the drama of *Othello* may be seen to conceal or to be coordinate with deep fantasies of maternal betrayal in *Macbeth* and *Lear*.[4] Here the emphasis falls not so much on the adult heterosexual relation (though there are such relations) as on the mother/son or the fantasy of the mother/son relation. In these plays, the perception of the masculine consciousness is that to be feminine is to be powerless, specifically in relation to a controlling or powerful woman. For Lear, rage as an expression of power acts as a defense against this awareness, while tears threaten not only the dreaded perception of himself as feminine and hence weak but also the breakdown of his psychic order.

> Life and death, I am ashamed
> That thou hast power to shake my manhood thus!
> That these hot tears, which break from me perforce,
> Should make thee worth them. Blasts and fogs upon thee!
> (I.iv.298–301)

> You think I'll weep.
> No, I'll not weep.
> I have full cause of weeping, but this heart
> Shall break into a hundred thousand flaws
> Or ere I'll weep. O Fool, I shall go mad! (II.iv.279–83)

156

> O, let me not be mad, not mad, sweet heaven!
> Keep me in temper; I would not be mad!   (I.v.45–46)

It is not Lear who annihilates his enemies, calling down curses on the reproductive organs of Goneril and Regan, but rather Lear who is being banished by the women on whom he had depended for nurturance. It is they who are the agents of power and destruction, allied with the storm, and he like Edgar, who is "unaccommodated man," a "poor, bare, forked animal" (III.iv.105–7), naked and vulnerable. That the condition of powerlessness gives rise to compassion in Lear is part of his dignity as a tragic hero. It does not, however, alter his perceptions of women as either good or bad mothers. If the banishment of Cordelia initiates a process by which Lear becomes psychotic, moreover, it may be argued that her return is essential to the restoration of his sanity. The presence or absence of Cordelia, like Othello's faith in Desdemona's fidelity, orders the hero's psychic universe. When Cordelia dies, Lear must either believe that she is not dead or die with her, being unable to withstand the condition of radical separation imposed by death.

The most powerful image of separation in *King Lear*, that of the child who is banished by his mother, is that of birth. "We came crying hither: / Thou know'st, the first time that we smell the air / We wawl and cry" (IV.vi.178–80). In this sense, the mother's first act of betrayal may be that of giving birth, the violent expulsion of her infant into a hostile environment. In other passages, a woman's body itself is perceived as a hostile environment.

> But to the girdle do the gods inherit,
> Beneath is all the fiend's.
> There's hell, there's darkness, there is the sulphurous pit.
>   (IV.vi.126–29)

> The dark and vicious place where thee he got
> Cost him his eyes.   (V.iii.173–74)

Intercourse imaged as violent intrusion into a woman's body may be designed to minimize the cost.

If it is birth itself, the condition of owing one's life to a woman and the ambivalence attending an awareness of dependence on women in general, which structures much of Lear's relations to his daughters, *Macbeth* may be read in terms of a systematic attempt on the part of the hero to deny such an awareness. The world constructed by Macbeth attempts to deny not only the values of trust and hospitality, perceived as essentially feminine, but to eradicate femininity itself.[5] Macbeth reads power in terms of a masculine mystique that has no room for maternal values, as if the conscious exclusion of these values would eliminate all conditions of dependence, making him in effect invulnerable. To be born of woman, as he reads the witches' prophecy, is to be mortal. Macbeth's program of violence, involving murder and pillage in his kingdom and the repression of anything resembling compassion or remorse within, is designed, like Coriolanus's desperate militarism, to make him author of himself.

The irony of *Macbeth*, of course, is that in his attempt to make himself wholly "masculine," uncontaminated, so to speak, by the womb, he destroys all source of value: honor, trust, and, to his dismay, fertility itself. It is his deep personal anguish that he is childless. The values associated with women and children, which he considers unmanly, come to be perceived as the source of greatest strength. It is procreation, in this play, rather than violence, which confers power. "The seeds of Banquo kings!" (III.i.70). To kill a child or to imagine such an act, as Lady Macbeth does in expressing contempt for her husband's vacillations, is to betray not only the bonds of human society, but to betray one's deepest self. To reject the conditions of weakness and dependence is to make oneself weak and dependent. Macbeth's relentless pursuit of power masks his insecurities, his anxieties, and ultimately his impotence. *Macbeth*, more clearly than any of the other tragedies, with the possible exception of *Coriolanus*, enacts the paradox of power in which the hero's equation of masculinity with violence as a denial or defense against femininity leads to his destruction.

Macbeth's attempt to avoid the perception of Lear that "we cry that we are come / To this great stage of fools" (IV.vi.182–83), that the human infant is radically defenseless and dependent on the nurturance of a woman, gradually empties his life of meaning, leading to his perception of it as "a tale / Told by an idiot . . . / Signifying nothing" (v.v.26–28). Of all the tragic heroes, moreover, Macbeth is the most isolated in his death, alienated from himself, his countrymen, his queen. He has become what he most feared, the plaything of powerful feminine forces, betrayed by the "instruments of darkness," the three witches.

"The Heart of Loss:" *Antony and Cleopatra*

Interwoven into the patriarchal structure of Shakespeare's tragedies is an equally powerful matriarchal vision. The two are even, I would argue, aspects of one another, both proceeding from the masculine consciousness of feminine betrayal. Both inspire a violence of response on the part of the hero against individual women, but more important, against the hero's ultimately damaging perception of himself as womanish. The concurrence of these themes is particularly evident in *Antony and Cleopatra*, a play that recalls the ritual marriage conclusion of the comedies as it deepens the sexual dilemma of the tragic hero.

Antony's relation both to Cleopatra and to Caesar may be read in terms of his anxieties about dominance, his fear of self-loss in any intimate encounter. Early in the play, Cleopatra uses this perception to her advantage by suggesting that for Antony to respond to the Roman messengers is to acknowledge his submission either to Caesar or to Fulvia. Her own tactics, of course, are manipulative and a form of dominance that Antony himself recognizes. "These strong Egyptian fetters I must break / Or lose myself in dotage" (I.ii.117–18). The advice of the soothsayer to Antony concerning his proximity to Caesar is similar in structure if not in content: "near him thy angel / Becomes afeard, as being o'erpow'red" (II.iii.20–21). When Antony returns to Egypt, he is in effect "o'er pow'red" by Cleopatra. "O'er my spirit / Thy full supremacy thou knew'st" (III.xi.58–59). "You did know / How much you were my conqueror, and that / My sword, made weak by my affection, would / Obey it on all cause" (65–68). Antony, like Romeo earlier, perceives himself as having been feminized by love. "O sweet Juliet, / Thy beauty hath made me effeminate / And in my temper soft'ned valor's steel!" (III.i.115–17). "O, thy vile lady! / She has robbed me of my sword" (IV.xiv.22–23).

If affection makes Antony weak, it also makes him suspicious of Cleopatra's fidelity. "For I am sure, / Though you can guess what temperance should be, / You know not what it is" (III.xiii.120–22). He falls easy prey to the conviction that Cleopatra has betrayed him to Caesar, making him the subject of sexual as well as political humiliation. "O, that I were / Upon the hill of Basan to outroar / The hornèd herd!" (126–28). In this light, Cleopatra becomes a "witch," a "spell," a "triple-turned whore."

> O this false soul of Egypt! This grave charm,
> Whose eye becked forth my wars, and called them home,
> Whose bosom was my crownet, my chief end,
> Like a right gypsy hath at fast and loose
> Beguiled me, to the very heart of loss.
> What, Eros, Eros! (IV.xii.25–30)

Antony, under the power of erotic attachment, like Othello feels himself to have been utterly betrayed. Under the impact of this loss, moreover, his sense of psychic integrity begins to disintegrate. "Here I am Antony, / Yet cannot hold this visible shape, my knave" (IV.xiv.13–14). Chaos is come again.

While the fiction of Cleopatra's death restores Antony's faith in her love, it does not restore his energy for life. Rather, the withdrawal of her presence destroys any vestige of interest he has in the world of the living. "Now all labor / Mars what it does; yea, very force entangles / Itself with strength" (IV.xiv.47–49). It is Cleopatra who not only dominates Antony's emotional life, but who invests his world with meaning. The fact that she, unlike Juliet, Ophelia, Desdemona, Cordelia, and Lady Macbeth, dies so long after her lover, not only reveals her as a complex figure in her own right, but also attests to her power to give imaginative shape to the hero's reality.

Cleopatra in many ways is the epitome of what is hated, loved, and feared in a woman by Shakespeare's tragic heroes. She is, on the one hand, the woman who betrays, a Circe, an Acrasia, an Eve, the Venus of *Venus and Adonis*. To submit to her, or to be seduced by her, is to die. She is the player queen, for whom adultery is also murder. She is a Goneril, a Lady Macbeth, a non-nurturing mother. What she takes, on the other hand, she also has the power to give. She is imaginative, fertile, identified with the procreative processes of the Nile. If Antony lives in our imagination, it is because of her "conception" of him. In this sense, she, like Desdemona and Cordelia, is the hero's point of orientation, his source of signification in the world. Union with her is both celebrated, as a curious comic counterpoint to the tragic structure of double suicide, and portrayed as a literal impossibility. Moreover, for this sexually powerful woman to escape censure, the fate of a Cressida or a Helen, she must negate her own strength, she must die. While Theseus's phallic sword, in Antony's hands, turns against himself, Cleopatra, like Juliet, will accept death "as a lover's pinch, / Which hurts, and is desired" (v.ii.295–96). Throughout Shakespeare's tragedies the imagery of heterosexual union involves the threat of mutual or self-inflicted violence.

Looked at from one angle, what Shakespeare's tragedies portray is the anguish and destruction attendant on a fairly conventional and culturally supported set of fictions regarding heterosexual encounter. The tragedies, as I read them, do not themselves support these fictions except to the extent that they examine them with such acute attention. The values that emerge from these plays are, if anything, "feminine," values dissociated from the traditional masculine categories of force and politics, focused instead on the significance of personal relationships, or the fact of human relatedness: the values of feeling, of kinship, of loyalty, friendship, and even romantic love. That the recognition of these values entails the destruction of the hero and everyone who matters to him attests perhaps to a kind of cultural determinism, or at least to the very great difficulty of re-imagining habitual modes of behavior. It is the basis in cultural fictions of certain kinds of heterosexual attitudes to which I now wish to turn.

On the Margins of Patriarchal Discourse

Shakespeare's tragic paradigms offer the possibility of a deconstructive reading of the rape metaphor that informs Theseus's words to his captured queen.[6] Violence against women as an aspect of the structure of male dominance in Shakespeare's plays may be seen to obscure deeper patterns of conflict in which women as lovers, and perhaps more important as mothers, are perceived as radically untrustworthy. In this structure of relation, it is women who are regarded as powerful and men who strive to avoid an awareness of their vulnerability in relation to women, a vulnerability in which they regard themselves as "feminine." It is in this sense that one may speak of a matriarchal substratum or subtext within the patriarchal text. The matriarchal substratum itself, however, is not feminist. What it does in Shakespeare's tragedies is provide a rationale for the manifest text of male dominance while constituting an avenue of continuity between these plays and the comedies in which women more obviously wield power.

The preceding analysis may be seen, moreover, to parallel the movement of psychoanalytic theory from an emphasis on oedipal to pre-oedipal stages of development. Roughly speaking, the shift has occurred in terms of a decrease of concern with father/son relations and a corresponding increase of concern with mother/son relations. (Although the shift from father to mother is clear in the work of such theorists as John Bowlby, Melanie Klein, Margaret Mahler, and D. W. Winnicott, the child or infant, partly for grammatical reasons, tends to be regarded as male).[7] Certainly it may be said that the theories of object-relations, narcissism, schizophrenia, and separation-individuation have more to do with the child's early relations with his mother than with his father. Whether or not these theories are read in consonance with Freud's formulation of the Oedipus complex, the shift in focus relocates the discussion of certain issues. This relocation, in turn, reveals new interpretive possibilities. Specifically, it reopens the question of femininity.

A deconstructive reading of the rape metaphor in Shakespeare's tragedies leads directly or indirectly to a discussion of the masculine perception of femininity as weakness. The macho mystique thus becomes a form of "masculine protest," or a demonstration of phallic power in the face of a threatened castration. It is for the male hero, however, that femininity signifies weakness, while actual women are perceived by him as enormously powerful, specifically in their maternal functions. It is not the female herself who is perceived as weak, but rather the feminized male. To project this problem back onto women, as Freud does when in his discussions of femininity he portrays the little girl as perceiving herself castrated, is to present it as incapable of resolution.[8] If femininity itself is defined as the condition of lack, of castration, then there is no way around the masculine equation that to be feminine is to be castrated, or as Antony puts it, to be robbed of one's sword.

It is the masculine consciousness, therefore, that defines femininity as weakness and institutes the structures of male dominance designed to defend against such an awareness. Shakespeare's tragedies, as I read them, may be viewed as a vast commentary on the absurdity and destructiveness of this defensive posture. While Shakespeare may be said to affirm the values of feeling and vulnerability associated with femininity, however, he does not in dramatic terms dispel the anxiety surrounding the figure of the feminized male. At this point, dramatic metaphors, I would say, intersect with cultural metaphors.[9]

Freud's views of femininity may be useful to the extent to which they articulate some deeply held cultural convictions. In one sense, what they do is reveal the basis of some powerful cultural metaphors, so powerful in fact that they continue to find formulation in the midst of our vastly different social and intellectual context. In the midst of profound structural changes in habits of philosophic and scientific thinking, as a culture we cling to the language of presence and absence, language and silence, art and nature, reason and madness to describe the relations between the terms masculine and feminine. It is as though the breakdown of hierarchical modes of thought, of vertical ways of imagining experience, finds its deepest resistance in our habits of imagining the relations between the sexes. Some, like the Jungian James Hillman, would even argue that in order to effect real changes in our intellectual formulations of reality, we must find ways of re-imagining femininity.[10] Sexual politics may lie at the heart of human culture, of our constantly shifting and evolving world views.

The preceding discussion, of course, rests on assumptions to which Freud would not have subscribed, chief among which is a hypothesis concerning the relation between cultural metaphors and the concept of a cultural unconscious. What I would like to propose is that the notion of the unconscious may be culture specific, that is to say, that the guiding metaphors of a given society or culture may legitimately be seen to express the structure of its unconscious assumptions, in the same way that the metaphoric structure of individual discourse may be seen to convey some of the unconscious freight of a given life. If Thomas Kuhn is correct in assuming that scientific revolutions are the result of paradigm shifts, or profound changes in our habits of imagining the world, then it may also be possible to consider the unconscious implications of certain habits of imagining.[11] Literary conventions may

then be viewed as aspects of these imaginative habits, as codifica-
tions of a certain spectrum of unconscious attitudes, at the same
time that they change and evolve, live and die according to their
relation to the society out of which they arise and to which they
respond. Cultural changes, to pursue the implications of Kuhn's
argument, are in effect profound metaphoric changes which in
turn involve changes in the structuring of the unconscious.

Literary history, may, in this light, be read psychologically.
The questions one might ask then would concern the spectrum of
psychic needs served by specific conventions and genres. Tracing
the uses of a convention would then also yield a literary version of
psychohistory. To offer an example close to the subject of this essay, I would like to pursue briefly some of the ramifications of the
rhetoric of courtly love.

It is interesting to observe the language of de Rougement,
who is so careful to situate the courtly love phenomenon in a historical sense, when he refers to the rhetorical trope of love as war.
"There is no need, for example, to invoke Freudian theories in
order to see that the war instinct and eroticism are fundamentally
allied: it is so perfectly *obvious* from the common figurative use
of language."[12] Obvious to whom? Is the war instinct, for instance, perceived as an aspect of the feminine psyche? Here the
common (and to many readers unquestioned) assumption that
reference to the male of the species includes women may be seen
to obscure a process by which a fundamentally "masculine" attitude is proposed as a universal norm. More important, however, is
the interpretive process by which de Rougemont reads a metaphor specific to a certain set of conventions, albeit powerful ones,
as an inalterable aspect of the unconscious life of the species. "All
this confirms the natural—that is to say, the physiological—connexion between the sexual and fighting instincts."[13]

It is this supposedly natural "connexion between the sexual and fighting instincts" that structures the language of the
courtly love lyric, as it structures the language of sexual encounter in Shakespeare. To term this rhetoric "conventional" is not to
demean it but rather to call attention to its psychological power
(which de Rougement himself agrees exists) at the same time that
one recognizes its mutability, its historicity. Images of sexual intercourse as an act of violence committed against women run

deep in our culture. The depth and persistence of these images, however, may tell us more about the anxieties of a culture in which femininity is conceived as castration and in which women are perceived paradoxically as a source of maternal power than it does about the actual or possible relations between the sexes.

Toward a Feminist Discourse

And, as I have hinted before, deconstruction must also take into account the lack of sovereignty of the critic himself. Perhaps this "will to ignorance" is simply a matter of attitude, a realization that one's choice of evidence is provisional, a self-distrust, a distrust of one's own power, the control of one's vocabulary, a shift from the phallocentric to the hymeneal.

Gayatri Chakravorty Spivak,
translator's preface, *Of Grammatology*

Literary history, finally, is an aspect of cultural history. Both attest to changing patterns of awareness, to the constant refiguring of our relation to our specific location in time and space, to our own historicity. If individual history, as Ortega y Gassset writes, may be conceived as a process of casting and living out or living through metaphors of the self, is it not possible to imagine cultural history in similar terms? [14] To interpret these metaphors, to read on the margins of discourse, is not only to engage in a process characteristic of psychoanalytic interpretation but also to become engaged in a fundamentally historical process, that of making what is unconscious conscious and thus altering and displacing the location of the unconscious. This process, obviously akin to that of psychotherapy, is not to be perceived statically as an attempt to eliminate the unconscious but rather as one to dislodge it, to transform its metaphoric base.

Psychoanalytic theory in this sense may also be read in the historical dimension, as a means of reading the unconscious figurings of a given life within a specific cultural moment. As such, it will of course be subject to change and will of course to some extent serve the interests of the society that supports it. I am not arguing here against psychoanalytic theory in any sense but rather *for* a recognition of its historicity. [15] While Freud's elaboration of the Oedipus complex may have served to assuage the neurotic dilemmas of his society, it does not serve the needs of contemporary feminism. In a society like ours in which most women can expect to work outside the home for a significant part of their lives, and to bear fewer than three children, the interpretive myths offered by Freud for women are increasingly pathological. In order to be useful, the theory must bear a demonstrable relation to perceived reality. To argue that the social reality of women should be altered in order to fit the theory is not only reactionary, but naïve. It would make more sense to pursue the directions of contemporary psychoanalytic theory toward a redefinition of femininity, assuming as I do that implicit within the current focus on the mother/child relation is a reawakening of interest in the question of femininity. There are even some theorists, like Dorothy Dinnerstein, who would argue that such a reformulation is necessary for cultural survival, given the destructiveness in political terms of the masculine mystique.[16]

What then, in psychoanalytic terms, would constitute the beginnings of feminist discourse? How is a woman, according to the painful elaborations of Julia Kristeva and others, to avoid the Scylla of silence or madness and the Charybdis of alienated or masculine discourse?[17] Gayatri Spivak has lately been suggesting that what we need is something like a Copernican revolution from the phallocentric formulation of femininity as absence to a gynocentric language of presence.[18] If it makes sense that the male child should perceive his own sex as primary and difference as an inferior version of himself, then it makes as much sense that the little girl should also initially perceive her sex as primary. That each sex should take itself as the norm is perhaps part of the Ptolemaic universe of children which must undergo several stages of decentering before maturity. Not to undergo this process of decentering is to elaborate structures of dominance and submission in which dominance becomes the mask of weakness and submission a subversive strategy in the mutual struggle for power. For a woman to read herself obliquely through the patriarchal discourse as "other" is to assent to this structure. For a critic, male or female, to read this discourse as representative of the true nature of masculinity or femininity is to accept this structure. For a femininist critic to deconstruct this discourse is simultaneously to recognize her own historicity and to engage in the process of dislocation of the unconscious by which she begins to affirm her own reality.

NOTES

1. *A Midsummer Night's Dream, The Complete Signet Classic Shakespeare*, ed. Sylvan Barnet (New York: Harcourt Brace Jovanovich, 1963, 1972), p. 530. Quotations from Shakespeare in this essay refer to this edition.

2. Two critics have dealt specifically with the relation between sex and violence in this play. A. K. Nardo notes that "To the youths who rekindle the feud on a point of honor, sex, aggression, and violence are inextricably united." While Juliet undergoes an extraordinary process of development, Nardo argues, she is ultimately unable to survive in this hostile atmosphere and is finally "thrust to the wall by the phallic sword her society has exalted." "Romeo and Juliet Up Against the Wall," *Paunch*, 48–49 (1977), 127–31. Coppélia Kahn in a more extensive consideration of this subject relates the ethic of the feud, in which sex and violence are linked, to the patriarchal structure of the society, commenting on the extent to which the conclusion of the play, associating death with sexual consummation, is also contained within this structure. Fate is thus not only a result of powerful social forces, but also of the individual subjective responses to these forces. "Coming of Age in Verona," *Modern Language Studies*, 8 (1977–78), 5–22, reprinted in this anthology.

3. Theodore Lidz represents Hamlet as torn between the impulse to kill his mother for having betrayed his father and the desire to win her to a state of repentance and renewed chastity. My reading of Hamlet is very much indebted to his analysis in *Hamlet's Enemy: Madness and Myth in Hamlet* (New York: Basic Books, 1975).

4. Murray Schwartz discusses the difficulty of the hero's recognition of his relation to a nurturing woman in "Shakespeare through Contemporary Psychoanalysis," *Hebrew University Studies in Literature*, 5 (1977), 182–98. While Lear's dilemma, according to Schwartz, results from a "refusal to mourn the loss of maternal provision" (p. 192), Macbeth's difficulty may be seen as the result of an attempt to usurp maternal functions and to control the means of nurturance himself.

5. My discussion of the ways in which masculinity and femininity are perceived in this play is indebted to Cleanth Brooks's classic essay on *Macbeth*, "The Naked Babe and the Cloak of Manliness," in *The Well Wrought Urn* (1947; rpt. London: Dobson Books, 1968), pp. 17–39. For Brooks, it is Macbeth's war on children which reveals most clearly his own weakness and desperation. In Brooks's view, the issue of manli-

ness is related ultimately to the theme of humanity or lack of it, but he does not raise questions about masculine and feminine stereotypes.

6. I would assent to the following description by Gayatri Spivak of the task of deconstruction: "To locate the promising marginal text, to disclose the undecidable moment, to pry it loose, with the positive lever of the signifier; to reverse the resident hierarchy, only to displace it; to dismantle in order to reconstitute what is always already inscribed. Deconstruction in a nutshell." Jacques Derrida, *Of Grammatology*, translator's preface (Baltimore: Johns Hopkins University Press, 1976), p. lxxvii. While Spivak points out that there is no end to this process in that the work of deconstruction is itself subject to deconstruction, she also notes that "as she deconstructs, all protestations to the contrary, the critic necessarily assumes that she at least, and for the time being, means what she says," p. lxxvii. While it may not be strictly necessary to borrow this terminology for the reading I am proposing, it may be useful to observe that any large-scale reinterpretation, from a minority position, of a majority view of reality must appear at least in the eyes of some as a "deconstruction."

7. Here, the problem inherent in the use of the masculine pronoun to refer to both sexes emerges. Textually speaking, the construction often obscures a shift of consideration from the development of the infant, male or female, to the exclusive development of the male infant. This convention is related to the cultural assumption by which the male of the species is taken as a norm, of which the female then becomes a variant. To remove this convention would not merely introduce a stylistic awkwardness (for some people at least), it would also reveal a fundamental awkwardness in the structure of an author's argument. While the male pronoun often *is* used generically to indicate both men and women, its use frequently serves to exclude consideration of the female without calling attention to the process by which she has been removed from the discussion.

8. Although Freud approaches the subject of femininity from different angles in his three major discussions of it, there is no question that he links the process of feminine development indissolubly to the recognition on the part of the little girl that she is castrated. It would seem at least reasonable to argue, however, that the presence or absence of a penis is of far greater significance to the boy or man, who feels himself subject to the threat of its removal, than it could ever be to the girl or woman, for whom such a threat can have little anatomical meaning. I wonder too, why, in Freud's argument, a little girl would be inspired to give up the manifestly satisfying activity of masturbation on the basis of the illusion of a loss—the assumption perhaps that she might have had more pleasure if she had once had a penis, of which she seems mysteriously to have been deprived? The problem which gives rise to these baroque speculations is, of course, Freud's assumption that there must be some reason why the little girl would with-

draw her love from her mother in order to bestow it upon her father. Freud can imagine no other reason than the little girl's recognition of her own inferiority and thus "penis envy," and her resentment of her mother, equally deprived, for not having provided her with the desired organ. There can be no heterosexual love, in this account, without the theory of feminine castration. One can understand, from this vantage point, why Freud was reluctant to give it up. See "Some Psychical Consequences of the Anatomical Distinction between the Sexes" (1925), "Female Sexuality" (1931), and "Femininity" (1933), *Standard Edition*, trans. and ed. James Strachey (London: Hogarth Press, 1961, 1964), XIX, 241–60; XXI, 221–46; XXII, 112–35. For various critiques of Freud, see also Roy Shafer, "Problems in Freud's Psychology of Women," *Journal of the American Psychoanalytic Association*, 22 (1974), 459–85; *Women and Analysis*, ed. Jean Strouse (New York: Grossman, 1974); *Psychoanalysis and Women*, ed. Jean Baker Miller (Baltimore: Penguin Books, 1973).

9. One might wish to argue that social, psychic, and literary structures are so intimately interwoven that the relation between plot and culture is like that between Hamlet and his fate, between a text which is given and that which is generated, enacted, in part, chosen. With this in mind, one might begin to speak of "patriarchal plots," the complex set of figures by which Western culture has elaborated its relation to the structures by which it lives. The question then becomes the extent to which a powerful social movement warps, flexes, alters, reimagines these essential structures, how genres are born, how transformed.

10. James Hillman, *The Myth of Analysis: Three Essays in Archetypal Psychology* (Evanston: Northwestern University Press, 1972), pp. 215–98.

11. Thomas Kuhn, *The Structure of Scientific Revolutions* (Chicago: University of Chicago Press, 1966).

12. Denis de Rougemont, *Love in the Western World*, trans. Montgomery Belgion (New York: Harcourt Brace, 1940, 1956), p. 243. I have chosen the passages from de Rougemont because they are central to the elucidation of the courtly love tradition and because they are so clearly, though unintentionally, biased. A more contemporary (and more complex) example of the same kind of bias might be found in the concluding chapters of Leo Bersani's *A Future for Astyanax: Character and Desire in Literature* (Boston: Little, Brown, 1976).

13. De Rougemont, *Love in the Western World*, p. 244.

14. Ortega y Gasset, *History as a System, and Other Essays Toward a Philosophy of History* (New York: Norton, 1941, 1961), pp. 165–233.

15. The following articles make a case for the relevance of Freud's personal history to the structure of his thought: Arthur Efron, "Freud's Self-Analysis and the Nature of Psychoanalytic Criticism," *The International Review of Psychoanalysis*, 4 (1977), 253–80; Jim Swan, "*Mater* and Nannie: Freud's Two Mothers and the Discovery of the

Oedipus Complex," *American Imago*, 31 (1974), 1–64; Patrick Mahony, "Friendship and Its Discontents," paper presented to the Canadian Psychoanalytic Society, Montreal, May 19, 1977. Freud's instrument of self-analysis, from the point of view of these critics, becomes a double-edged sword, a manifestation of his genius for the articulation of the structural principles of his own psyche, as well as a measure of the necessary limitation of his method. Murray Schwartz elucidates this point further in "Shakespeare through Contemporary Psychoanalysis." Juliet Mitchell might be seen to treat this subject on a large scale in *Psychoanalysis and Feminism* (New York: Pantheon, 1974), when she argues that the Oedipus complex acts as a structural representation of the psychic organization of patriarchal society.

16. Dorothy Dinnerstein, *The Mermaid and the Minotaur: Sexual Arrangements and Human Malaise* (New York: Harper & Row, 1976).

17. Julia Kristeva, who seems to accept the Lacanian explanation of the process of the child's induction into the symbolic order in Western culture, presents the position of women within this construct as one of agonized conflict in the opening chapters of *About Chinese Women*, trans. Anita Barrows (New York: Urizen Books, 1977). Shoshona Felman states the problem of defining a feminist discourse within a masculinist ethic as follows: "If, in our culture, the woman is by definition associated with madness, her problem is how to break out of this (cultural) imposition of madness *without* taking up the critical and therapeutic positions of reason: how to avoid speaking both as *mad* and as *not mad*. The challenge facing the woman today is nothing less than to 're-invent' language, to *re-learn how to speak*: to speak not only against, but outside of the specular phallocentric structure, to establish a discouse the status of which would no longer be defined by the phallacy of masculine meaning. An old saying would thereby be given new life: today more than ever, changing our minds—changing the mind—is a woman's prerogative." "Women and Madness: The Critical Phallacy," *Diacritics*, 5, No. 4 (1975), 2–10.

18. This statement derives from remarks made by Gayatri Spivak toward the end of a session at the 1977 MMLA convention in Chicago in which she spoke of "the womb as a tangible place of production," as the point of departure for a new discourse on femininity. She has suggested that since the work on which this comment is based is not yet in print, I refer to my memory of her statements. I wish to apologize in advance for any error of understanding on my part of her position.

Coming of Age in Verona

COPPÉLIA KAHN

I

Romeo and Juliet is about a pair of adolescents trying to grow up. Growing up requires that they separate themselves from their parents by forming with a member of the opposite sex an intimate bond which supersedes filial bonds. This, broadly, is an essential task of adolescence, in Renaissance England and Italy as in America today, and the play is particularly concerned with the social milieu in which these adolescent lovers grow up—a patriarchal milieu as English as it is Italian. I shall argue that the feud in a realistic social sense is the primary tragic force in the play—not the feud as agent of fate,[1] but the feud as an extreme and peculiar expression of patriarchal society, which Shakespeare shows to be tragically self-destructive.[2] The feud is the deadly *rite de passage* that promotes masculinity at the price of life. Undeniably, the feud is bound up with a pervasive *sense* of fatedness, but that sense finds its objective correlative in the dynamics of the feud and of the society in which it is embedded. As Harold Goddard says, ". . . the fathers are the stars and the stars are the fathers in the sense that the fathers stand for the accumulated experience of the past, for tradition, for authority, and hence for the two most potent forces that mold and so impart 'destiny' to the child's life

This essay is reprinted by permission, with revisions, from Modern Language Studies, *8 (1977–78), 5–22;* © *1978 by the Northeast Modern Language Association.*

... heredity and training. .... The hatred of the hostile houses in *Romeo and Juliet* is an inheritance that every member of these families is born into as truly as he is born with the name Capulet or Montague."[3]

That inheritance makes Romeo and Juliet tragic figures because it denies their natural needs and desires as youth. Of course, they also display the faults of youth: its self-absorption and reckless extremism, its headlong surrender to eros. But it is the feud which fosters the rash, choleric impulsiveness typical of youth by offering a permanent invitation to and outlet for violence. The feud is first referred to in the play as "their parents' strife and their parents' rage" and it is clear that the parents, not their children, are responsible for its continuance. Instead of providing social channels and moral guidance by which the energies of youth can be rendered beneficial to themselves and society, the Montagues and the Capulets make weak gestures toward civil peace while participating emotionally in the feud as much as their children do. While they fail to exercise authority over the younger generation in the streets, they wield it selfishly and stubbornly in the home. So many of the faults of character which critics have found in Romeo and Juliet are shared by their parents that the play cannot be viewed as a tragedy of character in the Aristotelian sense, in which the tragedy results because the hero and heroine fail to "love moderately."[4] Rather, the feud's ambiance of hot temper permeates age as well as youth; viewed from the standpoint of Prince Escalus, who embodies the law, it is Montague and Capulet who are childishly refractory.

In the course of the action, Romeo and Juliet create and try to preserve new identities as adults apart from the feud, but it blocks their every attempt. Metaphorically, it devours them in the "detestable maw" of the Capulets' monument, a symbol of the patriarchy's destructive power over its children. Thus both the structure and the texture of the play suggest a critique of the patriarchal attitudes expressed through the feud, which makes "tragic scapegoats" of Romeo and Juliet.[5]

Specifically, for the sons and daughters of Verona the feud constitutes socialization into patriarchal roles in two ways. First, it reinforces their identities as sons and daughters by allying them with their paternal household against another paternal household, thus polarizing all their social relations, particularly their marital choices, in terms of filial allegiance. They are constantly called upon to define themselves in terms of their families and to defend their families. Second, the feud provides a "psycho-sexual moratorium" for the sons,[6] an activity in which they prove themselves men by phallic violence on behalf of their fathers, instead of by the courtship and sexual experimentation that would lead toward marriage and separation from the paternal house. It fosters in the sons fear and scorn of women, associating women with effeminacy and emasculation, while it links sexual intercourse with aggression and violence against women, rather than with pleasure and love. Structurally, the play's design reflects the prominence of the feud. It erupts in three scenes at the beginning, middle, and end (I.i, III.i, v.iii) that deliberately echo each other, and the *peripeteia*, at which Romeo's and Juliet's fortunes change decisively for the worse, occurs exactly in the middle when Romeo in killing Tybalt faces the two conflicting definitions of manhood between which he must make his tragic choice.

It has been noted that *Romeo and Juliet* is a domestic tragedy but not that its milieu is distinctly patriarchal as well as domestic. Much of it takes place within the Capulet household, and Capulet's role as *paterfamilias* is apparent from the first scene, in which his servants behave as members of his extended family. That household is a charming place: protected and spacious, plentiful with servants, food, light, and heat, bustling with festivity, intimate and informal even on great occasions, with a cosy familiarity between master and servant. In nice contrast to it stands the play's other dominant milieu, the streets of Verona. It is there that those fighting the feud are defined as men, in contrast to those who would rather love than fight, who in terms of the feud are less than men. Gregory and Sampson ape the machismo of their masters, seeking insults on the slightest pretext so that they may prove their valor. In their blind adherence to a groundless "ancient grudge," they are parodies of the feuding gentry. But in Shakespeare's day, as servants they would be regarded as their master's "children" in more than a figurative sense, owing not just work but loyalty and obedience to their employers as legitimate members of the household ranking immediately below its children.[7] As male servants their position resembles that of the sons bound by their honor to fight for their families' names. Most important, their obvious phallic competitiveness in being quick to anger at an insult to their status or manhood, and quick to draw their swords and fight, shades into competitiveness in sex as well: "I strike quickly, being moved. . . . A dog of the house of Montague moves me. . . . Therefore I will push Montague's men from the wall and thrust his maids to the wall. . . . Me they shall feel while I am able to stand" (1.i.7, 9, 18–20, 30).[8] In this scene and elsewhere, the many puns on "stand" as standing one's ground in fighting and as erection attest that fighting in the feud demonstrates virility as well as valor. Sampson and Gregory also imply that they consider it their prerogative as men to take women by force as a way of demonstrating their superiority to the Montagues: ". . . women, being the weaker vessels, are ever thrust to the wall. Therefore I will push Montague's men from the wall and thrust his maids to the wall. . . . When I have fought with the men, I will be civil with the maids—I will cut off their heads. . . . the heads of the maids or their maidenheads. Take it in what sense thou wilt" (16–20, 24–25, 27–28). As the fighting escalates, Capulet and Montague finally become involved themselves, Capulet calling for a sword he is too infirm to wield effectively, merely because Montague, he claims, "flourishes his blade in spite of me." With the neat twist of making the masters parody the men who have been parodying them, the fighting ends as the Prince enters. At the cost of civil peace, all have asserted their claims to manhood through the feud.

Tybalt makes a memorable entrance in this first scene. Refusing to believe Benvolio's assertion that his sword is drawn only to separate the fighting servants, he immediately dares him to defend himself. To Tybalt, a sword can only mean a challenge to fight, and peace is just a word:

> What, drawn, and talk of peace? I hate the word
> As I hate hell, all Montagues, and thee.
> Have at thee, coward! (1.i.72–74)

In the first two acts, Shakespeare contrasts Tybalt and Romeo in terms of their responses to the feud so as to intensify the conflict Romeo faces in Act III when he must choose between being a man in the sanctioned public way, by drawing a sword upon an insult, or being a man in a novel and private way, by reposing an inner confidence in his secret identity as Juliet's husband.

In Act III, the fight begins when Tybalt is effectively baited by Mercutio's punning insults; from Mercutio's opening badinage with Benvolio, it is evident that he too is spoiling for a fight, though he is content to let the weapons be words. But words on the hot midday streets of Verona are effectively the same as blows that must be answered by the drawing of a sword. When Romeo arrives, Tybalt calls him "my man," "a villain," and "boy," all terms which simultaneously impugn his birth and honor as well as his manhood. Mercutio made words blows, but Romeo tries to do just the opposite, by oblique protestations of love to Tybalt, which must seem quite mysterious to him if he listens to them at all: "And so, good Capulet, whose name I tender / As dearly as mine own, be satisfied" (III.i.72–73). Romeo's puns of peacemaking fail where Mercutio's puns of hostility succeeded all too well. Only one kind of rigid, simple language is understood in the feud, a language based on the stark polarities Capulet-Montague, man-boy. No wonder Mercutio terms Romeo's response a "calm, dishonorable, vile submission" and draws on Tybalt: Romeo has allowed a Capulet to insult his name, his paternal heritage, his manhood, without fighting for them. Like Tybalt, Romeo owes a duty to "the stock and honor of his kin." When Mercutio in effect fights for him and dies, Romeo is overcome by the shame of having allowed his friend to answer the challenge which by the code of manly honor he should have answered himself. He momentarily turns against Juliet, the source of his new identity, and sees her as Mercutio sees all women:

> O sweet Juliet,
> Thy beauty hath made me effeminate,
> And in my temper soft'ned valor's steel!   (III.i.115–17)

In that moment, caught between his radically new identity as Juliet's husband, which has made him responsible (he thinks) for his friend's death, and his previous traditional identity as the scion of the house of Montague, he resumes the latter and murders Tybalt. As Ruth Nevo remarks, "Romeo's challenge of Tybalt is not merely an instance . . . of a rashness which fatally flaws his character. . . . On the contrary, it is an action first avoided, then deliberately undertaken, and it is entirely expected of him by his society's code."⁹ As much as we want the love of Romeo and Juliet to prosper, we also want the volatile enmity of Tybalt punished and the death of Mercutio, that spirit of vital gaiety, revenged, even at the cost of continuing the feud. Romeo's hard choice is also ours. Though the play is constantly critical of the feud as the medium through which criteria of patriarchally oriented masculinity are voiced, it is just as constantly sensitive to the association of those criteria with more humane principles of loyalty to family and friends, courage, and personal dignity.

Among the young bloods serving as foils for Romeo, Benvolio represents the total sublimation of virile energy into peacemaking, agape instead of eros; Tybalt, such energy channeled directly and exclusively into aggression; and Mercutio, its attempted sublimation into fancy and wit. (Romeo and Paris seek manhood through love rather than through fighting, but are finally impelled by the feud to fight each other.) That Mercutio pursues the feud though he is neither Montague nor Capulet suggests that feuding has become the normal social pursuit for young men in Verona. Through his abundant risqué wit, he suggests its psychological function for them, as a definition of manhood. Love is only manly, he hints, if it is aggressive and violent and consists of subjugating women, rather than being subjugated by them:

> If love be rough with you, be rough with love;
> Prick love for pricking, and you beat love down.
>
> (I.iv.27–28)
>
> Alas, poor Romeo, he is already dead: stabbed with a white wench's black eye; run through the ear with a love-song: the very pin of his heart cleft with the blind bow-boy's butt-shaft; and is he a man to encounter Tybalt?
>
> (II.iv.14–18)

The conflict between his conception of manhood and the one which Romeo learns is deftly and tellingly suggested in Romeo's line, "He jests at scars that never felt a wound" (II.i.1). Juliet is a Capulet, and Romeo risks death to love her; the trite metaphor of the wound of love has real significance for him. Mercutio considers love mere folly unworthy of a real man and respects only the wounds suffered in combat. Ironically, Mercutio will die of a real wound occasioned partly by Romeo's love, while Romeo, no less a man, will die not of a wound but of the poison he voluntarily takes for love.

Mercutio mocks not merely the futile, enfeebling kind of love Romeo feels for Rosaline, but all love. Moreover, his volley of sexual innuendo serves as the equivalent of both fighting and love. In its playful way, his speech is as aggressive as fighting, and while speech establishes his claim to virility, at the same time it marks his distance from women. As Romeo says, Mercutio is "A gentleman . . . that loves to hear himself talk and will speak more in a minute than he will stand to in a month" (II.iv.153–55). Mercutio would rather fight than talk, but he would rather talk than love, which brings us to his justly famed utterance, the Queen Mab speech. Like so much in this play, it incorporates opposites. While it is surely an isolated set piece, it is also highly characteristic of Mercutio, in its luxuriant repleteness of images and rippling mockery. While it purports to belittle dreamers for the shallowness of the wishes their dreams fulfill, it sketches the dreamers' world with loving accuracy, sweetmeats, tithe pigs, horses' manes and all. In service to the purest fancy, it portrays Mab's coach and accoutrements with workmanlike precision. It pretends to tell us dreams are "nothing but vain fantasy" but this pose is belied by the speaker's intense awareness that real people do dream of real things.[10] In short, Mercutio's defense against dreams gives evidence of his own urge to dream, but it also reveals his fear of giving in to the seething nighttime world of unconscious desires associated with the feminine; he prefers the broad daylight world of men fighting and jesting. Significantly, his catalogue of dreamers ends with a reference to the feminine mystery of birth, with an implied analogy between the birth of children from the womb and the birth of dreams from "an idle brain." He would like to think that women's powers, and desires for women, are as bodiless and inconsequential as the dreams to which they give rise, and to make us also think so he concludes his whole speech with the mock-drama of a courtship between the winds. For him the perfect image of nothingness is unresponsive and inconstant love between two bodies of air. But Mercutio protests too much; the same defensiveness underlies his fancy as his bawdry. Puns and wordplay, the staple of his bawdry, figure prominently in dreams, as Freud so amply shows; relying on an accidental similarity of sound, they disguise a repressed impulse while giving voice to it.[11]

II

In the feud, names (the signs of patriarchal authority and allegiance) are calls to arms, and words are blows. As Romeo and Juliet struggle to free themselves from the feud, their effort at first takes the form of creating new names for themselves to reflect their new identities. When they learn each other's names, they attend only to surnames, which signify the social constraints under which their love must exist. Romeo says, "Is she a Capulet? / O dear account! My life is my foe's debt" (I.v.119–20), and the Nurse tells Juliet, "His name is Romeo, and a Montague, / The only son of your great enemy" (I.v.138–39). Juliet's extended meditation on Romeo's name in the balcony scene begins with her recognition that for Romeo to refuse his name—to separate himself from the feud—he would have to deny his father (II.233–34); she moves from this unlikely alternative to a fanciful effort to detach the man from the name, and their love from the social reality in which it is embedded: " 'Tis but thy name that is my enemy. / Thou art thyself, though not a Montague" (II.i.238–39). Through the irony of Juliet's casual "but thy name," Shakespeare suggests both that it is impossible for Romeo to separate himself from his public identity as a Montague and that his public identity is nonetheless extraneous and accidental, no part of what he really is. The Romeo already transfigured by his love for Juliet is a different person and his name should reflect it. The exchange which Juliet proposes hints at this:

> Romeo, doff thy name;
> And for thy name, which is no part of thee,
> Take all myself. (II.ii.47–49)

In fact, his new identity as a man is to be based on his allegiance to her as her husband and not on his allegiance to his father. In the wedding scene, Romeo says with his desperate faith, "It is enough I may but call her mine" (II.vi.8), an ironic allusion to the fact that though she now has taken his surname in marriage, all he really can do is "call" her his, for the feud will not allow their new identities as husband and wife to become publicly known, as is all too apparent when Romeo's veiled references to Tybalt's name as one which he tenders as dearly as his own go uncomprehended in Act III.

Later, in Friar Lawrence's cell bemoaning his banishment, Romeo curses his name and offers literally to cut it out of his body as though it were merely physical and its hateful consequences could be amputated. Symbolically, he is trying to castrate himself; as a consequence of the feud he cannot happily be a man either by fighting for his name and family or by loving Juliet. Banished and apart from her, he will have no identity and nothing to live for. His obsession with his name at this point recalls Juliet's "'Tis but thy name that is my enemy." In the early moments of their love, both of them seek to mold social reality to their changed perceptions and desires by manipulating the verbal signifiers of that reality. But between Romeo's banishment and their deaths, both learn in different ways that not the word but the spirit can change reality. Juliet becomes a woman and Romeo a man not through changing a name but by action undertaken in a transformed sense of the self, requiring courage and independence.

Unmanned in the friar's cell by the thought of life without Juliet, Romeo hurls himself to the floor in tears and petulantly refuses to rise. The significance of this posture is emphasized by the Nurse's exclamation, "O, he is even in my mistress' case, / Just in her case!" (III.iii.84–85). Echoing the sexual innuendo of the play's first scene in a significantly different context, the Nurse urges him vigorously,

> Stand up, stand up! Stand, and you be a man.
> For Juliet's sake, for her sake, rise and stand!
> Why should you fall into so deep an O? (III.iii.88–90)

Friar Lawrence's ensuing philosophical speech is really only an elaboration of the Nurse's simple, earthy rebuke. The well-meaning friar reminds Romeo that he must now base his sense of himself as a man not on his socially sanctioned identity as a son of Montague, but on his love for Juliet, in direct conflict with that identity—a situation which the friar sees as only temporary. But this conflict between manhood as aggression on behalf of the father, and manhood as loving a woman, is at the bottom of the tragedy, and not to be overcome.

In patriarchal Verona, men bear names and stand to fight for them; women, "the weaker vessels," bear children and "fall backward" to conceive them, as the Nurse's husband once told the young Juliet. It is appropriate that Juliet's growing up is hastened and intensified by having to resist the marriage arranged for her by her father, while Romeo's is precipitated by having to fight for the honor of his father's house. Unlike its sons, Verona's daughters have, in effect, no adolescence, no sanctioned period of experiment with adult identities or activities. Lady Capulet regards motherhood as the proper termination of childhood for a girl, for she says to Juliet,

> Younger than you,
> Here in Verona, ladies of esteem,
> Are made already mothers. (1.iii.69–71)

and recalls that she herself was a mother when she was about her daughter's age. Capulet is more cautious at first: "Too soon marred are those so early made" (1.ii.13), he says, perhaps meaning that pregnancies are more likely to be difficult for women in early adolescence than for those even slightly older. But the pun in the succeeding lines reveals another concern besides this one:

> Earth hath swallowèd all my hopes but she;
> She is the hopeful lady of my earth. (1.ii.14–15)

Fille de terre is the French term for heiress, and Capulet wants to be sure that his daughter will not only survive motherhood, but produce healthy heirs for him as well.

Capulet's sudden determination to marry Juliet to Paris comes partly from a heightened sense of mortality which, when it is introduced in the first act, mellows his character attractively:

> Welcome, gentlemen! I have seen the day
> That I have worn a visor and could tell
> A whispering tale in a fair lady's ear,
> Such as would please. 'Tis gone, 'tis gone, 'tis gone.
> (1.v.23–26)

But he cannot give up his claim on youth so easily as these words imply. When he meets with Paris again after Tybalt's death, it is he who calls the young man back, with a "desperate tender" inspired by the thought that he, no less than his young nephew, was "born to die." Better to insure the safe passage of his property to an heir now, while he lives, than in an uncertain future. Even though decorum suggests but "half a dozen friends" as wedding guests so hard upon a kinsman's death, he hires "twenty cunning cooks" to prepare a feast, and stays up all night himself "to play the housewife for this once," insisting against his wife's better judgment that the wedding be celebrated not a day later. For him, the wedding constitutes the promise that his line will continue, though his own time end soon. Shakespeare depicts Capulet's motives for forcing the hasty marriage with broad sympathy in this regard, but he spares the anxious old man no tolerance in the scene in which Juliet refuses to marry Paris.

In Shakespeare's source, Arthur Brooke's versification of an Italian novella, the idea of marriage with Paris isn't introduced until after Romeo's banishment. In the play, Paris broaches his suit (evidently not for the first time) in the second scene and receives a temperate answer from Capulet, who at this point is a model of fatherly tenderness and concern:

> My child is yet a stranger in the world,
> She hath not seen the change of fourteen years;
> Let two more summers wither in their pride
> Ere we may think her ripe to be a bride.
> . . . .
> But woo her, gentle Paris, get her heart;
> My will to her consent is but a part.
> And she agreed, within her scope of choice
> Lies my consent and fair according voice. (I.ii.8–11, 16–19)

Significantly, though, this scene begins with Capulet acting not only as a father but also as the head of a clan; alluding to the recent eruption of the feud and the Prince's warning, he says lightly, ". . . 'tis not hard, I think, / For men so old as we to keep the peace." Only when his failure to exert effective authority over the inflammatory Tybalt results in Tybalt's death, an insult to the clan, does Capulet decide to exert it over his daughter, with compensatory strictness. Thus Shakespeare, by introducing the arranged marriage at the beginning and by making Capulet change his mind about it, shows us how capricious patriarchal rule can be, and how the feud changes fatherly mildness to what Hartley Coleridge called "paternal despotism."[12] After Tybalt's death, the marriage which before required her consent is now his "decree," and his anger at her opposition mounts steadily from an astonished testiness to brutal threats:

> And you be mine, I'll give you to my friend;
> And you be not, hang, beg, starve, die in the streets,
> For, by my soul, I'll ne'er acknowledge thee,
> Nor what is mine shall never do thee good.   (III.v.193–96)

Perhaps Shakespeare got the inspiration for these lines from Brooke's poem, where Capulet cites Roman law allowing fathers to "pledge, alienate, and sell" their children, and even to kill them if they rebel.[13] At any rate, it is clear that Capulet's anger is as violent and unreflective as Tybalt's, though he draws no sword against Juliet, and that the emotional likeness between age and youth in this instance is fostered by different aspects of the same system of patriarchal order.

Romeo finds a surrogate father outside that system, in Friar Lawrence, and in fact never appears onstage with his parents. Juliet, on the other hand, always appears within her parents' household until the last scene in the tomb. Lodged in the bosom of the family, she has two mothers, the Nurse as well as her real one. For Juliet, the Nurse is the oppposite of what the Friar is for Romeo; she is a surrogate mother within the patriarchal family, but one who is, finally, of little help in assisting Juliet in her passage from child to woman. She embodies the female self molded devotedly to the female's family role. The only history she knows is that of birth, suckling, weaning, and marriage; for her, earthquakes are less cataclysmic than these turning points of growth. She and Juliet enter the play simultaneously in a scene in which she has almost all the lines and Juliet less than ten, a disproportion which might be considered representative of the force of tradition weighing on the heroine.

The Nurse's longest speech ends with the telling of an anecdote (I.iii.35–48) which she subsequently repeats twice. It is perfectly in character: trivial, conventional, full of good humor but lacking in wit. And yet it epitomizes the way in which, in the patriarchal setting, woman's subjugation to her role as wife and mother is made to seem integral with nature itself:

And then my husband (God be with his soul!
'A was a merry man) took up the child.
"Yea," quoth he, "dost fall upon thy face?
Thou wilt fall backward when thou hast more wit;
Wilt thou not, Jule?" and by my holidam,
The pretty wretch left crying and said, "Ay."   (I.iii.39–44)

The story is placed between the Nurse's recollections of Juliet's weaning and Lady Capulet's statements that girls younger than Juliet are already mothers, as she herself was at Juliet's age. This collocation gives the impression of an uninterrupted cycle of birth and nurturance carried on from mother to daughter, under the approving eyes of fathers and husbands. The Nurse's husband, harmlessly amusing himself with a slightly risqué joke at Juliet's expense, gets more than he bargains for in the child's innocent reply. The Nurse finds the point of the story in the idea that even as a child, Juliet had the "wit" to assent to her sexual "fall"; she takes her "Ay" as confirmation of Juliet's precocious fitness for "falling" and "bearing." But in a larger sense than the Nurse is meant to see, "bearing" implies that it will be Juliet's fate to "bear" her father's will and the tragic consequences of her attempt to circumvent it. And in a larger sense still, all women, by virtue of their powers of bearing, are regarded as mysteriously close to the Earth, which, as Friar Lawrence says, is "Nature's mother," while men, lacking these powers, and intended to rule over the earth, rule over women also. As the Nurse says, "Women grow by men" (I.iii.95).

Against this conception of femininity, in which women are married too young to understand their sexuality as anything but passive participation through childbearing in a vast biological cycle, Shakespeare places Juliet's unconventional, fully conscious and willed giving of herself to Romeo. Harry Levin has pointed out how the lovers move from conventional formality to a simple, organic expressiveness that is contrasted with the rigid, arbitrary polarization of language and life in Verona.[14] Juliet initiates this departure in the balcony scene by answering Romeo's conceits, "love's light wings" and "night's cloak," with a directness highly original in the context:

Dost thou love me? I know thou wilt say "Ay";
And I will take thy word.   (II.ii.90–91)

Free from the accepted forms in more than a stylistic sense, she pledges her love, discourages Romeo from stereotyped love-vows, and spurs him to make arrangements for their wedding. As she awaits the consummation of their marriage, the terms in which she envisions losing her virginity parody the terms of male competition, the sense of love as a contest in which men must beat down women or be beaten by them:

> Come, civil night,
> Thou sober-suited matron all in black,
> And learn me how to lose a winning match,
> Played for a pair of stainless maidenhoods.   (III.ii.10–13)

She knows and values her "affections and warm youthful blood," but she has yet to learn the cost of such blithe individuality in the tradition-bound world of Verona. When the Nurse tells her that Romeo has killed Tybalt, she falls suddenly into a rant, condemning him in the same kind of trite oxymorons characteristic of Romeo's speech before they met (see especially I.i.178–86); such language in this context reflects the automatic thinking of the feud, which puts everything in terms of a Capulet-Montague dichotomy. But she drops this theme when a word from the Nurse reminds her that she now owes her loyalty to Romeo rather than to the house of Capulet:

> NURSE. Will you speak well of him that killed your cousin?
> JULIET. Shall I speak ill of him that is my husband?
> Ah, poor my lord, what tongue shall smooth thy name,
> When I, thy three-hours' wife, have mangled it?
> (III.ii.96–99)

Romeo's "name" in the sense of his identity as well as his reputation now rests not on his loyalty to the Montagues but on Juliet's loyalty to him and their reciprocal identities as husband and wife apart from either house.

Juliet's next scene (III.v), in which she no sooner bids farewell to Romeo than learns that she is expected to marry Paris, depicts another crucial development in her ability to use language creatively to support her increasing independence. As the scene opens, it is Juliet who would use words as a pretty refuge from harsh reality, renaming the lark a nightingale, the sunrise a meteor, as though words could stop time from passing, and it is

Romeo who gently insists that they accept their painful separation for what it is. But when her mother enters with bitter expressions of hatred toward Romeo, Juliet practices a skillful equivocation that allows her to appear a loyal Capulet while also speaking her heart about Romeo.

When her father's rage erupts moments later, however, Juliet is unable to say more than a few words on her own behalf. Seeking comfort and counsel from the Nurse, the only advice she receives is for expediency. The Nurse is so traditionally subservient to her master that she cannot comprehend a loyalty to Romeo that would involve opposing Capulet, and she has no idea of Juliet's growing independence of her father and commitment to Romeo. Juliet's disbelieving "Speak'st thou from thy heart?" and the Nurse's assuring reply underscore the difference between them as women. The Nurse has no "heart" in the sense that she has no self-defined conception of who she is or to whom she owes her fidelity; for her, affection and submission have always been one. As Coleridge said, she is characterized by a "happy, humble ducking under."[15] On the other hand, Juliet, now inwardly placing fidelity to Romeo above obedience to her father and thus implicitly denying all that family, society, and the feud have taught her, utters a lie in perfect calm to end her conversation with the Nurse. There is no way for her to speak the truth of her heart in her father's household, so she may as well lie. Though she will again employ equivocation in her stilted, stichomythic conversation with Paris later, her closing line, "If all else fails, myself have power to die," bespeaks a self-confidence, courage, and strength no longer dependent on verbal manipulations.

III

In this play ordered by antitheses on so many levels, the all-embracing opposition of Eros and Thanatos seems to drive the plot along.[16] The lovers want to live in union; the death-dealing feud opposes their desire. The tragic conclusion, however, effects a complete turnabout in this clear-cut opposition between love and death, for in the lovers' suicides love and death merge. Romeo and Juliet die as an act of love, in a spiritualized acting out of the ancient pun. Furthermore, the final scene plays off against each other two opposing views of the lovers' deaths: that they are consumed and destroyed by the feud, and that they rise above it, united in death. The ambivalence of this conclusion is worth exploring to see how it reflects the play's concern with coming of age in the patriarchal family.

It cannot be denied that, through the many references to fate, Shakespeare wished to create a feeling of inevitability, of a mysterious force stronger than individuals shaping their courses even against their will and culminating in the lovers' deaths. Yet it is also true that, as Gordon Ross Smith says, the play employs fate not as an external power, but "as a subjective feeling on the parts of the two lovers."[17] And this subjective feeling springs understandably from the objective social conditions of life in Verona. The first mention of fate, in the Prologue's phrase "fatal loins," punningly connects fate with feud and anticipates the rhyme uttered by Friar Lawrence, which might stand as a summary of the play's action:

> The earth that's Nature's mother is her tomb,
> What is her burying grave, that is her womb. . . .
>
> (II.iii.9–10)

The loins of the Montagues and the Capulets are fatal because the two families have established a state of affairs whereby their children are bound, for the sake of family honor, to kill each other. It is hardly necessary to recall how Romeo's first sight of Juliet is accompanied by Tybalt's "Fetch me my rapier, boy" or how (as I have shown) their very names denote the fatal risk they take in loving each other. Romeo's premonition, as he sets off for the Capulets' ball, that he will have "an untimely death," or Juliet's, as his banishment begins, that she will see him next in a tomb, are not hints from the beyond, but expressions of fear eminently realistic under the circumstances.

The setting and action of the final scene are meant to remind us of the hostile social climate in which the lovers have had to act. It begins on a bittersweet note as the dull and proper Paris approaches to perform his mangled rites, recapitulating wedding in funeral with the flowers so easily symbolic of a young and beautiful maiden, and symbolic of her expected defloration in marriage. By paralleling the successive entrances of Paris and Romeo, one who has had no part in the feud, the other who has paid so much for resisting it, both of whom love Juliet, Shakespeare suggests the feud's indifferent power over youth. Each character comes in with the properties appropriate to his task and enjoins the servant accompanying him to "stand aloof." Their ensuing sword-fight is subtly designed to recall the previous eruptions of the feud and to suggest that it is a man-made cycle of recurrent violence. Paris's challenge to Romeo,

> Stop thy unhallowèd toil, vile Montague!
> Can vengeance be pursued farther than death?
> Condemnèd villain, I do apprehend thee.
> Obey, and go with me; for thou must die.   (v.iii.54–57)

recalls Tybalt's behavior at the Capulets' ball, when he assumed Romeo's very presence to be an insult, and in Act III, when he deliberately sought Romeo out to get satisfaction for that insult. Romeo responds to Paris as he did to Tybalt, first by hinting cryptically at his true purpose in phrases echoing those he spoke in Act III:

> By heaven, I love thee better than myself,
> For I come hither armed against myself.   (v.iii.64–65)

Then once more he gives in to "fire-eyed fury" when Paris continues to provoke him and, in a gesture all too familiar by now, draws his sword.

Shakespeare prepares us well before this final scene for its grim variations on the Friar's association of womb and tomb. Juliet's moving soliloquy on her fears of waking alone in the family monument amplifies its fitness as a symbol of the power of the family, inheritance, and tradition over her and Romeo. She ponders "the terror of the place—"

> . . . a vault, an ancient receptacle
> Where for many hundred years the bones
> Of all my buried ancestors are packed.   (iv.iii.38–41)

In a "dismal scene" indeed, she envisions herself first driven mad by fear, desecrating these bones by playing with them, and then using the bones against herself to dash her brains out. This waking dream, like all the dreams recounted in this play, holds psychological truth; it bespeaks both Juliet's knowledge that in loving Romeo she has broken a taboo as forceful as that against harming the sacred relics of her ancestors, and her fear of being punished for the offense by the ancestors themselves—with their very bones.

As Romeo forces his way into the monument, he pictures it both as a monstrous mouth devouring Juliet and himself and as a womb:

> Thou detestable maw, thou womb of death,
> Gorged with the dearest morsel of the earth,
> Thus I enforce thy rotten jaws to open,
> And in despite I'll cram thee with more food. (v.iii.45–49)

When the Friar hastens toward the monument a few minutes later, his exclamation further extends the meanings connected with it:

> Alack, alack, what blood is this, which stains
> The stony entrance to this sepulcher?   (v.iii.140–41)

The blood-spattered entrance to this tomb that has been figured as a womb recalls both a defloration or initiation into sexuality, and a birth. Juliet's wedding bed is her grave, as premonitions had warned her, and three young men, two of them her bridegrooms, all killed as a result of the feud, share it with her. The birth that takes place in this "womb" is perversely a birth into death, a stifling return to the tomb of the fathers, not the second birth of adolescence, the birth of an adult self, which the lovers strove for.[18]

But the second part of the scene, comprising Romeo's death speech, the Friar's entrance and hasty departure, and Juliet's death speech, offers a different interpretation. Imagery and action combine to assert that death is a transcendent form of sexual consummation, and further, that it is rebirth into a higher stage of existence—the counterpart of an adulthood never fully achieved in life. That Shakespeare will have it both ways at once is perfectly in keeping with a play about adolescence in that it reflects the typical conflict of that period, which Bruno Bettelheim describes as "the striving for independence and self-assertion, and the opposite tendency, to remain safely at home, tied to the parents."[19] It is also similar to the ambivalent ending of *Venus and Adonis*, another work about youth and love, in which Venus's long-striven-for possession of Adonis takes the form of the total absorption of each person in the other, at the price of Adonis's death.[20]

It might be argued that Romeo and Juliet will their love-deaths in simple error caused by the mere chance of Brother John's failure to reach Romeo with the news of Juliet's feigned death and that chance is fate's instrument. But the poetic consistency and force with which their belief in death as consummation is carried out, by means of the extended play of words and actions on dying as orgasm, outweighs the sense of chance or of fate. The equation of loving with dying is introduced early; frequently, dying is linked to the feud, for instance in Juliet's reference to grave and wedding bed in Act I, scene v, restated in the wedding scene. Romeo's banishment produces an explosion of remarks linking wedding bed with tomb and the bridegroom Romeo with death.[21] The Friar's potion inducing a simulated death on the day of Juliet's wedding with Paris titillates us further with ironic conjunctions of death and marriage. But when Romeo declares, the instant after he learns of Juliet's supposed death, "Is it e'en so? Then I defy you, stars!" (v.i.24),[22] the context in which we have been led to understand and expect the lovers' death is transformed. Romeo no longer conceives his course of action as a way of circumventing the feud, which now has no importance for him. Rather, he wills his death as a means to permanent union with Juliet. When he says, in the same tone of desperate but unshakable resolve, "Well, Juliet, I will lie with thee tonight," as her lover and bridegroom he assumes his role in the love-death so amply foreshadowed, but that love-death is not merely fated; it is willed. It is the lovers' triumphant assertion over the impoverished and destructive world which has kept them apart. Romeo's ensuing conversation with the apothecary is full of contempt for a merely material world, and his confidence that he alone possesses Juliet in death is so serene that he indulges in the mordantly erotic fantasy that amorous Death keeps Juliet in the tomb "to be his paramour" (v.iii.102–5), recalling and dismissing the earlier conception of death as Juliet's bridegroom.

Shakespeare fills Romeo's last speech with the imagery of life's richness: the gloomy vault is "a feasting presence full of light," and Juliet's lips and cheeks are crimson with vitality. His last lines, "O true apothecary! / Thy drugs are quick. Thus with a kiss I die" (v.iii.120), bring together the idea of death as sexual consummation and as rebirth. Similarly, Juliet kisses the poison on his lips and calls it "a restorative." They have come of age by a means different from the rites of passage—phallic violence and adolescent motherhood—typical for youth in Verona. Romeo's death in the tomb of the Capulets rather than in that of his own fathers reverses the traditional passage of the female over to the male house in marriage and betokens his refusal to follow the code of his fathers. And it is Juliet, not Romeo, who boldly uses his dagger, against herself.[23]

NOTES

1. A long-standing interpretation of *Romeo and Juliet* holds that it is a tragedy of fate. F. S. Boas, *Shakespeare and His Predecessors* (London: J. Murray, 1896), p. 214; E. K. Chambers, *Shakespeare: A Survey* (London: Sidgwick and Jackson, 1925), pp. 70–71; E. E. Stoll, *Shakespeare's Young Lovers* (London: Oxford University Press, 1937), pp. 4–5; and G. L. Kittredge, ed., *Sixteen Plays of Shakespeare* (New York: Ginn, 1946), p. 674, are the most prominent of the many critics who have shared this view. Stopford Brooke, *On Ten Plays of Shakespeare* (London: Constable, 1905, pp. 36, 65), thinks that the quarrel between the houses is the cause of the tragedy, but sees it in moral rather than social terms as an expression of "long-continued evil." More recently, H. B. Charlton, "Experiment and Interregnum," *Shakespearian Tragedy* (Cambridge, Eng.: Cambridge University Press, 1948), pp. 49–63, calls the feud the means by which fate acts, but objects to it as such on the grounds that it lacks convincing force and implacability in the play. For an orthodox Freudian interpretation of the feud as a regressive, intrafamilial, narcissistic force that prevents Romeo and Juliet from seeking properly non-incestuous love objects, see M. D. Faber, "The Adolescent Suicides of Romeo and Juliet," *Psychoanalytic Review*, 59 (1972–73), 169–81.

2. As usual, Shakespeare portrays the milieu of his source in terms with which he and his audience are familiar; he is not at pains to distinguish the Italian family from the English. Here I accept Lawrence Stone's definition of the patriarchal family: "This sixteenth-century aristocratic family was patrilinear, primogenitural, and patriarchal: patrilinear in that it was the male line whose ancestry was traced so diligently by the genealogists and heralds, and in almost all cases via the male line that titles were inherited; primogenitural in that most of the property went to the eldest son, the younger brothers being dispatched into the world with little more than a modest annuity or life interest in a small estate to keep them afloat; and patriarchal in that the husband and father lorded it over his wife and children with the quasi-absolute authority of a despot." Stone, *The Crisis of the Aris-*

tocracy: 1558–1641, abridged ed. (London: Oxford University Press, 1971), p. 271.

3. Harold C. Goddard, *The Meaning of Shakespeare*, 2 vols. (Chicago: University of Chicago Press, 1951), I, 119.

4. This is a more recent critical tendency than that referred to in note 1, and is represented by Donald A. Stauffer, *Shakespeare's World of Images* (New York: Norton, 1949), pp. 56–57; Franklin M. Dickey, *Not Wisely But Too Well* (San Marino: Huntington Library, 1957), pp. 63–117; and Roy W. Battenhouse, *Shakespearean Tragedy: Its Art and Its Christian Premises* (Bloomington: University of Indiana Press, 1969), pp. 102–30. However, Dickey in his book and Paul N. Siegel in "Christianity and the Religion of Love in *Romeo and Juliet*," *Shakespeare Quarterly*, 12 (1961), 383, see the lovers' passion, flawed though it is, as the means by which divine order based on love is restored to Verona.

5. Siegel, "Christianity and the Religion of Love," p. 387, uses this phrase, but in a moral rather than social context; he sees them as scapegoats through whom their parents expiate their sins of hate and vengefulness.

6. The term is Erik Erikson's, as used in "The Problem of Ego Identity," *Psychological Issues*, No. 1 (1959), 103–5. He defines it partly through a description of George Bernard Shaw's self-imposed "prolongation of the interval between youth and adulthood" in his early twenties. His comments on "the social play of adolescents" further explain the purpose of such a moratorium and raise the questions I am raising with regard to the social function of the feud: "Children and adolescents in their presocieties provide for one another a sanctioned moratorium and joint support for free experimentation with inner and outer dangers (including those emanating from adult world). Whether or not a given adolescent's newly acquired capacities are drawn back into infantile conflict depends to a significant extent on the quality of the opportunities and rewards available to him in his peer clique, as well as on the more formal ways in which society at large invites a transition from social play to work experimentation, and from rituals of transit to final commitments . . ." (p. 118).

7. See Gordon Schochet, "Patriarchalism, Politics, and Mass Attitudes in Stuart England," *The Historical Journal*, 12 (1969), 413–41.

8. This quotation and subsequent ones are from *The Complete Signet Classic Shakespeare*, ed. Sylvan Barnet (New York: Harcourt Brace Jovanovich, 1963, 1972). Where relevant I have noted variant readings.

9. Ruth Nevo, "Tragic Form in *Romeo and Juliet*," *Studies in English Literature*, 9 (1969), 245.

10. Robert O. Evans, *The Osier Cage: Rhetorical Devices in Romeo and Juliet* (Lexington: University of Kentucky Press, 1966), argues that the Queen Mab speech deals with the real subjects of the play—money and place, the main reasons for marriage—and in the extended treat-

ment of the soldier which concludes its catalogue of Mab's victims "presents what in the milieu of *Romeo and Juliet* was a principal destructive force—violence" (p. 79).

11. Norman Holland, "Mercutio, Mine Own Son the Dentist," in *Essays on Shakespeare*, ed. Gordon Ross Smith (University Park: Pennsylvania State University Press, 1965), pp. 3–14, comments suggestively on the contrast between Mercutio and Romeo in this respect: "He jests at scars that fears to feel a wound—a certain kind of wound, the kind that comes from real love that would lay him low, make him undergo a submission like Romeo's. Mercutio's bawdry serves to keep him a noncombatant in the wars of love. . . . Not for Mercutio is that entrance into the tomb or womb or maw which is Romeo's dark, sexual fate" (pp. 11–12).

12. Quoted in *Romeo and Juliet: A New Variorum Edition*, ed. Horace Howard Furness (Philadelphia: Lippincott, 1871), p. 200n.

13. Arthur Brooke, *The Tragicall Historye of Romeus and Juliet* in *Narrative and Dramatic Sources of Shakespeare*, ed. Geoffrey Bullough, I (London: Routledge & Kegan Paul, 1957), p. 336, lines 1951–60.

14. Harry Levin, "Form and Formality in *Romeo and Juliet*," in *Twentieth Century Interpretations of Romeo and Juliet*, ed. Douglas Cole (Englewood Cliffs, N.J.: Prentice-Hall, 1970), 85–95.

15. *Coleridge's Writings on Shakespeare*, ed. Terence Hawkes (New York: Capricorn Books, 1959), p. 118. Coleridge adds to this phrase "yet resurgence against the check," but he is referring to the Nurse's garrulity in the first scene, when she persists in repeating her story against Lady Capulet's wishes.

16. This formulation is Levin's ("Form and Formality," p. 90), but he does not develop it. In a richly illuminating chapter of *Shakespeare and the Common Understanding* (New York: Free Press, 1967) titled "Eros and Death," Norman Rabkin treats *Venus and Adonis*, *Romeo and Juliet*, and *Antony and Cleopatra* as works which link "love, the most intense manifestation of the urge to life" with "the self-destructive yearning for annihilation that we recognize as the death wish" (p. 151). Rabkin finds this death wish inherent in the love of Romeo and Juliet itself; I find its source in the feud, seeing the lovers impelled to seek consummation in death only because the feud makes it impossible in life.

17. Gordon Ross Smith, "The Balance of Themes in *Romeo and Juliet*," *Essays on Shakespeare*, ed. Gordon Ross Smith (University Park: Pennsylvania State University Press, 1965), p. 39.

18. In "The 'Uncanny,'" Freud remarks that the fantasy of being buried alive while appearing to be dead is one of intrauterine existence (*Standard Edition*, trans. and ed. James Strachey [London: Hogarth Press, 1961, 1964], XVII, 244). The conflation of womb and tomb, birth and death throughout the play lends weight to this interpretation of the deaths and their setting.

19. Bruno Bettelheim, *The Uses of Enchantment: The Meaning and Importance of Fairy Tales* (New York: Knopf, 1976), p. 91.
20. See my article, "Self and Eros in *Venus and Adonis*," in *The Centennial Review*, 20 (1976), 351–71.
21. See III.ii.136–37; III.v.94–95, 141, 201–3.
22. The second quarto prints ". . . then I denie you starres," which, though it offers a different shade of meaning, still expresses Romeo's belief that he acts independently from fate.
23. In an interesting essay which stresses the importance of the family, "Shakespeare's Earliest Tragedies: *Titus Andronicus* and *Romeo and Juliet*," *Shakespeare Survey*, 27 (1974), 1–9, G. K. Hunter offers a different though related interpretation: "It is entirely appropriate that the 'public' wedding-bed of Romeo and Juliet (as against their previous private bedding) should be placed in the Capulet tomb, for it is there that Romeo may be most effectively seen to have joined his wife's clan, where their corporate identity is most unequivocally established" (p. 8).

A Heart Cleft in Twain

The Dilemma of Shakespeare's Gertrude

Rebecca Smith

Gertrude, in Shakespeare's *Hamlet*, has traditionally been played as a sensual, deceitful woman. Indeed, in a play in which the characters' words, speeches, acts, and motives have been examined and explained in myriad ways, the depiction of Gertrude has been remarkably consistent, as a woman in whom "compulsive ardure . . . actively doth burn, / And reason [panders] will" (III.iv. 86–88).[1] Gertrude prompts violent physical and emotional reactions from the men in the play, and most stage and film directors —like Olivier, Kozintsev, and Richardson—have simply taken the men's words and created a Gertrude based on their reactions. But the traditional depiction of Gertrude is a false one, because what *her* words and actions actually create is a soft, obedient, dependent, unimaginative woman who is caught miserably at the center of a desperate struggle between two "mighty opposites," her "heart cleft in twain" (III.iv.156) by divided loyalties to husband and son. She loves both Claudius and Hamlet, and their conflict leaves her bewildered and unhappy.

Three famous film versions of *Hamlet* illustrate the standard presentation, wherein Gertrude is a vain, self-satisfied woman of strong physical and sexual appetites. Thus, Grigori Kozintsev (1964) shows her gazing into a hand mirror and arranging her hair as she chastens Hamlet for the particularity of his grief in the face of the commonness of death. Tony Richardson (1969) repeatedly shows her eating and drinking. Jack Jorgens's description in *Shakespeare on Film* is vividly accurate: "Richardson's film shows the bed as a 'nasty sty' where overweight Claudius and pallid Gertrude drink blood-red wine and feast with their dogs on greasy chicken and fruit."[2] Gertrude sustains herself throughout the play with frequent goblets of greedily swilled wine.

In the same way, in the Olivier *Hamlet* (1948), the dramatic symbol for Gertrude is a luxurious canopied bed. This bed is one of the first and last images on the screen and emphasizes both Gertrude's centrality in the play and Olivier's interpretation of the centrality of sexual appetite in Gertrude's nature. Even her relationship with her son is tinged with sexuality. Olivier's Hamlet brutally hurls Gertrude—the ultimate sexual object—onto her bed, alternating embraces and abuse in the accusatory closet scene. In Richardson's and Kozintsev's film versions, the sexual passion between Claudius and Gertrude receives similarly emphatic treatment. For example, Richardson has Claudius and Gertrude conduct much royal business from their bed; and in one particularly obvious scene, Kozintsev's Gertrude is led by Claudius through the midst of people scantily costumed as satyrs and nymphs and dancing in frenzied celebration. She is then literally pushed into a darkened room, whereupon Claudius moves toward her (and the camera) with a lustfully single-minded expression on his face. The misrepresentations that these film versions of Gertrude perpetuate take their cues from respected critical interpretations of Gertrude,[3] which seem to assume that only a deceitful, highly sexual woman could arouse such strong responses and violent reactions in men, not a nurturant and loving one, as is Shakespeare's Gertrude.

Gertrude, like Hamlet, is a character who undergoes subtle but significant changes between Shakespeare's sources and his play, changes which increase her complexity and ambiguity. In the earliest Amleth/Hamlet stories, Gertrude clearly is culpable. In Saxo Grammaticus's twelfth-century *Historiae Danicae*, Gerutha/Gertrude marries Feng/Claudius, who is the known murderer of her husband. François de Belleforest, in his sixteenth-century retelling of the story in the *Histoires Tragiques*, makes one important addition to the depiction of Gertrude: he states that the Queen committed adultery with her brother-in-law during her marriage to the King.[4] Finally, in the *Ur-Hamlet*, significant actions by Gertrude reinforce the suspicion of her culpability: "After the death of Corambis (Polonius) she blames herself for Hamlet's madness, and believes that she is thereby punished for her incestuous re-marriage, or else that her marriage, by depriving Hamlet of the crown, has driven him mad from thwarted ambition. Hamlet upbraids her for her crocodile tears, and urges her to assist in his revenge, so that in the King's death her infamy should die."[5] In this earlier version, Gertrude promises to "conceale, consent, and doe my best / What stratagem soe're thou shalt deuise," and she sends Hamlet warnings by Horatio, thus taking direct steps to aid Hamlet's revenge and thereby rid herself of guilt.[6]

As Kenneth Muir points out, Shakespeare's play apparently follows the main lines of the *Ur-Hamlet* (with its secret murder, doubtable ghost, feigned and real madness, play-within-a-play, closet scene, killing of the Polonius/Corambis figure, voyage to England, suicide of Ophelia, and fencing match with Laertes— Shakespeare's additions including only the pirates, Fortinbras, and possibly the gravediggers).[7] The changes that Shakespeare does make in the structure and characters of the play demand attention as significant indicators of a redirection that adds subtlety and thematic complexity: melodrama is replaced by tragedy. In Shakespeare's *Hamlet*, many questions about Gertrude arise that cannot be fully answered: the murder of old Hamlet is not public knowledge, but does Gertrude know, or at least suspect? Is she guilty of past adultery as well as current incest? Does the closet scene demonstrate her acknowledgment of sexual guilt, and does she thereafter align herself with Hamlet in his quest for revenge and thus shun Claudius's touch and bed? Indeed, does Gertrude demonstrate change and development in the course of the play, or is she incapable of change?

Finding answers to these questions about Gertrude is complicated by the fact that in *Hamlet* one hears a great deal of discussion of Gertrude's personality and actions by other characters. She is a stimulus for and object of violent emotional reactions in the ghost, Hamlet, and Claudius, all of whom offer extreme descriptions of her. The ghost expresses simultaneous outrage, disgust, and protectiveness in his first appearance to Hamlet: "Let not the royal bed of Denmark be / A couch for luxury and damned incest. / But howsomever thou pursues this act, / Taint not thy mind, nor let thy soul contrive / Against thy mother aught" (I.v.82–86). The ghost first asks Hamlet for revenge, describes his present purgatorial state, spends ten lines sketchily outlining the secret murder, and then begins a vivid sixteen-line attack on the sexual relationship of Claudius and Gertrude (42–57). He returns to a brief description of the actual murder only because he "scent[s] the morning air, / Brief let me be" (58–59). Before he disappears, he returns to the topic of Gertrude's sexual misdeeds, but again admonishes Hamlet to "leave her to heaven." The ghost's second appearance to Hamlet is prompted by the need for further defense of Gertrude. Hamlet's resolution when he is preparing to visit his mother's bedchamber after "The Mousetrap," to "be cruel, not unnatural," to "speak [daggers] to her, but use none" (III.ii.395–96), seems to be failing. His frenzied attack on Gertrude gains verbal force and violence (which, on stage, is usually accompanied by increasing physical force and violence) until the ghost intervenes. Hamlet shares the ghost's obsession with Gertrude's sexuality, but is dissipating the energy that should be directed toward avenging his father's murder in attacking Gertrude for, he claims, living "In the rank sweat of an enseamed bed, / Stew'd in corruption, honeying and making love / Over the nasty sty!" (III.iv.93–95). The ghost must intervene to whet Hamlet's "almost blunted purpose" of revenge and to command Hamlet to protect Gertrude, to "step between her and her fighting soul," since "conceit in weakest bodies strongest works" (111–14).

Hamlet's violent emotions toward his mother are obvious from his first soliloquy, in which twenty-three of the thirty-one lines express his anger and disgust at what he perceives to be Gertrude's weakness, insensitivity, and, most important, bestiality: "O most wicked speed: to post / With such dexterity to incestious [*sic*] sheets" (I.ii.156–57). Gertrude's apparent betrayal of his idealized Hyperion father, not the actual death, has given rise to Hamlet's melancholy state at the first of the play. A. C. Bradley's analysis of the cause of Hamlet's sickness of life and longing for death is vividly corroborative: "It was the moral shock of the sudden ghastly disclosure of his mother's true nature, falling on him when his heart was aching with love, and his body doubtless weakened by sorrow. . . . Is it possible to conceive an experience more desolating to a man such as we have seen Hamlet to be; and is its result anything but perfectly natural? It brings bewildered horror, then loathing, then despair of human nature."[8]

Later, when the ghost tells Hamlet that Claudius, Gertrude's second husband, is the murderer of her first, his generalized outrage at women increases and spreads. His sense of betrayal is soon further fed by the unexpected rejection of his love by Ophelia, who obeys the commands of her brother and father that result from their one-dimensional conception of a woman as a sexual "object." Laertes advises Ophelia that "best safety lies in fear" (I.iii.43), and Polonius, in a mean-minded speech, demands her immediate rejection of Hamlet's apparently "honorable" (111) espousals of love. To all of this, Ophelia replies, "I shall obey, my lord" (136). Hereafter, Hamlet is described by Ophelia as behaving quite strangely (II.i.74–97), and he is heard by the audience speaking to Ophelia abusively or coarsely, as he does to his mother. His experiences lead him to attack what he perceives to be the brevity of women's love (I.ii.129–59; III.ii.154), women's wantonness (III.i.145), and the ability that women have to make "monsters" of the men (III.i.138) over whom they have so much power. Indeed, in the sea of troubles that may lead one to seek an end to life, "despis'd love" (III.i.71) is fourth in the list of heartaches.

Claudius creates an impression of Gertrude for the audience because she is the object of violent conflicting emotions for him as she is for the ghost and Hamlet. She is, he says, "My virtue or my plague" (IV.vii.13). He suffers under a "heavy burthen" (III.i.53) of guilt, but he refuses to give up "those effects for which I did the murther: / My crown, mine own ambition, and my queen" (III.iii.54–55). He speaks respectfully to Gertrude throughout the play, and tells Laertes that one of the reasons for his toleration of Hamlet's extraordinary behavior is his love for Gertrude:

> The Queen his mother
> Lives almost by his looks, and for myself—
> My virtue or my plague, be it either which—
> She is so [conjunctive] to my life and soul,
> That, as the star moves not but in his sphere,
> I could not but by her.   (IV.vii.11–16)

In Belleforest's version of the Hamlet story, the Claudius figure kills the King ostensibly to save the life of the Queen, his mistress. In Shakespeare's *Hamlet*, Gertrude's attractiveness for Claudius is one of the causes—and his sexual possession of her one of the results—of the murder of old Hamlet. To possess Gertrude, Claudius is brazenly willing to risk the displeasure of "the general gender" (IV.vii.18) who bear great love for young Hamlet and does not hesitate to displace him on the throne by marrying Gertrude—"our sometime sister, now our queen, / Th'imperial jointress to this warlike state" (I.ii.8–9). Claudius is as obsessed by Gertrude as the two Hamlets are, and—although he clearly loves her—he shares the Hamlets' conception of Gertrude as an *object*. She is "possess'd" as one of the "effects" of his actions (III.iii.53–54) and is thereafter "Taken to wife" (I.ii.14). It may then seem contradictory that he does not forcibly stop Gertrude from drinking the poisoned wine, but there are, in the context of the final scene of the play, many strong reasons for his self-restraint. Therefore, one has no reason to assume that his lecture to Laertes on the ephemerality of love—which "Dies in his own too much" (IV.vii.118)—arises out of his experiences with Gertrude.

Although she may have been partially responsible for Claudius's monstrous act of fratricide and although her marriage to Claudius may have been indirectly responsible for making a "monster" of Hamlet, Gertrude is never seen in the play inducing anyone to do anything at all monstrous. Jan Kott's assertion notwithstanding—that Gertrude "has been through passion, murder, and silence. . . . suppress[ing] everything inside her," so that one senses "a volcano under her superficial poise"⁹—when one closely examines Gertrude's actual speech and actions in an attempt to understand the character, one finds little that hints at hypocrisy, suppression, or uncontrolled passion and their implied complexity.

Gertrude appears in only ten of the twenty scenes that comprise the play; furthermore, she speaks very little, having less dialogue than any other major character in *Hamlet*—a mere 157 lines out of 4,042 (3.8 percent).¹⁰ She speaks plainly, directly, and chastely when she does speak, using few images except in the longest of her speeches, which refer to Hamlet's and Ophelia's relationship (III.i.36–41 and v.i.243–46), to Ophelia's death (iv.vii.166–83), to her sense of unspecified guilt (iv.v.17–20), and to Hamlet's madness in the graveyard (v.i.284–88). Gertrude tells Ophelia before the spying scene that she hopes that the "happy cause of Hamlet's wildness" is Ophelia's "good beauties." If so, she trusts that Ophelia's "virtues" can effect a cure (iii.i.39–40); and later, when relaying the news of Ophelia's death, Gertrude characteristically disdains liberality and creates her bittersweet pictures in the language of the "cull-cold maids." Gertrude's brief speeches include references to honor, virtue, flowers, and a dove's golden couplets; neither structure nor content suggests wantonness. Gertrude's only mildly critical comments are in response to the verbosity of Polonius ("More matter with less art"—ii.ii.95) and that of the Player Queen ("The lady doth protest too much, methinks"—iii.ii.230).

Gertrude usually asks questions (ten questions in her approximately forty-five lines of dialogue in the closet scene) or voices solicitude for the well-being and safety of other characters. She divides her concern between Claudius and Hamlet; indeed, Claudius observes that she "lives almost by his [Hamlet's] looks" (iv.vii.12). Her first speeches are to Hamlet, admonishing an end to his "particular" grief and pleading that he stay in Denmark with her: "Let not thy mother lose her prayers, Hamlet, / I pray thee stay with us, go not to Wittenberg" (i.ii.118–19). In her second appearance on stage, she directs Rosencrantz and Guildenstern "to visit / My too much changed son" (ii.ii.35–36) in an attempt to discover the cause of his change. However, in the same scene she also demonstrates her perspicuity by intuitively, and correctly, analyzing Hamlet's behavior: "I doubt it is no other but the main, / His father's death and our [o'erhasty] marriage" (ii.ii.56–57). Gertrude's dialogue gains atypical force when she must defend both Claudius (iv.v.110–11, 117, 129) and Hamlet (v.i.264, 273, 284–88) to Laertes, and in her desperate defense of Hamlet to Claudius when he asks of Hamlet's whereabouts after the murder of Polonius. Hamlet, she says, killed Polonius because of a "brainish apprehension" and "weeps for what is done" (iv.i.11, 27).

Gertrude's actions are as solicitous and unlascivious as her language. She usually enters a scene with the King, and she is alone on stage only with Hamlet in the closet scene and with mad Ophelia (both times expressing feelings of some kind of guilt). She repeatedly leaves scenes after being ordered out by Claudius, which he does both to protect her from the discovery of his guilt and to confer with her privately about how to deal with Hamlet. Little proof for the interpretation of Gertrude as a guileful and carnal woman emerges from her other textually implicit actions, as, for example, when she sorrowfully directs the attention of Polonius and Claudius to Hamlet: "But look where sadly the poor wretch comes reading" (II.ii.168). She acquiesces in the plan to determine the cause of Hamlet's extraordinary behavior by spying on him, using Ophelia as a decoy, and leaves when ordered to, so the plan can be carried out, saying, "And for your part, Ophelia, I do wish / That your good beauties be the happy cause / Of Hamlet's wildness. So shall I hope your virtues / Will bring him to his wonted way again, / To both your honors" (III.i.36–41). She later sends messengers to Hamlet to bring him to her after "The Mousetrap" and attempts to deal roundly with him, but she is forced to sit down and to contrast the pictures of her first husband and Claudius (III.iv.34, 53). Even after her encounter with Hamlet in the closet scene, she apparently attempts to restrain Laertes physically when he madly bursts in to accuse Claudius of killing Polonius ("Let him go, Gertrude, do not fear our person" IV.v.123). She accepts a sprig of rue from Ophelia, to be worn "with a difference" (IV.v.183), and later scatters flowers on Ophelia's grave. It also is observable from the text that she offers Hamlet a napkin with which to wipe his face during the fencing match and wipes his face for him once. Finally, and most important, she drinks the poisoned wine and dies onstage, using her dying words to warn Hamlet of the poison (v.ii.291, 309–10), but not accusing Claudius. Although both the ghost and Hamlet repeatedly speak in vivid language of her gamboling between incestuous sheets (and presumably she does sometimes share a bed with Claudius), the text never states or implies that Gertrude gives or receives the wanton pinches or "reechy kisses" (III.iv.183–84) that so obsess, enrage, and disgust the imaginations of Hamlet and the ghost.

Her own words and actions compel one to describe Gertrude as merely a quiet, biddable, careful mother and wife. Nonetheless, one can still examine Gertrude's limited actions and reactions to answer the knotty interpretative question of Gertrude's culpability in the murder of her first husband. When speaking to Hamlet, the ghost does not state or suggest Ger-

trude's guilt in his murder, only in her "falling-off" from him to
Claudius (I.v.47). When Hamlet confronts her after "The Mousetrap," she asks in apparent innocence, "What have I done, that
thou dar'st wag thy tongue / In noise so rude against me?"
(III.iv.39–40). She has not been verbally guileful before, so one has
no reason to suspect her of duplicity in this instance. And when
Hamlet informs her that old Hamlet was murdered by Claudius,
she does not indicate prior knowledge. Instead, she exclaims in
horror, "As kill a King!" (30), and pleads for the third time that
Hamlet mitigate his attack: "No more!" (101). She is not aware of
any personal guilt, and she does not want to hear of the guilty
deeds of one of the men she loves.

Clearly, Gertrude's innocence of involvement in the murder is most strongly suggested. However, many critics have interpreted the text differently, asserting that at the least Gertrude is
guilty of having had a sexual relationship with Claudius before
the murder of her husband because the ghost uses the word *adulterate*[11] when describing Claudius and asserts, in reference to
Gertrude, that "[lust], though to a radiant angel link'd, / Will [sate]
itself in a celestial bed / And prey on garbage" (I.v.55–57). But if
Gertrude had been involved in an adulterous affair with Claudius,
she would surely have known that she was "conjunctive" to his
"life and soul" and that he was ambitious. She might therefore
have suspected him to be capable of murder in order to obtain her
and the crown (which a marriage to her would assure him), but
she has no such suspicions. The ghost does use the past tense to
describe Claudius's and Gertrude's sexual liaison. Claudius "*won*
to his shameful lust" Gertrude's will: "O Hamlet, what [a] falling-
off *was* there" (45–47, emphasis added). Still, it is not clear if the
ghost is referring to a time before his murder or if the past to
which he refers is that period since his death, during which
Claudius has won and married Gertrude. Hamlet's anger and disgust at Gertrude's hasty marriage and the dexterity with which
she moved to "incestious sheets"—feelings expressed even before
he had talked with the ghost or knew of the murder—further support the interpretation that Gertrude was not guilty of a sexual
liaison with Claudius before her husband's murder, but that her
hasty, apparently careless betrayal of the memory of her first husband is what, in Hamlet's eyes, "makes marriage vows / As false

as dicers' oaths" (III.iv.44–45). Indeed, in the closet scene Hamlet never accuses her of adultery, but abhors her choice of an "adulterate" second husband: "Could you on this fair mountain leave to feed, / And batten on this moor? . . . what judgment / Would step from this to this?" (67–71).

Although Gertrude is not an adulterer, she has been "adulterated" by her contact, even innocently in marriage, with Claudius. Similarly, his crimes and deceit have, in fact, made Gertrude guilty of incest.[12] In order to marry, Claudius and Gertrude would have been required to obtain a dispensation to counteract their canonical consanguinity or affinity. Obviously, if his crime of fratricide were publicly known—as it is by the ghost and Hamlet—Claudius's dispensation to marry his victim's wife, his sister-in-law, certainly would not have been granted. Therefore, one could assert that the relationship between Claudius and Gertrude is incestuous because the dispensation was based on false pretenses and would not have been granted if the truth were known. Because they know the truth, the ghost and Hamlet persist in terming the relationship incestuous; but Gertrude has married in innocence and good faith, not as a party to the deception.

Gertrude does readily admit her one self-acknowledged source of guilt—that her marriage was "o'erhasty," but in all other instances she feels guilt only after Hamlet has insisted that she be ashamed.[13] And it is not ever completely clear to what Gertrude refers in the closet scene when she mentions the black spots on her soul—if it is a newly aroused awareness of her adulterate and incestuous relationship, if it is her marriage to a man whom Hamlet so clearly despises, or if it is merely her already lamented o'erhasty marriage:

> O Hamlet, speak no more!
> Thou turn'st my [eyes into my very] soul,
> And there I see such black and [grained] spots
> As will [not] leave their tinct.   (III.iv.88–91)

Hamlet's violent cajolery in the closet scene has created unaccustomed feelings of guilt in this accommodating woman, who wants primarily to please him. However, she has not pleased Hamlet by acting in a way that pleased Claudius—by marrying him so soon after her husband's death and in spite of their consanguinity. For Hamlet, her act "roars so loud and thunders in the index" (III.iv.52), and his displeasure has "cleft" the Queen's heart "in twain" (156) because she obviously loves both Hamlet and Claudius and feels pain and guilt at her inability to please both.

Hamlet is commanded by the ghost to moderate his attack, to "step between her and her fighting soul" because of Gertrude's "amazement" and because of the force of imagination in a weak body (III.iv.112–14). It is even possible that Gertrude's "fighting soul" results not only from an awakened sense of guilt at Hamlet's words but also from the conflict between her persistent, extreme love for her son and her momentary terror of him. After all, in the preceding 115 lines, Hamlet has certainly demonstrated emotional, and probably physical, brutality toward Gertrude; indeed, she has called for help in fear that he will murder her (21). Hamlet has stabbed Polonius and shown little remorse, and he continues the extraordinary behavior that prompts her amazement:

> Alas, how is't with you,
> That you do bend your eye on vacancy,
> And with th' incorporal air do hold discourse?
> Forth at your eyes your spirits wildly peep,
> And as the sleeping soldiers in th' alarm,
> Your bedded hair, like life in excrements,
> Start up and stand an end. O gentle son,
> Upon the heat and flame of thy distemper
> Sprinkle cool patience. Whereon do you look?
>
> (III.iv.116–24).

Since the beginning of the play, Hamlet has been obsessed with Claudius's and Gertrude's guilt, and it is this which precipitates his distempered behavior. Indeed, judged without Hamlet's strong predisposition, Gertrude's behavior at "The Mousetrap" would lead no one to believe that she has seen herself reflected in the Player Queen. However, Hamlet believes that she has—and Hamlet is a powerful first-person force in the play who encourages one to see all events and people from his perspective, nearly compelling one to see Gertrude's one-line response to the play's action as an admission of guilt: "The lady doth protest too much, methinks" (III.ii.230). Gertrude's remark at this play-within-the-play can be given another interpretation that may be more accurate, in view of Gertrude's accommodating, dependent personality: her words are not a guileful anticipation and deflection of comparisons between herself and the Player Queen. Instead, being a woman of so few words herself, Gertrude must sincerely be irritated by the Player Queen's verbosity, just as she was earlier by that of Polonius. Obviously, Gertrude believes that quiet women best please men, and pleasing men is Gertrude's main interest. Indeed, Gertrude's concern to maintain a strong relationship with two men is demonstrated by her only other lines at the play—brief lines—asking her "dear Hamlet" to sit beside her (108) and voicing distress for Claudius's obvious consternation at the end of the play: "How fares my lord?" (267). After the play, Gertrude is, according to Guildenstern, "in most great affliction of spirit" (311–12) and calls Hamlet for a chastening session in her room for two reasons: the conference, with Polonius as spy, had already been planned before the presentation of the play; and more important, she is quite upset because one of the men for whom she cares greatly has "much offended" (III.iv.9) the other. In no way, by word or act, does she indicate that the play has spontaneously created any sense of guilt in her.

Obviously, this analysis of Gertrude's behavior does not suggest any changes or clear moral development in her. After the play-within-the-play and the closet scene, Gertrude agrees to Hamlet's request that she not "ravel all this matter out," since he is "essentially . . . not in madness, / But mad in craft" (III.iv.186–88). She says, "I have no life to breathe / What thou has said to me" (198–99). And she is true to her word. She does not unravel it to Claudius, whom Hamlet hates and fears. However, she is immediately seen in the next scene telling Claudius of something else—the murder of Polonius—and defending Hamlet in his apparent madness; and although she is true to Hamlet, the scene nonetheless works to undercut her position as an honest woman. That Gertrude does not promise Hamlet to refrain from going to Claudius's bed may possibly suggest an admission of guilt about the relationship. Those who claim that Gertrude does admit to committing adultery and incest cite her one self-revealing aside, four lines in which she directly grieves for her sinful, sick soul and self-destructive, fearful guilt:

To my sick soul, as sin's true nature is,
Each toy seems prologue to some great amiss,
So full of artless jealousy is guilt,
It spills itself in fearing to be spilt. (IV.v.17–20)

But the nature of this lamented guilt remains unclear; it is apparently unfelt until aroused by Hamlet's attack. If it arises out of the conflict between her love for Claudius and her remorse for betraying the memory of her first husband, she obviously chooses, like Claudius, to "retain th'offense" (III.iii.56), because she soon thereafter tries physically and verbally to protect Claudius from Laertes.

Gertrude has not moved in the play toward independence or a heightened moral stance; only her divided loyalties and her unhappiness intensify. Given the presentation of Gertrude in Shakespeare's text, it is impossible to see the accuracy of Olivier's and Kozintsev's film presentations and of many stage depictions that show Gertrude shrinking after Act Three from Claudius's touch because of her newly awakened sense of decency and shame. Nor does the text suggest, as Olivier does in his film, that she is suspicious of the pearl that Claudius drops in Hamlet's wine goblet. Gertrude does not drink the wine to protect Hamlet or to kill herself because of her shame; she drinks it in her usual direct way to toast Hamlet's success in the fencing match, after first briskly and maternally advising him to wipe his face. In fact, Gertrude's death is symbolic of the internal disharmony caused by her divided loyalties. In order to honor Hamlet, she directly disobeys Claudius for the first time:

QUEEN. The Queen carouses to thy fortune, Hamlet.
HAMLET. Good Madam!
KING.   Gertrude, do not drink.
QUEEN. I will, my lord, I pray you pardon me.
KING. [Aside.] It is the pois'ned cup, it is too late.
                                                    (v.ii.289–92)

Gertrude dies asserting that she is poisoned and calling out for her "dear Hamlet," but still not attacking Claudius.

Gertrude's words and actions in Shakespeare's *Hamlet* create not the lusty, lustful, lascivious Gertrude that one generally sees in stage and film productions but a compliant, loving, unimaginative woman whose only concern is pleasing others: a woman who seemed virtuous (I.v.46), and who would, so Hamlet asserts, hang on her first husband, "As if increase of appetite had grown / By what it fed on" (I.ii.143–45). This same careful woman, soon after her husband's death, "with remembrance of" herself (7), marries his brother—probably because of her extremely dependent personality—and tries to relieve her much-loved son's melancholy by counseling him in temporality: "Thou know'st 'tis common, all that lives must die, / Passing through nature to eternity" (72–73). As these and most of her other lines demonstrate, Gertrude may be the object of violent emotions, but she displays no passion, only quietly consistent concern for the well-being of the two other characters: Claudius and, most profoundly, Hamlet. She is easily led, and she makes no decisions for herself except, ironically, the one that precipitates her death. Her personality is, both figuratively and literally, defined by other characters in the play. Because of her malleability and weakness, the distorted image created and reflected by others—not the one created by her own words and actions—has predominated.

In creating Gertrude, Shakespeare clearly diverged from the sources he followed quite closely in other areas, making her of a piece with the rest of the play—that is, problematic. But Gertrude is problematic not because of layers of complexity or a dense texture such as that of Hamlet but because, as with the ghost, Shakespeare does not provide all the "answers," all the necessary clues that would allow one to put together her character and fully understand her speech, actions, and motivations. Still, Gertrude is not a flat, uninteresting character as a result of her limited range of responses and concerns. Gertrude's words and acts interest the audience because, obviously, she is of extreme interest to the combatants in the play—the ghost, Hamlet and Claudius—all of whom see her literally and in quite heightened terms as a sexual *object*. However, if she were presented on stage and film as only her own words and deeds create her, Gertrude might become another stereotypical character: the nurturing, loving, careful mother and wife—malleable, submissive, totally dependent, and solicitous of others at the expense of herself. This is still a stereotype, but a more positive one than that of the temptress and destroyer—self-indulgent and soulless. And certainly it more accurately reflects the Gertrude that Shakespeare created.

NOTES

1. William Shakespeare, *Hamlet,* in *The Riverside Shakespeare,* ed. G. Blakemore Evans et al. (Boston: Houghton Mifflin, 1974). All further references are to this edition.
2. Jack Jorgens, *Shakespeare on Film* (Bloomington: Indiana University Press, 1977), p. 27.
3. The "received" critical opinion of Gertrude is most clearly stated by Ernest Jones, *Hamlet and Oedipus* (Garden City, N.Y.: Doubleday, 1954). He says that the Queen's "markedly sensual nature . . . is indicated in too many places in the play to need specific reference, and is generally recognized" (p. 91). Other influential critics have interpreted her similarly. A. C. Bradley, *Shakespearean Tragedy* (London: Macmillan, 1956), says that the "ghastly disclosure" of Gertrude's true nature is a moral shock to Hamlet. She marries Claudius not for state reasons or out of family affection; instead, her marriage shows "an astounding shallowness of feeling [and] an eruption of coarse sensuality, 'rank and gross,' speeding posthaste to its horrible delight" (pp. 118–20). H. D. F. Kitto, *Form and Meaning in Drama* (1956), rpt. in part in *Shakespeare Criticism: 1935–1960,* ed. Anne Ridler (Oxford: Oxford University Press, 1970), states that "a mad passion . . . swept [Gertrude] into the arms of Claudius" (p. 158). Similarly, L. C. Knights, *An Approach to "Hamlet"* (London: Chatto and Windus, 1961), describes the court's qualities as "coarse pleasures," "moral obtuseness," "sycophancy," "base and treacherous plotting," and "brainless triviality": "This is the world that revolves round the middle-aged sensuality of Claudius and Gertrude" (p. 42). Harry Levin, *The Question of Hamlet* (London: Oxford University Press, 1959), contrasts Ophelia (virginal, "faithful daughter and sister") to Gertrude (adulterous, corrupted, "faithless mother and wife") who is "associated with the artificial enticement of cosmetics" (p. 66). J. Dover Wilson, *What Happens in Hamlet* (Cambridge: Cambridge University Press, 1935), insists that Hamlet knows that Gertrude is "a criminal, guilty of the filthy sin of incest," and finally comes to see her "as rotten through and through" (p. 44). And, in the same vein, E. M. W. Tillyard, *Shakespeare's Problem Plays* (Toronto: University of Toronto Press, 1968), comments on the "lascivious and incestuous guilt of Gertrude" which has "made the world ugly" for Hamlet (pp. 21–22).
   In contrast, it is interesting to note that some earlier *women* writers have been more generous to Gertrude. Consider the evaluation by Lillie Buffum Chace Wyman in an appendix to *Gertrude of Denmark:*

An Interpretive Romance (Boston: Marshall Jones, 1924), p. 238. Wyman says, "The critics have generally denouced Gertrude's second marriage as sinful in its very nature. It is rather absurd to echo Hamlet so completely as to this. Such an opinion certainly has been very dominant in some ages and some countries. It is doubtful, however, whether it was ever so universally an accepted belief as to make it certain that Shakespeare intended that such a mountain of odium should be heaped upon her, as writers have been piling up for centuries. In this connection, it may be noted that the Roman Catholic Church upheld the marriage of Katharine to Henry the Eighth. And certainly Shakespeare, however Anglican he may have been personally, did not represent Katharine as a loathsome creature in his drama on that subject, and he did permit Henry's courtiers to jeer at the King's pretence of scruple." Rosamond Putzel in "Queen Gertrude's Crime," *Renaissance Papers, 1961*, ed. George Walton Williams (Durham, N.C.: Southeastern Renaissance Conference, 1962), pp. 37–46, argues that the evidence in the play does not prove that Gertrude committed adultery and that her characterization suggests that she did not.

4. Saxo Grammaticus, *Amleth*, and F. de Belleforest, *The Hystorie of Hamblet, Prince of Denmarke*, in *Hamlet*, Norton Critical Edition, ed. Cyrus Hoy (New York: Norton, 1963), pp. 123–41.

5. Kenneth Muir, *Shakespeare's Sources* (London: Methuen, 1961), p. 112. See also Geoffrey Bullough, "Introduction" to *Hamlet* in *Narrative and Dramatic Sources of Shakespeare*, VII (London: Routledge & Kegan Paul, 1973), pp. 3–59.

6. Muir, *Shakespeare's Sources*, p. 112.

7. *Ibid.*, p. 114. See also Frank Kermode, "Introduction" to *Hamlet*, in *The Riverside Shakespeare*, pp. 1136–37.

8. Bradley, *Shakespearean Tragedy*, pp. 118–19.

9. Jan Kott, *Shakespeare Our Contemporary*, trans. Boleslaw Taborski (Garden City, N.Y.: Doubleday/Anchor, 1966), p. 61.

10. Line counts and percentage from Marvin Spevack, *A Complete and Systematic Concordance to the Works of Shakespeare*, III (Hildesheim: Georg Olms, 1968), 828, 751.

11. The adjective *adulterate* denotatively refers to something that makes other things inferior, impure, or corrupted by its addition and need not be limited to a specific reference to sexual intercourse between a married person and someone who is not that person's spouse. Bertram Joseph, *Conscience and the King* (London: Chatto and Windus, 1953), defines *adulterate* by reference to Renaissance sources, namely, Thomas Wilson, who states in his *Christian Dictionary* (1612) that adultery means "all manner of uncleanness, about desire of sex, together with occasion, causes, and means thereof, as in the 7th Commandment," and Perkins, who says in *A Golden Chain* (1616) that adultery means "as much as to do anything, what way so ever," that stains one's own chastity or that of another. Joseph also quotes from the homily "Against Whoredom and Uncleanness" in *Certain Ser-*

mons or Homilies (1623), which defines adultery as "all unlawful use of those parts, which be ordained for generation" (p. 17). Clearly, the ghost's use of the word *adulterate* may refer to Claudius's impurity resulting from his lust for Gertrude and the corruption that he spreads to Gertrude when she becomes his wife, not necessarily to a sexual liaison between the two before old Hamlet's murder.

12. See Jason P. Rosenblatt, "Aspects of the Incest Problem in *Hamlet*," *Shakespeare Quarterly*, 29 (1978), 349–64, for a thorough analysis of the sixteenth-century religious controversy on consanguineous marriages.

13. It is significant that without Hamlet's guidance, Gertrude herself lacks conscious awareness of guilt. Shakespeare may thus demonstrate in Gertrude the commonplace judgment of his society that women must rely on men for guidance and support. Richard Hooker, for example, speaks of the giving of women in marriage as a customary reminder of "the very imbecility of their nature and sex" which "doth bind them to be always directed, guided and ordered by others . . ."; see his *Of the Laws of Ecclesiastical Polity*, V. lxxiii. 5 (London: Dent, 1954), II, p. 393. Such conventional assumptions about female "imbecility" may help to explain both Hamlet's anger at Gertrude and the ghost's charity toward her. However, as Carolyn Heilbrun has pointed out, Gertrude is no imbecile. While Heilbrun accepts the ghost's description of Gertrude as lustful, she urges that the Queen "is also intelligent, penetrating, and gifted with a remarkable talent for concise and pithy speech." See "The Character of Hamlet's Mother," *Shakespeare Quarterly*, 8 (1957), 201–6.

Women and Men in *Othello*

"What should such a fool / Do with so good a woman?"

CAROL THOMAS NEELY

"Almost damned in a fair wife" is Leslie Fiedler's alternate title for his chapter on *Othello* in *The Stranger in Shakespeare*. In it he asserts of the women in the play: "Three out of four, then, [are] weak, or treacherous, or both."[1] Thus he seconds Iago's misogyny and broadens the attack on what Leavis has called "The Sentimentalist's *Othello*," the traditional view of the play held by Coleridge, Bradley, Granville-Barker, G. Wilson Knight, John Bayley, Helen Gardner, and many others.[2] These "Othello critics," as I shall call them, accept Othello at his own high estimate. They are enamored of his "heroic music" and, like him, are overwhelmed by Iago's diabolism, to which they devote much of their analysis.[3] Like Othello, they do not always argue rationally or rigorously for their views and so are vulnerable to attacks on their romanticism or sentimentality. Reacting against these traditionalists, the "Iago critics" (Eliot, Empson, Kirschbaum, Rossiter, and Mason, as well as Fiedler and Leavis) take their cues from Iago.[4] Like him, they are attracted to Othello, unmoved by his rhetoric, and eager to "set down the pegs that make this music."[5]

This essay is reprinted, with revisions, from Shakespeare Studies, *10 (1978), 133–58.*

They attack Othello at his most vulnerable point, his love. They support their case by quoting Iago's estimates of Othello, and they emphasize Iago's realism and "honesty" while priding themselves on their own.[6] Their realism or cynicism gives them, with Iago, an apparent invulnerability. But, like Othello critics, they share the bias and blindness of the character whose perspective they adopt. Most damaging, both groups of critics, like both Othello and Iago, badly misunderstand and misrepresent the women in the play.[7]

Iago critics implicitly demean Desdemona, for if Othello's character and love are called into question, then her love for him loses its justification and validity. Explicitly they have little to say about her.[8] Othello critics idealize her along with the hero, but like him they have a tendency to see her as an object. The source of her sainthood seems a passivity verging on catatonia: "Desdemona is helplessly passive. She can do nothing whatever. She cannot retaliate even in speech; no, not even in silent feeling. . . . She is helpless because her nature is infinitely sweet and her love absolute. . . . Desdemona's suffering is like that of the most loving of dumb creatures tortured without cause by the being he adores."[9] Iago critics, finding the same trait, condemn Desdemona for it: "But the damage to her symbolic value is greater when we see her passively *leaving everything to Heaven*. She ought in a sense to have *embodied* Heaven, given us a human equivalent that would 'make sense' of Heaven. For this task she had the wrong sort of purity."[10]

When Desdemona is credited with activity, she is condemned for that too; she is accused of being domineering, of using witchcraft, of rebelliousness, disobedience, wantonness.[11] Whatever view critics take, discussion of her is virtually an afterthought to the analysis of the men. Emilia and Bianca are still more neglected and are invariably contrasted with Desdemona.[12]

Such neglect has resulted not merely in misreadings of the women's characters and roles but in distorted interpretations of the entire play. Both Othello and Iago critics have tended to see good versus evil as the play's central theme, Othello versus Iago as the play's central conflict, and hence the major tragedies as its most important context. In order to correct this emphasis, I will show that the play's central theme is love—especially marital love; its central conflict is between the men and the women; and contexts quite as illuminating as the tragedies are its source, Cinthio's *Gli Hecatommithi* and, especially, Shakespeare's preceding comedies.[13] Within *Othello* it is Emilia who most explicitly speaks to this theme, recognizes this central conflict, and inherits from the heroines of comedy the role of potential mediator. She is dramatically and symbolically the play's fulcrum. It is as an Emilia critic, then, that I should like to approach the play, hoping to perceive it with something like her good-natured objectivity.

Gli Hecatommithi* may have provided *Othello* with its theme and organizing principle as well as with its plot. The battle of the sexes in marriage is its central motif dominating the frame, the subject matter, and the arrangement of the tales. In the introduction the company debates whether harmony can be achieved in marriage. Ponzio denies this, supporting his view with platitudes Iago would relish: "Better bury a woman than marry her"; "For there to be peace between husband and wife, the husband must be deaf and the wife blind." Fabio, the group's leader, asserts instead that "the only rational love is that which has marriage as its goal, and that this is the quiet of true and wise lovers, coupled together, cooling their amorous flames with sage discourse and in legitimate union."[14] *Othello* similarly presents marriage as potentially strife-ridden or potentially harmonious. In *Gli Hecatommithi* the debate continues in the tales, and in the Third Decade it is intensified by the inflammatory subject matter—the infidelity of husbands and wives. The seventh tale, *Othello's* source, is a rebuttal of the sixth, in which a husband discovers his wife's infidelity and, as the company judges, most prudently (*"prudentissimamente,"* p. 317) arranges to have her drowned so that it appears accidental. In the eighth tale, a contrast to the two preceding it, harmony supersedes warfare. A wife forgives her unfaithful husband and wins him back, behaving with a prudence (*"la prudenza,"* p. 325) exactly the opposite of that of the husbands in tales six and seven. *Othello* similarly rings changes on the theme of male and female in a series of parallel and contrasting couples—Desdemona/Othello, Emilia/Iago, Bianca/Cassio—along with fantasy couples—Roderigo/Desdemona, Cassio/Desdemona, Othello/Emilia. Throughout the tales of the Third Decade it is most often the men who intensify the conflicts, practicing infidelity or taking revenge on wives they suspect of infidelity; the wives, even when wronged, often succeed in mending the relationships. The women in *Othello* similarly seek to secure harmonious relationships but fail to do so.

Their predecessors in this task are the heroines of Shakespearean comedy, to which *Othello* shows pervasive and profound resemblances.[15] Though it is almost always assumed that *Othello* is dominated by a tightly meshed plot, the play seems, like many of the comedies, loosely plotted, held together by theme. The conflicts introduced in the first act between Desdemona and her father and between Venetians and Turks evaporate before they are under way, exactly as do those between Hermia and Egeus in *Midsummer Night's Dream* and between Duke Frederick and Duke Senior in *As You Like It*. As in the comedies, these early plot developments are presented in a flat, stereotyped way; they seem almost an excuse to get the characters to the woods or to Cyprus where the play's real conflicts emerge. Once on Cyprus, however, Act II is in many ways a repetition of Act I.[16] Iago plots the remainder of the play, but his scheme is slight, repetitive, and flawed. It has been found lacking in both motive (like Rosalind's plot in *As You Like It*) and goal (like Don John's plot in *Much Ado about Nothing*). Although the play's increasing intensity is undeniable, there is little actual plot development between the end of the first phase of the temptation scene (III.iii.281) and the attempt on Cassio's life in Act V. Iago's temptation of Othello, like Rosalind's education of Orlando, is not merely linear. Both are continually starting over; they are repeated variations on opposite themes: Iago works to induce fantasy and Rosalind to dispel it. Neither entirely succeeds. Iago's plot, like those of the comedies, rests on coincidence and absurdity. The handkerchief is like the givens of the comedies—the fairy juice, the caskets, the disguises, the identical twins; it is trivial and ridiculous but symbolically all-important. The play develops out of the opposition of attitudes, viewpoints, and sexes. As in the comedies, no single character or viewpoint prevails.

The structure, too, imitates that of the pastoral comedies in its movement from an urban center to an isolated retreat with resultant intensity, freedom, breakdown, and interaction of disparate characters.[17] Though Othello refers to Cyprus as a "town of war" (II.iii.204), once the threats of Turks and storm are lifted, it is instead Venus's isle, a place for celebration—relaxation, drinking, eating (dinner arrangements are a frequent topic of conversation here as in Arden), flirting, sleeping, lovemaking. In the comedies, the potential corruption of these activities is suggested in witty banter, in songs, in comic simile and metaphor; in *Othello*, this corruption becomes literal.

The play is a terrifying completion of the comedies. In them, realism and romanticism, lust and love, desire and illusion, love and friendship, cuckoldry and marriage, masculinity and femininity are held in precarious balance. The men's propensities for folly, cuckoldry, promiscuity, and cruelty are "laugh[ed] to scorn" (*As You Like It*, iv.ii.19); through mockery they are both acknowledged and made powerless. In all of the comedies "The cuckoo then, on every tree, / Mocks married men" (*Love's Labour's Lost*, v.ii.896–97), and mockery grounds and strengthens love. In *Othello*, instead, "villainy hath made mocks with love" (v.ii.152), parodying and perverting love to destroy it. Many of the comedies begin, as *Othello* does, in a masculine world—isolated, rigid, hostile, foolish. But the women enter, take control, and by their "high and plenteous wit and invention" (iv.i.185) transform the men from foolish lovers into—we hope—sensible husbands. The women prepare the way for the harmonious endings symbolized by the consummation of a marriage—in the fairy-blessed beds of the *Midsummer Night's Dream* couples, the re-won beds of Bassanio and Portia, Gratiano and Nerissa in *Merchant of Venice*, the "well-deservèd bed" (v.iv.190) of Silvius and the rest in *As You Like It*. In *Othello*, the women's wit is constrained, their power over men is lost, and the men are transformed downwards—"to be now a sensible man, by and by a fool, and presently a beast!" (ii.iii.296–97). In the romantic comedies the men, while foolish, are not beasts, and their follies are reined and dispelled by the witty heroines. In the dark comedies, the men are almost too foolish (Bassanio, Bertram) or too bestial (Shylock, Angelo) for the happy endings to be possible or satisfying. The women must work too hard, and the men are not changed enough for either sex to be entirely likable or for their reconciliations to be occasion for rejoicing. In *Othello*, the men's murderous fancies are untouched by the women's affection, wit, and shrewishness. The play ends as it began, in a world of men—political, loveless, undomesticated.[18]

The men in *Othello* extend and darken the traits of the

comedy heroes. They are, in Emilia's words, "murderous cox-comb[s]" (v.ii.234). Three out of the five attempt murder; five out of the five are foolish and vain. Roderigo, most obviously a cox-comb, shows in exaggerated fashion the dangerous combination of romanticism and cynicism and the dissociation of love and sex which all the men share. He is the conventional Petrarchan lover: love is a "torment," death a "physician" (i.iii.308–10), Desde-mona "full of most blest condition" (ii.i.247), and consummation of their relationship securely impossible. Yet he easily accepts Desdemona's supposed adultery and the necessity of Cassio's murder; his casual cynicism comes to outdo Iago's: "'Tis but a man gone" (v.i.10). The other men have similarly divided views of women. Brabantio shifts abruptly from protective affection for the chaste Desdemona—"A maiden never bold of spirit / So still and quiet, that her motion / Blush'd at her self" (i.iii.94–96)—to physical revulsion from the sexuality revealed by her elope-ment—"I had rather to adopt a child than get it" (i.iii.191). Cas-sio's divided view is more conventionally accommodated. He ide-alizes the "divine Desdemona" (ii.i.73), flirting courteously and cautiously with her and rejecting Iago's insinuations about her sexuality; this side of women is left to Bianca, who is a "monkey" and a "fitchew" (iv.i.127, 144) and is used and degraded for it. Othello's conflict regarding women is more profound, and the other men's solutions are not open to him. Because of his mar-riage and because of his integrity, he cannot, like Roderigo, assert Desdemona's chastity and corruptibility simultaneously; he can-not, like Cassio, direct his divided emotions toward different ob-jects or, like Brabantio, disown the problem.

Othello's shifts from the idealization of women to their degradation are "extravagant and wheeling" (i.i.136). Iago is their catalyst, but Othello makes the task easy. At the play's start, Othello's idealistic love needs, like that of the comedy heroes, some realistic grounding in the facts of sex. For Othello sex is sec-ondary and potentially either frivolous or debilitating:

> no, when light-wing'd toys,
> And feather'd Cupid, foils with wanton dullness
> My speculative and active instruments,
> That my disports corrupt and taint my business,
> Let housewives make a skillet of my helm,

And all indign and base adversities
Make head against my reputation!　　　　　(1.iii.268–74)

Marriage and its impending consummation naturally pose a threat to this idealistic love. Othello's greeting on Cyprus reveals his preference for a perpetually unconsummated courtship:

If it were now to die,
'Twere now to be most happy, for I fear
My soul hath her content so absolute,
That not another comfort, like to this
Succeeds in unknown fate.　　　　　(II.i.189–93)

In response Desdemona asserts instead quotidian joys:

The heavens forbid
But that our loves and comforts should increase,
Even as our days do grow.　　　　　(II.i.193–95)

Perhaps she, like Rosalind or Viola or the women in *Love's Labour's Lost*, might have tempered Othello's idealism. Instead, it is nudged by Iago into its antithesis—contempt for women, disgust at sexuality, terror of cuckoldry, the preference for literal death instead of metaphorical "death." The acceptance of cuckoldry and sexuality found in the comedies—"As horns are odious, they are necessary" (*As You Like It*, III.iii.49–50)—is impossible for Othello. Instead he turns Petrarchan imagery against Desdemona—"O thou black weed, why art so lovely fair?" (IV.ii.69), praising and damning her simultaneously. His conflicts are resolved, his needs to idealize and degrade her momentarily reconciled only when he kills her, performing a sacrifice which is also a murder.[19]

Iago, though primarily the manipulator of these conflicts in the other men, is also the victim of his own. His cynical generalizations are, like those of Jaques, the parody and inverse of the romantics' claims; they are self-conscious, self-aggrandizing, and divorced from reality: "my Muse labours, / And thus she is deliver'd" (II.i.127–28). Like the other men, he accepts generalizations—especially generalizations about women—as true, provided they are "apt and of great credit" (II.i.282), "probable and palpable to thinking" (1.ii.76). Like the others, he is careful not to contaminate his fantasies with facts. Roderigo does not court

Desdemona in person, Cassio does not sue for his position directly, Othello does not immediately confront Desdemona and Cassio with his suspicions, and Iago never tries to ascertain whether Emilia is promiscuous.[20] In fact he has little contact with the women in the play. He is at ease in Act II, engaging Desdemona in witty banter, but he is subdued and almost speechless in Act IV when confronted with her misery and fidelity. Like Brabantio, Iago assumes that "consequence" will "approve" his "dream" (II.iii.58) and ignores evidence to the contrary.

Even protected as it is from reality, Iago's cynicism has cracks just as Othello's idealism does. He has a grudging admiration for Desdemona's "blest condition" (III.i.47), Othello's "constant, noble, loving nature" (II.i.284), and Cassio's "daily beauty" (v.i.19). He aspires to Cassio's job and Othello's "content" and tries to identify with their love for Desdemona—"now I do love her too" (II.i.286), though this love is immediately subsumed under notions of lust and revenge. The tension between his theoretical misogyny and his occasional intimations of Desdemona's virtue drive him to resolve the conflict, to turn that virtue "into pitch" (II.iii.351) just as his verses extravagantly praise the deserving woman, the better to be able to diminish her. Othello's conflict has the opposite issue; he murders Desdemona to redeem her from degradation.

The women in *Othello* are not murderous, and they are not foolishly idealistic or foolishly cynical as the men are. From the start they, like the comedy heroines, combine realism with romance, mockery with affection. Bianca comically reflects the qualities of the women as Roderigo does those of the men. The play explicitly identifies her with the other women in the overheard conversation about her which Othello takes to be about Desdemona and in her response to Emilia's attack: "I am no strumpet, but of life as honest / As you, that thus abuse me" (v.i.121–22). At this point, Iago tries to fabricate evidence against Bianca just as Othello, in the scene immediately following, fabricates a case against Desdemona. Bianca's active, open-eyed, enduring affection is similar to that of the other women. She neither romanticizes love nor degrades sex. She sees Cassio's callousness but accepts it wryly—"'Tis very good, I must be circumstanc'd" (III.iv.199). She mocks him to his face, but not behind his back as he does her. Her active pursuit of Cassio is in contrast to his indifference, to Roderigo's passivity, and to Othello's naïveté. When jealous, she accuses Cassio openly and continues to feel affection for him. The play's humanization of her, much like, for example, that of the bourgeois characters at the end of *Love's Labour's Lost*, underlines the folly of the male characters who see her as merely whore.

Emilia articulates the balanced view which Bianca embodies—"and though we have some grace, / Yet have we some revenge" (IV.iii.92–93). She, like other Shakespearean shrews, especially Beatrice and Paulina, combines sharp-tongued honesty with warm affection. Her views are midway between Desdemona's and Bianca's and between those of the women and those of the men. She rejects the identification with Bianca yet sympathizes with female promiscuity. She corrects Desdemona's occasional naïveté but defends her chastity. Although she comprehends male jealousy and espouses sexual equality, she seems remarkably free of jealousy herself. She wittily sees cuckoldry and marital affection as compatible: "who would not make her husband a cuckold, to make him a monarch?" (IV.iii.74–75). She understands but tolerates male fancy; the dangers of such tolerance become evident in this play as they never do in the comedies.

Desdemona's and Emilia's contrasting viewpoints in the willow scene have led critics to think of them as opposites, but they have much in common. When we first see them together, they encourage and participate in Iago's misogynist banter but reject his stereotypes. Desdemona here defends Emilia from Iago's insults just as Emilia will ultimately defend Desdemona from Othello's calumny. While Desdemona is no shrew (though she might be said to approach one in the matter of Cassio's reinstatement), her love is everywhere tempered by realism and wit like that of the comedy heroines. During courtship she hides, as they did, behind a sort of disguise—not literal male dress but the assumption of a pose of docility and indifference that conceals her passion from both her father and Othello. Like Iago's deserving woman she is one that could "think, and ne'er disclose her mind, / See suitors following, and not look behind" (II.i.156–57). Eventually, though, she takes the lead in the courtship as the heroines do; she finds an excuse to be alone with Othello, mocks him by speaking of him "dispraisingly" (III.iii.73), and traps him into a proposal using indirection not unlike Rosalind's with Orlando (I.iii.161–66).[21]

After marriage, as during courtship, Desdemona's love tempers romance with realism. She is indifferent to Cassio's elaborate compliments (II.i.87–88). She rejects Othello's desire to stop time, emphasizing instead love's growth.[22] Her healthy, casual acceptance of sexuality is evident in her banter with Iago (II.i.109–64) and with the clown (III.iv.1–18),[23] in her affirmation that she "did love the Moor, to live with him" (I.iii.248), and in her refusal to postpone consummation of "the rites for which I love him" (I.iii.257). She will not allow herself to be idealized nor will she romanticize Othello. She had spoken "dispraisingly" of him during courtship (III.iii.73), and she mocks him gently after marriage:

> Tell me, Othello: I wonder in my soul,
> What you could ask me, that I should deny?
> Or stand so mammering on?
> . . . .
> Shall I deny you? no, farewell, my lord.   (III.iii.69–71, 87)

She reminds herself, in an emphatically short line:

> nay, we must think
> Men are not gods;
> Nor of them look for such observances
> As fits the bridal. . . .   (III.iv.145–48)

Her concise statement about her love reveals its balance and health:

> I saw Othello's visage in his mind,
> And to his honours, and his valiant parts
> Did I my soul and fortunes consecrate. . . .   (I.iii.252–54)

She loves Othello for his body and mind, for his reputation and actions; she consecrates herself to him spiritually and practically.

Desdemona's spirit, clarity, and realism do not desert her entirely in the latter half of the play as many critics and performances imply. In the brothel scene, she persistently questions Othello to discover exactly what he accuses her of and even advances a hypothesis about her father, linking with herself the "state-matters" (III.iv.153) which may have transformed Othello.

Throughout the scene she defends herself as "stoutly" (III.i.45) as she had earlier defended Cassio:

> If to preserve this vessel for my lord
> From any hated foul unlawful touch,
> Be not to be a strumpet, I am none.   (IV.ii.85–87)

Her naïveté and docility in the willow scene are partly a result of her confusion and exhaustion but perhaps also partly a protective facade behind which she waits, as she did during courtship, while determining the most appropriate and fruitful reaction to Othello's rage. The conversation and the song with its alternate last verses explore alternate responses to male perfidy—acceptance *"Let nobody blame him, his scorn I approve"*—or retaliation *"If I court moe women, you'll couch with moe men"* (IV.iii.51, 56). Emilia supports retaliation—"The ills we do, their ills instruct us so" (103)—though, like Bianca, she practices acceptance. Desdemona's final couplet suggests that she is groping for a third response, one that is midway between "grace" and "revenge," one that would be more active than acceptance yet more loving than retaliation: "God me such usage send, / Not to pick bad from bad, but by bad mend!" (104–5). The lines are a reply to Emilia and a transformation of an earlier couplet of Iago's: "fairness and wit; / The one's for use, the other using it" (II.i.129–30). Desdemona will put fairness and wit to "use" in a sense that includes and goes beyond the sexual one, acknowledging and using "bad" to heal it. Her earlier command to have the wedding sheets put on her bed seems one expression of this positive usage. Just before her death, as in the brothel scene, she strives to "mend" Othello's debased view of her, transforming the "sins" he accuses her of into "loves I bear to you"; but he recorrupts them: "And for that thou diest" (V.ii.40–41).

Vanity is the central characteristic of coxcombs and is at the root of the men's murderousness in *Othello*. In the comedies, lovers like Orsino, Orlando, and Bassanio suffer their foolishness gladly, but in this play men must destroy the women who make fools of them. Jaques satirizes their particular brand of vanity in the portrait of the soldier in his seven ages speech: "Full of strange oaths and bearded like the pard, / Jealous in honor, sudden and quick in quarrel, / Seeking the bubble reputation / Even in the cannon's mouth" (II.vii.149–52). Shakespeare himself, through the men in *Othello*, questions or perhaps even satirizes conventional Renaissance notions about honor and reputation.[24] Cassio, of course, explicitly voices the men's concern with "the bubble reputation" and reveals how central their position and image are to their sense of identity: "I ha' lost my reputation! I ha' lost the immortal part, sir, of myself, and what remains is bestial" (II.iii.254–56). At the same time the men view reputation as detachable; it is a matter of rank or place, something conferred—or removed—by others. Hence Iago continues to care about the rank of lieutenant in spite of his continuing intimacy with Othello. Cassio equally relishes his title: "The lieutenant is to be saved before the ancient," he boasts (II.iii.103). Othello must fire Cassio for appearances' sake and because Montano "is of great fame in Cyprus" (III.i.46). Othello's dependence on others' "rich opinion" (II.iii.186) creates conflict in his love; "feather'd Cupid" potentially threatens "reputation" in the first act, and later he finds the scorn due the cuckold almost as difficult to bear as the loss of Desdemona.

Although they are neither "bearded like a pard" nor "full of strange oaths," the men in this play, in their vanity, desire the swaggering manliness which such characteristics conjure up. Iago successfully plays on the others' nervousness about their "manliness," driving them to acts of "malicious bravery" (I.i.100). He jovially calls them "man" while questioning their manhood or urging new proofs of it. He goads Cassio into "manly" drunkenness and good fellowship—"What, man, 'tis a night of revels, the gallants desire it" (II.iii.39). He urges Othello, "Good sir, be a man" (IV.i.65). He flatters Roderigo's manly pride: "if thou hast that within thee indeed, which I have greater reason to believe now than ever, I mean purpose, courage, and valour, this night show it" (IV.ii.213–16). His suggestive battle cries to Roderigo imply a connection between sexual and martial prowess: "Wear thy good rapier bare, and put it home. . . . fix most firm thy resolution" (V.i.2, 5); perhaps the gull's melodramatic attack on Cassio is "satisfying" even beyond Iago's "reasons," compensating him for his lack of sexual success. Inversely, cuckoldry invalidates Othello's military glories, and only the murder of Desdemona and his own suicide restore his pride in his "occupation."

Since the reputation and manliness which the men covet is achieved in competition with others, all of them are "jealous in honor"—indeed are "easily jealous" (v.ii.346) in every sense of the word. Brabantio is possessive, watchful, enraged to have the object of his esteem taken from him. Iago is critical and envious and resentful—of Cassio's position and "daily beauty" (v.i.19), of Othello's love and power, perhaps even of Roderigo's wealth and rank. Othello is sexually possessive and envious and suspicious—of Cassio, of Emilia, and (too briefly) of Iago as well as of Desdemona. While overhearing Cassio and Iago mock Bianca, Othello's wounded vanity, obsessive jealousy, and competitive concern for reputation and manliness coalesce in his terse asides with their complicated sexual/martial double entendres:

Do you triumph, Roman, do you triumph?
. . . .
So, so, so, so; laugh that wins.
. . . .
Ha' you scor'd me? Well.
. . . .
I see that nose of yours, but not that dog I shall throw 't to.
(IV.i.118, 122, 126, 140)[25]

But although Othello vows to murder Cassio, he does not do so, and Iago and Roderigo together bungle the attempt. The cowardice, clumsiness, and insecurity which belie male pretensions to valor are manifested, comically—as in the *Twelfth Night* duel—in the hesitation of Lodovico and Gratiano to answer Roderigo's and Cassio's cries for help: "Two or three groans; it is a heavy night, / These may be counterfeits, let's think 't unsafe / To come into the cry without more help" (v.i.42–44). Even after Iago's entrance, they still hang back, ascertaining his identity (51) but ignoring his cry (thus allowing him to murder Roderigo), introducing themselves (67), discovering Cassio's identity (70), and finally coming to his side following Bianca, who has just entered (75). They still offer no assistance but only perfunctory sympathy and an anticlimactic explanation: "I am sorry to find you thus, I have been to seek you" (81).

Male friendship, like male courage, is, in the play, sadly deteriorated from the Renaissance ideal. In romance and comedy the world of male friendship in which the work opens (in, for example, the *Arcadia*, *Two Gentlemen*, *Merchant of Venice*, *Love's Labour's Lost*) is shattered and transcended by romantic love. As

Othello begins, romantic love already dominates, but friendship is reasserted in perverted form. Iago's hypocritical friendship for all of the men, which aims to gratify his own will and gain power over them, is the model for male friendship in the play. Brabantio's "love" for Othello evaporates when his friend marries his daughter. Roderigo intends to use Iago though he is worse used by him. Othello has no hesitation in cashiering Cassio and ordering his death. The men's vanity, their preoccupation with rank and reputation, and their cowardice render them as incapable of friendship as they are of love.

The women, in contrast, are indifferent to reputation and partially free of vanity, jealousy, and competitiveness. Desdemona's willingness "to incur a general mock" is evident in her elopement and her defense of it, and her request to go to Cyprus. Emilia braves scorn to defend her mistress: "Let heaven, and men, and devils, let 'em all, / All, all cry shame against me, yet I'll speak" (v.ii.222–23). If Cassio's description of Bianca corresponds at all to fact, she too ignores reputation, comically, to pursue him—"she haunts me in every place. . . . she falls thus about my neck, . . . So hangs, and lolls, and weeps upon me" (iv.i.131–37)— and we see her brave the confusion of the night and the ugliness of Iago's insinuations to come to Cassio's side when he is wounded. Bianca's jealousy is also in contrast to the men's; instead of corroding within, it is quickly vented and dissipates, leaving her affection for Cassio essentially untouched. Furthermore, she makes no effort to discover her rival, to obtain "proof," or to get revenge. Likewise Emilia, though expert at noting and analyzing jealousy, seems untouched by it herself. Even her argument for the single standard is good natured; it contains little hatred of men and no personal animosity toward Iago.

Desdemona is neither jealous nor envious nor suspicious. She is not suspicious or possessive about Othello's job, his intimacy with Iago, or his "love" for Cassio but supports all three. She seems entirely lacking in the sense of class, race, rank, and hierarchy which concerns the men and is shared by Emilia, who refuses to be identified with Bianca. She treats her father, the Duke, Othello, Cassio, Iago, Emilia, even the clown, with precisely the same combination of politeness, generosity, openness, and firmness. Emilia's and Desdemona's lack of competitiveness, jealousy, and class consciousness facilitates their growing intimacy, which culminates in the willow scene. The scene, sandwiched between two exchanges by Iago and Roderigo, sharply contrasts the genuine intimacy of the women with the hypocritical friendship of the men. Emilia's concern for Desdemona is real and her advice well meant, whereas Iago's concern for Roderigo is feigned, his advice deadly—"whether he kill Cassio, / Or Cassio him, or each do kill the other, / Every way makes my game" (v.i.12–14). Roderigo accepts Iago's "satisfying reasons" (9), finding them sufficient to justify murder; Desdemona rejects Emilia's reasonable justification of adultery without rejecting the concern which prompts her to offer it. In the willow scene intimacy stretches from Emilia and Desdemona to include Barbary and the protagonist of the song; in the Roderigo/Iago scenes enmity reaches Cassio. In this play romantic love is destroyed by male friendship which itself soon disintegrates. Meanwhile, friendship between women is established and dominates the play's final scene. Othello chooses Iago's friendship over Desdemona's love temporarily and unwittingly; Emilia's choice of Desdemona over Iago is voluntary and final. Though the stakes here are higher, the friendship of Desdemona and Emilia is reminiscent of the frank, warm, witty, female friendships in the comedies—for example, between Rosalind and Celia, Beatrice and Hero, Portia and Nerissa—and of the sympathy that certain of these heroines feel even for rivals—Julia for Silvia, Viola for Olivia, Helena for Diana.

In spite of the men's vanity and competitiveness and their concern for honor and reputation, when they do act, they persistently place the blame for their actions outside themselves. Even Cassio, while abusing himself for his drunkenness, comes to personify that drunkenness as a "devil," something which invades him. Roderigo blames Iago for his failure to prosper: "Iago hurt [me]. Iago set [me] on" (v.ii.329–30). Iago, at the last, instead of boasting of the execution of his grand design (as, for example, Satan does in *Paradise Lost*), tries to shift responsibility for it elsewhere—to Bianca, to Emilia, and finally, even after the facts are known, to Othello: "I told him what I thought, and told no more / Than what he found himself was apt and true" (v.ii.177–78). Othello's longing for passivity and his denial of responsibility are intertwined throughout the play. He both sees himself as passive and desires passivity. His narrative history before the senate, the basis for our original impression of the heroic Othello, describes, when closely examined, what he has suffered rather than what he has done; he speaks of "moving accidents by flood and field; / Of hair-breadth scapes 'i th' imminent deadly breach; / Of being taken by the insolent foe; / And sold to slavery, and my redemption thence" (I.iii.135–38), and of his subsequent enslavement by Desdemona, whom he entertained with similar tales, for example, "of some distressed stroke / That my youth suffer'd" (I.iii.157–58). His farewell to arms is, curiously, a farewell to "content," to "the tranquil mind" (III.iii.354), and to the instruments of war; it is they who are seen as active and heroic, not himself. His vow of revenge, likening him to the "compulsive course" of the "Pontic sea" (III.iii.460–61), reveals the longing for external control that underlies the heroic stance. In a parallel passage after his error is revealed, he again wants to be swept along by a current even if the agency is hell-fire: "Blow me about in winds, roast me in sulphur, / Wash me in steep-down gulfs of liquid fire!" (V.ii.280–81). Two of his significant actions in the play—the dismissal of Cassio and the murder of Desdemona—are, in a sense, "compulsive," achieved, as he himself notes, only when passion "Assays to lead the way" (II.iii.198) and he feels out of control. Even at his suicide, when he is in control, he sees himself as "you" rather than "I," object rather than actor, as "being wrought, / Perplex'd in the extreme, . . . one whose subdued eyes, . . . Drops tears as fast as the Arabian trees / Their medicinal gum . . ." (V.ii.346–51). In the anecdote which accompanies his suicide he is actor and acted upon, hero and victim, and his action is again violent and enraged. Earlier he placed responsibility for his actions elsewhere—on the moon which "makes men mad" (V.ii.112), on his "fate" (266), and on Iago who "perplex'd" him; now, even while acknowledging his unworthiness, he is taking credit for punishing himself.

Desdemona's self-recriminations must be seen in the light of Othello's evasions. Critics have found them puzzling, excessive, intolerable, even neurotic;[26] perhaps they are all of these. But her unwarranted self-accusations—"beshrew me much, Emilia, / I was (unhandsome warrior as I am) / Arraigning his unkindness with my soul; / But now I find I had suborn'd the witness, / And he's indicted falsely" (III.iv.148–52)—and her false assumption of responsibility for her death—"Nobody, I myself, farewell" (v.ii.125)—provide the sharpest possible contrast to the men's excuses. Her last request, "Commend me to my kind lord," not only conveys her forgiveness but is one final active effort to mend and renew the relationship. Othello, at the last, responds to it as he dies "upon a kiss."

From the beginning, Desdemona has viewed love as risk and challenge; she has initiated while Othello has responded. She is neither the "rose" or "chrysolite" of Petrarchan convention seen by Othello nor the saint extolled by critics. She sets the stage for her wooing by an extraordinarily active listening which Othello naturally notices and describes; she would "with a greedy ear / Devour up my discourse" (1.iii.149–50). She engenders his love by her own—"She lov'd me for the dangers I had pass'd, / And I lov'd her that she did pity them" (167–68); she proposes and elopes. She is the one who challenges her father directly, who determines to go to Cyprus. She moves after marriage to bring the lovers' idiom down to earth, using all of her "plenteous wit and invention" at their reunion and in the discussion of Cassio. All the characters in the play make mention of her energizing power. Cassio, hyperbolically, attributes to her the ability to influence recalcitrant nature:

> Tempests themselves, high seas, and howling winds,
> The gutter'd rocks, and congregated sands,
> Traitors ensteep'd, to clog the guiltless keel,
> As having sense of beauty, do omit
> Their common natures, letting go safely by
> The divine Desdemona.   (ii.i.68–73)

Othello is awed by her power to move man and beast—"she might lie by an emperor's side, and command him tasks. . . . O, she will sing the savageness out of a bear" (iv.i.180–81, 184–85). Iago, in soliloquy, attributes to her unlimited power over Othello—"she may make, unmake, do what she list" (ii.iii.337). And Desdemona herself, vowing support for Cassio, reveals her sense of her own persistence and force:

> If I do vow a friendship, I'll perform it
> To the last article; my lord shall never rest,
> I'll watch him tame, and talk him out of patience;

His bed shall seem a school, his board a shrift,
I'll intermingle every thing he does
With Cassio's suit.   (III.iii.21–26)

But Desdemona does not educate Othello as the falconer does the
falcon, the teacher the pupil, or the priest the penitent. The wom-
en, for all their affection, good sense, and energy, fail to transform
or be reconciled with the men. The first reason for this is that the
sexes, so sharply differentiated in the play, badly misunderstand
each other. The men, as we have seen, persistently misconceive
the women; the women fatally overestimate the men. Each sex,
trapped in its own values and attitudes, misjudges the other. Iago
acts on the hypothesis that women, on the one hand, share his
concern with reputation and propriety—"Be wise, and get you
home" (v.ii.224) he orders Emilia—and, on the other, enact his
salacious fantasies. Othello assumes that just as he is the stereotypical soldier, foreigner, older husband, so Desdemona will be
the stereotypical mistress, Venetian, young bride. He responds to
Iago's claim to knowledge about Desdemona—"knowing what I
am, I know what she shall be"—with comic enthusiasm: "O,
thou art wise, 'tis certain" (iv.i.73–74). Likewise, the women attribute their own qualities to the men. Desdemona projects her
own lack of jealousy onto Othello. Emilia attributes to Iago her
own capacity for empathy: "I know it grieves my husband, / As if
the case were his" (III.iii.3–4). Even Bianca, because she does not
view herself as a whore in her relationship with Cassio, is surprised that he should treat her as one.

 The men see the women as whores and then refuse to toler-
ate their own projections. The women recognize the foolishness
of the men's fancies but are all too tolerant of them. Emilia steals
the handkerchief for the sake of Iago's "fantasy" (III.iii.303) and
assures the success of his plot. Desdemona's salutation to Othello
in Act III is lamentably prophetic—"be it as your fancies teach
you, / Whate'er you be, I am obedient" (89–90). He leaves her to be
instructed in her whoredom. The failure of the women's power
can be more fully understood by examining the handkerchief
which is its symbol.

 Both Othello's original description of the handkerchief and
its part in the plot reveal that it is a symbol of women's civilizing
power. It has passed from female sibyl to female "charmer" to

Othello's mother to Desdemona. Othello is merely a necessary intermediary between his mother and his wife—"she dying, gave it me / And bid me, when my fate would have me wive, / To give it her" (III.iv.61–63). Its creator, the sibyl, who "In her prophetic fury sew'd the work," and its next owner, the Egyptian charmer who "could almost read / The thoughts of people," place the source of its power in women's intuitive knowledge. This knowledge enables them to use and control sexuality. The middle ground which they find between lust and abstinence (as the men in the play cannot do) is suggested in the description of the process by which the handkerchief is made. The worms which did "breed" the silk, emblems of death, sexuality, and procreation, are "hallow'd." The thread which the worms spin naturally from themselves is artificially improved, "dyed in mummy" which is "conserve[d] of maiden's hearts." The handkerchief then represents sexuality controlled by chastity. Its function is to induce love and control it:

> . . . she told her, while she kept it
> 'Twould make her amiable, and subdue my father
> Entirely to her love: but if she lost it,
> Or made a gift of it, my father's eye
> Should hold her loathly, and his spirits should hunt
> After new fancies   (III.iv.56–61)

It represents women's ability to moderate men's erratic (and erotic) "fancies," to "subdue" their promiscuity, and perhaps, by extension, their vanity, romanticism, jealousy, and rage as well. These fancies are associated here, as in the comedies, with men's deluded and capricious "eye." At the play's beginning, Desdemona, like the comedy heroines, has this ability in abundance, as Othello affirms:

> Excellent wretch, perdition catch my soul,
> But I do love thee, and when I love thee not,
> Chaos is come again.   (III.iii.91–93)

But the handkerchief is lost, the female power it symbolizes evaporates, and comedy gives way to tragedy.[27]

After the handkerchief's original loss, all of the characters, men and women alike, symbolically misuse and misinterpret it; as a result, all the love relationships in the play are disrupted. The abuse begins as Othello pushes it aside, rejecting Desdemona's loving attempt to heal the "pain" on his forehead, and Emilia picks it up to give it to her husband.[28] In Iago's hands its function is reversed; it is used to give Iago power over Othello and Desdemona and to induce in him loathing for her. Iago's first mention of it incites Othello to reject love and embrace vengeance (III.iii.441–86). Now the hero proceeds to reinterpret the handkerchief as *his* love token—a pledge of his love and of Desdemona's fidelity—"She is protectress of her honour too, / May she give that?" (IV.i.14–15). Hence its loss provides "proof" of his suspicions. The reinterpretation continues in his altered description of its history in the last act. As he uses it to support his "cause" against Desdemona, it becomes "the recognizance and pledge of love, / Which *I* first gave her; ... an antique token / *My father gave my mother*" (V.ii.215–18, emphasis added). It is now a symbol of the male love which Desdemona has betrayed; hence she must be punished—"Yet she must die, else she'll betray more men" (V.ii.6).[29]

Desdemona, too, alters her view of the handkerchief. Instinctively using it to cure Othello's pain, she almost succeeds. She "loves" the handkerchief (III.iii.297) and recognizes the danger of its loss. But when pressed by Othello, she rejects its significance—"Then would to God that I had never seen it!" (III.iv.75). Her rejection reflects the failure of her power. In Desdemona's earlier discussion of Cassio she was in control; now her persistence is foolish and provokes Othello's rage. Even in the early part of this scene Desdemona deftly parries and "mends" Othello's ugly insinuations, turning his implied vices into virtues:

> OTHELLO. . . . . this hand is moist, my lady.
> DESDEMONA. It yet has felt no age, nor known no sorrow.
> . . . .
> OTHELLO. For here's a young and sweating devil here,
>   That commonly rebels: 'tis a good hand,
>   A frank one.
> DESDEMONA. You may indeed say so,
>   For 'twas that hand that gave away my heart. (III.iv.32–41)

But after the tale of the handkerchief she loses the initiative. She tries to regain it by—just barely—lying and by changing the subject. But the attempt to calm and heal Othello fails. Her lie, like

Ophelia's similarly well-intentioned lie to Hamlet, signals the loss of her maiden's power and innocence; it confirms—Othello believes—his notions about female depravity as Ophelia's lie confirms Hamlet's similar views. Both women, rejected by their lovers, do not regain the initiative in the relationship.

The handkerchief next creates conflict in the Iago/Emilia and Cassio/Bianca relationships. Both men use it, as Othello has done, to consolidate their power over women. When Emilia regrets its theft, Iago snatches it from her and dismisses her, "Be not you known on 't" (III.iii.324). Cassio similarly gives orders to Bianca regarding it and dismisses her (III.iv.188–89). She, though jealous, agrees to copy the work; her willingness to be "circumstanc'd" (199) is a flaw which all the women share. Later, however, she returns the handkerchief in a scene that is a parallel and contrast to that when the handkerchief was lost. Bianca, like Othello, is jealous. The handkerchief is flung down here as it was pushed aside there, and it lies on the stage ignored by the couple, who go off to a possible reconciliation. But Bianca's refusal to be used by the handkerchief or by Cassio leads to a truce and a supper engagement, whereas Othello's refusal to be healed by it had opened the breach in his relationship with Desdemona which would culminate in her murder.

Eventually the handkerchief's original function is reestablished; it becomes the vehicle through which civilizing control is returned to the women. The reference to it by Othello in the last scene enlightens Emilia; it ends Iago's domination of her, engenders her accusations of Othello and Iago, and provides her (and through her, Othello) with positive proof of Desdemona's chastity. Emilia, stealing the handkerchief, is the catalyst for the play's crisis; revealing its theft, she is the catalyst for the play's denouement.

The reiteration of "husband" and "mistress" in the last scene emphasizes the play's central division and the "divided duty" of Emilia. Like her mistress in the play's first act, she shifts her allegiance unhesitatingly. Instead of tolerating both Iago's "fancy" and Desdemona's virtue, she denounces the one and affirms the other. She questions Iago's manliness: "Disprove this villain, if thou be'st a man; / He says thou told'st him that his wife was false, / I know thou didst not, thou art not such a villain" (v.ii.173–75). Then she rejects the wifely virtues of silence, obedience, and prudence which are demanded of her: "I will not charm my tongue, I am bound to speak" (185). A few lines later she adds, " 'Tis proper I obey him, but not now: / Perchance, Iago, I will ne'er go home" (197–98). Her epithet just before she is stabbed appropriately refers to all the men in the play—to Iago, to whose taunts it is a response; to Othello, who responds to it; and to Cassio, Roderigo, and Brabantio as well: "O murderous cox-comb! what should such a fool / Do with so good a woman?" (234–35). Emilia, another "good woman," dies without self-justi-fication or calls for revenge; instead she testifies to Desdemona's innocence and love just as her mistress had done at her own death. Emilia's request to be laid by her mistress, her reiteration of the willow song, and her own attempts to "by bad mend" com-plete her identification with Desdemona.

Thus in the last scene the gulf between men and women widens. Emilia's confession is not just a refusal of obedience; it destroys Iago's plot and refutes his philosophy, which requires that she act according to her own self-interest. Iago's Othello-like response to his wife's betrayal is to call her "villainous whore" and stab her in a vengeful fury, thus validating her confession and her epithet. With his power evaporated, philosophy repudiated, and guilt revealed, he has no reason to talk and nothing to say; it is his tongue which is "charmed," not hers. After the stabbing he makes no further reference to Emilia, nor does she to him; all connections between them are severed. Bianca has been earlier separated from Cassio, and she is absent from the last scene. We can perhaps assume that Cassio, in his new post, will be even less eager to be "woman'd" (III.iv.193) or "damn'd in a fair wife" (I.i.21) than he was earlier.

The division between Othello and Desdemona remains, though it is not absolute. Desdemona, as we have seen, strives to sustain the relationship up to the moment of her death, and in the last scene Othello does move away from the men and toward the women. Othello, like Desdemona and Emilia, dies testifying to love, whereas Iago lives, silent. Othello, like the women, stays to acknowledge at least partial responsibility for his actions, while Iago flees, accepting none. But Othello cannot abandon his mas-culine identity by asserting a new one: "That's he that was Othello; here I am" (v.ii.285). Instead of applying Emilia's accusation to himself, he stabs Iago; the two men are one in their desire to place guilt elsewhere and eliminate its bearer. With Iago's exit Othello grows concerned, characteristically, with his honor and a suicide weapon. Emilia's death, though it reenacts Desdemona's, is a mere parenthesis in his search, scarcely noticed by him. The "grimly comic little practical joke"[30] he plays on Montano is reminiscent of Iago's larger, grimmer, and not so comic plot. Although male bombast is virtually silenced at the end of this play as it is in the comedies—Iago "never will speak word" (305) and the terseness and precision of Roderigo's dying epithet for Iago ("O inhuman dog") are equalled in Cassio's epitaph for the dead Othello ("For he was great of heart")—Othello's rhetoric continues unchecked. His last speech is his own brand of Iago's "motive-hunting." Throughout the scene, he persists in seeing himself and Desdemona as ill-fated, unlucky. Desdemona is still imagined as the remote, passive, perfect object of romantic love. He says she is "cold, cold, my girl, / Even like thy chastity" (276–77) and associates her with "monumental alabaster" (5), with an "entire and perfect chrysolite" (146), and with a "pearl" (348). He leaves the play as he had entered it, extolling his services to the state (cf. I.ii.17 ff.), confessing, asking for justice and judgment (cf. I.iii.122–25), telling stories about his past, and putting his "unhoused free condition" into its ultimate "confine" for love of Desdemona. Because his character remains essentially unchanged (he still combines romanticism and cynicism, confidence and insecurity, love and folly), his relationship with Desdemona remains symbolically—as perhaps literally—unconsummated.

Indeed, as in the comedies, most of the characters remain where they started—or return there. Here there is not even the tentative movement beyond folly that we find in the comedy heroes. Roderigo was upbraiding Iago in the play's first lines and is still doing so in the letter that is his last communication. Cassio has again received a promotion and is again caught up in events which he does not comprehend. Brabantio, had he lived, likely would have responded to Desdemona's death exactly as he did to her elopement: "This sight would make him do a desperate turn" (v.ii.208). Iago, like Jaques, Malvolio, and Shylock, the villains of the comedies, is opaque and static . His cryptic last word, "what you know, you know" (304), reveals no more about him than did his explanatory soliloquies. Desdemona, just before her death, challenges Othello as she had challenged her father and defends herself with the same straightforward precision she used before the Senate:

> And have you mercy too! I never did
> Offend you in my life, . . . never lov'd Cassio,
> But with such general warranty of heaven,
> As I might love: I never gave him token.   (v.ii.59–62)

Bianca comes forth to seek Cassio at her last appearance as at her first; both times she frankly declares her affection and is brusquely dismissed. Emilia's function and attitudes do change, however, though her character perhaps does not. She moves from tolerating men's fancies to exploding them and from prudent acceptance to courageous repudiation. She ceases to function as a reconciler of the views of the men and the women, and the separation between them becomes absolute.

The play's ending is less like tragedy than like cankered comedy. The *Liebestod* is not mutual and triumphant as in the tragedies of love; indeed the final speech does not even refer to the love of Desdemona and Othello. It does not look backward over the events of the play, creating the sense of completion and exhaustion found in *King Lear*; it does not look forward to the new beginning promised in *Macbeth*. As in the comedies, the men are chastened and their rhetoric somewhat subdued, but they remain relatively unchanged. They do not go forth to do penance like the men in the abortive comedy *Love's Labour's Lost*; even that play's tentative movement toward transformation and reconciliation is absent here. The conflict between the men and the women has not been eliminated or resolved. The men have been unable to turn the women's virtue into pitch, but the women have been unable to mend male fancy. So the comic resolution of male with female, idealism with realism, wit with sex is never achieved. The play concludes, not with symmetrical pairing off, but with one final triangle: Emilia, Desdemona, and Othello dead on the wedding sheets. Instead of the images of fertile marriage beds which the comedies provide, we are made here to look with Iago, ominously a survivor, at the "tragic lodging of this bed"; "lodging" here, with its resonance from other Shakespearean uses,[31] concludes the play on the note of arrested growth, devastated fertility. "The object poisons sight"; it signifies destruction without catharsis, release without resolution. The pain and division of the ending are unmitigated, and the clarification it offers is intolerable. "Let it be hid" is our inevitable response.

NOTES

1. Leslie Fiedler, *The Stranger in Shakespeare* (New York: Stein and Day, 1972), p. 169. The three he refers to are Emilia, Bianca, and Barbary. His description of Desdemona after her marriage as "a passive, whimpering Griselda" (p. 142) suggests that his statistics might more accurately be put at four out of four.

2. F. R. Leavis, "Diabolic Intellect and the Noble Hero or The Sentimentalist's *Othello,*" in *The Common Pursuit* (London: Chatto & Windus, 1952), pp. 136–59; *Coleridge's Shakespearean Criticism,* ed. Thomas M. Raysor (Cambridge, Mass.: Harvard University Press, 1930), I. 121–25; A. C. Bradley, *Shakespearean Tragedy,* 2d ed. (London: Macmillan, 1964), pp. 175–242; H. Granville-Barker, *Prefaces to Shakespeare* (London: B. T. Batsford, 1958), II, 3–149; G. Wilson Knight, *The Wheel of Fire* (1930; rpt. London: Oxford University Press, 1946), pp. 107–31; John Bayley, *The Characters of Love* (New York: Basic Books, 1960), pp. 125–201; Helen Gardner, "The Noble Moor," *Proceedings of the British Academy,* 41 (1955), 189–205.

3. On Othello's music, see especially Knight, *Wheel of Fire,* pp. 107–18, and Bayley, *Characters of Love,* pp. 150–59. On Iago, see especially Bradley, *Shakespearean Tragedy,* pp. 207–37, and Knight, pp. 125–26.

4. T. S. Eliot, "Shakespeare and the Stoicism of Seneca," *Selected Essays* (New York: Harcourt Brace, 1950), pp. 110–11; A. P. Rossiter, *Angel with Horns* (New York: Theatre Arts, 1961), pp. 189–208; H. A. Mason, *Shakespeare's Tragedies of Love* (New York: Barnes & Noble, 1970), pp. 59–161; William Empson, "Honest in *Othello*" in *The Structure of Complex Words* (London: Chatto & Windus, 1951), pp. 218–49; Leo Kirschbaum, "The Modern Othello," *ELH,* 11 (1944), 283–96.

5. *Othello,* Arden Shakespeare, ed. M. R. Ridley (Cambridge, Mass.: Harvard University Press, 1958), ii.i.200. All *Othello* quotations are from this edition, for I find persuasive Ridley's arguments for using the 1622 Quarto rather than the First Folio as his copy text. All other plays are quoted from *The Complete Signet Classic Shakespeare,* Sylvan Barnet, gen. ed. (New York: Harcourt Brace Jovanovich, 1963, 1972).

6. For such quotations see Fiedler, *Stranger in Shakespeare,* p. 158, and Mason, *Tragedies of Love,* pp. 75–76. On Iago's honesty, see Empson, "Honest in *Othello,*" and Mason, p. 75.

7. "Everyone in the play fails to understand her [Desdemona], and fails

her. . . ." Philip Edwards, *Shakespeare and the Confines of Art* (London: Methuen, 1968), p 123.

8. Neither Rossiter nor Leavis mentions Desdemona except as the object of Othello's love or jealousy. Even in D. A. Traversi's more general discussion in *An Approach to Shakespeare*, 2d ed. (Garden City, N.Y.: Doubleday, 1956), she is the subject of only a couple of sentences.

9. Bradley, *Shakespearean Tragedy*, p. 179. See also Granville-Barker, *Prefaces*, p. 124; Knight, *Wheel of Fire*, pp. 119–20.

10. Mason, *Tragedies of Love*, p. 147. See also Fiedler, *Stranger in Shakespeare*, passim.

11. Robert Dickes, "Desdemona: An Innocent Victim?" *American Imago*, 27 (1970), 279–97; Fiedler, *Stranger in Shakespeare*, pp. 141–42; Richard Flatter, *The Moor of Venice* (London: William Heinemann, 1950), pp. 72–74; G. Bonnard, "Are Othello and Desdemona Innocent or Guilty?" *English Studies*, 30 (1949), 175–84; Jan Kott, *Shakespeare Our Contemporary* (with three new essays), trans. Boleslaw Taborski (Garden City, N.Y.: Doubleday/Anchor, 1966), pp. 118–19.

12. This is true even in R. B. Heilman's *Magic in the Web* (Lexington: University of Kentucky Press, 1956) and in Marvin Rosenberg's *The Masks of Othello* (Berkeley: University of California Press, 1961), books which seek for Desdemona a middle ground between passivity and aggressiveness and which frequently illuminate the details of the play.

13. I do·not mean to suggest that critics have not noted that love is a theme in the play. This theme is, of course, at the center of John Bayley's study of *Othello* in *The Characters of Love*. Helen Gardner emphasizes the play's concern with the union of romantic love and marriage in "The Noble Moor" as well as in her useful survey of criticism, "'Othello': A Retrospect, 1900–67," in *Shakespeare Survey*, 21 (1968), 1–11. Rosalie Colie in "*Othello* and the Problematics of Love" in *Shakespeare's Living Art* (Princeton, N.J.: Princeton University Press, 1974), pp. 148–67, brilliantly sees *Othello* as an "unmetaphoring" and a reanimation of the conventions of Renaissance love lyrics.

14. The translation is Geoffrey Bullough's in *Narrative and Dramatic Sources of Shakespeare*, VII (London: Routledge & Kegan Paul, 1973), 239. Subsequent Italian quotations are from M. Giovanbattista Giraldi Cinthio, *De Gli Hecatommithi* (Vinegia: G. Scotto, 1566), vol. I. Page numbers are given in the text and translations are my own.

15. Superficial resemblances to comedy have often been noted. Barbara Heliodora C. De Mendonça in "'Othello': A Tragedy Built on a Comic Structure," *Shakespeare Survey*, 21 (1968), 31–38; and Richard Zacha, "Iago and the *Commedia dell' arte*," *Arlington Quarterly*, 2 (Autumn, 1969), 98–116, discuss the play's similarities of subject, plot, and character with the *commedia dell'arte*. Mason, *Tragedies of Love*, pp. 73–97, and Fiedler, *Stranger in Shakespeare*, pp. 43–55, show how the first act or the first two acts form a Shakespearean comedy in miniature.

16. Mason, *Tragedies of Love*, pp. 73–97, esp. p. 88.
17. See Alvin Kernan, Introduction to *Othello* in *The Complete Signet Classic Shakespeare*, and Fiedler, *Stranger in Shakespeare*.
18. Fiedler, *Stranger in Shakespeare*, p. 194.
19. See Winifred M. T. Nowottny's excellent discussion of the way in which the murder reconciles Othello's conflicts in "Justice and Love in *Othello*," *University of Toronto Quarterly*, 21 (1951–52), esp. pp. 340–44.
20. We are reminded of Orlando, who writes poems on trees instead of seeking Rosalind.
21. Othello, along with many critics, fails to see that her approach is calculated and witty.
22. Rosalind likewise educates Orlando in the necessities of time. In *Othello* Bianca as well as Desdemona stresses its passage. Compare her "What, keep a week away? seven days and nights?"; "I pray you bring me on the way a little, / And say, if I should see you soon at night" (III.iv.171, 195–96) with Desdemona's "Why then to-morrow night, or Tuesday morn, / Or Tuesday noon, or night, or Wednesday morn" (III.iii.61–62).
23. Critics have been surprisingly intolerant of this episode, but Rosalind, Portia, and the ladies in *Love's Labour's Lost* engage more wholeheartedly in such banter without compromising their reputations.
24. David L. Jeffrey and Patrick Grant suggest in "Reputation in *Othello*," *Shakespeare Studies*, 6 (1970), 197–208, that Othello corrupts the ideal of reputation, desiring "bad fame" rather than "good fame," secular rather than heavenly glory. It seems difficult to determine whether the characters are to be viewed as debasing the ideal or whether it is the ideal itself which Shakespeare is questioning. At any rate, Curtis Brown Watson, in *Shakespeare and the Renaissance Concept of Honor* (Princeton, N.J.: Princeton University Press, 1960), pp. 209–11, 377–79, oversimplifies the relationship of the men in *Othello* to the ideals of honor and reputation. They are clearly not straightforward representatives of these ideals.
25. Editors have been unclear about the precise implications of "Roman" and "triumph," but the latter perhaps contains a sexual innuendo as in Sonnet 151: "My soul doth tell my body that he may / Triumph in love; flesh stays no farther reason, / But, rising at thy name, doth point out thee, / As his triumphant prize." "Scor'd" seems to mean not only "defaced," as it is usually glossed, but also to have its contemporary meaning of "outscored," perhaps with sexual undertones. There is no *OED* citation for this sense before 1882, but "score" in the sense "to add up" is used punningly and bawdily in *All's Well that Ends Well*: "When he swears oaths, bid him drop gold, and take it; / After he scores, he never pays the score. / Half won is match well made; match and well make it; / He ne'er pays after-debts, take it before" (IV.iii.228–31). The first "score" is glossed by Ribner, in *The Complete Works of Shakespeare*, ed. Irving Ribner and George Lyman Kittredge (Wal-

tham, Mass.: Xerox College Publishing, 1971), p. 461, as "(a) obtains goods on credit, (b) hits the mark, as in archery," and perhaps some of the latter sense is present in the *Othello* passage too. Othello's reference to throwing Cassio's nose to an unseen dog has also puzzled editors. Plucking, tweaking, or cutting off the nose was an act of humiliation and revenge, and here Othello imagines himself getting back at Cassio for his "triumph." But "nose" appears frequently in the plays with bawdy implications—in Mercutio's Queen Mab speech, in the tavern scenes in *2 Henry IV*, in the banter between Charmian, Iras, and Alexas in *Antony and Cleopatra*, and in *Troilus and Cressida*, where Troilus is described by Helen as "In love, i' faith, to the very tip of the nose" (III.i.125)—and it seems likely that the bawdy sense is intended here, especially as the preceding line is, "Now he tells how she pluck'd him to my chamber." It is perhaps possible that, on this level of meaning, the "dog" Othello does not see and to whom he will throw Cassio's "nose" is Desdemona. At any rate, sex and combat seem fused and confused here as in Othello's other asides.

26. Dickes, "Desdemona, an Innocent Victim?" and Stephen Reid, "Desdemona's Guilt," *American Imago*, 27 (1970), 279–97, 245–62.

27. It is noteworthy that in Shakespeare's plays this power belongs almost always to maidens—to the women in *Love's Labour's Lost*, to Rosalind, Portia, Viola, Perdita, Marina, and Miranda. In married women it is in abeyance (Gertrude), used against them (Titania), perverted (Goneril, Regan, Lady Macbeth), or lost (Desdemona, Helena, Hermione, Imogen). Cleopatra is an exception to this generalization as to every other; she retains her power long after losing her maiden status.

28. Shakespeare's alteration of his source, removing Iago from an active role in the theft of the handkerchief and dramatizing its loss in these particular circumstances, emphasizes the handkerchief's symbolism and the active role played by Desdemona and Emilia in the misunderstandings that follow from its original loss.

29. Critics also wilfully reinterpret—and misinterpret—the handkerchief. G. R. Elliott asserts that Othello gave it to her "with the secret hope that it would hold her faithful to him, as faithful as his 'amiable . . . mother' (56, 59) was to his father until her death" and explains further in a footnote the basis of this assertion: "It is surely obvious that Othello's dying mother in bidding him to give the handkerchief to his future wife was concerned for the faithfulness, not of her son, but of that unknown woman," *Flaming Minister: A Study of Othello* (Durham, N.C.: Duke University Press, 1953), p. 146. David Kaula, in "Othello Possessed: Notes on Shakespeare's Use of Magic and Witchcraft," *Shakespeare Studies*, 2 (1966), is relieved when Othello alters his story of the handkerchief's history: "Nevertheless, the fact that Othello's *father* now becomes the one who gave his mother the handkerchief converts it into a more plausible love token than the horrific thing contrived by the superannuated sibyl in her prophetic fury. In

communication once more with the civilized representatives of the Venetian order, Othello, even though he has yet to suffer his awakening, is returning to a more normal view of love and marriage" (pp. 126–27). While I cannot accept this view of the handkerchief, much in the article is illuminating, especially the discussion (p. 125) of the implications of the augmented first syllable of "handkerchief," "hank," whose meanings include "a restraining or curbing hold; a power of check or restraint" (*OED*. 4, fig. a).

30. Granville-Barker, *Prefaces*, p. 89.
31. See *Richard II*, iii.iii.161; *2 Henry VI*, iii.ii.176; and *Macbeth*, iv.i.55, where "lodging" is used to describe the destruction of young corn on the brink of maturity (as it still is today in central Illinois). Ridley cites these parallels in his detailed and informative note on the word in the Arden edition (p. 197) demonstrating that Quarto's "lodging" is richer than Folio's more familiar "loading."

Lady Macbeth
"Infirm of purpose"

JOAN LARSEN KLEIN

In the Elizabethan marriage service, in the Elizabethan homily on
marriage, in books like Vives's *Instruction of a Christen Woman*
and Tilney's discourse on marriage, women were said to be weaker than men in reason and physical strength, prone to fears and
subject to the vagaries of their imaginations. The second account
of the creation in Genesis even suggests that the perfect woman
was an afterthought, created later than the perfect man, shaped
from his rib in order to forestall his loneliness and to be a "helpe
meet for him" (Chapter II, verse 20).[1] The serpent was able to seduce Eve, many theologians said, because she was the weaker ves-
sel. When she seduced Adam, they concluded, she reversed the
order and denied the purpose of her own creation. On account of
the original created estate of woman and the curse of the Fall,
therefore, it was said that women were bound by nature and law
to obey their husbands as well as their God. Only when husbands
acted in opposition to divine law, said all the treatises, could their
wives disobey them. Then, however, the chief duty of good wives
was to try lovingly to bring their errant husbands back into virtuous ways.[2]

 Lady Macbeth violates her chief duty to her husband and
her God when she urges Macbeth to murder his king. For these
and other reasons, most critics believe that Lady Macbeth, the

*An earlier version of this essay was presented at a Special Session
on Feminist Criticism of Shakespeare at the MLA Annual Convention,
December 1977, Chicago, Illinois.*

"fiend-like queen" (v.viii.69),[3] lapses from womanliness.[4] I want to suggest, however, that Shakespeare intended us to think that Lady Macbeth, despite her attempt to unsex herself, is never able to separate herself completely from womankind—unlike her husband, who ultimately becomes less and worse than a man. At the beginning Lady Macbeth embodies certain Renaissance notions about women. But when she wills actions that are opposed to the dictates of charity and fails in her chief duty, her wifely roles of hostess and helpmate are perverted. She is deprived of even these perverted roles in the banquet scene as Macbeth abandons his roles of host and husband. Her occupation gone, Lady Macbeth is left anguished, alone, and guilty in ways which are particularly "feminine."

Lady Macbeth embodies in extremity, I think, the Renaissance commonplace that women reflect God's image less clearly than men and that consequently women are less reasonable than men. Right reason enables mankind to choose between good and evil and thus to know right from wrong.[5] Lady Macbeth, however, seems to have repudiated whatever glimmerings of right reason she might once have possessed. She does not consider the ethical or the religious aspects of murder. She seems to believe, for instance, that ambition is attended with "illness" (i.v.18). That which one craves "highly," she says, cannot be got "holily" (18–19). The dying grooms' prayers for blessing and Macbeth's inability to say "Amen," she insists, must not be considered "so deeply" (ii.ii.26–29). She refuses, in fact, to think of "These deeds . . . After these ways" (32–33). Thus she seems to have forgotten or repudiated the dictates of reason and her own conscience. Shakespeare may even intend us to conclude that she has renounced her God.

Having put away the knowledge of good, Lady Macbeth is without charity. She is without, in other words, the virtue enjoined on mankind by Christ when He told man to love his neighbor as himself, the virtue which gave man the will to act upon his knowledge of good.[6] Macbeth himself appears to be imperfectly rational and infected in will. That the witches wait for no other purpose than to meet him suggests that he has long since opened his mind to demonic temptation, for "that olde and craftie enemie of ours, assailes none . . . except he first finde an entresse reddy for him."[7] In fact, it is Macbeth who seems originally to have thought of murdering Duncan (see I.vii.47–48). Yet Macbeth, unlike Lady Macbeth, can at first perceive goodness. He knows that "Duncan . . . hath been / So clear in his great office" (I.vii.16–18) and that Banquo is royal "of nature" (III.i.50). He also, for one short moment, seems to understand that charity, not cruelty, ought to motivate human action and that pity, not cruelty, is strong—that pity strides the blast and tears drown the wind. His momentary vision of pity as a newborn babe, furthermore, evokes not only the image of Christ triumphant but also the emblem of charity—a naked babe sucking the breast.[8] We should remember, however, that charity was associated more often with women than it was with men because women, like children, were thought to be physically weak: "hit is natural for women to be kynde and gentyll / bicause they be feble / and nede the ayde of other," said Vives (sig. M^v). But the woman who denies her nature and is consumed with "outragious ire and cruelte," said Vives, "hit is jeoperdye / leest she be distroyed / and have everlastynge payne / bothe in this lyfe / and in an other" (sig. M^v-Mii). Portia argues for mercy; Cordelia practices it. It is Macbeth, however, not Lady Macbeth, who has right reason enough to glimpse both the strength of pity and its chief resting place. But he never acts upon his vision and she never sees it.

Having apparently denied her God, Lady Macbeth puts her trust in the murdering ministers of Hell. Thus she disobeys the first rule of marriage as it was formulated in the sixteenth century. A wife, said Tilney in the language of natural fruition common to *Macbeth*, must trust wholly in God: a wife "must being of hir selfe weake, and unable besides hir owne diligence, put hir whole trust in the first . . . author thereof, whome if she serve faythfullye, wyll no doubt, make thys Flower [of Friendship in holye Matrimonie] to spring up in hir aboundantly" (sig. E[7]). Nothing in life can prosper, say all the authorities, when faith is dead, and the commandments of Christ denied.[9] Thus, despite her wish to aid her husband, Lady Macbeth cannot give him that lasting companionship under God which the *Homilies* saw as true marriage. Furthermore, although Lady Macbeth may once have had a child, its absence from her life and her willingness to contemplate its destruction contradict the *Homilies'* view that children are an end of marriage, a blessing upon their parents, and a means of enlarging God's kingdom.[10] Macbeth at first tries crookedly to keep to the ways of faith even as he dwells on the prospect of damnation and feels the loss of grace: "Wherefore could not I pronounce 'Amen'?" he asks (II.ii.30). But Lady Macbeth refuses from the outset to consider the first author of her being, the last judge of her actions, and the life to come.

Perhaps because of her separation from God, Lady Macbeth is as mistaken about her own nature as she is about her marriage. She says she could dash out the brains of her suckling child. She thinks of wounding with her keen knife. But she has no child and can not murder the sleeping Duncan. She begs to be unsexed, but is never able to assume in fact what she wrongly believes is the masculine attribute of "direst cruelty" (I.v.41). Lady Macbeth, therefore, cannot act out of cruelty. But she refuses to act out of what Latimer called "charitable" love.[11] As she forfeits the power for good which derives from the practice of pity, she is left only with loss and weakness. She is further enfeebled to the point of madness by what Bright called the awareness of sin.[12] Along this path to despair, she does not even seem to notice that she also loses her husband. But Macbeth loses too. He exchanges the fellowship of his badly founded marriage to Lady Macbeth for union with the weird sisters. He exchanges his hopes for men-children born to his wife for the grisly finger of a birth-strangled babe and tormenting visions of the crowned children of other men.

Despite Lady Macbeth's heavy ignorance of Christian marriage, she conceives of herself almost exclusively as a wife, a helpmate. Thus she epitomizes at the same time that she perverts Renaissance views of the woman's role. Macbeth, she says, shall be what he is "promised" (I.v.15). "Great Glamis" must have the "golden round"(20,26). When Lady Macbeth reads Macbeth's letter, she speaks not to herself but to her husband: "Thou wouldst be great . . . wouldst not play false, / And yet wouldst wrongly win" (16–20). (Macbeth, on the contrary, absents himself in soliloquy even in company.) Lady Macbeth will "chastise" Macbeth with the "valor" of her tongue so that he, not she, might have what he wants (25). Nowhere does she mention Macbeth's implied bribe—that she, too, has been promised "greatness" (12). When Lady Macbeth later speaks to Macbeth in person, she measures what she takes to be his love for her by his willingness to murder. But love for Lady Macbeth never figures in Macbeth's stated desires for the kingdom or for an heir. Nor does he give in to her persuasions out of love. On the contrary, he responds to her only when she impeaches his manliness and arouses his fear. "If we should fail?" (I.vii.59), he asks. In a grim perversion of married companionship, Lady Macbeth responds by assuming the feminine role of comforter and helper: "we'll not fail" (61). But Macbeth never includes Lady Macbeth in any of his visions of the deed successfully done.

Although Lady Macbeth always thinks of herself as a wife, Macbeth thinks of himself as a husband only when she forces him to do so. Otherwise he is concerned solely for himself: "I am Thane of Cawdor . . . My thought . . . Shakes . . . my single state of man" (I.iii.133–40). (The witches recognize Macbeth's self-interest better than Lady Macbeth does; they never discuss her with him.) In his soliloquy during the first banquet, Macbeth uses the royal *we* proleptically when he describes his readiness to jump the life to come and the first person singular when he thinks about his own ambition and his present relationship to a loving king. Nowhere in this soliloquy does he speak of a wife or future queen. When Macbeth goes to murder Duncan, it is the fatal vision of his own mind that materializes before him. The "I" sees the dagger of his own fantasy and the "I" draws the dagger of steel. After the murder of Duncan, there is almost no husband to talk to a wife, for Lady Macbeth can scarcely reach Macbeth. "What do you mean?" (II.ii.39), she asks him. "Be not lost / So poorly in your thoughts" (70–71), she begs him, quite uselessly. After the murder of Banquo, Macbeth is wholly dominated by self: "For mine own good / All causes shall give way" (III.iv.135–36).

In spite of the view of some critics that Lady Macbeth is the evil force behind Macbeth's unwilling villainy, she seems to epitomize the sixteenth-century belief that women are passive, men active: "nature made man more strong and couragiouse, the woman more weake fearefull and scrupulouse, to the intente that she for her feblenesse shulde be more circumspecte, the man for his strengthe moche more adventurouse."[13] It is Macbeth, the man, who must be the "same in [his] own act and valor / As [he is] in desire" (I.vii.40–41), Macbeth, who must "screw [his] courage to the sticking point" (60). Lady Macbeth's threats of violence, for all their force and cruelty, are empty fantasies. It is Macbeth who converts them to hard reality. He does so in terms of his single self and his singular act: "I am settled, and bend up / Each corporal agent to this terrible feat" (79–80).

One can suggest, I think, that the virtues which Lady Macbeth sees as defects in Macbeth's character and obstacles to his success are in fact the better parts of her own being—which she determines to suppress. She says that she fears Macbeth's nature because "It is too full o' th' milk of human kindness" (i.v.15), but we have never seen Macbeth "kind." On the contrary, we were told about a man whose sword "smoked with bloody execution" and were shown a man whose thought was taken over by murderous "imaginings" (i.ii.18; i.iii.138). It is Lady Macbeth who knows "How tender 'tis to love the babe that milks" her (i.vii.55). It is Lady Macbeth who could not kill because she remembered her father as he slept. Thus it is Lady Macbeth, not Macbeth, who feels the bonds of kind, Lady Macbeth who has, as women were supposed to have, something of the milk of human kindness in her, and who, to rid herself of it, begs murdering ministers to come to her woman's breasts and take that milk "for gall" (i.v.46). She also begs those demonic ministers to stop up in her "th' access and passage to remorse" and thus forestall the "compunctious visitings of nature" which result when bonds of kind are violated (i.v.42–43; "compunction"=the stings of conscience, *OED*, 1). But Lady Macbeth's prayers are never granted by any of the murdering ministers we see waiting on nature's mischief. Unlike Macbeth and until her own suicide, Lady Macbeth does not succeed in breaking that great bond which keeps him pale and ties her to her kind.

Remorse and guilt finally overtake Lady Macbeth. But she manages for a short time to slow their advent by occupying herself with the practical details of murder. Indeed, Lady Macbeth's preparations for and clearing up after Duncan's murder become a frightening perversion of Renaissance woman's domestic activity. As Vives said, "the busynes and charge within the house lyeth upon the womans hande" (sig. Kii^v).[14] Unlike Goneril, Regan, Cordelia, and Desdemona—all of whom take to the field of battle—Lady Macbeth waits for Macbeth at home, where good-conduct books told her to stay: "whan her husbande is forth a dores, than kepe her house moche more diligently shutte" (Vives, sig. Kii^v). At home, Lady Macbeth remembers to give "tending" to the

messenger who comes with the news of Duncan's arrival (I.v.35).
She remembers that the king "that's coming / Must be provided
for" (I.v.64–65). She is called "hostess," "Fair and noble hostess"
(I.vi.10, 24, 31). As she connives at murder, she thinks to assail
the grooms with "wine and wassail" (I.vii.64). Even the images
she uses to describe her domestic battleground evoke the limbeck
and fumes of home-brewed liquor (I.vii.66–67). Before Duncan's
murder, it is Lady Macbeth who unlocks the king's doors and lays
the daggers ready—although Macbeth draws one of his own. After
the murder, it is Lady Macbeth who smears the grooms with
blood. In her last act as housekeeper, Lady Macbeth remembers to
wash Duncan's blood off their hands and to put on nightgowns.

As soon as Duncan's murder is a public fact, Lady Macbeth
begins to lose her place in society and her position at home. She
does so because there is no room for her in the exclusively male
world of treason and revenge. Therefore, her true weakness and
lack of consequence are first revealed in the discovery scene. Lady
Macbeth's feeble and domestic response, for instance, to the news
she expected to hear—"What, in our house?" (II.iii.84)—is very
different from the cries and clamors she said she would raise.
When she asks Macduff the domestic question, "What's the business" that wakes the "sleepers of the house?" (77–79), he refuses
to answer a "gentle lady": "'Tis not for you to hear what I can
speak" (79–80). It is apparent, therefore, that Lady Macbeth has
as little place in the male world of revenge as she had in the male
world of war. Thus it may be that her faint is genuine, a confirmation of her debility. On the other hand, if her faint is only
pretended in order to shield Macbeth, it is still a particularly feminine ploy. True or false, it dramatically symbolizes weakness. It
has the further effect of removing her from the center of events to
the periphery, from whence she never returns. It is characteristic
that Macbeth, busy defending himself, ignores his lady's fall.
Only Banquo and Macduff in the midst of genuine grief take time
to "Look to the lady" (115, 121).

After Macbeth becomes king, he, the man, so fully commands Lady Macbeth that he allows her no share in his new business. No longer his accomplice, she loses her role as housekeeper.
Macbeth plans the next feast, not Lady Macbeth. It is Macbeth
who invites Banquo to it, not Lady Macbeth, who had welcomed
Duncan to Inverness by herself. When Macbeth commands his

nobles to leave him alone, Lady Macbeth withdraws silently and unnoticed along with them (III.i.39–43). Macbeth does not tell Lady Macbeth that he plans to murder Banquo before his feast or even that he wanted Macduff to attend it. Although Macbeth needed Lady Macbeth to keep house during Duncan's murder, he disposes of Banquo well outside the castle walls. Thus Lady Macbeth is now neither companion nor helpmate. Finally, in the great banquet scene, she loses even her faltering role as hostess. Because Macbeth is there beyond her reach and her comprehension, she is powerless. Ross, not Lady Macbeth, gives the first command to rise. When Lady Macbeth twice tries to tell the nobles that Macbeth has been thus since his youth, no one pretends to believe her. When she attempts to preserve the "good meeting" (III.iv.109), even Macbeth ignores her. As soon as she is forced by Macbeth's actions to give over her last role, she dissolves in confusion the very society upon whose continuance that role depends. With her husband out of her reach and society in shambles, Lady Macbeth no longer has any reason for being.

As soon as Macbeth abandons her company for that of the witches, Lady Macbeth is totally alone. In fact, Macbeth's union with the witches symbolizes the culmination of Lady Macbeth's loss of womanly social roles as well as her loss of home and family. But her growing isolation had been apparent from the moment her husband became king. Unlike Portia or Desdemona or even Macbeth himself, Lady Macbeth was never seen with friends or woman-servants in whose presence she could take comfort. Even when she appeared in company, she was the only woman there. Consequently, once she begins to lose her husband, she has neither person nor occupation to stave off the visitings of nature. All she has is time, time to succumb to that human kindness which, said Bright, no one could forget and remain human.[15] Thus, in Lady Macbeth's short soliloquy before Macbeth's feast, even though she still talks in terms of "we," she seems to be speaking only of herself. Alone and unoccupied, she is visited by the remorse and sorrow she had hoped to banish:

> Naught's had, all's spent,
> Where our desire is got without content.
> 'Tis safer to be that which we destroy
> Than by destruction dwell in doubtful joy.   (III.ii.4–7)

Lady Macbeth's existence now is circumscribed by the present memory of past loss. Absent from her mind is the sense of future promise she had anticipated before Duncan's murder when she thought herself transported beyond the "ignorant present" and felt "The future in the instant" (I.v.55–56). In her words we also hear, I think, what Bright calls the afflictions of a guilt-ridden conscience, that "internal anguish [which] breve[s] us of all delight" in "outward benefits."[16] Even after Macbeth joins Lady Macbeth, her words seem to continue her own thoughts, not to describe his: "Why do you keep alone, / Of sorriest fancies your companions making" (III.ii.8–9). For we know, as Lady Macbeth does not, that Macbeth is thinking of the coming murder of Banquo, not the past murder of Duncan. We know his recent companions have been murderers, not "fancies." Only Lady Macbeth suffers now the "repetition" of the "horror" of Duncan's death which Macduff had feared "in a woman's ear / Would murder as it fell" (II.iii.76, 81–82).[17] When Lady Macbeth thinks to quiet her husband, she does so with advice she has already revealed she cannot herself take: "Things without all remedy / Should be without regard" (III.ii.11–12). But Macbeth no longer needs her advice: "Duncan is in his grave," he says, "nothing, / Can touch him further" (22–26). Thus Shakespeare shows us that the differences between husband and wife are extreme. Macbeth wades deeper and deeper in blood in order to stifle the tortures of a mind which fears only the future: Banquo's increasing kingliness, Fleance and his unborn children, all living things and their seed. Lady Macbeth, her husband's "Sweet remembrancer" (III.iv.37), does little else but think of horrors past: of the "air drawn" dagger which led Macbeth to Duncan (62), of the king slaughtered and her hands bloodied, of Banquo dead and Lady Macduff in realms unknown.

In the banquet scene, Lady Macbeth's words reveal an increase in weakness, emphasize the loss of her womanly roles, and lay bare her present isolation. Her scolding, for instance, is no more than a weak, futile imitation of the cruelty of her earlier goading. Her images, correspondingly, are more obviously feminine: "these flaws and starts," she tells Macbeth, "would well become / A woman's story at a winter's fire, / Authorized by her grandam" (III.iv.63–66). But her images also evoke a kind of homeliness and comfort she can never know: the security that other women feel when they sit at their warm hearths and tell tales to their children. In fact, Lady Macbeth's words describe the comforts of a home she so little knows that she uses the picture her words evoke to castigate a man who will soon destroy the only real home we see in the play. Thus it is not surprising that Lady Macbeth at the end of the banquet scene does not seem to realize that Macbeth is leaving her as well as the community of men in order to join the unsexed witches in an unholy union— one wherein they joy to "grieve his heart" (IV.i.110). As soon as Macbeth joins the witches, Lady Macbeth no longer has any place anywhere. Offstage, she is neither wife, queen, housekeeper, nor hostess. When we see her next, she will have lost the memories of motherhood and childhood she remembered so imperfectly and used so cruelly at the beginning of the play. She will also have lost that fragmented glimpse of womanly life she repudiates during her last banquet.

In her sleepwalking scene, Lady Macbeth exists (for she cannot be said to *live*) in the perpetual darkness of the soul which no candle can enlighten, although she has a taper by her continually. This is the darkness of the soul which, said Bright, "is above measure unhappy and most miserable."[18] Cut off from grace, Lady Macbeth is without hope. Like the damned in the *Inferno*, she exists solely within the present memory of past horrors. In fact, her existence seems to exemplify—but only in relation to herself—medieval definitions of eternal time as the everlasting "now," the present during which all things that have happened or will happen are happening.[19] For she relives outside of any temporal sequence all Macbeth's murders and senses, as if damnation were an already accomplished fact, that "Hell is murky" (V.i.33). Without grace, Lady Macbeth cannot envision a world outside her own where Lady Macduff might possess another kind of being. Nor can she conceive of a power greater than that which she still seems to think she and Macbeth possess, a power which might call theirs "to accompt" (34–35). In the prison of her own anguish, she is ignorant of good and the God she long ago renounced. This is the illness that Bright said no physic could cure: "Here no medicine, no purgation, no cordiall, no tryacle or balme are able to assure the afflicted soule and trembling heart."[20] This is the infection of the mind which the physician hired by Macbeth says only a divine can cure—although Shakespeare shows us no priest in Scotland.

It is painfully ironic that Lady Macbeth, who had once thought that drink could make "memory, the warder of the brain," into a fume and sleep into something "swinish" (I.vii.64–67), can now neither forget her guilt nor sleep the sleep of oblivion. Unlike Macbeth, however, who revealed his guilt before the assembled nobility of Scotland, Lady Macbeth confesses hers when she is alone. She does so because she has always been, as women were supposed to be, a private figure, living behind closed doors. She also reveals her anguish in sleep partly because she has no purposeful waking existence and partly, as Banquo said, because in repose the fallen, unblessed nature "gives way" to "cursèd thoughts" (II.i.8–9; see also v.i.67–68).[21] Macbeth's guilty soul is as public as his acts. Lady Macbeth's is as private as memory, tormented by a self whose function is only to remember in isolation and unwillingly the deeds done by another. So tormented is Lady Macbeth that the gentlewoman—the first we ever see tending her—says she would not have that heart in her "bosom for the dignity of the whole body" (v.i.50–51).

Our final glimpse into the afflicted and brainsick mind of Lady Macbeth reveals that her doctor is either mistaken or lying when he says she is troubled with "thick-coming fancies" (v.iii.38). Her madness is not that melancholy which springs from delusion, but rather than which stems from true and substantial causes.[22] Her mind, like her being as mother, child, wife, and hostess, has also been twisted by her destructive longing for Macbeth to murder cruelly and deliberately. When we see Lady Macbeth at the end, therefore, she is "womanly" only in that she is sick and weak. All the valor of her tongue is gone, as is her illusion of its power. The hands which she cannot sweeten with the perfumes of Arabia are the little hands of a woman. As long as she lives, Lady Macbeth is never unsexed in the only way she wanted to be unsexed—able to act with the cruelty she ignorantly and perversely identified with male strength. But she has lost that true strength which Shakespeare says elsewhere is based on pity and fostered by love.

She is not now—perhaps she never was—of real concern to her lord, whom she remembers and speaks to even as she sleepwalks. Macbeth does not think of her as he prepares himself for war. When her doctor forces Macbeth to speak about her troubled mind, Macbeth renounces physic on his own account, not hers.

"I'll none of it," he says (v.iii.47). It is ironic, therefore, that Lady Macbeth, offstage and neglected, is able at the last to unsex herself only through the act of self-murder—in contrast to her husband, whose single attribute now is the "direst cruelty" she begged for, who wills himself to murder others tomorrow after tomorrow so long as he sees "lives" (v.vii.2). The cry of women which rises at his wife's death is no more than another proof to him that he is fearless, that no "horrors" can move him. (v.v.13). Even her death to him is only a "word," a word for which he has no "time" (v.v.18).

Notes

1. All biblical quotations are to the Breeches edition of the Geneva Bible (London: Christopher Barker, 1599).
2. Renaissance texts on the role of women universally called for wifely submission, but with varying emphases. "An Homilie of the state of Matrimonie," in *Certaine Sermons Appoynted by the Quenes Majesty, to be Declared and Read, by al Parsons, Vicars, & Curates, Everi Sunday and Holiday, in their Churches* [*Homilies*, 2 vols.] (London: Richard Jugge, and John Cawood, 1563), II, 253–63, declares, "Ye wives, be ye in subjection to obey your own husband" (fol. 256). Lewes Vives, in *A Very Frutefull and Pleasant Boke Called the Instruction of a Christen Woman*, trans. Richarde Hyrde (London: Thomas Berthelet, c. 1531), sig. Yii^v, goes so far as to claim that "Nature her selfe cryeth and commandeth / that the woman shalbe subject & obedient or sturdy." See also Edmund Tilney, *A Brief and Pleasant Discourse of Duties in Mariage, called the Flower of Friendshippe* dam: Theatrum Orbis Terrarum, 1974), fol. liiii^r-v, explicitly links the necessity for wifely obedience to Eve's transgression, although he puts limits on that obedience: "First / doth Paul speake of the obedience / that maried wemen owe to their husbandes. Let the wemen saieth he be in subjection that is to saye / servyable & obedient unto their husbandes . . . Wherout it foloweth / that the sayde obedience extendeth not unto wickednesse & evell / but unto that which is good / honest / and comely . . . For Adam was first made and then Eva. And Adam was not disceaved but the woman was disceaved / and brought in the transgression . . . therefore god to punishe the synne / humbled her / made her fearefull and subdued her." Elyot and Tilney also teach wives to resist their husbands' evil counsel, but advise them to do so without appearing to be disobedient. See Sir Thomas Elyot, *The Defence of Good Women*, ed. Edwin Johnston Howard (London: Berthelet, 1540; rpt. Oxford, Ohio: Anchor Press, 1940), p. 57: "And if she

measure it to the will of her husbande, she doth the more wisely: except it may tourne them both to losse or dishonestye. [Y]et than shuld she seme rather to give him wise counsaile, than to appere dissobedient or sturdy." See also Edmund Tilney, *A Brief and Pleasant Discourse of Duties in Mariage, called the Flower of Friendshippe* (London: Henrie Denham, 1568), sig. Eiiii^v-[E5]. (Where appropriate, throughout this essay, I have regularized *i* and *j*, *u* and *v*, in accordance with modern usage.)

3. This citation and subsequent ones are to *Macbeth*, ed. Alfred Harbage, in William Shakespeare, *The Complete Works*, Alfred Harbage, gen. ed. (Baltimore: Penguin, 1969).

4. Coleridge is among the few critics who insist upon Lady Macbeth's femininity. See especially Collier's transcripts of the "Lectures on Shakespere and Milton, 1813–14," in *Lectures and Notes on Shakspere and Other English Poets* (London: George Bell, 1897), pp. 469–70: "The lecturer alluded to the prejudiced idea of Lady Macbeth as a monster; as a being out of nature and without conscience: on the contrary . . . So far is the woman from being dead within her, that her sex occasionally betrays itself in the very moment of dark and bloody imagination. A passage where she alludes to 'plucking her nipple from the boneless gums of her infant,' though usually thought to prove a merciless and unwomanly nature, proves the direct opposite. . . . Had she regarded this with savage indifference, there would have been no force in the appeal; but her very allusion to it, and her purpose in this allusion, shows that she considered no tie so tender as that which connected her with her babe." Ellen Terry, of course, played Lady Macbeth as entirely feminine, even "pre-Raphaelite," as Dennis Bartholomeusz said in *Macbeth and the Players* (Cambridge: Cambridge University Press, 1969), p. 206. A few other critics also discuss the humanity and femininity of Lady Macbeth: see Willard Farnham in *Shakespeare's Tragic Frontier* (1950; rpt., New York: Barnes & Noble, 1973), p. 110; D. W. Harding in "Women's Fantasy of Manhood: A Shakespearian Theme," *Shakespeare Quarterly*, 20 (1969), 246; and Larry S. Champion in *Shakespeare's Tragic Perspective* (Athens: University of Georgia Press, 1976), pp. 182–83. For representatives of the opposing view, see G. Wilson Knight, *The Wheel of Fire* (London: Oxford University Press, 1930), p. 168: Lady Macbeth "is an embodiment—for one mighty hour—of Evil absolute and extreme"; W. M. Merchant, "'His Fiend-like Queen,'" *Shakespeare Survey*, 19 (1966), 75, 77: Lady Macbeth's invocation of murdering ministers "is a formal stage in demonic possession"; "her submission to demonic powers" condemns "her in the rest of the play to a merely passive damnation." See also Paul A. Jorgensen, *Our Naked Frailties: Sensational Art and Meaning in Macbeth* (Berkeley: University of California Press, 1971), p. 163. Representatives of similar but less extreme positions are Cleanth Brooks, "The Naked Babe and the Cloak of Manliness," in *The Well Wrought Urn* (New York: Reynal & Hitch-

cock, 1947), p. 34; William Rosen, *Shakespeare and the Craft of Tragedy* (Cambridge, Mass.: Harvard University Press, 1960), pp. 73–77; Derek Traversi in *Troilus and Cressida to The Tempest*, 3d ed. rev. (1938; rpt. London: Hollis & Carter, 1969), II, 129; Clifford Davidson in *The Primrose Way: A Study of Shakespeare's Macbeth* (Conesville, Iowa: John Westburg, 1970), pp. 10–11.

5. Vives said, for instance, that "in wedlocke the man resembleth the reason / and the woman the body" (Sig. Yiii). Elyot said that "Reason is the principall parte of the soule divine and immortal, wherby man dothe discerne good from yll . . . reason . . . to man is so propre, that lackinge it, he loseth his denomination" (*The Defence of Good Women*, p. 41). See also Hooker, *Of the Laws of Ecclesiastical Polity*, I.vii.4, (London: J. M. Dent, 1907), p. 171.

6. Alexander Nowell in *A Catechisme* (London: John Daye, 1570; facs. rpt. Delmar, N.Y.: Scholars' Facsimiles & Reprints, 1975), fols. 17^v, 19, said that the "summe of the lawe" expounded by Christ is "not in absteyning onely from injurie and evill doing, but in love and charitie." All men, even enemies, he said, "are knit to us with the same bond, wherewith God hath coupled together all mankind." See also I. Cor. xiii:13: "now abideth faith, hope *and* love . . . but the chiefest of these *is* love."

7. James I, *Daemonologie* (Edinburgh: Robert Walde-grave, 1597; facs. rpt. Amsterdam: Theatrum Orbis Terrarum, 1969), p. 32.

8. On images of the last judgment, see Nowell: "Christ shall come in the cloudes of the heaven . . . And at the horrible sound, and dredfull blast of trumpet all the dead . . . shall appere before his throne to be judged, every one for him selfe to geve accompt of their life" (fol. 41^v). On the emblem of charity see, for instance, Spenser's description of Charissa, *F.Q.*I.x.30–31: "She was a woman . . . Full of great love . . . Her necke and brests were ever open bare, / That ay thereof her babes might sucke their fill." *The Works of Edmund Spenser, A Variorum Edition*, ed. Edwin Greenlaw et al. (Baltimore: Johns Hopkins Press, 1932), I, 131.

9. Evil men "neither have any trust in hys [God's] goodnesse and mercy toward them, nor any recourse to hys grace, nor enter into any endevour to obey hys will. Therefore their fayth, although they dout not of the truth of the worde of God, is called a dead fayth, for that like a drye and dead stocke it never bringeth forth any fruites of godly life, that is, of love to God, and charitie toward men" (Nowell, *A Catechisme*, fol. 23^v).

10. Marriage "is instituted of God, to thintent that man & woman should live lawfully in a perpetuall frendly felowship, to bryng forth fruite, and to avoyde fornication . . . Furthermore, it is also ordeyned, that the Churche of God and his kingdome, might by this kynde of lyfe, be conserved & enlarged, not only in that god geveth children by his blessing, but also in that they be brought up by the parentes godly, in the knowledge of Gods worde, that this the knowledge of God and

true religion, myght be delyvered by succession from one to another, that finally, many myght enjoye that everlastyng immortalitie" (fol. 253). See also Tilney, *Discourse*, sig. [A8].

11. Latimer in his sermon on John 15 said that "this charitable love, is so necessary, that when a man hath her, without all other things it will suffice him. Agayn, if a man have all other things and lacketh that love, it will not help him, it is all vayn and lost." *Frutefull Sermons* (London: John Daye, 1578), sig. [AAi^v].

12. See T. Bright, *A Treatise of Melancholie* (London: Thomas Vautrollier, 1586; facs. rpt. New York: Columbia University Press, 1940), Chap. xxxii, "Of the affliction of conscience for sinne," pp. 184–87. See also Chap. xxxiii, "Whether the conscience of sinne and the affliction thereof be melancholy or not," pp. 187–93: "such is the estate of all defiled consciences with hainous crimes; whose harts are never free from that worme, but with deadly bite thereof are driven to dispaire" (pp. 193–94); "the issue of this affliction is eternall punishment . . . extended . . . to all, neither that of the body only, but of the soule . . . so once shaken by the terrours of Gods wrath, and blasted with that whirlewinde of his displeasure, falleth and with it driveth the whole frame of our nature into extreame miserie and utter confusion" (p. 190).

13. Elyot, *The Defence of Good Women*, p. 36.

14. See also Bullinger, *The Christen State of Matrimonye*, Chap. xix, fols. lxiii–lxvii: "Of convenient Carefulnes and just keping of the house lyke Christen folke." "What so ever is to be done without the house / that belongeth to the man / & the woman to studye for thinges within to be done" (fol. lxiii^v).

15. Bright, *Treatise*, p. 193.

16. *Ibid.*, p. 185.

17. Lady Macbeth understood that thinking of murder after "these ways . . . will make us mad" (II.ii.33); she also saw in Macbeth's vision of the loss of sleep the brainsickness that would soon characterize her own inability to sleep without the effects of waking (II.ii.45). At this point Lady Macbeth exemplifies additional sixteenth-century assumptions about women, just as Macbeth, now set on his murderous "way," does about men: "For the woman is a weake creature, not endued with like strength and constancie of mynde, therefore they be the sooner disquieted, and they be the more prone to all weake affections and dispositions of mynde, more then men be, and lyghter they be, and more vayne in theyr fantasies and opinions" (*Homilies*, II, fol. 255). See also Lewes Lavater, *Of Ghostes and Spirites Walking by Nyght*, trans. R.H. (London: Henry Benneyman, 1572), p. 14.

18. Bright, *Treatise*, p. 186.

19. See, for instance, Augustine, *Confessions*, trans. William Watts, Loeb Classical Library (1631; Cambridge, Mass.: Harvard University Press,

1961), II, Bk. xi, 23, 232, 248: "quod semper est praesens . . . non sunt nisi praesentia." See also Nowell, *A Catechisme*, fol. 42^{r-v}.
20. Bright, *Treatise*, p. 189.
21. Thomas Nashe, although he is not a trustworthy authority, is vivid on this point: "As touching the terrors of the night, they are as many as our sinnes. The Night is the Divells Blacke booke, wherein hee recordeth all our transgressions. Even, as when a condemned man is put into a darke dungeon, secluded from all comfort of light or companie, he doth nothing but despairfully call to minde his gracelesse for-mer life, and the brutish outrages and misdemeanours that have throwne him into that desolate horrour: so when Night in her rustie dungeon hath imprisoned our ey-sight, and that we are shut seperatly in our chambers from resort, the divell keepeth his audit in our sin-guilty consciences, no sense but surrenders to our memorie a true bill of parcels of his detestable impieties. The table of our hart is turned to an index of iniquities, and all our thoughts are nothing but texts to condemne us." *The Terrors of the Night Or, A Discourse of Apparitions* (London: John Danter, 1594), sig. B^{r-v}.
22. See Bright: "Whatsoever molestation riseth directly as a proper object of the mind, that in that respect is not melancholicke, but hath a far-ther ground then fancie, and riseth from conscience, condemning the guiltie soule of those ingraven lawes of nature, which no man is voide of, be he never so laborous . . . Of this kinde Saule was possessed . . . and Judas the traytor, who tooke the revenge of betraying the innocent uppon him selfe with his owne handes." *Treatise*, p. 193.

Shakespeare's Female Characters as Actors and Audience

MARIANNE NOVY

At the center of Shakespeare's comedies there is frequently a female character who is acting a part, whether disguising herself as a boy or pretending in some more subtle fashion. These characters usually play roles that provide counter-roles for the men and draw them into participation. By the end of the play, characters of both sexes can be alternately actors and audience, cooperating in a relationship of mutuality.[1] The women's acting has been deed as well as pretense; their fictions have helped express some kind of truth. When the men finally discover that the women have pretended false identities, no shadow falls on the celebration.

In the tragedies, however, the image of the woman as actor is more problematic. The heroes' suspicion of female pretense darkens their view of the women, whether pretending or not. The men's own acting—whether deed or pretense—discourages female participation. When Shakespeare's tragic women do act, the men find it difficult to cooperate or be audience. Thus, the tragic women are often confined to being audience for the hero,

An earlier version of this essay was presented at the Special Session on Shakespearean Metadrama at the MLA Annual Convention, December 1977, Chicago, Illinois, and reproduced for distribution to participants in the session by the Department of English, University of Rochester.

mediating the offstage audience's sympathy with their own, as
Ophelia does for Hamlet, Desdemona for Othello, and even Lady
Macbeth for Macbeth. Furthermore, because of the men's suspicion of female pretense, the sympathy the female characters express often cannot reach them; the women are like the tragic audience in their sense of powerlessness and separateness.

To Hamlet, for example, even his mother's tears for his father seem "unrighteous" (I.ii.154) because of her subsequent re-
marriage.[2] He is enraged by the pretenses he sees in women—
"God hath given you one face, and you make yourselves another"
(III.i.143–44), he says to Ophelia. But Ophelia's shifting responses
are less controlled pretense than the result of her inability to transcend the role of audience, whether to brother, father, or lover.
Even in the nunnery scene, on stage for her father and Claudius,
she phrases her hurt at Hamlet's rejection as a kind of compliment on his acting.

> HAMLET. I did love you once.
> OPHELIA. Indeed, my lord, you made me believe so. . . .
> HAMLET. I loved you not.
> OPHELIA. I was the more deceived.   (III.i.115–16, 119–20)

At the end of his attack, though she is "of ladies most deject and
wretched" (III.i.155), her tone is much more one of sympathy for
Hamlet—"Th'observed of all observers, quite, quite down!"
(154)—than of concern for herself. It has been argued that Ophelia
and similar heroines speak such lines not in their own person but
to guide audience reaction to the hero. The words do guide audiences to sympathy, but they also say something about the au-
dience-actor nature of Ophelia's relationship with Hamlet; she is
a mediator between him and the offstage audience. It is characteristic of them that when they watch a play together, Hamlet
cannot bear to be just a spectator, while Ophelia is a spectator to
both him and the play. She must go mad in order to escape social
restrictions and take center stage.

At the beginning of *Othello*, Desdemona seems likely to be
more successful as both actor and audience. The beginning of
their love, as Othello lyrically describes it, seems the epitome of
an ideal actor-audience relationship. "She loved me for the dangers I had passed, / And I loved her that she did pity them"
(I.iii.167–68). With her gestures, tears, and sympathy, her re-

sponse to his storytelling is an actor's dream. Like the theater audience, furthermore, she identifies with him; she wishes, ambiguously, "That heaven had made her such a man" (163), and he recalls that she would "With a greedy ear / Devour up my discourse" (149–50). Her listening is such an intense and incorporative activity that Othello can only compare it to eating, just as Norman Holland compares an attentive theater audience to a child wishing to merge with a mother who feeds it.[3]

Desdemona, however, goes beyond the audience's responsiveness. Because of the restrictions of her society, her acting-as-doing requires acting-as-pretending, and her abilities in both coalesce. In the emotional moment we have just heard Othello describe, she resourcefully finds a way to initiate courtship while seeming to him merely to be hinting:

> She thanked me;
> And bade me, if I had a friend that loved her,
> I should but teach him how to tell my story,
> And that would woo her.   (I.iii.163–66)

Later examples of the two forms of acting, now separated, do not work so well. Her pretense that her handkerchief is not lost and her commitment to Cassio—"If I do vow a friendship, I'll perform it / To the last article" (III.iii.21–22)—both contribute to Othello's anger at her. In reaction, she again assumes the role of audience, trying to understand Othello, sympathizing with him, imagining him in pain.

> Something sure of state
> . . . .
> Has puddled his clear spirit. . . .
> . . . . let our finger ache, and it endues
> Our other, healthful members even to a sense
> Of pain.   (III.iv.140, 143, 146–48)

But rather than seeing *her* pain, Othello describes her tears as "well-painted passion" (IV.i.250) and casts her in the role of a prostitute who can act to suit her customer's fancy. "Sir, she can turn, and turn, and yet go on / And turn again; and she can weep, sir, weep" (IV.i.246–47). She keeps trying to break into his nightmare world, to ask for a specific accusation so she can defend herself—but his insistence that she is false means that none of her words can persuade him; if he doubts her honesty in the Elizabethan sense of sexual fidelity, he can never believe in the honesty of her words. She lives in a society where women are always suspect, and Iago has used her own love and survival techniques against her: "She that, so young, could give out such a seeming / To seel her father's eyes up close as oak—" (III.iii.209–10).

At the end she is still trying to act—both to conceal her feelings and to mend the situation—but she is also still the sympathetic audience who adds to her song the line, "Let nobody blame him; his scorn I approve" (IV.iii.50).

> EMILIA. I would you had never seen him!
> DESDEMONA. So would not I. My love doth so approve him
>   That even his stubbornness, his checks, his frowns—
>   Prithee unpin me—have grace and favor in them.
>   (IV.iii.17–20)

Her last combination of acting with audiencelike sympathy occurs after her apparent death, when she speaks upon Emilia's return.

> EMILIA. O, who hath done this deed?
> DESDEMONA. Nobody—I myself. Farewell.
>   Commend me to my kind lord.   (V.ii.124–26)

Even in this absurd attempt to claim Othello's guilt as her own, he sees only sinful pretense: "She's like a liar gone to burning hell!" (V.ii.130). After he discovers her truth, his words still suggest inability to appreciate her integration of sympathy and acting. He speaks of her as a kind of rejecting audience—"This look of thine will hurl my soul from heaven" (275)—identifies her chastity with coldness, and finally describes her as a pearl, an image of beauty and value with an absence of animate energy.

Different as Lady Macbeth is from Desdemona, she has a similar vicarious interest in her husband's achievements and similar sympathy for his sufferings. Pursuing their goals involves both women in pretense and stirs their resourcefulness in crises. But Macbeth's progressive insistence on acting on his own turns Lady Macbeth into an isolated and powerless audience.

Initially she advises him to pretend innocence and can herself pretend quite effectively to be a loving hostess and a grieved one after the death of Duncan. But basically she is dependent on

Macbeth's acting. Though he calls her his "dearest partner of greatness" (I.v.10–11) it is *his* greatness, his manhood, his ambition she speaks about even in her soliloquies. Her own ambition is expressed through playing the encouraging and taunting wife, concerned about her husband's career and self-esteem—a much more complex version of the unquenchable burning for a crown of her counterpart in Holinshed. As Robert Egan has suggested, her influence on him here is very much the audience's influence on an actor.[4] Furthermore, her words express one attitude the offstage audience can take to Macbeth—complicity and vicarious satisfaction in his self-assertion. After the murders, her role as audience and voice for some audience attitudes is clearer; since Macbeth will not let her help in his future plans or even tell her what they are, in their scene alone together (III.ii) all she can do is sympathize with him and encourage him in his plans to play the jovial host. In the banquet scene she tries to keep the show going on by improvising when he can't hide his reactions to Banquo's ghost, but her performance is useless without his cooperation. Afterward she is audience again—the clearest feeling in her few words is sympathy: "You lack the season of all natures, sleep" (III.iv.141). But Macbeth has grown so withdrawn that he can scarcely accept even her sympathy, let alone her cooperative acting. She now, like Ophelia, can take center stage only when her rational consciousness is suspended. Macbeth finally reacts to her suicide by speaking not about her but about the meaninglessness of life. His words expressing discomfort in his own role also suggest his growing inability to be a responsive audience to her or to anyone else.

> The time has been my senses would have cooled
> To hear a night-shriek, and my fell of hair
> . Would at a dismal treatise rouse and stir
> As life were in't . . . .
> Life's but a walking shadow, a poor player
> That struts and frets his hour upon the stage. . . .
>
> (v.v.10–13, 24–25)

While *Lear* includes two women who exemplify the pretense most tragic heroes fear, it gives the suspicion of that pretense not to the hero but to Cordelia, who censors her own words by it. She disclaims "that glib and oily art / To speak and purpose not" (1.i.224–25); she exemplifies what Jonas Barish calls the non-theatrical protagonist, characterized by rectitude rather than plenitude.[5] While other tragedies, like *Othello*, generally combine female pretense and female attempts at autonomy, so that we may be confused about which infuriates the hero more, here the two are separated and it is clear that what Lear resents is the challenge to his desire for control. It should be noted, furthermore, that Cordelia refuses not only to pretend, but also to say anything that might be interpreted as pretense. The kind of acting that she refuses in the first scene is the emotional expression, on cue, of feelings that are really hers. She loves Lear, but she does not want him to control her expression of that love.

But as Lear, cast out from society, becomes more critical of its pretenses, Cordelia, freed from her father's commands, expresses her feelings of love for him more openly. Shakespeare includes a choral scene to draw our attention to this: when Kent and the Gentleman discuss her reactions to the letters about her father, their descriptions and questions at times sound like those of a theater critic.

> KENT. Did your letters pierce the Queen to any demonstra-
> tion of grief?
> GENTLEMAN. Ay, sir. She took them, read them in my pres-
> ence,
> And now and then an ample tear trilled down
> Her delicate cheek. . . .
> KENT.   O, then it movèd her?
> GENTLEMAN. Not to a rage. Patience and sorrow strove
> Who should express her goodliest. . . .
> Faith, once or twice she heaved the name of father
> Pantingly forth, as if it pressed her heart.
>
> (IV.iii.9–13, 15–17, 25–26)

Kent and the Gentleman are extraordinarily interested in her expression of her feelings; this scene prepares us for what we will see in her later appearance and makes a link between the role of actor and the role of audience. For Cordelia, in expressing her feelings for Lear, is also playing the role of audience here and in the next scene. In her sympathy for Lear, she is providing a voice, a mediation for the sympathy of the offstage audience. But at the same time her words and gestures accomplish something onstage—they give the recognition, love, and forgiveness that Lear needs and asks for.

> LEAR. As I am a man, I think this lady
>   To be my child Cordelia.
> CORDELIA.   And so I am! I am!
> LEAR. Be your tears wet? Yes, faith. I pray weep not.
>   If you have poison for me, I will drink it.
>   I know you do not love me; for your sisters
>   Have (as I do remember) done me wrong.
>   You have some cause, they have not.
> CORDELIA.   No cause, no cause.
>   (IV.vii.68−75)

She moves from audiencelike sympathy to its expression in tears, words, and gestures that finally reach Lear; she is even willing to use the verbal pretense of "No cause, no cause."

In an essay on Lear and the theatrical experience, Stanley Cavell asks, ". . . what is the difference between tragedy in a theater and tragedy in actuality? In both, people in pain are in our presence. But in actuality acknowledgment *is* incomplete, . . . unless we put ourselves in their presence, reveal ourselves to them."[6] For the theater audience, however, no self-revelation to those they see suffering is expected or possible. Many of the examples of sympathy expressed by the women discussed here have been more like those of a theater audience—incomplete by the standards of actuality—because they have been expressed in the hero's absence; even in speaking to the hero, Lady Macbeth and Ophelia often maintain something of the audience's refusal to acknowledge themselves. Few as her words are, however, Cordelia's acknowledgment of her relationship to Lear is extraordinarily powerful and seems complete. In this reunion scene each can be moved by the other, like an audience, and can express feelings, like an actor, in a kind of mutual dependence. But Cordelia reaches Lear here partly because she has proved herself by her earlier refusal to say anything that could be construed as pretense. Only in *Antony and Cleopatra* does the man enjoy the woman's ability to pretend as much as he suspects it.

Antony and Cleopatra is the only Shakespearean tragedy

that focuses on and indeed glorifies the woman as actor in both senses, doer and pretender, and, not coincidentally, as sexually active. Whether she is asking for a declaration of love from Antony or asking him to return to Rome, Cleopatra is likely to be role-playing. Antony does at times angrily accuse her of deception, but she, unlike the other heroines so accused, makes similar accusations to him:

> Good now, play one scene
> Of excellent dissembling, and let it look
> Like perfect honor.   (I.iii.78–80)

Much more than the other tragic heroes, each of them can be mollified; their ability to forgive and start over is closely related to their ability to play many different roles. Furthermore, each of them can also be appreciative audience to the other.

> Fie, wrangling queen!
> Whom every thing becomes—to chide, to laugh,
> To weep; whose every passion fully strives
> To make itself, in thee, fair and admired.   (I.i.48–51)

> His legs bestrid the ocean: his reared arm
> Crested the world; his voice was propertied
> As all the tunèd spheres, and that to friends. . . .
>   (v.ii.82–84)

Each, in describing the other, creates and shares the audience's admiration for the other; Cleopatra, especially, becomes artist as well as audience and actor. In the last of her visions, before her death modeled on Antony's ideals, the barriers between roles dissolve and each can be both actor and audience at once.

> Methinks I hear
> Antony call: I see him rouse himself
> To praise my noble act. I hear him mock
> The luck of Caesar. . . .   (v.ii.282–85)

A skeptic may always refuse to believe in the love between Antony and Cleopatra. Love can never be proved with mathematical certainty; attempts to show it can always be taken as pretense or self-deception. As Janet Adelman has suggested, the trust required of an audience to believe in love onstage is analogous to the trust required of lovers to believe in each other.[7] In *Hamlet*, *Othello*, *Macbeth*, and *Lear*, the heroes tragically fail to achieve or maintain their trust in the women who love them; they regain it, if at all, when it is too late. In *Antony and Cleopatra*, by contrast, the lovers, for all their jealousy and wrangling, are always willing to forgive each other and start over after their fights; thus they accept the ambiguities in each other and in their relationship, and paradoxically achieve something more like trust than do any of the other couples. The role that each plays allows for and indeed demands the partnership of a free and independent person.

Why this sharp contrast between Shakespeare's comic and tragic men (with Antony in between) in their attitude toward woman as actors (in most of the tragic heroes a suspicion that works to confine women to being audience, in most of the comic heroes acceptance and participation)? The difference is clearly related not only to genre but also to gender; women in the tragedies have no obsessive suspicion about men as actors. According to Michael Goldman, all major dramatic characters are actors in the extended sense that they "go beyond ordinary bounds in ways that remind us of acting. They are capable of some kind of seductive, hypnotic, or commanding expression."[8] Thus audiences onstage and off see in them the *otherness* of the professional actor. The character as actor is strange, exotic, and therefore an object of both repulsion and attraction. I would suggest that within Shakespeare's tragedies, the women's reaction to the men as actors shows much more the positive side of that ambivalence—the sympathy and admiration. The tragic heroes' attitude to the women as actors shows mostly the negative side. There the suspicion of the actor as other coalesces with what Simone de Beauvoir sees as the general cultural suspicion of the woman as other.[9] Much that Goldman says about one group could apply to both: "The community focuses on them, makes them a cynosure, enjoys seeing them dressed up in their proper costumes at the proper times. But always the attraction springs from and exists in tension with an implied hostility. . . . They are elevated above the community by the role they take on, but their elevation exposes them [like women on a pedestal]; they serve at their audience's pleasure."[10]

Furthermore, for both women and actors, being seen as

other also implies being identified with sexuality and physicality. Conditions of childbearing and traditions of child-rearing associate women with the body; women have been seen as sexual temptresses since Eve became an archetype, and that females were excessively lustful was an Elizabethan commonplace.[11] Actors too, more directly than almost any other artists, use their own bodies in their work, and have historically been attacked by moralists for their sexual behavior.[12]

Shakespeare seems to have recognized and used further similarities between actors and women. Both are often seen not only as separate and alien but also as sources of diversion. When Hamlet says, "Man delights not me" (II.ii.305), the two possibilities for entertainment that occur to him and his companions are women and actors. Both are traditionally expected to survive by pleasing and are therefore dependent on others.[13] Thus in Shakespeare women often express a sense of kinship with the fool; Viola praises Feste: "He must observe their mood on whom he jests, / The quality of persons, and the time" (III.i.60−61). The necessity to please leads to much of the role-playing of which women are accused, which in turn makes them seem more strange and foreign to men who cannot determine what feelings are behind the roles. Paradoxically, however, this dependence on pleasing other people inclines both women and actors to study faces closely for clues to feelings and thus contributes to the ability of both groups to be audience as well, a point to which we shall return later.

Even in childhood, according to the psychologist Philip Weissman, "girls engage in play acting and play action more universally and with more spontaneous freedom than does the average boy."[14] He further notes that acting begins when the infant "takes on the role of the mother, amusing her by borrowing her identity."[15] Identification with the mother is easier for girls because they are of the same sex; this ease of identification, perhaps combined with other restrictions, may be a cause of girls' early affinity for acting as well as of women's general greater ease in identifying with others, whether we see this as flexibility or weakness.[16] According to Weissman's theory, a man who becomes an actor is developing aspects of himself which originate in his identification with his mother; this kind of development is open to most women. The actor experiences "lack of differentiation of self from nonself"; his choice of profession is aimed at working out his uncertainty about how to define himself.[17] Goldman notes the universality of this need for self-definition, but if the actor, as he says,[18] lives closer to it, so do women. A consistent, and related, charge against actors has been "ontological subversiveness."[19] As Goldman paraphrases it, "A man is supposed to have only *one* being; what kind of creature can shift identities at will?"[20] This same criticism can apply to women, whether they play only traditional feminine roles and mystify by their adaptability or flirtation, or play traditional masculine roles and try to transcend conventional limits.

These similarities may help to explain why male actors have been effective in playing female roles in so many societies: their own experience of dependence and identification helps them in their interpretation, and since they are already "other" as actors, the audience sees them in many ways as it sees women. My point here is not simply that actors are androgynous, but that traditional masculine and feminine qualities exist in everyone to some degree, and that the condition of actors mirrors the potentiality we all have to go beyond these categories—beyond all dichotomies—a potentiality threatening to believers in a neatly ordered world. As Jonas Barish points out, the anti-theatrical prejudice "belongs to . . . a conservative ethical emphasis in which the key terms are those of order, stability, constancy, and integrity, as against a more existentialist view that prizes exploration, process, growth, flexibility, variety, and versatility of response."[21] The world view suggested by the anti-theatrical prejudice is the same one that would keep women silent and "in their place."

Paradoxically, this world view is also part of the world view of the typical Shakespearean tragic hero, actor though he is. He tries to be an actor-as-doer; he feels sullied by the necessity of pretending. He hates female pretense—what he sees in Ophelia, Gertrude, or Desdemona—in part because it exemplifies a way of life he is trying to transcend; he values constancy and integrity much as, like Macbeth, he may depart from them. The guiltier he feels about his own pretenses, the harder it is for him to trust any woman. And the tragic genre itself is in accord with his emphasis on integrity.

The spirit of Shakespearean comedy, however, is much closer to Barish's "existentialist view." The basic explanation for the different treatment of women as actors in Shakespearean comedy and Shakespearean tragedy may be that most of the qualities which, as we have seen, are associated with both women and actors are more highly valued or more easily accepted in comedy than in tragedy. Sexuality, physicality, diversion, dependence, flexibility, compromise—all of these are much more at home in the comic world than in the tragic.

Yet actors and women are also associated with one quality that tragedy values—concern for feeling—and this concern relates closely to the characterization of women rather than men as sympathetic audiences. It is partly because emotions and their expression are so important in tragedy that the ability of the actor—or the woman—to express emotions felt only briefly or not at all is such a threat. It is a commonplace of Elizabethan times as well as our own that women are allowed by convention to cry when men are not; actors are also expected to express emotions—in their performances—more often than other people do in life. Members of a theater audience too are there partly for the sake of the feelings they experience and may allow themselves to cry (or laugh) more freely than at other times. In concern for feelings actors and audience meet; to the extent they can respond to the feelings that an actor expresses, spectators momentarily transcend their ambivalence toward the actor's otherness. As I have suggested, in Shakespearean tragedy it is most often the female characters who provide the audience with a model for this attitude. Their love of the hero powerfully moves the offstage audience to sympathize with him, to experience the positive side of their ambivalence. Shakespeare's women accept the otherness of the actor in the men they love.

Perhaps we can see this most clearly when Shakespeare uses different kinds of otherness to overlap with the otherness of the actor. Many of the characteristics shared by women and actors are also shared by members of racial minority groups. Certainly one of the reasons for the power of *Othello* is the juxtaposition of the black man, who knows he is seen as foreign, with the woman whom he sees as foreign and whom, partly under pressure of his society's expectations about his passionate nature, he punishes for embodying all the passions he wishes to deny in himself. Similarly, both Elizabethan and modern writings show a set of stereotypes for old people which overlaps with those for women and actors, and the confrontations between Lear and his daughters owe some of their power to this coincidence.[22] The two plays that emphasize most the hero's sufferings because of his membership in an alien group are the two plays that emphasize most the woman's ability to sympathize as well as to act. It is as if Desdemona and Cordelia recognize the link between themselves and the hero in sharing this experience of being considered other (and thus transform it into sympathy), while Goneril and Regan recognize it and reject their own possible reflection in Lear. "I pray you, father, being weak, seem so" (II.iv.196), says Regan, using words frequently directed at women.

Although women in the comedies are more often actors than those in the tragedies, and when they are audience it is frequently to wit rather than to feeling, there too we see women as onstage audiences responding with sympathy to an actor's emotions. For example, in *Two Gentlemen of Verona*, Julia, in her boy's disguise, tells a story about herself to Silvia, now pursued by Julia's fiancé Proteus.

> . . . at that time I made her [Julia] weep agood,
> For I did play a lamentable part.
> Madam, 'twas Ariadne passioning
> For Theseus' perjury and unjust flight,
> Which I so lively acted with my tears
> That my poor mistress, movèd therewithal,
> Wept bitterly; and would I might be dead,
> If I in thought felt not her very sorrow! (IV.iv.163–70)

Julia imagines the boy actor playing the role of a deserted woman, arousing the tears of a deserted woman (herself) in the audience, and responding to those tears with sympathy. The story arouses further sympathy in Silvia—"Alas, poor lady, desolate and left" (IV.iv.172)—and Silvia's response in turn arouses admiration and gratitude that restrain Julia's instinctive feelings of competition.

Of course, not all female audiences in Shakespeare are this sympathetic; Hippolyta, watching the mechanicals perform *Pyramus and Thisbe*, says, "This is the silliest stuff that ever I heard" (V.i.208). But her mockery is much less than what Demetrius, Lysander, and Theseus give that play, and in *Love's Labor's Lost* there is an even more obvious contrast between the mockery of the lords and the gracious response of the Princess to the Nine

Worthies' Pageant. In neither situation do the ladies in the audience try to take over the focus of attention from the actors the way the men do.

Goneril and Regan aside, most of Shakespeare's women act using the same feelings that make them responsive audiences, and when they act they are concerned about the feelings of *their* audiences. In both comedy and tragedy, we can see the link between women's roles as actor and audience when their admiration or sympathy leads them to express themselves, directly or through a disguise, and to actively reach out. In the comedies, the concluding rituals and marriages that result from the mutuality of this process symbolize the acceptance of compromise, dependence, physicality, ambiguity; in the tragedies, the central characters must die to prove that their emotions are felt with constancy and not simply pretended. In both comedy and tragedy, Shakespeare's women gain their dramatic power because they seem to live so close to the conflict between the desires to keep and to lose the self, between individuality and merging with others, and between integrity and flexibility, a conflict that is part of the basis for the human interest in the theater.

NOTES

1. I use the term "actor" rather than "actress" throughout because "actor" is the generic term; see Casey Miller and Kate Swift, *Words and Women* (New York: Anchor, 1976), p. 50. On mutuality in the comedies, see my article, " 'And You Smile Not, He's Gagged': Mutuality in Shakespearean Comedy," *Philological Quarterly*, 55 (1976), 178–94.
2. All quotations from the plays are taken from *William Shakespeare: The Complete Works*, Alfred Harbage, gen. ed., (Baltimore: Penguin, 1969).
3. Norman Holland, *The Dynamics of Literary Response* (New York: Oxford University Press, 1968), pp. 75–79.
4. Robert Egan, "His Hour upon the Stage: Role-Playing and Suffering in *Macbeth*," delivered at the 1975 International Shakespeare Association Conference.
5. Jonas Barish, "The Anti-Theatrical Prejudice," *Critical Quarterly*, 8 (1966), 343.
6. Stanley Cavell, *Must We Mean What We Say?* (New York: Scribners, 1969), p. 332. See also Helene Keyssar, "I Love You. Who Are You? The Strategy of Drama in Recognition Scenes," *PMLA*, 92 (1977), 297–306.

7. Janet Adelman, *The Common Liar* (New Haven: Yale University Press, 1973), pp. 106–13.
8. Michael Goldman, *The Actor's Freedom* (New York: Viking, 1975), p. 17.
9. Simone de Beauvoir, *The Second Sex*, trans. H. M. Parshley (New York: Bantam, 1961), p. xvi. Leslie Fiedler, *The Stranger in Shakespeare* (New York: Stein and Day, 1972), discusses woman as other, but he often identifies Shakespeare's attitude too closely with that of his male characters. Some affinities between women and the theater are noted in Juliet Dusinberre's *Shakespeare and the Nature of Women* (New York: Barnes & Noble, 1975), pp. 11, 247.
10. Goldman, *The Actor's Freedom*, pp. 12–13.
11. See Dorothy Dinnerstein, *The Mermaid and the Minotaur: Sexual Arrangements and Human Malaise* (New York: Harper & Row, 1976); Louis B. Wright, *Middle-Class Culture in Elizabethan England* (1935; rpt. Ithaca: Cornell University Press, 1958), esp. pp. 465–507; Carroll Camden, "Iago on Women," *Journal of English and Germanic Philology*, 48 (1949), 57–71.
12. Barish, "Anti-Theatrical Prejudice," p. 330.
13. See Elizabeth Janeway, *Man's World, Woman's Place* (New York: Morrow, 1971), pp. 112–13.
14. Philip Weissman, *Creativity in the Theater* (New York: Basic Books, 1965), p. 19.
15. *Ibid.*, p. 14.
16. Nancy Chodorow, "Family Structure and Feminine Personality," in *Woman, Culture and Society*, ed. Michelle Z. Rosaldo and Louise Lamphere (Stanford: Stanford University Press, 1974), p. 44.
17. Weissman, *Creativity in the Theater*, pp. 13–14.
18. Goldman, *The Actor's Freedom*, p. 122.
19. Barish, "Anti-Theatrical Prejudice," p. 331.
20. Goldman, *The Actor's Freedom*, p. 9.
21. Barish, "Anti-Theatrical Prejudice," p. 342.
22. See Lawrence Stone, "Walking Over Grandma," *New York Review of Books*, 24 (May 12, 1977), 10–16.

A Penchant for Perdita on the Eighteenth-Century English Stage

IRENE G. DASH

When *The Winter's Tale* finally gained acceptance on the eighteenth-century stage, it was not as Shakespeare's full-length play but in abbreviated versions derived from the last two acts. On March 25, 1754, John Rich presented a musical farce, *The Sheep Shearing or Florizel and Perdita*, by MacNamara Morgan, as an afterpiece at Covent Garden.[1] Two years later, David Garrick presented his version of the play, also entitled *Florizel and Perdita*, at Drury Lane.[2] As their titles suggest, both versions center on the sheepshearing, pastoral scenes of the last two acts. Garrick's, however, has far greater pretensions than does Morgan's. Presented as the main piece in a double bill with another work derived from Shakespeare, *Catherine and Petruchio*, it pledges to "lose no Drop of that immortal Man!"[3] By eliminating the gap of sixteen years, however, it amputates most of the first three acts—a contradiction that Garrick's critics were quick to observe. Nevertheless, the actor-manager had discovered the key to *The Win-*

This essay is reprinted, with revisions, from Studies in Eighteenth Century Culture, 6 (1977), 331–46.

ter's Tale's theatrical potential; his version remained popular until the close of the century.

Earlier attempts to revive the full-length play had had limited success. Giffard's famous "first-time-acted-in-a-hundred-years" production during the season of 1740–41 and Rich's the following season at Covent Garden survived nine and five performances respectively.[4] Nor was Hull's five-act version in 1771 applauded.[5] For even after audiences and critics no longer insisted on the unities, only the pastoral adaptations drew their support. Several factors explain this development: the cultural and intellectual atmosphere of the 1730s and '40s; the work of the early textual editors; but most of all, the character of the women in the plays.

With the publication in 1739 of William Smith's first direct English translation of Longinus's *On the Sublime*, poets, playwrights, and painters began to reexamine their aims.[6] Smith's works prepared "the way for the ultimate rejection" of the neoclassical rules.[7] Suddenly the outdoors—external nature and simple rural characters—provided new and vital sources of inspiration. Seeking to evoke from their readers an emotional response approximating the sublime experience described by Longinus, poets indulged in vivid descriptions of nature's minutest changes. To compensate for the diminution of action and wit, they expanded their poems to include philosophical musings, discovering analogues to man's behavior in the constantly changing cycles of nature. Descriptions of natural phenomena were interspersed with contemplative passages on life and death and the transitoriness of man's existence. In Perdita's analogy of the flowers of the seasons to the ages of man, in the description of the storm at sea, and in the behavior of the natural rustic characters at the sheepshearing, *The Winter's Tale* fit the new mold. In 1747, it was therefore natural for William Warburton, responding to the new intellectual climate, to commend for special reader attention the speeches of the rustics—the natural Clown, the rough, semi-civilized Old Shepherd, and the idealized Shepherdess—presaging the versions of the 1750s.[8] Before his work, Pope too had laid the groundwork for the pastoral adaptations when he subdivided the scenes in Shakespeare's plays into brief scenic units. Particularly in IV.iv, where he created eight scenes, breaking down the long nine-hundred-line sheepshearing episode, Pope revealed a theatrical potential previously unrealized.[9]

On the whole, however, the first eighteenth-century editors indicated a progression of interest from the earlier to the later sections of the play: from the women of its potentially tragic first acts to Perdita, who dances, strews flowers, and philosophizes at the sheepshearing. Rowe, for example, introduced excessive punctuation into the dramatically explosive sections. Because he himself was a writer of she-tragedies, one can only suspect that he hoped, through a plethora of dashes and exclamation points added to male speeches, to enhance the emotional intensity of responses to Hermione and therefore of her appeal to contemporary audiences. Because he did not tamper with her text, however, she withstood his attempts, remaining aloof and self-contained.[10] Pope, too, revealed a bias for the early sections. Designating as memorable only two speeches, he chose Polixenes' reverie on the father-son relationship—"He's all my exercise, my mirth, my matter" (I.ii.165−71)—and Paulina's condemnation of Leontes— "A thousand knees, / Ten thousand years together . . . could not move the gods / To look that way thou wert" (III.ii.205−12).[11]

The discovery of flaws in Paulina's character, and a heightened sensitivity to some of the play's more sexually outspoken language, marked the next step in textual responses to the play. Theobald challenged the propriety of Paulina's calling the king a fool (III.ii.184): "It is certainly too gross and blunt in Paulina, tho' She might impeach the King of Fooleries in some of his past Actions and Conduct, to call him downright a Fool. And it is much more pardonable in her to arraign his Morals, and the Qualities of his Mind, than rudely to call him *Idiot* to his Face."[12] Thomas Hanmer questioned the authenticity of the italicized sections of the following passage, labeling them "spurious," while Warburton deleted these lines from his text, attributing their authorship to "some profligate player":[13]

It is a bawdy planet, that will strike
Where 'tis predominant; *and 'tis powerful, think it,*
From east, west, north, and south. Be it concluded,
No barricado for a belly. Know't,
It will let in and out the enemy,

With bag and baggage. Many thousand on's
Have the disease, and feel't not.

(I.ii.201−7; emphasis added)

Although this speech, with its inferences of sexuality and promiscuity, was the only one excised by editors, the mid-century revisers by discarding the first three acts accepted the implications of the precedent. But by removing the first half of the play, they cut out Leontes' passion-wracked passages, his intense spurts of jealousy, and his arrogance. Since characters in drama are defined by their interaction with other characters, the omission of the early scenes affected not only the portrait of Leontes but also those of Hermione and Paulina. Contrast, action, and re-action all help to project an image. Hermione's strength becomes unnecessary if there is no challenge, no contest, for her to face. And Paulina's role as the voice of conscience also loses its meaning. By revising, excising, and emending, both Morgan and Garrick substituted weak women for strong, and strong men for weak.

I believe that this is an important reason for the comparative popularity of the pastoral versions over those of the full-length productions of *The Winter's Tale.* However, it was not simply the strength of these women that was abrasive, for statistics on the popularity of Shakespeare's plays during the second half of the eighteenth century indicate that among repertory favorites were *Macbeth, The Merchant of Venice, As You Like It, Much Ado about Nothing,* and *Cymbeline.*[14] All have strong women. All save *Macbeth* have attractive, triumphant women, resembling those in *The Winter's Tale.* With the exception of Portia, however, none of the other women challenges the notion of the acquiescent wife. Imogen's dilemma results from her accepting too readily the message relayed through Iachimo. Rosalind and Beatrice, while they entertain us with their wit during the premarital and highly acceptable "chase," never hint at any prospect of irregular patterns of behavior after marriage. Just as their actions during the play, although brave and enchanting, conform to archetypal patterns of female coquetry, so their post−wedding ceremony demeanor may be expected to conform to acceptable stereotypes. In Hermione and Paulina, however, Shakespeare creates two married women who challenge male rule and reject male domination of female life experience.

The most outspoken of them, Paulina, exhibits a fearlessness and self-confidence that suggest her later role as the scourge of Leontes. It is she who charges the King's lords to follow her—"be second" to her—in defying their sovereign. And it is she who, alternating between scorn and appeasement, promises first, "I have come to bring him sleep," then remonstrates:

> 'Tis such as you
> That creep like shadows by him, and do sigh
> At each his needless heavings—such as you
> Nourish the cause of his awaking.   (II.iii.33–36)

Shakespeare also establishes her credentials earlier, at her first appearance in the jail scene. Through the jailer we hear of her virtue, "a worthy lady, / And one whom much I honour" (II.ii.5–6). We also perceive that she is considered a threat, for the jailer has "express commandment" (8) to bar her entry. Her reputation precedes her. It is worth observing that although Hermione's scene with her women immediately precedes the jail scene, Paulina's first entrance is reserved for a scene of her own. Contrasted with the muted humble character of the jailer, her brilliance, wit, and sophistication sparkle. Thus introduced, neither as a lady-in-waiting to the Queen nor as a member of Hermione's staff, Paulina functions as an independent, a woman with a staff of her own. "So please you, madam, / To put apart *these your attendants*, I / Shall bring Emilia forth" (12–14; emphasis added).

The characterization then moves from second person comments on her to positive examples of Paulina's strength when she convinces the jailer to relinquish the infant:

> This child was prisoner to the womb and is
> By law and process of great Nature thence
> Freed, and enfranchised; not a party to
> The anger of the king, nor guilty of,
> If any be, the trespass of the queen.   (II.ii.58–62)

Her ingenuity and mental acumen have defined the legal limits of the jail; her introduction is thus complete. The woman who strides into the King's chamber in the next scene is someone we know. Although the range of her capacities is still a mystery to us—and will remain so until the play's closing scene—we know that her challenge to the men to "be second" to her in courage and imaginative action is not empty ranting.

But this Paulina, the woman who cries out, even at her husband, "Unvenerable be thy hands, if thou / Tak'st up the princess, by that forcèd baseness / Which he has put upon 't!" (II.iii.76–78), is not the Paulina of Garrick's version. In imposing a unity of place as well as time on *The Winter's Tale*, the eighteenth-century actor-dramatist brought Paulina to Bohemia, there to accept the protection of Polixenes. In Garrick's text her function as the conscience of Leontes disappears. Ironically, her great speech, commended by Pope in 1725, is transferred to Leontes, who, weeping with self-pity, exclaims:

> *I can't* repent these things, for they are heavier
> Than all *my* woes can stir: *I must* betake *me*
> To nothing but despair—a thousand knees
> Ten thousand years together, naked, fasting,
> Upon a barren mountain, and still winter,
> In storms perpetual, could not move the gods
> To look *this* way *upon me*.   (p. 11)[15]

With a few changes of pronouns from "thou" to "I," Garrick creates a repentant, sorrowful, and sorrowing male to be loved and forgiven. Paulina he transforms into a dependent, displaced person who has "fled with her effects, for safety of her life, to Bohemia" (p. 4). No longer is her great dramatic moment concentrated in the trial scene. Instead it has been shifted to the close of the play. No longer does her strength lie in intellectual power and righteous outrage. Instead the emphasis rests on Paulina as magician and Paulina the old woman who bemoans her single state: "I an old turtle, / Will wing me to some wither'd bough, and there / My mate, that's never to be found again, / Lament 'till I am lost" (p. 65). Although the lines are Shakespeare's, the characterization is Garrick's. For he has exorcised the scourge of Leontes and made the King his own man. If Garrick has also subverted the intention of the text, he has nevertheless enhanced its appeal to eighteenth-century audiences.

The second woman, Hermione, does not, on her first appearance, impress the reader or auditor as an independent, strong, self-confident person. She belongs to that race of human beings whose inner strength surfaces only during periods of trial. Thus, when we first meet her, she is happy, complacent, relaxed, and utterly womanly. In her physical being, large with child near the end of her pregnancy, she expresses visually as well as in her words a dependent, sexist role. Significantly, her first words are spoken in response to her husband's command: "Tongue-tied, our queen? Speak you" (I.ii.27). Although in their bantering quality her words do not suggest a woman fearful of her husband, they do reinforce the first impression that this is a female who sees her primary role as wife to her husband, and hostess for his home and kingdom. Her wit and ingenuity are in the service of Leontes. Ironically, her success as wife and hostess proves her undoing; employing coquetry, charm, and the familiar skills expected of a woman, she convinces Polixenes to linger longer in Sicilia. Her mocking threats win Polixenes—but lose Leontes. The charm of her request and the warmth of her pursuit illuminate her womanliness. And it is this womanly loveliness that Leontes wants to possess wholly.

As the scene progresses, Shakespeare gives lines to Hermione that also suggest a sexuality and passion capable of arousing further the jealousy of her husband. Although the following passage is considered one of the cruxes of the play, defying absolute comprehension, it evokes images, although fleeting and temporary, that provide further insights into the character of Hermione. Persistently begging for a series of answers to her questions with, "What! Have I twice said well? When was 't before?" she admits delight in being praised, exclaiming:

> Our praises are our wages—you may ride's
> With one soft kiss a thousand furlongs, ere
> With spur we heat an acre. (I.ii.90, 94–96)

The images are there: kiss, ride, spur, heat. And they suggest the sensuality of the speaker herself.

This concept of the womanly woman is reinforced in the following scene, that in the Queen's chamber. There we view the petulant, somewhat fatigued Hermione dismissing her son to the care of her women. Not until her life is challenged does Hermione reveal the core of strength that is to sustain her—first through the trial, then through sixteen years in seclusion. As she leaves her

chamber in this scene, it is no longer the fatigued woman seeking
rest whom we hear, but the regal Queen consoling her women:

> Do not weep, good fools;
> There is no cause; when you shall know your mistress
> Has deserved prison, then abound in tears,
> As I come out.   (II.i.118–21)

She remains statuesque, calm, and reserved.

Hermione, then, is perceived first as a woman—the sexual
bias of her role emphasized by the physical self that she carries
through the first scenes. But Hermione develops emotionally during the play. When she comes to the court in the third act, she
carries herself with remarkable restraint and calm, insisting on
her own innocence at the trial. Did adversity kindle this inner
strength? Or was it a quality belonging to the daughter of a king
but submerged to help her conform to the female role she was
physically destined to play? "The Emperor of Russia was my father" (III.ii.117), she asserts, implying that she should be respected and honored as an equal. Standing before a court of men
and a hostile husband, however, she recognizes the impossibility
of winning a just verdict. Nevertheless, the Queen persists: "My
life stands in the level of your dreams, / Which I'll lay down"
(III.ii.79–80)—but she never does. Instead, after fainting at the
news of her son's death, she chooses to disappear, refusing to be a
breeder of disposable children. That her reason for seclusion cen-
ters on the return of the infant, Perdita, is obvious in the single
speech uttered during the play's closing moments:

> You gods look down,
> And from your sacred vials pour your graces
> Upon my daughter's head! Tell me, mine own,
> Where hast thou been preserved? Where lived? How found
> Thy father's court? For thou shalt hear that I,
> Knowing by Paulina that the oracle
> Gave hope thou wast in being, have preserved
> Myself to see the issue.   (v.iii.121–28)

But Shakespeare's Hermione, like his Paulina, disappears
from the versions usually performed during the second half of the
eighteenth century. Not present at all in Morgan's version, she
differs from Shakespeare's mature queen in Garrick's version.

There she appears only in the last scene, and her single speech, quoted above, is divided into several parts. Adding new material as well, Garrick alters the dominant theme. Instead of a mother's joy at the restoration of a daughter, the scene revolves around a wife's ecstacy over reunion with a husband. First asking for blessings on both Florizel and Perdita, then insisting that all present pray "Before this swelling flood o'er-bear our reason" (p. 64), Hermione finally exclaims: "This firstling *duty* paid, let transport loose, / My lord, my king,—there's distance in those names, / My husband!" (p. 65, emphasis added). There's no question of the source of Hermione's greatest joy. Garrick makes explicit what may or may not have been implicit in Hermione's embracing of Leontes in Shakespeare's drama. Moreover Hermione's words— the grouping together of "My lord, my king . . . / My husband"— suggest a subservience not indicated in the closing scene of *The Winter's Tale*. For Garrick revives the wifely Hermione of the early scenes and buries the more mature, self-reliant woman of the third and fifth acts. Furthermore, his technique illustrates Arthur Sherbo's thesis for the creation of a sentimental drama. Sherbo argues that repetition and prolongation of certain elements account for a drama's fall into that "debased literary genre."[16] By prolonging Hermione's effusive greeting to her daughter, extending the prayers to include Florizel, and inserting a multiplicity of references to husband, lord, and king, the eighteenth-century adapter alters the tone and transforms an unusually reserved scene into one bathed in sentimentality.

Because Garrick "knew the temper of his audiences better than any other manager, possibly, that has ever lived," he was able to develop a successful formula for the statue scene.[17] Paradoxically, however, Hermione was not always retained in stage productions of *Florizel and Perdita*—probably because Garrick's work was a pastoral and as such was often abbreviated to conform to the requirements of time or personnel for a total evening's program.[18] But the success of this revision was not lost on subsequent producers and managers of *The Winter's Tale*. Even when, as in Kemble's case, a form of the full-length play was revived and the pastoral emphasis discarded in favor of the tragic, Garrick's transformation of the character of Hermione was adopted.[19]

Perdita, too, was slightly modified for eighteenth-century audiences. Fewer textual revisions were necessary in her lines, however, because in many ways Perdita's behavior resembles that of the idealized stereotypical woman. Despite the fact that she epitomizes the pastoral shepherdess of the "golden age," since she is endowed with beauty, wisdom, courage, and innocence, and illustrates the ascendancy of "nature over nurture," she does defer with humility to the man she loves, a characteristic of the more human, and conventional, woman in love. Even in the contrasting of her private remonstrance to Florizel to return to his father with her public expansive declaration of love, she acts according to acceptable patterns. If Perdita is a little forward in her declaration—

> O, these I lack
> To make you garlands of, and my sweet friend,
> To strew him o'er and o'er!
> . . . .
> . . . like a bank for Love to lie and play on,   (IV.iv.127–30)

—she is quick to retract, attributing her arrogance to the "robe" of queen which does "change [her] disposition" (IV.iv.135).

Perdita has some qualities, however, which link her to the two older women of the play. She exhibits self-confidence and individuality, particularly when confronting moral issues. Even if the issues seem somewhat removed from reality, as in the reference to bastard flowers—gillyvors—she insists:

> I'll not put
> The dibble in earth, to set one slip of them,
> No more than were I painted, I would wish
> This youth should say 'twere well, and only therefore
> Desire to breed by me.   (IV.iv.99–103)

Although Polixenes is her guest, she refuses to play the perfect hostess. Again, when she cautions that the peddler "use no scurrilous words in's tunes" (IV.iv.215), she projects the portrait of the upright moral maiden. Finally, after Polixenes unmasks, her generalization about humanity—"The selfsame sun that shines upon his court / Hides not his visage from our cottage" (448–49)—indicates a view that all people are basically equal. Her comment courageously contrasts with Polixenes' damning outburst.

Nevertheless, Shakespeare's Perdita is not without moral imperfections. She has no scruples about leaving her father and brother in a rather dangerous predicament. Nor does she consider the possible "moral" consequences of traveling alone with Florizel. Although she retreats temporarily, "I'll queen it no inch farther, / But milk my ewes, and weep" (iv.iv.453–54), she is easily convinced by Florizel's "Lift up thy looks; / From my succession wipe me, father, I / Am heir to my affection" (483–85).

Because Perdita is the core figure of Garrick's and Morgan's versions, it is important to be aware of these particular responses of hers; the adapters were. Conscious of her conformity as well as her nonconformity, they excised when she seemed too independent; they emended when she sounded too outspoken; and they invented when she seemed unaware of her moral obligations. Thus her debate with Polixenes over bastard flowers disappears from their texts. Reference to "maidenheads" becomes "maiden honours" and "Maiden blushes."[20] Finally, in a work that resembles a Harlequin entertainment more closely than it approximates Shakespeare's drama, Morgan imposes morality by bringing a priest to the sheepshearing. Garrick weighs down Perdita with a sense of guilt for the division of father from son:

> Alas! I've shown too much
> A maiden's simpleness; I have betray'd,
> Unwittingly divorc'd a noble prince
> From a dear father's love. (p. 41)

From self-doubt to dependency is a short step. We note that Perdita leans "heavily on Florizel's bosom" during the closing scene. To the Prince's observation of her weakness, "My princely shepherdess! / This is too much for hearts of thy soft mold" (p. 63), Garrick adds her overly modest apology:

> I am all shame
> And ignorance itself, how to put on
> This novel garment of gentility. (p. 66)

Florizel, the strong male, supports her, promising to teach her the ways of the court.

Since some form of Garrick's or Morgan's version appeared for a total of ninety-six performances on an average of every two years during the second half of the eighteenth century, the persistence of these revivals indicates a penchant for Perdita and for the values she symbolized. An attempt was made in 1771 to revive the full-length play. Inspired probably by the new attitude to-

ward the neoclassical rules in the theater and by the support inherent in Samuel Johnson's "Preface" (1765), Thomas Hull revised the play, including the time span of sixteen years. The comments prefacing the text and the pseudo-literary footnotes
explaining excisions, however, disclose the real estimate of the
work and the continued rejection of the women whom Shakespeare created. After commending Garrick's version, the editor
observes that "the present copy has been studiously prun'd and
regulated, by the ingenious Mr. Hull, . . . who has certainly made
it much more bearable than the author left it." We are then told
that it will never do well on the stage because it requires good actors "who find too small a scope for impressive, creditable exer-
tion; save what belongs to Florizel, Perdita, and Autolicus."[21]
This reference to the roles of Florizel, Perdita, and Autolicus prepares us for what we are to find in the text. For although the first
three acts have been restored, they are skeletal. The main emphasis remains with the pastoral last two acts, those developed by
Garrick and Morgan.

It is difficult for us today to understand this lack of interest
in the psychologically challenging portraits of Leontes, Paulina,
and Hermione as they debate Hermione's faithfulness or the infant's parentage. But Hull's version shows little sympathy for the
play's older characters. Grouped together, Polixenes and Hermione are described as "watergruel character[s], equally distant
from giving pleasure or disgust" (p. 154). The scene that sparks
Leontes' jealousy—Hermione's successful invitation to Polixenes—"tho' curtailed, is still too long, quibbling and flat, conceived in terms, on the queen's side, rather childishly low, then
maturely royal" (p. 156). The humanity of these first scenes with
the imposition of family relationships on monarchy, as a foil for
the later plot development, escapes the commentators. Preoc-
cupied with the weakness of Hermione and probably conditioned
by the more familiar stage characterizations of the time, they
miss the implications of the scene. Rejecting also the bantering
between Mamillius and the Queen's women in the bedroom
scene, as "one of the trifling excrescences which Shakespeare
suffered to shoot from his luxuriant genius" (p. 164), the editor
chooses to delete references to the physical and emotional weight
of Hermione's pregnancy in a drama that is as much about children and infidelity as about pastoral innocence and beauty. Fi-

nally, when he excises lines of Leontes that show him to be "little better than a bedlamite" (pp. 156–57), the editor alters the "balance of power"—of inner power—between the men and the women.

Thus the penchant for Perdita in the eighteenth century took two forms: concentration on those sections of the play that revolved around the most conforming of the three women, Perdita, and rejection of those sections where the strength and conviction of Paulina and Hermione most clearly shine. Although the full-length play was returned to the stage in the nineteenth century, the eighteenth-century versions, particularly Garrick's, left a residue of influence on interpretations of the women. This was logical. For, in comparison with the short-lived productions of the whole work in the 1740s and in 1771, the versions of the fifties had prolonged theatrical exposure. In them, the images of the women who remained were altered to conform to acceptable female patterns. Bowing, therefore, to the power of the men who rewrote their roles and to the spectators who applauded their actions, the strong, self-reliant women of *The Winter's Tale* relinquished the stage.

NOTES

1. George Winchester Stone, Jr., *The London Stage*, part 4 (Carbondale: Southern Illinois University Press, 1962), I, 416. This work will hereafter be cited as *LS4*.
2. *LS4*, II, 521.
3. David Garrick, *Florizel and Perdita* (London: Tonson, 1758), prologue. Page numbers from this edition will subsequently be included in the text.
4. Charles Beecher Hogan, *Shakespeare in the Theatre, 1701–1800* (Oxford: Clarendon Press, 1952), I, 457–58.
5. *Ibid.*, II, 680–81.
6. Dionysius Longinus, *On the Sublime*, trans. from the Greek, with Notes and Observations by William Smith, 2d ed. corrected and rev. (London: Dod, 1743), pp. 135–40, 151–55, 169.
7. John William Hey Atkins, *English Literary Criticism: 17th and 18th Centuries* (1951; rpt. London: University Paperbacks, 1966), p. 186.
8. William Warburton, ed., *The Works of Shakespear in Eight Volumes* (London: Knapton, Birt et al., 1747), III. Warburton enclosed in quotation marks all the speeches that he felt were memorable. For a more complete analysis see Irene Dash, "Changing Attitudes toward Shake-

speare as Reflected in Editions and Staged Adaptations of *The Winter's Tale* from 1703 to 1762," Diss. Columbia University 1971, chap. 4.

9. Irene Dash, "The Touch of the Poet," *Modern Language Studies*, 4 (Fall 1974), 59–64.

10. Nicholas Rowe, ed., *The Works of Mr. William Shakespear* (London: Tonson, 1709), II. For a fuller discussion of Rowe's exact changes, see Dash, "Changing Attitudes," chap. 2.

11. All references will be to *The Winter's Tale*, ed. Frank Kermode (New York: New American Library, 1963).

12. Lewis Theobald, ed., *The Works of Shakespeare* (London: n.p., 1733), III, 106.

13. Sir Thomas Hanmer, ed., *The Works of Shakespear* (Oxford: Bettersworth, Hitch, et al., 1744), II; Warburton ed., III, 287. Warburton's excision is of lines 203–6, "From East . . . baggage."

14. Hogan, *Shakespeare*, II, 716–19.

15. The italicized words are Garrick's alteration of Shakespeare's text, III.ii.206–12.

16. Arthur Sherbo, *English Sentimental Drama* (East Lansing: Michigan State University Press, 1957), pp. vii, 32–71.

17. George Winchester Stone, Jr., "Garrick, and an Unknown Operatic Version of *Love's Labour's Lost*," *Review of English Studies*, 15 (July 1939), 328.

18. Because Hermione did not always appear in the staged versions, Stone in *LS4* and Hogan in *Shakespeare in the Theatre* do not always agree on whether to attribute a specific production to Morgan or Garrick. See Irene Dash, "Garrick or Colman?" *Notes and Queries*, 216 (April 1971), 154, for exact comparison of productions. Further evidence of the elimination of Hermione from Garrick's text appears in the copy of the play included in David Garrick, *Dramatic Works* (London: A. Miller, 1798), I, 242–75. There the entire last section, the statue scene, is omitted.

19. William Shakespeare, *The Winter's Tale*, adapted for the stage by J. P. Kemble (London, 1811). This is Folger Prompt *WT* 25.

20. Garrick's "maiden honours," p. 21; MacNamara Morgan's "Maiden blushes," "Florizel and Perdita" (1754), Larpent Manuscript Collection no. 110, Huntington Library, San Marino, California.

21. William Shakespeare, *The Winter's Tale* (London: printed for John Bell, 1773), V, introduction. This separate issue of the play, which was planned from the start, follows the same text and pagination as the Bell 1774 *Works*.

The Miranda Trap

Sexism and Racism in Shakespeare's *Tempest*

LORIE JERRELL LEININGER

Shakespeare's *Tempest* was first performed before King James I at Whitehall in November of 1611. It was presented a second time at the court of King James early in 1613, as part of the marriage festivities of James's daughter Elizabeth, who, at the age of sixteen, was being married to Frederick the Elector Palatine. The marriage masque within *The Tempest* may have been added for this occasion. In any case, the Goddess Ceres' promise of a life untouched by winter ("*Spring come to you at the farthest / In the very end of harvest!*" IV.i.114–15)[1] and all the riches the earth can provide ("*Earth's increase, foison plenty*") was offered to the living royal couple as well as to Ferdinand and Miranda.

Elizabeth had fallen dutifully in love with the bridegroom her father had chosen for her, the youthful ruler of the rich and fertile Rhineland and the leading Protestant prince of central Europe. Within seven years Frederick was to become "Frederick the Winter King" and "The Luckless Elector," but in 1613 he was still the living counterpart of Ferdinand in *The Tempest*, even as Elizabeth was the counterpart of Miranda. Like Miranda, Elizabeth was beautiful, loving, chaste, and obedient. She believed her fa-

An earlier version of this essay was presented at a Special Session on Problems in Racism and Sexism as Reflected in Shakespeare at the MLA Annual Convention, December 1977, Chicago, Illinois.

ther to be incapable of error, in this sharing James's opinion of himself. Miranda in the play is "admired Miranda," "perfect," "peerless," one who "outstrips all praise"; Elizabeth was praised as "the eclipse and glory of her kind," a rose among violets.[2]

What was the remainder of her life to be like? Elizabeth, this flesh-and-blood Miranda, might have found it difficult to agree that "We are such stuff / As dreams are made on; and our little life / Is rounded with a sleep" (IV.i.156–58). The future held thirteen children for her, and forty years as a landless exile. Her beloved Frederick died of the plague at the age of thirty-six, a plague spreading through battle camps and besieged cities in a Europe devastated by a war which appeared endless—the Thirty Years War, in which whole armies in transit disappeared through starvation and pestilence. The immediate cause of this disastrous war had been Frederick and Elizabeth's foolhardy acceptance of the disputed throne of Bohemia. Politically inept, committed to a belief in hierarchical order and Neoplatonic courtliness, the new king and queen failed to engage the loyalty of the Bohemians or to prepare adequately for the inevitable attack by the previously deposed king.

While the happiness of the young lovers in *The Tempest* depended upon their obedience to Miranda's father, the repeated political and military failures of Elizabeth and Frederick were exacerbated by their dependence upon the shifting promises of King James. Elizabeth experienced further tragedy when two of her sons drowned, the eldest at the age of fifteen in an accident connected with spoils from the New World, the fourth son in a tempest while privateering in the New World. There was no Prospero-figure to restore them to life magically.

The Princess Elizabeth, watching *The Tempest* in 1613, was incapable of responding to clues which might have warned her that being Miranda might prove no unmixed blessing: that even though Miranda occupies a place next to Prospero in the play's hierarchy and appears to enjoy all of the benefits which Caliban, at the base of that hierarchy, is denied, she herself might prove a victim of the play's hierarchical values. Elizabeth would be justified in seeing Miranda as the royal offspring of a ducal father, as incomparably beautiful (her external beauty mirroring her inward virtue, in keeping with Neoplatonic idealism), as lovingly educated and gratefully responsive to that education, as chaste (her chastity symbolic of all human virtue), obedient and, by the end of the play, rewarded with an ideal husband and the inheritance of two dukedoms. Caliban, at the opposite pole, is presented as the reviled offspring of a witch and the Devil, as physically ugly (his ugly exterior mirroring his depraved inner nature), as racially vile, intrinsically uneducable, uncontrollably lustful (a symbol of all vice), rebellious, and, being defined as a slave by nature, as justly enslaved.

Modern readers have become more attentive than Elizabeth could have been in 1613 to clues such as Prospero's address to Miranda, "What! I say, / My foot my tutor?" (I.ii.471–72). The crucial line is spoken near the end of the scene which begins with Prospero's and Ariel's delighted revelation that the tempest was raised through Prospero's magic powers and then continues with the demonstration of Prospero's ability to subjugate the spirit Ariel, the native Caliban, and finally the mourning Prince Ferdinand to his will. Miranda's concern is engaged when Prospero accuses Ferdinand of being a spy, a traitor and usurper; Prospero threatens to manacle Ferdinand's head and feet together and to force him to drink salt water. When Ferdinand raises his sword to resist Prospero's threats, Prospero magically deprives him of all strength. Miranda, alarmed, cries,

> O dear father,
> Make not too rash a trial of him, for
> He's gentle, and not fearful. (I.ii.469–71)

Prospero's response is,

> What! I say,
> My foot my tutor? (I.ii.471–72)

Miranda is given to understand that she is the foot in the family organization of which Prospero is the head. Hers not to reason why, hers but to follow directions: indeed, what kind of a body would one have (Prospero, or the play, asks) if one's foot could think for itself, could go wherever it pleased, independent of the head?

Now it is true that Prospero is acting out a role which he knows to be unjust, in order to cement the young couple's love by placing obstacles in their way. Miranda, however, has no way of knowing this. Prospero has established the principle that stands whether a father's action be just or unjust: the daughter must submit to his demand for absolute unthinking obedience.

But might not being a "foot" to another's "head" prove advantageous, provided that the "head" is an all-powerful godlike father who educates and protects his beloved daughter? Some ambiguous answers are suggested by the play, particularly in the triangular relationship of Prospero, Miranda, and Caliban.

When Prospero says to Miranda,

We'll visit Caliban my slave, who never
Yields us kind answer,

Miranda's response is,

'Tis a villain, sir,
I do not love to look on. (1.ii.310–12)

Miranda fears Caliban, and she has reason to fear him. The play permits either of two interpretations to explain the threat which Caliban poses. His hostility may be due to his intrinsically evil nature, or to his present circumstances: anyone who is forced into servitude, confined to a rock, kept under constant surveillance, and punished by supernatural means would wish his enslavers ill.[3] Whatever Caliban's original disposition may have been when he lived alone on the isle—and we lack disinterested evidence—he must in his present circumstances feel hostility toward Prospero and Miranda. Miranda is far more vulnerable to Caliban's ill will than is her all-powerful father.

Prospero responds to Miranda's implicit plea to be spared exposure to Caliban's hostility with the *practical* reasons for needing a slave:

But, as 'tis,
We cannot miss him: he does make our fire,
Fetch in our wood, and serves in offices
That profit us. What, ho! slave! Caliban! (1.ii.312–15)

A daughter might conceivably tell her loving father that she would prefer that they gather their own wood, that in fact no "profit" can outweigh the uneasiness she experiences. Miranda, however, is not free to speak, since a father who at any time can silence his daughter with "What! My foot my tutor?" will have educated that "foot" to extreme sensitivity toward what her father does or does not wish to hear from her. Miranda dare not object to her enforced proximity to a hostile slave, for within the play's universe of discourse any attempt at pressing her own needs would constitute both personal insubordination and a disruption of the hierarchical order of the universe of which the "foot/head" familial organization is but one reflection.

Miranda, admired and sheltered, has no way out of the cycle of being a dependent foot in need of protection, placed in a threatening situation which in turn calls for more protection, and thus increased dependence and increased subservience.

Miranda's presence as the dependent, innocent, feminine extension of Prospero serves a specific end in the play's power dynamics. Many reasons are given for Caliban's enslavement; the one which carries greatest dramatic weight is Caliban's sexual threat to Miranda. When Prospero accuses Caliban of having sought "to violate / The honour of my child" (1.ii.349–50), Caliban is made to concur in the accusation:

> O ho, O ho! Would't had been done!
> Thou didst prevent me; I had peopled else
> This isle with Calibans.   (1.ii.351–53)

We can test the element of sexual politics at work here by imagining, for a moment, that Prospero had been cast adrift with a small son instead of a daughter. If, twelve years later, a ship appeared bearing King Alonso and a marriageable daughter, the play's resolution of the elder generation's hatreds through the love of their offspring could still have been effected. What would be lost in such a reconstruction would be the sexual element in the enslavement of the native. No son would serve. Prospero needs Miranda as sexual bait, and then needs to protect her from the threat which is inescapable given his hierarchical world—slavery being the ultimate extension of the concept of hierarchy. It is Prospero's needs—the Prosperos of the world—not Miranda's, which are being served here.

The most elusive yet far reaching function of Miranda in the play involves the role of her chastity in the allegorical scheme. Most critics agree that the chastity of Miranda and Ferdinand in the fourth act symbolizes all human virtue ("Chastity is the quality of Christ, the essential symbol of civilization"[4]), while Caliban's lust symbolizes all human vice.

The first result of this schematic representation of all virtue and vice as chastity and lust is the exclusion from the field of
moral concern the very domination and enslavement which the
play vividly dramatizes. The exclusion is accomplished with phe-
nomenal success under the guise of religion, humanism, and Neoplatonic idealism, by identifying Prospero with God (or spirit, or
soul, or imagination), and Caliban with the Devil (or matter,
body, and lust). Within the Christian-humanist tradition, the superiority of spirit over matter, or soul over body, was a commonplace: body existed to serve soul, to be, metaphorically, enslaved by soul. In a tradition which included the *Psychomachia*,
medieval morality plays, and Elizabethan drama, the "higher" and
"lower" selves existing within each person's psyche had been represented allegorically in the form of Virtues and Vices. A danger
inherent in this mode of portraying inner struggle lay in the possibility of identifying certain human beings with the Vice-figures,
and others (oneself included) with the representatives of Virtue.
Such identification of self with Virtue and others with Vice led to
the great Christian-humanist inversion: the warrant to plunder,
exploit and kill in the name of God—Virtue destroying Vice.

It was "only natural" that the educated and privileged be
identified with virtue and spirit, and that those who do society's
dirty work, and all outsiders, be identified with vice and matter.
Ellen Cantarow has analyzed the tendency of allegory to link virtue with privilege and sin with misfortune, making particular
power relationships appear inevitable, "natural" and just within a
changeless, "divinely ordained" hierarchical order;[5] Nancy Hall
Rice has analyzed the manner in which the artistic process of embodying evil in one person and then punishing or destroying that
person offers an ersatz solution to the complex problem of evil,
sanctioning virulent attacks on social minorities or outcasts;[6]
and Winthrop D. Jordan has discussed the tendency of Western
civilization to link African natives, for example, with precon-
ceived concepts of sexuality and vice. Jordan speaks of "the ordered hierarchy of [imputed] sexual aggressiveness": the lower
one's place on the scale of social privilege, the more dangerously
lustful one is perceived as being.[7]

Thus in *The Tempest*, written some fifty years after England's open participation in the slave trade,[8] the island's native is
made the embodiment of lust, disobedience, and irremediable

evil, while his enslaver is presented as a God-figure. It makes an enormous difference in the expectations raised, whether one speaks of the moral obligations of Prospero-the-slave-owner toward Caliban-his-slave, or speaks of the moral obligations of Prospero-the-God-figure toward Caliban-the-lustful-Vice-figure. In the second instance (the allegorical-symbolic), the only requirement is that Prospero be punitive toward Caliban and that he defend his daughter Miranda's chastity—that daughter being needed as a pawn to counterbalance Caliban's lust. In this symbolic scheme, Miranda is deprived of any possibility of human freedom, growth or thought. She need only *be* chaste—to exist as a walking emblem of chastity. This kind of symbolism is damaging in that it deflects our attention away from the fact that real counterparts to Caliban, Prospero, and Miranda exist—that real slaves, real slave owners, and real daughters existed in 1613 for Shakespeare's contemporaries and have continued to exist since then.

To return to one of those daughters, Miranda's living counterpart Elizabeth Stuart, at whose wedding festivities *The Tempest* was performed: it appears likely that King James's daughter and her bridegroom were influenced in their unrealistic expectations of their powers and rights as future rulers by the widespread Jacobean attempt to equate unaccountable aristocratic power with benevolent infallibility and possibly by the expression of that equation in *The Tempest*. In our own century the play apparently continues to reflect ongoing societal confusions that may seduce women—and men—into complicity with those who appear to favor them while oppressing others. Can we envision a way out? If a twentieth century counterpart to Miranda were to define, and then confront, *The Tempest*'s underlying assumptions—as, obviously, neither the Miranda created by Shakespeare nor her living counterpart in the seventeenth century could do—what issues would she need to clarify? Let us invent a modern Miranda, and permit her to speak a new Epilogue:

"My father is no God-figure. No one is a God-figure. My father is a man, and fallible, as I am. Let's put an end to the fantasy of infallibility.

"There is no such thing as a 'natural slave.' No subhuman laborers exist. Let's put an end to *that* fantasy. I will not benefit from such a concept presented in any guise, be it Aristotelian, biblical, allegorical, or Neoplatonic. Three men are reminded of Indians when first they see Caliban; he might be African, his mother having been transported from Algiers. I will not be used as the excuse for his enslavement. If either my father or I feel threatened by his real or imputed lust, we can build a pale around our side of the island, gather our own wood, cook our own food, and clean up after ourselves.

"I cannot give assent to an ethical scheme that locates all virtue symbolically in one part of my anatomy. My virginity has little to do with the forces that will lead to good harvest or to greater social justice.

"Nor am I in any way analogous to a foot. Even if I were, for a moment, to accept my father's hierarchical mode, it is difficult to understand his concern over the chastity of his *foot*. There is no way to make that work. Neither my father, nor my husband, nor any one alive has the right to refer to me as his foot while thinking of himself as the head—making me the obedient mechanism of his thinking. What I do need is the opportunity to think for myself; I need practice in making mistakes, in testing the consequences of my actions, in becoming aware of the numerous disguises of economic exploitation and racism.

"Will I succeed in creating my 'brave new world' which has people in it who no longer exploit one another? I cannot be certain. I will at least make my start by springing 'the Miranda-trap,' being forced into unwitting collusion with domination by appearing to be a beneficiary. I need to join forces with Caliban—to join forces with all those who are exploited or oppressed—to stand beside Caliban and say,

As we from crimes would pardon'd be,
Let's work to set each other free."

NOTES

1. This quotation and subsequent ones are from *The Tempest*, Arden Shakespeare, ed. Frank Kermode (Cambridge, Mass.: Harvard University Press, 1958).
2. "The eclipse and glory of her kind" is the closing line of Sir Henry Wotton's poem, "On His Mistress, The Queen of Bohemia," in *The Poems of Sir Walter Raleigh . . . with those of Sir Henry Wotton and*

other Courtly Poets from 1540–1650, ed. John Hannah (London: Bell and Sons, 1892), pp. 95–96. "A rose among violets" is a paraphrase of the third verse of that poem; the compliment was often quoted.

3. That the spirit Ariel, the figure contrasted to Caliban in the allegorical scheme, is a purely imaginary construct for whom no human counterparts exist helps to obscure the fact that human counterparts for Caliban did indeed exist. A community of free blacks had been living in London for over fifteen years at the time of the writing of *The Tempest.* The first Indian to have been exhibited in England had been brought to London during the reign of Queen Elizabeth's grandfather, Henry VII. For a full discussion of the historical background see Chapter II of my dissertation, "The Jacobean Bind: A Study of *The Tempest, The Revenge of Bussy D'Ambois, The Atheist's Tragedy, A King and No King* and *The Alchemist,* the Major Plays of 1610 and 1611, in the Context of Renaissance Expansion and Jacobean Absolutism," University of Massachusetts/Amherst, 1975. For more on the effects of the ambiguity surrounding the definition of Caliban as an abstract embodiment of evil and as an inhabitant of a newly discovered island see Chapter III of the same work, which considers *The Tempest* in relation to seventeenth- and twentieth-century imperialism.

Four critics, among others, who have dealt with the colonial aspects of *The Tempest* and have focused upon Caliban and his enslavement as moral concerns are O. Mannoni, *Prospero and Caliban: The Psychology of Colonization,* trans. Pamela Powesland (New York: Praeger, 1956); Philip Mason, *Prospero's Magic: Some Thoughts on Class and Race* (London: Oxford University Press, 1962), pp. 75–97; Roberto Fernández Retamar, "Caliban," *Massachusetts Review,* 15 (Winter-Spring 1974), 7–72; and Kermode, "Introduction," *The Tempest.* While Kermode observes that Shakespeare, and more generally Renaissance writers, held contradictory attitudes toward Indians, viewing them on one hand as inhabitants of a golden age, with no *meum* or *tuum,* and on the other hand as human beasts in whom one could place no trust, he nevertheless arrives at the conclusion that "the confusion of interests characteristic of the subject is harmoniously reflected in Shakespeare's play" (p. xxxi)—a "harmony" more likely to be acceptable to those who are at ease with the historical reality of conquest and enslavement than by those who, like Caliban's living counterparts, have been conquered, enslaved, or colonized. It is puzzling that even an article as sensitive as Harry Berger, Jr.'s "Miraculous Harp: A Reading of Shakespeare's *Tempest,*" in *Shakespeare Studies,* 5 (1969), 253–83, in its exploration of the contradictory elements in Prospero's character—his tendency to see himself as a god, his limited knowledge of human nature, his pleasure in dominating others, and his preference for, and success in, dealing with projected embodiments of pure evil—falls short of focusing upon the dramatization of enslavement itself as an ethical concern. I explore this question, posed in general terms, in my "Cracking the

Code of *The Tempest*," *Bucknell Review*, 25 (Spring 1979), issue on "Shakespeare: Contemporary Critical Approaches," ed. Harry R. Garvin and Michael D. Payne.

4. Irving Ribner, "Introduction" to Shakespeare's *Tempest*, ed. George Lyman Kittredge, rev. Ribner (Waltham, Mass.: Blaisdell, 1966), p. xv.

5. Ellen Cantarow, "A Wilderness of Opinions Confounded: Allegory and Ideology," *College English*, 34 (1972), 215–16.

6. Nancy Hall Rice, "Beauty and the Beast and the Little Boy: Clues about the Origins of Sexism and Racism from Folklore and Literature," Diss. University of Massachusetts/Amherst 1974, p. 207.

7. Winthrop D. Jordan, *The White Man's Burden: Historical Origins of Racism in the United States* (New York: Oxford University Press, 1974), p. 196.

8. See, for example, accounts of the 1562–68 slaving voyages of Sir John Hawkins (one with Sir Francis Drake) which appear in Richard Hakluyt's *Principall Navigations Voiages and Discoveries of the English Nation* (London, 1589; facs. rpt. Cambridge: Cambridge University Press, 1965), Part Two, 521–22, 526–29, 531–32, 553–54, 562–64.

"O sacred, shadowy, cold, and constant queen"

Shakespeare's Imperiled and Chastening Daughters of Romance

CHARLES FREY

Shakespeare's plays often open with generational conflicts that point up distressing consequences of patriarchy. We find fathers and husbands treating children and wives as mere property or appurtenances of themselves (for example, the Duke of Milan in *The Two Gentlemen of Verona*; Egeus in *A Midsummer Night's Dream*; several men in *The Taming of the Shrew* and *The Merry Wives of Windsor*; the Capulets; Lear; Brabantio). We see children greedy for patrimony (Oliver in *As You Like It*; various characters in the Histories; Edmund, Goneril, and Regan in *Lear*) or "lovers" greedy for dowry (suitors of Kate, Portia, and Anne Fenton; Angelo in *Measure for Measure*; Burgundy in *Lear*). The elder generation often adheres, moreover, to a code of revenge or war in

This essay is reprinted by permission, with revisions, from the South Atlantic Bulletin, *43, No. 4 (November 1978), 125–40; © 1978* South Atlantic Modern Language Association.

which it seeks to over-involve the younger generation (*Titus Andronicus, Romeo and Juliet, I Henry IV, Hamlet, Lear*), so that the procreative process becomes interrupted by misdefinitions of roles or unfortunate expectations of family loyalty and "inheritance." Sons, in particular, become tragic losers in this patriarchal overdetermination of loyalties, because they are, typically, used up in fighting feuds of their fathers; the desire for primogenitural progeny becomes thwarted when the male line is forfeited in parental wars. The particular conflict between values of war (or protection of family) and love (or extension of family) shows up most clearly in tragedies such as *Romeo and Juliet* and *Hamlet*. In *Lear, Othello,* and *Macbeth,* plays shot through with sexual and familial confusion and unwholesomeness, we see the inability of an authoritarian, aggressive male to enter reciprocal, fruitful relations with women or to foster life or line.

Given such often-disastrous results generated by the system of near-absolute male authority, a major issue in Shakespeare's plays is "What part may women play simply to survive, and then, beyond that, what part may women play to right at least some of the wrongs of patriarchy?" In what follows, I shall examine Shakespeare's evolving depictions of daughters' responses to the familial pressures outlined here. I shall consider particularly the plights and flights of daughters in Shakespeare's later plays, daughters who respond to expectations of love and matrimony in surprisingly contradictory, and modern, or perhaps timeless, ways.

To say, initially, that Shakespeare's women are to some degree victims of patriarchy is not to say that, among the range of Shakespeare's characters, one finds a dearth of spirited, knowing women; one has but to think of Rosalind or Beatrice or Viola or Helena, or of Cordelia, Cleopatra, and Imogen. Such women manage to assert themselves, however, *in spite of* the odds against them, as heroic exceptions to the more general rule of depressing male domination. To take the most significant theme, think of how often and how keenly Shakespeare concentrates upon the perversity of fathers' claims to direct their daughters' destinies in marriage. We hear throughout the plays of proprietary acts and attitudes taken by fathers in regard to or rather disregard of their daughters.

I beg the ancient privilege of Athens:
As she is mine, I may dispose of her;
Which shall be either to this gentleman,
Or to her death. . . .

          (Midsummer Night's Dream, 1.i.41−44)

A' Thursday let it be—a' Thursday, tell her,
She shall be married to this noble earl.
Will you be ready? do you like this haste?

          (Romeo and Juliet, III.iv.20−22)

    This is for all:
I would not, in plain terms, from this time forth
Have you so slander any moment leisure
As to give words or talk with the Lord Hamlet.
Look to't, I charge you. Come your ways.

          (Hamlet, 1.iii.131−35)

Thou must to thy father, and be gone from Troilus.

          (Troilus and Cressida, IV.ii.91)[1]

To the father's combined claims of legal and emotional interest in the daughter's marriage choice, the Elizabethans were, obviously, well-attuned. So intense, moreover, is the emotional investment of Shakespeare's fathers in their daughters' love that the thwarting of the fathers' expectations often brings forth imprecations and diatribes of surpassing bitterness:

I would my daughter were dead at my foot, and the jewels in her ear!

          (Merchant of Venice, III.i.87−89)

Do not live, Hero, do not ope thine eyes;
For did I think thou wouldst not quickly die,
Thought I thy spirits were stronger than thy shames,
Myself would, on the rearward of reproaches,
Strike at thy life.

          (Much Ado about Nothing, IV.i.123−27)

Look to't, think on't, I do not use to jest.
Thursday is near, lay hand on heart, advise.
And you be mine, I'll give you to my friend;

And you be not, hang, beg, starve, die in the streets,
For, by my soul, I'll ne'er acknowledge thee,
Nor what is mine shall never do thee good.

(*Romeo and Juliet*, iii.v.189–94)

The barbarous Scythian,
Or he that makes his generation messes
To gorge his appetite, shall to my bosom
Be as well neighbor'd, pitied, and reliev'd,
As thou my sometime daughter.

(*King Lear*, i.i.116–20)

Examples of such bitterness could be multiplied from other plays, and such multiplication would merely serve to support one's natural response and question: Why? Why do Shakespeare's fathers often hate their daughters so ambitiously, with a hate that borders on disintegration and madness? Part of the answer lies, no doubt, in the special relations between father and only or best-loved daughter. More important is the concomitant absence, at least in the plays quoted above, of any sons.

Some of the fathers mention their reliance upon their daughters for comfort and security in old age. Thus the Duke in *The Two Gentlemen of Verona* says: ". . . I thought the remnant of mine age / Should have been cherish'd by her child-like duty" (iii.i.74), and Lear says, "I lov'd her most, and thought to set my rest / On her kind nursery" (i.i.123). Such considerations—of emotional and economic security and of political control and generational extension of line—help to dictate the father's interest in the choice of his daughter's marriage partner. Lack of sons not only may make plain the father's need for the daughter's support and thus for a congenial son-in-law, it also may turn the son-in-law into substitute son, the inheritor of family power and values. When the daughter chooses radically against the father's will, she effectively shuts him off from patriarchal domination of the son-in-law and consequent sonlike extension of his power and values. In the earlier comedies, the daughter's choice does not really extend beyond the father's range. Who can tell a Lysander from a Demetrius? When the choice does extend vastly beyond the father's range, as in the case of Jessica and Shylock, the results, for the father at least, are tragic.

In the earlier comedies, the society with which we are presented at the opening does not need fundamental revision, and the daughter's choice of a partner, even if against her father's will, serves eventually to confirm existing values. In tragedies such as *Romeo and Juliet*, *Othello*, and *Lear*, where the order existing at the outset is often superficial, narrow, or grown archaic, the daughter marries someone far beyond her father's range who challenges his sociopolitical security. Romeo's family is the age-old enemy of Juliet's family; Brabantio finds Othello repugnant as a son-in-law; France is inevitably under suspicion as rival or enemy of Lear's England, which he indeed invades later in the play. Given these special circumstances, fathers such as Capulet (though he may be on the brink of giving up the feud), Brabantio, and Lear cannot or will not think to extend their line through their daughters. Yet they have little alternative. Dreams they might have of patrilineal extension are shattered by their daughters' choice of marriage partners. Their resultant rage may be better understood in this light, as may its terrible consequences.

Terrible as the consequences are in terms of individual deaths, the revolts in the tragedies of daughters against their fathers' wills become essential elements in the whole process of loss and at least partial redemption that marks the tragic catharsis.[2] In Shakespeare's tragedies, as in his comedies, a daughter who defines herself *against* her father, who takes a husband, as it were, in spite of him, usually becomes associated with regenerative forces and outcomes. Where the problem, or part of it, is to break the death-dealing feud or prejudice of the father, the daughter manages to help, but in the tragedies she helps in a way that costs very dearly. Viewed in the most basic terms of patriarchal expectations, tragedies such as *Romeo and Juliet* and *Hamlet* portray fathers who employ sons to carry on their concerns, to enforce their continuing image in patrilineal succession but also to fight in the fathers' feuds. Where sons are denied to such patriarchal fathers, they may become resentful or seek substitutes. Macbeth may be analyzed usefully from this perspective. Macbeth, whose ambition to be king is threatened by Duncan's election of his son as successor, does manage to become king, but he himself has no son and remains threatened not only by Malcolm but by Banquo's line, prophesied to succeed to the throne. Macbeth becomes cast in the role of one who kills the sons of others. Unable to reach Malcolm, he attempts through hired killers to murder Banquo's son (as well as Banquo) and almost succeeds. His killers do kill Macduff's son, onstage, and finally, near the end of the play, we see Macbeth himself hack down Siward's son, "Young Siward." The most significant fact about Macduff, who at last kills Macbeth, is that Macduff is "not of woman born," as if only such a person could get around Macbeth's malevolence against issue. Lear, too, has no son, but our first glimpse of him is in the act of arranging to acquire appropriate sons-in-law. He thinks to extend his line through daughters. Two of them, however, turn out to be his enemies, and the third marries France, who becomes Britain's enemy, albeit in a war of "liberation." Still, as in *Romeo and Juliet*, the daughter's choice of a husband who is independent of her father's influence proves a catalyst, though a bitter one, for the changes necessary to a revitalization of the home society. Thus the tragedies rather insistently criticize the patriarch's own attempts to manipulate sons or sons-in-law for his own interest.

In the romances, these themes intensify. Here problems of sons as tragic victims of their fathers' feuds are largely eliminated (save, possibly, for the example of Mamillius in *The Winter's Tale*). In *Pericles, Cymbeline, Winter's Tale*, and *Tempest*, such sons are nonexistent, lost, or killed, and only daughters are looked to for continuation of the central family. Pericles, Cymbeline, Leontes, and Prospero all have enmities in which they could tragically involve any sons of theirs, but when each such son appears to be eliminated (together with the wives of the fathers), the relation between each father and his sole daughter becomes central. The function of each daughter is not to represent, as a son might, the father in the father's battles but rather to leave home, travel widely, perhaps marry the son of her father's chief enemy (as in *Winter's Tale* and *Tempest*), and return home to instill virtues of forgiveness and the lesson of pardon in the father. The solution for patriarchal overcontrol and quasi-incestuous inwardness thus seems to be a dramatic destruction of the progenitive center and an explosion outward through time and space that leads to regroupings at the end and visions of a wide incorporative harmony.

It seems apparent that Shakespeare in these four romances celebrates a view of women as protectors and givers of life in a very special sense. Daughters such as Imogen, Perdita, and Miranda not only marry in ways that heal enmities but also they prove their love viable in settings that harbor lustful or permissive appetites, that is, they encounter in "nature" a rapacious Cloten or Caliban or a bawdy Autolycus but they remain chaste and eventually chasten the appetites of their true lovers. Marina, of course, chastens even the brothel. Often we see these daughters, moreover, rising from sleep and seeming death, as if to prove their miraculous power to awaken fresh life.

In all the romances (as in other Shakespearean plays), lesser characters may be seen as representing in part components within the psyche of a central character. Each father—Pericles, Cymbeline, Leontes, Prospero—works out his emotional maturation, partly through recognition of his daughter as she embodies nature's powers to renew itself rhythmically and human powers to delay acting upon desires that else might become confused and blighted. Recognition of this sort is not easily won, however, and the romances are notable for their repeated images of fathers trying to dominate their daughters as well as to learn from them. In *Pericles*, Antiochus commits incest with his daughter. Cymbeline berates Imogen and orders her locked in her chamber. Prospero admonishes Miranda to listen and to obey. In the instant before recognizing his daughter, Pericles pushes her back. Leontes, too, makes menacing gestures at the infant Perdita whom he denies is his, and later, still not knowing her, he makes a kind of romantic overture in her direction (v.i.223). The passionate interaction of all of the romance fathers and daughters perhaps thus necessitates in psychic terms the far journey of each daughter away from home and the taking a husband in each case so clearly set apart from the father.

Despite these apparently happy solutions to problems of patriarchal domination, and though the romances have witnessed in our supposedly liberated age a mounting tide of enthusiasm, they may be more patriarchal and patrilineal in perspective than Shakespearean interpreters have yet cared or dared to recognize. To ask the following question is to ask, in some respects, how many children had Lady Macbeth, but still: Is not the engendering of a daughter in each romance taken implicitly as a guilty act which signals the impotence of the father or his receipt of divine displeasure? Else why should he have lost or in the course of the play lose wife and any sons he may have had? Kings need sons.

When they produce daughters, in a patrilineal society, they do less than the optimum to further a secure succession. When their sons die or they produce a daughter or daughters alone, they become as vulnerable as Henry the Eighth, who says, according to Shakespeare:

> First, methought
> I stood not in the smile of heaven, who had
> Commanded nature, that my lady's womb,
> If it conceiv'd a male-child by me, should
> Do no more offices of life to't than
> The grave does to th' dead; for her male issue
> Or died where they were made, or shortly after
> This world had air'd them. Hence I took a thought
> This was a judgment on me, that my kingdom
> (Well worthy the best heir o' th' world) should not
> Be gladded in't by me. Then follows, that
> I weighed the danger which my realms stood in
> By this my issue's fail, and that gave to me
> Many a groaning throe.
>
> (*Henry VIII*, ii.iv.187–200)

In *Pericles*, *Cymbeline*, *Winter's Tale*, and *Tempest*, each leader of the state is threatened with similar "issue's fail." The plays might seem to strike at patriarchal chains when they take up the device of extending a family not through sons but through a daughter's adventure in finding a son-in-law. Through this infusion of fresh male blood, the plays seem to say, a king can more truly revitalize his kingdom. And, given the English experience with Henry the Eighth and his children, the pattern of the saving daughter might well be regarded as much more than an anomalous and irrelevant residue of folktale origins of the romances. Shakespeare could be saying, in the style of Lear's Edmund, "Now, gods, stand up for daughters!" Still, assuming that Shakespeare (who himself lost a son and, judging from the terms of his will, looked wistfully to his daughters for continuance of his line) has raised in the romances a kind of argument for daughters otherwise demeaned by patriarchalism, are not the daughters exalted more as potential wives and father-comforters than as persons in their own right? Marina, Imogen, Perdita, and Miranda are, to be sure, spirited and, at times, independent. Consider Marina speaking to Boult in the bawdy house:

> Thou art the damned door-keeper to every
> Custrel that comes inquiring for his Tib.
> To the choleric fisting of every rogue
> Thy ear is liable; thy food is such
> As hath been belch'd on by infected lungs.
>
> *(Pericles*, IV.vi.165–69)

Or Imogen speaking of Posthumus and Cloten:

> I would they were in Afric both together,
> Myself by with a needle, that I might prick
> The goer-back.
>
> *(Cymbeline*, I.i.167–69)

Or Perdita:

> I was about to speak, and tell him plainly
> The self-same sun that shines upon his court
> Hides not his visage from our cottage, but
> Looks on alike. Will't please you, sir, be gone?
> I told you what would come of this.
>
> *(Winter's Tale*, IV.iv.443–47)

Or Miranda: calling Caliban "abhorred slave" to his face, breaking her father's command that she not tell her name to Ferdinand, and accusing Ferdinand of false play at chess. Despite such displays, however, the chief *function* of the daughter in each romance is to bring home a husband and to teach or permit her father a newfound love and forgiveness made possible and believable amid the restored patriarchal security. At the end of each romance, the daughter's father explicitly rejoices over the presence of his son-in-law. Pericles says to his wife: "Thaisa, / This prince, the fair-betrothed of your daughter, / Shall marry her at Pentapolis" (v.iii.70–72). Cymbeline says: "We'll learn our freeness of a son-in-law: / Pardon's the word to all" (v.v.421–22). Leontes' last act is to introduce Florizel to Hermione: "This' your son-in-law, / And son unto the King, whom heavens directing / Is troth-plight to your daughter" (v.iii.149). Prospero tells Alonso of his "hope to see the nuptial / Of these our dear-belov'd solemnized . . ." (v.i.309–10).

In terms of what their worlds and plays obviously expect of them, Shakespeare's daughters of romance have done well, and Shakespeare has, in a sense, "solved" problems of overcontrolling fathers and overrebellious daughters that appeared in tragedies such as *Romeo and Juliet*, *Othello*, and *Lear*. In place of patrilineal succession, we have a new procreative process in which direct male issue are bypassed—perhaps as too competitive, aggressive, promiscuous, or death-dealing—in favor of virginal daughters who promise to win reinvigoration of the family through outside stock which is now more readily accepted by the fathers than it was before. The daughters themselves, however, are hardly permitted the alternative of *not* choosing a mate. To do so would be unthinkable. They must take mates to save and extend the families of their fathers, who remain so much in evidence. After working out this "solution" in the romances, Shakespeare went on, nonetheless, to consider the matter further (as was his custom) and even to question the solution.

In *Henry VIII*, we find the familiar romance patterns of ostracized queen, restorative daughter, and great hopes for the younger generation, but now the daughter, Elizabeth, becomes exalted in virginal radiance:

> Good grows with her;
> In her days every man shall eat in safety
> Under his own vine what he plants, and sing
> The merry songs of peace to all his neighbors.
> God shall be truly known, and those about her
> From her shall read the perfect ways of honor,
> And by those claim their greatness, not by blood.
> Nor shall this peace sleep with her; but as when
> The bird of wonder dies, the maiden phoenix,
> Her ashes new create another heir
> As great in admiration as herself,
> So shall she leave her blessedness to one
> (When heaven shall call her from this cloud of darkness)
> Who from the sacred ashes of her honor
> Shall star-like rise as great in fame as she was,
> And so stand fix'd. (v.iv.32–47)

If we compare Elizabeth to the heroines of the preceding four romances, we find that the romance pattern is transcended. Though the father's search for male issue remains important, is never more important than here, the daughter need now elect no husband to fulfill her function. She becomes herself a "pattern to all princes," and this, it seems stressed, is "not by blood" but by "honor," meaning, among other things, her sexual purity. Cranmer continues:

> Would I had known no more! but she must die,
> She must, the saints must have her; yet a virgin,
> A most unspotted lily shall she pass
> To th' ground, and all the world shall mourn her.
>
> (v.iv.59–62)

Praise of woman beyond or even in opposition to the supposed virtues of marriage and childbearing seems to be Shakespeare's purpose not only in his depiction of Elizabeth but also in his treatment of Katherine in *Henry VIII*. Katherine, who "failed" to give Henry the male issue he so desperately wanted, follows the lead of Buckingham and Wolsey by converting her secular fall into spiritual ascent. On her sickbed (iv.ii), she learns to forgive Wolsey; meditating on "celestial harmony," she falls asleep and sees a heavenly vision that promises "eternal happiness." She asks that, when she is dead, she be "us'd with honor" and strewn with "maiden flowers." All this fits the general tenor of the play as it suggests the vanity of earthly pageantries, the paltriness of bodily appetites, and the insufficiency of love's whole enterprise. Reminiscent of *The Tempest*, and reaching perhaps beyond, is the strange power of *Henry VIII* to present bodily and earthly life, especially in the getting of children, as somehow inconsequential, even petty. In its revelation of brave but diaphanous masques, of vain attempts to solidify the stage and state of earthly shows, the play points heavenward. Miranda's admirable chastity evolves toward Elizabeth's sacred virginity.

In *The Two Noble Kinsman* (which for present purposes I treat as dominated by Shakespeare's conception and handling),[3] Shakespeare, from the outset, makes his heroine one of Diana's great devotees. Emilia describes her affection for a childhood companion in these terms:

> The flow'r that I would pluck
> And put between my breasts (O then but beginning

To swell about the blossom), she would long
Till she had such another, and commit it
To the innocent cradle, where phoenix-like
They died in perfume. On my head no toy
But was her pattern, her affections (pretty,
Though happily her careless wear) I followed
For my most serious decking. Had mine ear
Stol'n some new air, or at adventure humm'd one
From musical coinage, why it was a note
Whereon her spirits would sojourn (rather dwell on)
And sing it in her slumbers. This rehearsal
(Which, ev'ry innocent wots well, comes in
Like old importment's bastard) has this end,
That the true love 'tween maid and maid may be
More than in sex dividual.   (I.iii.66–82)

Asked later to choose as husband either Arcite or Palamon, Emilia decides, momentarily, that her "virgin's faith has fled" (IV.ii.46), she loves them both, but, still later, when the two kinsmen are about to fight for her hand, she prays at the altar of Diana:

O sacred, shadowy, cold, and constant queen,
Abandoner of revels, mute, contemplative,
Sweet, solitary, white as chaste, and pure
As wind-fann'd snow, who to thy female knights
Allow'st no more blood than will make a blush,
Which is their order's robe: I here, thy priest,
Am humbled 'fore thine altar. O, vouchsafe,
With that rare green eye—which never yet
Beheld thing maculate—look on thy virgin,
And sacred silver mistress, lend thine ear
(Which nev'r heard scurril term, into whose port
Ne'er ent'red wanton sound) to my petition,
Season'd with holy fear. This is my last
Of vestal office; I am bride-habited,
But maiden-hearted.   (V.i.137–51)

We could say that Shakespeare simply took his plays and themes in no special order, as they came to him. The evolution of his heroines toward virgin faith would remain, nonetheless, to be accounted for. The entire action and atmosphere of *The Two Noble Kinsmen* help account for Emilia's lack of love. Arcite and Palamon are made to seem simpleminded, outer-directed followers of Mars and Venus, respectively, but the best exposure of the post-romance attitude occurs in two prayers that Arcite and Palamon give just before Emilia's. Arcite prays to a Mars of destruction and waste, the "decider / Of dusty and old titles," whose "prize / Must be dragg'd out of blood" (v.i.63–64, 42–43). Palamon prays to a Venus who commands the rage of love throughout man and woman unkind, whose "yoke . . . is heavier / Than lead itself, stings more than nettles," who incites gross geriatric lusts, and "whose chase is this world, / And we in herds thy game" (95–97). Through these debased, decadent visions of chivalric and courtly ideals, Arcite and Palamon develop further Shakespeare's critique of patriarchalism and the potential murderousness and sterility that often accompany its political, social, and sexual hierarchies. Small wonder that Emilia, faced with two such votaries, chooses to remain "maiden-hearted."

Shakespeare's post-romance has moved far beyond the paradigmatic plots of *Pericles*, *Cymbeline*, *Winter's Tale*, and *Tempest* in which the needs of a society for restoration, needs embodied in its leader, are answered by the restorative instincts of the leader's daughter. For Emilia, as for Elizabeth the Queen, choice of a marriage partner is dictated neither by a father's will nor by resistance to it. Remote from the dynamics of patripotestal interests, left to her own devices, Emilia displays no sense of familial drive. Lacking a father, a brother, or other male to define herself against, the daughter tends perhaps to resist marriage or to see it as especially troublesome. In contrast to Emilia, moreover, we find in this play the Jailer's Daughter, whose father wants her to marry her Wooer but who loves her father's prisoner (Palamon) and even frees him from her father's prison. She thus represents a filial pattern seen in the comedies. Irony descends again, however, as the Jailer's Daughter loses Palamon and goes mad. In this late stage in his career, Shakespeare enters an especially problematic zone in his conception of our romantic instincts and their functioning.

In the tragedies, Shakespeare's lovers—Juliet, Desdemona, Cleopatra—exercise free and vivid imaginative powers and make real, in some sense, the vigorous wide-embracing males with whom they flee, fight, and die. In the romances, the daughters no longer display the tragic force of will that finds and loses itself in an all-consuming love. They become subordinated to the pattern of generational renewal prompted by needs of their inescapable fathers. Their husbands, too, are conceived in terms of function rather than given an independence of being. They lack, consequently, the splendid wilfullness and freedom of self-definition possessed by Romeo, Othello, and Antony. Lysimachus, Posthumus Leonatus, Florizel, and Ferdinand become, like the societies they inhabit, chastened and subdued by redemptive responsibilities their betrotheds place upon them. This is a typical pattern in such dramatic romances as *Alcestis*, *The Beggar's Opera*, *When We Dead Awaken*, *The Caucasian Chalk Circle*, and *The Cocktail Party*.[4] Women are made to undertake journeys that will redeem their families and societies from some version of sterility, but the redemptive journey and return renders both husband and society strangely quiet, meditative, less lusty and more spiritual. For Antony and Cleopatra (and perhaps even for Romeo and Juliet or Othello and Desdemona) one could almost substitute Mars and Venus, their heterosexuality and the vigor of their interchange is so strong, but for Ferdinand and Miranda and other Romance couples one would prefer, at best, Apollo and Diana.

In Shakespeare's post-romance, Diana appears to win. After the womanizing excesses of Henry the Eighth, the virgin faith and phoenix-project of Elizabeth sound persuasive, and, given the unconvincing, fatuous romanticalities of Arcite and Palamon, Emilia's chaste reserve appears appropriate. But societies are not renewed by chaste reserve, and Shakespeare, whose great subject has always been the renewal of family and society, is unlikely to settle, finally, for so sterile a solution. Emilia is made, at the end, to accept Palamon, the devotee of Venus, and, though the ending is hardly celebratory in tone, what makes the union of Palamon and Emilia acceptable, I submit, is the preceding incident of the Jailer's Daughter. Her idealizing eagerness for Palamon in part subjects him to ironic scrutiny but also in part marks the preservation in the play of an essential, sincere, and effective romantic imagination. That is, in the Jailer's Daughter and, through her in Palamon, we see that a creative passion of this romantic or romance-ic sort must be heeded and welcomed. The

Jailer, Doctor, and Wooer give in to the Daughter, humor her passion, and try their best to shape her world to her liking. She responds well and takes the Wooer for Palamon. The Doctor promises, convincingly, that by these means the Daughter will in three or four days become "right again."

The Two Noble Kinsmen, then, simultaneously attacks and defends romantic imagination, attacks the moribund mythologizing of Arcite and Palamon as embodied in their prayers to Mars and Venus, and purges their conception of humanity as passive and powerless before secret forces of hate and love raging in the blood, even to senility. The play first substitutes, for Arcite and Palamon, Emilia set on contemplative purity and blamelessness, praying to her sacred mistress, Diana, the "constant queen, / Abandoner of revels" (v.i.137–38). Then the play celebrates more positively and warmly the laughable but vital madness of the Jailer's Daughter, who makes the world try to create her imagined love before her eyes. Love is thus purged and renewed. The perverse and uncreative passions must yield to shadowy cold "Diana." Emilia is never a shining vital heroine. She seems to represent a stage in the development of successively more chaste, virginal heroines away from, say, Cleopatra through the likes of Imogen, Perdita, and Miranda, to Margaret, Elizabeth (as imaged in *Henry VIII*), and beyond. But Emilia, unlike Elizabeth, does marry. And her marriage is made possible and believable, I suggest, because its aim and function are supported by the warmer eagerness of the Jailer's Daughter toward Palamon and love.

Further investigation into Shakespeare's treatment of these acts and themes might seem foreclosed at this point by the absence of any more plays to contemplate. There are, however, significant links or overlaps between *The Two Noble Kinsmen* and the Cardenio episode in *Don Quixote*, the episode upon which is based, almost certainly, the lost play *Cardenio*, attributed to Shakespeare and Fletcher in a significant "blocking entry" of the Stationer's Register and acted by the King's Men in 1613.[5] Cardenio falls in love with Lucinda, but Cardenio's friend Ferdinand (who had betrothed himself to Dorothea and jilted her), by a series of strategems, contrives to marry Lucinda in Cardenio's supposed absence. Lucinda, at any rate, submits to a marriage ceremony with Ferdinand, and Cardenio, who returns just in time to spy upon the ceremony, is so horror-struck that he flees to the wilds where he meets Don Quixote and relates his misfortunes. It turns out that Dorothea, Ferdinand's betrothed, also comes to the wilds. She meets the friends of Don Quixote, and they persuade her to help them humor his madness by pretending to be a damsel in distress whom Don Quixote can aid. After elaborately playing up to Don Quixote's chivalric whims, Dorothea, Cardenio, Sancho Panza, the Barber, and the Curate bring Don Quixote to an inn where, eventually, Ferdinand and Lucinda also arrive. After the inevitable recognition, Lucinda is restored to Cardenio and Dorothea to Ferdinand. In chart form, striking similarities between the plots of *The Two Noble Kinsmen* and the conjectural *Cardenio* may be observed:

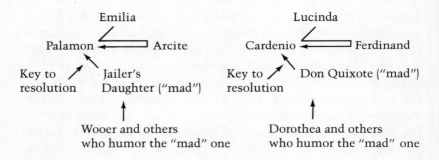

"I saw her first," says Palamon to Arcite (ii.ii.160) concerning Emilia. Cardenio saw Lucinda first. But both "first" lovers appear to lose out in dramatic fashion to their more active, scheming rivals. In each case the rival's intervention appears institutionally sanctioned, as when Arcite wins the battle at the pillar and is given Emilia by Theseus and, similarly, Ferdinand marries Lucinda in a church ceremony. Then there is the eventual return of the heroine to her first love but not before he is aided in each case by a mad romantic. The Jailer's Daughter frees Palamon and brings him food in the forest; Don Quixote, meeting Cardenio in the wilds, embraces him, gives him food, and vows to serve him. In each case the mad romantic's passionate desire to serve a disconsolate lover is finally gratified by friends who, through impersonations, humor the mad fancies and change the world so as to satisfy their intention.

When Palamon asserts his prior claim to Emilia, saying to Arcite, "You must not love her" (II.ii.161), Arcite replies:

> I will not, as you do—to worship her
> As she is heavenly and a blessed goddess;
> I love her as a woman, to enjoy her,
> So both may love. (II.ii.162–65)

In *The Two Noble Kinsmen* and the conjectural *Cardenio*, the first lover is relatively passive, a worshiper of woman rather than an enjoyer. The second lover, more lusty-active, "wins" the woman but has less right and is presented with less sympathetic interiority of love. The mad romantics, the Jailer's Daughter and Don Quixote, intervene and support with intensity of conviction the worth and quest of the first lover. Both Emilia and Lucinda, moreover, are represented as rather passive and shrinking, tossed between extremes of ineffective spiritual esteem from one man and primarily physical lust from another. In each story the development of the main plot lies secretly in the hands, or minds, of the subplot characters—Jailer's Daughter and Don Quixote— who must, as it were, dream the main plot onward, substituting their creative faith, their active idealizing eagerness, for the split love of the main characters.

Both *The Two Noble Kinsmen* and the *Cardenio* story are, in one sense, satires. The state of mind that overcomes the impasse of love which is split into effete worship and Mars-like rapacity is a state of mind represented as madness, an unthinkable dedication of unified mind and heart, spirit and flesh. But behind the satire, in each case there lies, I suggest, the secret project of resuscitating the romance-ic spirit. Shakespeare, like Cervantes, may have seen ahead in his very last works to an age of satire looming up on the horizon, but he also honored, as did Cervantes, the unquenchable desire of romantic will to purge and renew itself toward some version, no matter how strangely won, of ongoing and productive love. Ever since *All's Well* and *Measure for Measure*, if not before, Shakespeare had honored the beleaguered maiden's often-instinctive retreat to Diana, to the purer precincts of that shadowy queen, and never was this honor made more telling than in *The Two Noble Kinsmen*, but Shakespeare made Emilia—wrought even beyond Diana with impossi-

ble longings ("Were they metamorphis'd / Both into one," v.iii.84–
85)—yield, finally, to her fated marriage. As Emilia exits hand in
hand with Palamon, there linger still the singsong cracked remarks, the deepest hopes and fears of the Jailer's Daughter:

> DAUGH. We shall have many children. . . .
>
> . . . .
>
> WOOER. Come, sweet, we'll go to dinner,
>   And then we'll play at cards.
> DAUGH.   And shall we kiss too?
> WOOER. A hundred times.
> DAUGH.   And twenty?
> WOOER.   Ay, and twenty.
> DAUGH. And then we'll sleep together?
> DOCT.   Take her offer.
> WOOER. Yes, marry, will we.
> DAUGH.   But you shall not hurt me.
> WOOER. I will not, sweet.
> DAUGH.   If you do, love, I'll cry.
>
>   (v.ii.95–112)

Shakespeare understood and made vivid, as have few artists before or since, the spirit of the maiden phoenix that flutters
up periodically in women, if not in men as well, and he traced
with surpassing skill the intricacies of that endless dance where
daughters escape and follow, reject and recreate, their once and
future fathers.

NOTES

1. See also, e.g., *Merry Wives of Windsor*, IV.vi.23; *Othello*, I.iii.192;
   Lear, I.i.113; *Cymbeline*, I.ii.131. Quotations are from the *Riverside
   Shakespeare*, ed. G. B. Evans (Boston: Houghton Mifflin, 1974).
2. One may observe that in a tragedy where a daughter, such as Ophelia,
   fails to assert herself against her father's dictate, the sense of nature
   redeemed, of human nature and society revitalized, may be diminished, as when the relatively limited Fortinbras takes over at the end
   of *Hamlet*.
3. Just what portion, if any, of *The Two Noble Kinsmen* John Fletcher
   may be responsible for is as yet undetermined. Shakespeare is generally credited with scenes I.i–I.ii, III.i, IV.i.34–173, and v.iii–v.iv,

which include the scene introducing the Jailer's Daughter and the addresses of Arcite, Palamon, and Emilia to Mars, Venus, and Diana. Paul Bertram, *Shakespeare and the Two Noble Kinsmen* (New Brunswick, N.J.: Rutgers University Press, 1965), argues at length that the entire play is by Shakespeare.

4. These plays are collected, together with *The Tempest*, in *Dramatic Romance: Plays, Theory, and Criticism*, ed. Howard Felperin (New York: Harcourt, 1973). I am indebted to Howard Felperin for this collocation and for thoughts it has fostered.

5. In discussing *Cardenio*, I refer to the plot of the Cardenio story as contained in the first part of Cervantes' novel, translated by Thomas Shelton in 1612. The Court Chamber Account and Court (Greenwich) account indicate that *Cardenio* was presented twice by the King's Men in 1613; see E. K. Chambers, *William Shakespeare: A Study of Facts and Problems* (Oxford: Clarendon, 1930), II, 343. On September 9, 1653, the publisher Humphrey Moseley registered "The History of Cardennio, by Mr. Fletcher and Shakespeare" in the Stationer's Register; see Chambers, I, 539–42. Lewis Theobald published a play, *Double Falsehood*, in 1728, and alleged that it was based upon manuscripts of a play by Shakespeare that dealt with the Cardenio story. Opinions vary as to whether Theobald really could have adapted or did adapt his play from such a manuscript; see John Freehafer, "*Cardenio*, by Shakespeare and Fletcher," *PMLA*, 84 (1969), 501–12, and Harriet C. Frazier, *A Babble of Ancestral Voices: Shakespeare, Cervantes, and Theobald* (The Hague: Mouton, 1974). Theobald's play excludes Don Quixote.

Women and Men in Shakespeare
A Selective Bibliography

Carolyn Ruth Swift Lenz,
Gayle Greene,
and Carol Thomas Neely

This bibliography is designed to be compact enough to be useful to students with a general interest in nonsexist approaches to Shakespeare and inclusive enough to be helpful to scholars with more specific research concerns. It lists Shakespeare criticism in English which is feminist or otherwise appropriate to the concerns of those interested in the position of women, in relations between men and women, and in love, sexuality, courtship, marriage, and the family in Shakespeare. We have included items which are original contributions to Shakespeare criticism and which are, for the most part, nonsexist in their language and orientation. Most of the entries have been published since 1960, but some earlier works are included, especially those by women critics who felt (as do some contemporary feminist critics) that their gender gave them a special perspective on Shakespeare. Material on the historical position of women in the period is excluded but is to be found in the following related bibliographies: "Shakespeare and Women: A Bibliography," ed. Robert C. Steensma, *Shakespeare Newsletter*, 12, No. 2 (April 1962), 12; "Women in Shakespeare: A Bibliography," *Shakespeare Newsletter*, 27, No.

Carolyn Ruth Swift Lenz, Gayle Greene, and Carol Thomas Neely

5/6 (Nov./Dec. 1977), 39; "Bibliography of Women in the English Renaissance," ed. Norma Greco and Ronaele Novotny, University of Michigan *Papers in Women's Studies*, 1, No. 2 (June 1974); "List of Works Cited" in Juliet Dusinberre, *Shakespeare and the Nature of Women* (Barnes & Noble, 1975), pp. 309–17. Each of these complementary bibliographies is selective in a somewhat different way. The two *Shakespeare Newsletter* bibliographies cite only works on women and emphasize critical works, although some entries on women in the period are included. In the first, most of the items were published between 1900 and 1960; the supplement lists items published between 1962 and 1976. The Dusinberre bibliography includes material on the drama from 1590 to 1625, but its emphasis is on Renaissance and twentieth-century material on the historical position of women in the period. The usefully annotated "Bibliography of Women in the English Renaissance" also stresses historical and biographical material in its four divisions: Women Writers, Women in Relation to Male Writers, Female Characters in Literature, and Women in Their Cultural and Historical Setting. Unlike the Dusinberre and Greco/Novotny bibliographies, ours includes only criticism of Shakespeare and Shakespeare in performance; unlike the *Shakespeare Newsletter* bibliographies, this one focuses on important feminist or nonsexist contributions to criticism. It excludes works in languages other than English, *Shakespeare Newsletter* entries, and most dissertations. For more complete listings, readers should consult the annual bibliographies in *PMLA* and in *Shakespeare Quarterly* (annotated). We recognize that we may have overlooked relevant items and invite readers to send Carolyn Lenz listings which may be included in a revised edition of the bibliography or in a supplement to it. The divisions of this bibliography are identical with those of the annual PMLA bibliography: General Works, Comedies (general), Histories (general), Tragedies (general), and Individual Plays and Other Works.

GENERAL

Andresen-Thom, Martha. "Thinking About Women and Their Prosperous Art: A Reply to Juliet Dusinberre's *Shakespeare and the Nature of Women.*" *Shakespeare Studies*, 11 (1978), 259–76.

Avery, Emmett L. "The Shakespeare Ladies Club." *Shakespeare Quarterly*, 7 (1956), 153–58.

Bamber, Linda Vigderman, "Comic Women, Tragic Men: Genre and Sexuality in Shakespeare's Plays." *Dissertation Abstracts International*, 36 (1975), 2212A (Tufts University, 1974).

Bandel, Betty. "Ellen Terry's Foul Papers." *Theater Survey*, 10 (1969), 43–52.

———. *Shakespeare's Treatment of the Social Position Of Women*. Diss. Columbia University, 1951. Facsimile, Doctoral Dissertation Series, Publication No. 2793. Ann Arbor: University Microfilms, 1975.

Barton, Anne. "The Feminist Stage," rev. of *Shakespeare and the Nature of Women*, by Juliet Dusinberre. *Times Literary Supplement*, 24 Oct. 1975, p. 1259. For responses to the review, including letters from Barton and Dusinberre, see *Times Literary Supplement*, 24 Nov. 1975, p. 1420; 5 Dec. 1975, p. 1463; 19 Dec. 1975, p. 1516.

Bean, John C. "Passion versus Friendship in The Tudor Matrimonial Handbooks and Some Shakespearean Implications." *Wascana Review*, 9 (1974), 231–40.

Bland, D. S. "The Heroine and the Sea: An Aspect of Shakespeare's Last Plays." *Essays in Criticism*, 3 (1953), 39–44.

Bullough, Geoffrey. "Shakespeare the Elizabethan." *Proceedings of the British Academy*, 50 (1964), 121–41.

Cather, Willa. "Willa Cather on Shakespeare." *Prairie Schooner*, 38 (1964), 65–74.

Charney, Maurice, and Hanna Charney. "The Language of Madwomen in Shakespeare and His Fellow Dramatists." *Signs*, 3 (1977), 451–60.

Clarke, Mary Cowden. *The Girlhood of Shakespeare's Heroines*. 3 vols. London: W. H. Smith, 1850–55; rpt. New York: AMS, 1974.

———. "Shakespeare as the Girl's Friend." *Shakespeareana*, 4 (1887), 355–69.

Colie, Rosalie. *Shakespeare's Living Art*. Princeton, N.J.: Princeton University Press, 1974.

Cook, Ann Jennalie. "The Mode of Marriage in Shakespeare's England." *Southern Humanities Review*, 11 (1977), 126–32.

Danks, K. B. "Shakespeare's Second Best Bed." *Notes and Queries*, NS 2 (1955), 227.

Davies, William R. *Shakespeare's Boy Actors*. London, 1939; rpt. New York: Russell and Russell, 1964.

Doran, Madeleine. *Endeavors of Art: A Study of Form in Elizabethan Drama*. Madison: University of Wisconsin Press, 1954.

Draper, John. "Shakespeare's Ladies in Waiting." *Neophilologus*, 49 (1965), 255–62.

Dusinberre, Juliet. *Shakespeare and the Nature of Women*. New York: Barnes & Noble, and London: Macmillan, 1975.

Elliott Leigh-Noel, M. *Shakespeare's Garden of Girls*. London: Remington, 1885.

Ewbank, Inga-Stina. "Shakespeare's Portrayal of Women: A 1970's View." *Shakespeare: Pattern of Excelling Nature*. Ed. David Bevington and Jay L. Halio. Newark: University of Delaware Press, and London: Associated University Presses, 1978, pp. 222–29.

Fiedler, Leslie A. *The Stranger in Shakespeare*. New York: Stein and Day, 1972.

Fowler, Elaine W. "The Earl of Bedford's 'Best' Bed." *Shakespeare Quarterly*, 18 (1967), 80.

Garber, Marjorie. "Coming of Age in Shakespeare." *Yale Review*, 66 (1977), 517–33.

Gross, George C. "Mary Cowden Clarke, 'The Girlhood of Shakespeare's Heroines', and the Sex Education of Victorian Women." *Victorian Studies*, 16 (1972), 37–58.

Halio, Jay L. "'Perfection' and Elizabethan Ideas of Conception." *English Language Notes*, 1 (1964), 179–82.

Harding, D. W. "Women's Fantasy of Manhood: A Shakespearean Theme." *Shakespeare Quarterly*, 20 (1969), 245–53.

Hibbard, G. R. "Love, Marriage, and Money in Shakespeare's Theatre and Shakespeare's England." *The Elizabethan Theatre*, VI. Ed. G. R. Hibbard. Hamden, Conn.: Shoe String Press, 1977, pp. 134–55.

Holland, Norman N. *Psychoanalysis and Shakespeare*. New York: McGraw-Hill, 1966.

Hurstfield, Joel. "Shakespeare, Historical Criticism, and the Historian." *Shakespeare Newsletter*, 25 (Nov. 1975), 42.

Jameson, Anna B. *Shakespeare's Heroines: Characteristics of Women*. London: Saunders & Otley, 1832; rpt. New York: AMS Press, 1971; Philadelphia: R. West, 1973; Folcroft, Pa.: Folcroft Library Editions, 1973; New York: Gordon Press, 1978.

Jamieson, Michael. "Shakespeare's Celibate Stage." *Papers, Mainly Shakespearean*. Ed. George Ian Duthie. Aberdeen University Studies, No. 147. Edinburgh: Oliver and Boyd, 1964, pp. 21–39.

Kahn, Coppélia. *Man's Estate: Male Identity in Shakespeare*. Berkeley: University of California Press, 1980.

Kiernan, V. G. "Human Relationships in Shakespeare." *Shakespeare in a Changing World*. Ed. Arnold Kettle. New York: International Publishers, 1964, pp. 43–64.

Lyons, Charles R. *Shakespeare and the Ambiguity of Love's Triumph*. Mouton: The Hague, 1971.

MacKenzie, Agnes Mure. *The Women in Shakespeare's Plays*. London: William Heinemann, 1924; New York: Doubleday, Page, 1924; rpt. Folcroft, Pa.: Folcroft Library Editions, 1973.

McAleer, John J. "Sarah Siddons—Shakespearean Preceptress." *Shakespeare Newsletter*, 14 (Sept. 1964), 65.

McKewin, Carol. "Shakespeare Liberata: Shakespeare, The Nature of Women, and the New Feminist Criticism." *Mosaic*, 10, No. 3 (1977), 157–64.

Martin, Helena Faucit. *On Some of Shakespeare's Female Characters*.

Edinburgh and London: W. Blackwood and Sons, 1885; rpt. Philadelphia: R. West, 1973; New York: AMS, 1970.

Mowat, Barbara A. "Images of Woman in Shakespeare's Plays." *Southern Humanities Review*, 11 (1977), 145–57.

Pendlebury, B. J. "Happy Ever After: Some Aspects of Marriage in Shakespeare's Plays." *Contemporary Review*, 227 (1975), 324–28.

Ranald, Margaret Loftus. "'As Marriage Binds, and Blood Breaks': English Marriage and Shakespeare." *Shakespeare Quarterly*, 30 (1979), 68–81.

Richmond, Velma Bourgeois. "Shakespeare's Women." *Midwest Quarterly*, 19 (1977–78), 330–42.

Rossiter, A. P. *Angel with Horns and Other Shakespeare Lectures*. Ed. Graham Story. London: Longmans, 1961.

Salter, Nancy Kay Clark. "Masks and Roles: A Study of Women in Shakespeare's Drama." *Dissertation Abstracts International*, 36 (1975), 1535A (University of Connecticut).

Saxon, Patricia Jean. "The Limits of Assertiveness: Modes of Female Identity in Shakespeare and the Stuart Dramatists." *Dissertation Abstracts International*, 38 (1977), 7349A–50A (University of Texas at Austin).

Schwartz, Murray M. "Shakespeare through Contemporary Psychoanalysis." *Hebrew University Studies in Literature*, 5 (1977), 182–98.

Schwartz, Murray M., and Coppélia Kahn. *Representing Shakespeare: New Psychoanalytic Essays*. Baltimore, Md.: Johns Hopkins University Press, 1980.

Sexton, Joyce H. *The Slandered Woman in Shakespeare*. English Literary Studies, No. 12. Victoria, B.C.: University of Victoria, 1978.

Shapiro, Susan C. "Shakespeare's View of Motherhood," *CEA Forum*, 8 (April 1978), 8–10.

Shakespeare Jahrbuch (Weimar), 113 (1977). Several articles in English and German devoted to the subject of women in Shakespeare.

Sinnott, Bethany Strong. "The Father-Daughter Theme in Shakespeare's Plays." *Dissertation Abstracts International*, 34 (1972), 339A (University of North Carolina at Chapel Hill).

Spencer, T. J. B. "Shakespeare and the Noble Woman." *Shakespeare Jahrbuch* (Heidelberg), 1966, 49–62.

Sproat, Kezia Bradford Vanmeter. "A Reappraisal of Shakespeare's View of Women." *Dissertation Abstracts International*, 36 (1975), 3664A (Ohio State University).

Stockton, Eric W. "The Adulthood of Shakespeare's Heroines." *Shakespearean Essays*. Ed. Alwin Thaler and Norman Sanders. Special No. 2 of *Tennessee Studies in Literature*. Knoxville: University of Tennessee Press, 1964, pp. 161–80.

Suddard, S. Mary. *Keats, Shelley, and Shakespeare*. Cambridge, England: Cambridge University Press, 1912; rpt. Folcroft, Pa., Folcroft Library Editions,n.d.

Terry, Dame Ellen. *Four Lectures on Shakespeare*. Ed. Christopher St. John. London: Martin Hopkinson, 1932; rpt. Philadelphia, Pa.: R. West, 1978.

————. *The Story of My Life: Recollections and Reflections*. London and New York: 1908; also published as *Ellen Terry's Memoirs*. London, 1932; rpt. New York: B. Blom, 1969; New York: Arno, 1978.

Vyvyan, John. *Shakespeare and Platonic Beauty*. London: Chatto & Windus, 1961; New York: Barnes and Noble, 1961.

Webster, Margaret. *Shakespeare Today*. London: Dent, 1942, 1957; also published as *Shakespeare without Tears*, New York: Whittlesey House, and London: McGraw Hill, 1942; rpt. New York: G. P. Putnam, 1975.

Wright, Lewis B. "The Reading of Renaissance English Women." *Studies in Philology*, 28 (1931), 139–56.

COMEDIES

Clubb, Louise George. "Woman as Wonder: A Generic Figure in Italian and Shakespearean Comedy." *Studies in the Continental Background of Renaissance English Literature: Essays Presented to John L. Lievsay*. Ed. Dale B. J. Randall and George W. Williams. Durham, N.C.: Duke University Press, 1967, pp. 109–32.

Gilbert, Miriam Anne. "The Shrew and the Disguised Girl in Shakespeare's Comedies." *Dissertation Abstracts International*, 30 (1970), 2967A (Indiana University, 1969).

Greer, Germaine. *The Female Eunuch*. New York: McGraw-Hill, 1971.

————. "The Ethic of Love and Marriage in Shakespeare's Early Comedy." Diss. Cambridge University, 1967.

Gunning, Elizabeth Rose. "The Motherless Heroines in Shakespeare's Comedies." Master's thesis, Brown University, 1961.

Hartwig, Joan. *Shakespeare's Tragicomic Vision*. Baton Rouge: Louisiana State University Press, 1972.

Hoy, Cyrus. "Fathers and Daughters in Shakespeare's Romances." *Shakespeare's Romances Reconsidered*. Ed. Carol McGinnis Kay and Henry E. Jacobs. Lincoln: University of Nebraska Press, 1978, pp. 77–90.

Hunter, G. K. *Shakespeare: The Late Comedies*. Writers and Their Work, No. 143. London: Longmans, Green, 1962.

Hyland, Peter. "Shakespeare's Heroines: Disguise in the Romantic Comedies." *ARIEL: A Review of International English Literature*, 9, No. 2 (1978), 23–39.

Jensen, Ejner J. "The Changing Faces of Love in English Renaissance Comedy." *Comparative Drama*, 6 (1972–73), 294–309.

Leggatt, Alexander. *Shakespeare's Comedy of Love*. London: Methuen, 1974.

Mowat, Barbara A. *The Dramaturgy of Shakespeare's Romances*. Athens: University of Georgia Press, 1976.

Nelson, Timothy, S.A. "The Rotten Orange: Fears of Marriage in Comedy from Shakespeare to Congreve." *Southern Review* (Adelaide), 8 (1975), 205–6.

Novy, Marianne L. "'And You Smile Not, He's Gagged': Mutuality in Shakespearean Comedy." *Philological Quarterly*, 55 (1976), 178–94.

———. "Recognition Scenes and Their Thematic Significance in Shakespeare's Romantic Comedies." *Dissertation Abstracts International*, 34 (1973), 3422A (Yale University).

Peter, Lilian Augustine. "Woman as Educative Guardian in Shakespeare's Comedies." *Dissertation Abstracts International*, 36 (1976), 7443A (Indiana University, 1975).

Phialas, Peter G. *Shakespeare's Romantic Comedies: The Development of Their Form and Meaning*. Chapel Hill: University of North Carolina Press, 1966.

Wheeler, Richard P. *Shakespeare's Development and the Problem Comedies: Turn and Counter-Turn*. Berkeley: University of California Press, 1980.

HISTORIES

Pierce, Robert B. *Shakespeare's History Plays: The Family and the State*. Columbus: Ohio State University Press, 1971.

TRAGEDIES

Bamber, Linda Vigderman. See above, *General*.

Heilman, Robert B. "Manliness in the Tragedies: Dramatic Variations." *Shakespeare 1564–1964: A Collection of Modern Essays*. Ed. Edward Bloom. Providence: Brown University Press, 1964, pp. 19–37.

Rackin, Phyllis. *Shakespeare's Tragedies*. New York: Frederick Ungar, 1978.

Stilling, Roger. *Love and Death in Renaissance Tragedy*. Baton Rouge: Louisiana State University Press, 1976.

INDIVIDUAL PLAYS AND OTHER WORKS

All's Well That Ends Well

Bennett, Josephine Waters. "New Techniques of Comedy in *All's Well That Ends Well*." *Shakespeare Quarterly*, 18 (1967), 337–62.

Bergeron, David M. "The Mythical Structure of *All's Well That Ends Well*." *Texas Studies in Literature and Language*, 14 (1973), 559–68.

Calderwood, James L. "The Mingled Yarn of *All's Well*." *Journal of English and Germanic Philology*, 62 (1963), 61–76.

Dennis, Carl. "*All's Well That Ends Well* and the Meaning of *Agape*." *Philological Quarterly*, 50 (1971), 75–84.

Everett, Barbara. Introduction. *All's Well That Ends Well*. Harmondsworth, Eng.: Penguin, 1970.

Gorfain, Phyllis. "Riddles and Reconciliation: Formal Unity in *All's Well That Ends Well*." *Journal of the Folklore Institute*, 13 (1976), 263–81.

Hill, W. Speed. "Marriage as Destiny: An Essay on *All's Well That Ends Well*." *English Literary Renaissance*, 5 (1975), 344–59.

Layman, B. J. "Shakespeare's Helena, Boccaccio's Giletta, and the Riddles of 'Skill' and 'Honesty.'" *English Miscellany*, 23 (1972), 39–53.

Magee, William H. "Helena, a Female Hamlet." *English Miscellany*, 22 (1971), 31–46.

Pearce, Frances N. "In Quest of Unity: A Study of Failure and Redemption in *All's Well That Ends Well*." *Shakespeare Quarterly*, 25 (1974), 71–88.

Ranald, Margaret Loftus. "The Betrothals of *All's Well That Ends Well*." *Huntington Library Quarterly*, 26 (1963), 179–82.

Shalvi, Alice. "The Pursuit of Honor in *All's Well That Ends Well*." *Studies in English Language and Literature* (Scripta Hierosolymitana), 17. Ed. Alice Shalvi and A. A. Mendilow. Jerusalem: Magnes Press, Hebrew University, 1966, pp. 9–34.

Shapiro, Michael. "'The Web of Our Life': Human Frailty and Mutual Redemption in *All's Well That Ends Well*." *Journal of English and Germanic Philology*, 71 (1972), 514–26.

Warren, Roger. "Why Does It End Well? Helena, Bertram, and the Sonnets." *Shakespeare Survey*, 22 (1969), 79–92.

Welsh, Alexander. "The Loss of Men and Getting of Children: 'All's Well That Ends Well' and 'Measure for Measure.'" *Modern Language Review*, 73 (1978), 17–28.

Wheeler, Richard P. "The King and the Physician's Daughter: *All's Well That Ends Well* and the Late Romances." *Comparative Drama*, 8 (1974–75), 311–27.

———. "Marriage and Manhood in *All's Well That Ends Well*." *Bucknell Review*, 21 (1973), 103–24.

Antony and Cleopatra

Adelman, Janet. *The Common Liar: An Essay on Antony and Cleopatra*. New Haven, Conn.: Yale University Press, 1973.

Barton, Anne. "*Nature's Piece 'Gainst Fancy": The Divided Catastrophe in "Antony and Cleopatra*." Inaugural Lecture, Bedford College. London: University of London, 1973.

Bonjour, Adrien. "From Shakespeare's Venus to Cleopatra's Cupids." *Shakespeare Survey*, 15 (1962), 73–80.

Donno, Elizabeth. "Cleopatra Again." *Shakespeare Quarterly*, 7 (1956), 227–33.

Dunbar, Georgia S. "The Verse Rhythms of Antony and Cleopatra." *Style*, 5 (1971), 231–45.

Fitz, L. T. "Egyptian Queens and Male Reviewers: Sexist Attitudes in *Antony and Cleopatra* Criticism." *Shakespeare Quarterly*, 28 (1977), 297–316.

Grindon, Rosa. *A Woman's Study of Antony and Cleopatra*. Manchester: Sherratt & Hughes, 1909.

Hamilton, Donna B. "*Antony and Cleopatra* and the Tradition of Noble Lovers." *Shakespeare Quarterly*, 24 (1973), 245–51.

Hapgood, Robert. "Hearing Shakespeare: Sound and Meaning in *Antony and Cleopatra*." *Shakespeare Survey*, 24 (1971), 1–12.

Harris, Duncan S. "'Again for Cydnus': The Dramaturgical Resolution of *Antony and Cleopatra*." *Studies in English Literature*, 17 (1977), 219–31.

Jamieson, Michael. See above, *General*.

Kuriyama, Constance Brown. "The Mother of the World: A Psychoanalytic Interpretation of Shakespeare's *Antony and Cleopatra*." *English Literary Renaissance*, 7 (1977), 324–51.

Lloyd, Michael. "Cleopatra as Isis." *Shakespeare Survey*, 12 (1959), 88–94.

Morris, Helen. "Queen Elizabeth I 'Shadowed' in Cleopatra." *Huntington Library Quarterly*, 32 (1969), 271–78.

Nevo, Ruth. "The Masque of Greatness." *Shakespeare Studies*, 3 (1968), 111–28.

Payne, Michael. "Erotic Irony and Polarity in *Antony and Cleopatra*." *Shakespeare Quarterly*, 24 (1973), 265–79.

Pearson, Norman Holmes. "*Antony and Cleopatra*," in *Shakespeare: of an Age for All Time*. Yale Shakespeare Festival Lectures, ed. Charles Tyler Prouty. Hamden, Conn.: Shoe String Press, 1954, pp. 125–147.

Rackin, Phyllis. "Shakespeare's Boy Cleopatra, the Decorum of Nature, and the Golden World of Poetry." *PMLA*, 87 (1972), 201–12.

Rinehart, Keith. "Shakespeare's Cleopatra and England's Elizabeth." *Shakespeare Quarterly*, 23 (1972), 81–86.

Schanzer, Ernest. "'Antony and Cleopatra' and The Countess of Pembroke's 'Antonius.'" *Notes and Queries*, 201, NS 3 (1956), 152–54.

Shapiro, Stephen A. "The Varying Shore of the World: Ambivalence in *Antony and Cleopatra*." *Modern Language Quarterly*, 27 (1966), 18–32.

Stirling, Brents. "Cleopatra's Scene with Seleucus: Plutarch, Daniel, and Shakespeare." *Shakespeare Quarterly*, 15 (1964), 299–311; rpt. in *Shakespeare 400*, ed. James G. McManaway, New York: Holt, Rinehart and Winston, 1964, pp. 299–311.

Stull, Joseph S. "Cleopatra's Magnanimity: The Dismissal of the Messenger." *Shakespeare Quarterly*, 7 (1956), 73–78.

Traci, Philip J. *The Love Play of Antony and Cleopatra*. The Hague: Mouton, 1970.

Williamson, Marilyn L. *Infinite Variety: Antony and Cleopatra in Renaissance Drama and Earlier Tradition*. Mystic, Conn.: L. Verry, 1974.

———. "Patterns of Development in *Antony and Cleopatra*." *Tennessee Studies in Literature*, 14 (1969), 129–39.

As You Like It

Beckman, Margaret Boerner. "The Figure of Rosalind in *As You Like It*." *Shakespeare Quarterly*, 29 (1978), 44–51.

Frey, Charles. "The Sweetest Rose: *As You Like It* as Comedy of Reconciliation." *New York Literary Forum*, 1 (1978), 167–83.

Kuhn, Maura Slattery. "Much Virtue in *If*," *Shakespeare Quarterly*, 28 (1977), 40–50.

Jamieson, Michael. See above, *General*.

Kelly, Thomas. "Shakespeare's Romantic Heroes: Orlando Reconsidered." *Shakespeare Quarterly*, 24 (1973), 12–24.

Comedy of Errors

Barber, C. L. "Shakespearean Comedy in *The Comedy of Errors*." *College English*, 25 (1964), 493–97.

Coriolanus

Adelman, Janet. "'Anger's My Meat': Feeding, Dependency, and Aggression in *Coriolanus*." *Shakespeare: Pattern of Excelling Nature*. Ed. David Bevington and Jay L. Halio. Newark: University of Delaware Press, 1978, pp. 108–24.

Berry, Ralph. "Sexual Imagery in *Coriolanus*." *Studies in English Literature*, 13 (1973), 301–16; rpt, with some alterations, in Ralph Berry, *Shakespearean Metaphor*, Totowa, N.J.: Rowman and Littlefield, 1978, pp. 88–100.

Bryan, Margaret B. "Volumnia—Roman Matron or Elizabethan Huswife." *Renaissance Papers*, 1972. Ed. Dennis G. Donovan and A. Leigh Deneef. Durham, N.C.: Southeastern Renaissance Conference, 1973, pp. 43–58.

Cymbeline

Carr, Joan. "*Cymbeline* and the Validity of Myth," *Studies in Philology*, 75 (1978), 316–30.

Camden, Carroll. "The Elizabethan Imogen." Rice Institute Pamphlet. *Studies in English*, 38, No. 1 (April 1951), 1–17.

Hamlet

Bligh, John. "The Women in the Hamlet Story." *Dalhousie Review*, 53 (1973), 275–85.

Camden, Carroll. "On Ophelia's Madness." *Shakespeare Quarterly*, 15, No. 2 (1964), 247–55; rpt. in *Shakespeare 400*, ed. James G. McManaway, New York: Holt, Rinehart and Winston, 1964, pp. 247–55.

Carlisle, Carol J. "Hamlet's 'Cruelty' in the Nunnery Scene: The Actors' Views." *Shakespeare Quarterly*, 18 (1967), 129–40.

Eissler, K. R. *Discourse on Hamlet and 'Hamlet'*. New York: International Universities Press, 1971.

Falk, Doris V. "Proverbs and the Polonius Destiny." *Shakespeare Quarterly*, 18 (1967), 23–36.

Heilbrun, Carolyn. "The Character of Hamlet's Mother." *Shakespeare Quarterly*, 8 (1957), 201–6.

Hogrefe, Pearl. "Artistic Unity in *Hamlet*." *Studies in Philology*, 46 (1949), 184–95.

Jenkins, Harold. "Hamlet and Ophelia." *Proceedings of the British Academy*, 49 (1963), 135–51.

Jofen, Jean B. "Two Mad Heroines: A Study of the Mental Disorders of Ophelia in *Hamlet* and Margarete in *Faust*." *Literature and Psychology*, 11 (1961), 70–71.

Klein, Joan Larsen. "'Angels and Ministers of Grace': *Hamlet* IV, v-vii." *Allegorica*, 1, No. 2 (1976), 156–76.

Leverenz, David. "The Woman in Hamlet: An Interpersonal View." *Signs*, 4 (1978), 291–308.

Lyons, Bridget Gellert. "The Iconography of Ophelia." *English Literary History*, 44 (1977), 60–74.

Maxwell, Baldwin. "Hamlet's Mother." *Shakespeare Quarterly*, 15 (1964), 235–46; rpt. in *Shakespeare 400*, ed. James G. McManaway, New York: Holt, Rinehart and Winston, 1964, pp. 235–46.

Nosworthy, J. M. "Hamlet and the Pangs of Love." *The Elizabethan Theatre*, IV. Ed. G. R. Hibbard. Hamden, Conn.: Shoe String Press, 1974, pp. 41–56.

Putzel, Rosamond. "Queen Gertrude's Crime." *Renaissance Papers*, *1961*. Ed. George Walton Williams. Durham, N.C.: Southeastern Renaissance Conference, 1962, pp. 37–46.

Seaman, John E. "The 'Rose of May' in the Unweeded Garden." *Études Anglaises*, 22 (1969), 337–45.

Seng, Peter J. "Ophelia's Songs in *Hamlet*." *Durham University Journal*, 56, NS 25 (1964), 77–85.

Shudofsky, M. Maurice. "Sarah Bernhardt on *Hamlet*." *College English*, 3 (1941), 293–95.

Tracy, Robert. "The Owl and the Baker's Daughter: A Note on *Hamlet* IV.v.42–43." *Shakespeare Quarterly*, 17 (1966), 83–86.

Wagner, Linda Welshimer. "Ophelia: Shakespeare's Pathetic Plot Device." *Shakespeare Quarterly*, 14 (1965), 94–97.

White, R. S. "The Tragedy of Ophelia." *ARIEL: A Review of International English Literature*, 9, No. 2 (1978), 41–53.

Henry IV

Bueler, Lois E. "Falstaff in the Eye of the Beholder." *Essays in Literature, University of Denver*, 1, No. 1 (1973), 1–12.

Roberts, Jeanne A. "Prince Hal as a Model for Professional Women." *Agnes Scott Alumnae Quarterly*, 52, No. 4 (1974), 6–12.

Henry V

Williamson, Marilyn L. "The Courtship of Katherine and the Second Tetralogy." *Criticism*, 17 (1975), 326–34.

Henry VI

Ashcroft, Dame Peggy. "Margaret of Anjou." *Shakespeare Jahrbuch* (Heidelberg), 1973, 7–9.

Bevington, David M. "The Domineering Female in *I Henry VI*." *Shakespeare Studies*, 2 (1966), 51–58.

Boas, Frederick S. "Joan of Arc in Shakespeare, Schiller, and Shaw." *Shakespeare Quarterly*, 2 (1951), 35–45.

Duncan-Jones, E. E. "Queen Katherine's Vision and Queen Margaret's Dream." *Notes and Queries*, 201, NS 8 (1961), 142–43.

French, A. L. "Joan of Arc and *Henry VI*." *English Studies*, 49 (1968), 425–29.

Williams, Gwyn. "Suffolk and Margaret: A Study of Some Sections of Shakespeare's *Henry VI*." *Shakespeare Quarterly*, 25 (1974), 310–33.

Windt, Judith H. "Not Cast in Other Womens Mold: Strong Women Characters in Shakespeare's *Henry VI* Trilogy, Drayton's *England's Heroical Epistles* and Jonson's Poems to Ladies." *Dissertation Abstracts International*, 35 (1974), 3777A–78A (Stanford University).

Henry VIII

Duncan-Jones, E. E. See above, *Henry VI*.

Julius Caesar

Faber, M. D. "Lord Brutus' Wife: A Modern View." *Psychoanalytic Review*, 52, No. 2 (1965), 109–15.

Velz, John W. "'Nothing Undervalued to Cato's Daughter': Plutarch's Porcia in the Shakespeare Canon." *Comparative Drama*, 11 (1977), 303–15.

Velz, John W., and Sarah C. Velz. "Publius, Mark Antony's Sister's Son." *Shakespeare Quarterly*, 26 (1975), 69–74.

King Lear

Alexander, Peter. "A Case of Three Sisters." *Times Literary Supplement*, 8 July 1965, p. 588. For response by S. F. Johnson see *TLS* 2 Sept. 1965, p. 761.

Blaydes, Sophia B. "Cordelia: Loss of Insolence." *Studies in the Humanities*, 5, No. 2 (1976), 15–21.

Craik, T. W. "Cordelia as 'Last and Least' of Lear's Daughters." *Notes and Queries*, 201, NS 3 (1956), 11.

Doran, Madeleine. "Elements in the Composition of *King Lear*." *Studies in Philology*, 30 (1933), 34–58.

Driscoll, James P. "The Vision of King Lear." *Shakespeare Studies*, 10 (1977), 159–89.

Dundes, Alan. "'To Love My Father All': A Psychoanalytic Study of the Folktale Source of *King Lear*." *Southern Folklore Quarterly*, 40 (1976), 353–66.

Greenfield, Thomas A. "Excellent Things in Women: The Emergence of Cordelia." *South Atlantic Bulletin*, 42, No. 1 (1977), 44–52.

Guyol, Hazel Sample. "A Temperance of Language: Goneril's Grammar and Rhetoric." *English Journal*, 55 (1966), 316–19.

Isenberg, Arnold. "Cordelia Absent." *Shakespeare Quarterly*, 2 (1951), 185–94.

Jayne, Sears. "Charity in *King Lear*." *Shakespeare Quarterly*, 15 (1964), 277–88.

Melchior, Barbara. "'Still Harping on My Daughter.'" *English Miscellany*, 11 (1960), 59–74.

Novy, Marianne. "Patriarchy, Mutuality, and Forgiveness in *King Lear*." *Southern Humanities Review*, 13 (1979), 281–92.

Oates, Joyce Carol. "'Is This the Promised End?' The Tragedy of *King Lear*." *Journal of Aesthetics and Art Criticism*, 33 (1974), 19–32.

Reid, Stephen. "In Defense of Goneril and Regan." *American Imago*, 27 (1970), 226–44.

Love's Labour's Lost

Montrose, Louis A. "'Sport by sport o'erthrown': *Love's Labour's Lost* and the Politics of Play." *Texas Studies in Language and Literature*, 18 (1977), 528–52.

Nelson, Timothy G. A. "The Meaning of *Love's Labour's Lost*." *Southern Review* (Adelaide), 4 (1971), 179–91.

Roesen, Bobbyann. "*Love's Labour's Lost.*" *Shakespeare Quarterly*, 4 (1953), 411–26.

Macbeth

Barron, David B. "The Babe That Milks: An Organic Study of Macbeth." *American Imago*, 17 (1960), 133–61.

Biggins, Dennis. "Sexuality, Witchcraft, and Violence in *Macbeth.*" *Shakespeare Studies*, 8 (1975), 255–77.

Boyd, Catherine Bradshaw. "The Isolation of Antigone and Lady Macbeth." *Classical Journal*, 47 (1952), 174–77, 203.

Carlisle, Carol J. "The Macbeths and the Actors." *Renaissance Papers: 1958, 1959, 1960*. Ed. George Walton Williams. Durham, N.C.: Southeastern Renaissance Conference, 1961, pp. 46–57.

Donohue, Joseph W., Jr. "Kemble and Mrs. Siddons in *Macbeth*: The Romantic Approach to Tragic Character." *Theatre Notebook*, 22 (1968), 65–86.

Elliott, Leigh-Noel M. *Lady Macbeth: A Study*. London: Wyman, 1884.

Ewbank, Inga-Stina. "The Fiend-Like Queen: A Note on 'Macbeth' and Seneca's 'Medea.'" *Shakespeare Survey*, 19 (1966), 82–94.

French, Marilyn. "Macbeth at My Lai: A Study of the Value Structure of Shakespeare's *Macbeth.*" *Soundings*, 58 (1975), 54–68.

Goode, Bill. "How Little the Lady Knew Her Lord: A Note on *Macbeth.*" *American Imago*, 20 (1963), 349–56.

Major, Tamás. "Lady Macbeth—The Stage Manager's Letter to the Actress." *New Hungarian Quarterly*, 5 (Spring 1964) 68–70.

Merchant, W. Moelwyn. "'His Fiend-Like Queen.'" *Shakespeare Survey*, 19 (1966), 75–81.

Ramsey, Jarold. "The Perversion of Manliness in *Macbeth.*" *Studies in English Literature*, 13 (1973), 285–300.

Sadler, Lynn Veach. "The Three Guises of Lady Macbeth." *College Language Association Journal*, 19 (1975), 10–19.

"Sarah Siddons as Lady Macbeth: Two Contemporary Accounts." *Theatre Quarterly*, 1, No. 3 (1971), 25–26.

Taylor, Michael. "Ideals of Manhood in *Macbeth.*" *Études Anglaises* 21 (1968), 337–48.

Williams, Edith Whitehurst. "In Defense of Lady Macbeth." *Shakespeare Quarterly*, 24 (1973), 221–23.

Measure for Measure

Birje-Patil, J. "Marriage Contracts in *Measure for Measure.*" *Shakespeare Studies*, 5 (1969), 106–11.

Diffey, Carole T. "The Last Judgment in *Measure for Measure.*" *Durham University Journal*, 35 (1974), 231–37.

Geckle, George L. "Shakespeare's Isabella." *Shakespeare Quarterly*, 22 (1971), 163–68.

Greco, Anne. "A Due Sincerity." *Shakespeare Studies*, 6 (1970), 151–73.

Harding, Davis P. "Elizabethan Betrothals and *Measure for Measure*." *Journal of English and Germanic Philology*, 49 (1950), 139–58.

Hyman, Lawrence W. "Mariana and Shakespeare's Theme in *Measure for Measure*." *University Review*, 31 (1964), 123–27.

Leech, Clifford. "'More Than Our Brother Is Our Chastity.'" *Critical Quarterly*, 12 (1970), 73–74.

Nagarajan, S. "*Measure for Measure* and Elizabethan Betrothals." *Shakespeare Quarterly*, 14 (1963), 115–19.

Owen, Lucy. "Mode and Character in *Measure for Measure*." *Shakespeare Quarterly*, 25 (1974), 17–32.

Skura, Meredith. "New Interpretations for Interpretation in *Measure for Measure*." *Boundary 2*, 7, No. 2 (1979), 39–59.

Smith, Gordon Ross. "Isabella and Elbow in Varying Contexts of Interpretation." *Journal of General Education*, 17 (1965), 63–78.

Trombetta, James. "Versions of Dying in *Measure for Measure*." *English Literary Renaissance*, 6 (1976), 60–76.

Welsh, Alexander. See above, *All's Well That Ends Well*.

Merchant of Venice

Hamill, Monica J. "Poetry, Law, and the Pursuit of Perfection: Portia's Role in *The Merchant of Venice*." *Studies in English Literature*, 18 (1978), 229–43.

Hill, R. F. "'The Merchant of Venice' and the Pattern of Romantic Comedy." *Shakespeare Survey*, 28 (1975), 75–87.

Jiji, Vera M. "Portia Revisited: The Influence of Unconscious Factors upon Theme and Characterization in *The Merchant of Venice*." *Literature and Psychology*, 26 (1976), 5–15.

Novy, Marianne. "Giving, Taking, and the Role of Portia in *The Merchant of Venice*." *Philological Quarterly*, forthcoming.

Pearlman, E. "Shakespeare's Freud and the Two Usuries, or, Money's a Meddler." *English Literary Renaissance*, 2 (1972), 217–36.

Sklar, Elizabeth S. "Bassanio's Golden Fleece." *Texas Studies in Literature and Language*, 18 (1976), 500–9.

Smith, Fred Manning. "Shylock on the Rights of Jews and Emilia on the Rights of Women." *West Virginia University Bulletin*, Series 47, No. 11.I, Philological Papers, Vol. 5 (May 1947), 32–33.

The Merry Wives of Windsor

Bruce, Dorothy Hart. "*The Merry Wives* and Two Brethren." *Studies in Philology*, 39 (1942), 265–78.

Carroll, William. "'A Received Belief': Imagination in *The Merry Wives of Windsor*." *Studies in Philology*, 74 (1977), 186–215.

Grindon, Rosa. *In Praise of Shakespeare's Merry Wives of Windsor*. Manchester: Sherratt & Hughes, 1902.

Haller, Eleanor Jean. "The Realism of *The Merry Wives*." *West Virginia University Bulletin*, Series 37, No. 11.I, West Virginia University Studies, III, Philological Papers, Vol. 2 (May 1937), 32–38.
Roberts, Jeanne Addison. *Shakespeare's English Comedy: "The Merry Wives of Windsor" in Context*. Lincoln: University of Nebraska Press, 1978.

A Midsummer Night's Dream

Faber, M. D. "Hermia's Dream: Royal Road to *A Midsummer Night's Dream*." *Literature and Psychology*, 22 (1972), 179–90.
Lewis, Allan. "*A Midsummer Night's Dream*—Fairy Fantasy or Erotic Nightmare?" *Educational Theater Journal*, 21 (1969), 251–58.
Nemerov, Howard. "The Marriage of Theseus and Hippolyta." *Kenyon Review*, 18 (1956), 633–41.
Pearson, D'Orsay W. "'Unkinde' Theseus: A Study in Renaissance Mythography." *English Literary Renaissance*, 4 (1974), 276–98.

Much Ado about Nothing

Barker, Clive. "Marxist Interpretation of Shakespeare: A Director's Comments." *Shakespeare Jahrbuch* (Weimar), 114 (1978), 115–22.
Blythe, David. "Beatrice's 'Clod of Wayward Marl.'" *Notes and Queries*, 25, No. 2 (1978), 134.
Crighton, Andrew B. "Hercules Shaven: A Centering Mythic Metaphor in *Much Ado about Nothing*." *Texas Studies in Language and Literature*, 16 (1975), 619–26.
Dennis, Carl. "Wit and Wisdom in *Much Ado about Nothing*." *Studies in English Literature*, 13 (1973), 223–37.
Everett, Barbara. "*Much Ado about Nothing*." *Critical Quarterly*, 3 (1961), 319–35.
Gardner, C. O. "Beatrice and Benedick." *Theoria*, 49 (1977), 1–17.
Prouty, Charles T. "The Sources of *Much Ado about Nothing*: A Critical Study, Together with the Text of Peter Beverley's *Ariodanto and Ieneura*." New Haven, Conn.: Yale University Press, 1950.
Rose, Steven. "Love and Self-Love in *Much Ado about Nothing*." *Essays in Criticism*, 20 (1970), 143–50.
Shapiro, Susan C. "The Originals of Shakespeare's Beatrice and Hero." *Notes and Queries*, 25, No. 2 (1978), 133–34.

Othello

Adamowski, T. H. "The Aesthetic Attitude and Narcissism in *Othello*." *Literature and Psychology*, 18 (1968), 73–81.
Baker, Harry T. "The Fair Cassio." *Philological Quarterly*, 6 (1927), 89–90.
Bayley, John. *The Characters of Love: A Study in the Literature of Person-*

ality. New York: Basic Books, and London: Constable, 1960, pp. 127–201.

Bishop, Sharon. "Another Look at Desdemona, Heroine of Dry Dreams." *Paunch*, 23 (1965), 5–9.

Boose, Lynda Elizabeth. "'Lust in Action': *Othello* as Shakespeare's Tragedy of Human Sexuality." *Dissertation Abstracts International*, 37 (1977), 7136A-7137A (University of California, Los Angeles, 1976).

———. "Othello's Handkerchief: 'The Recognizance and Pledge of Love.'" *English Literary Renaissance*, 5 (1975), 360–74.

Camden, Carroll. "Iago on Women." *Journal of English and Germanic Philology*, 48 (1949), 57–71.

Doran, Madeleine. "Good Name in *Othello*." *Studies in English Literature*, 7 (1967), 195–217.

Everett, Barbara. "Reflections on the Sentimentalist's *Othello*." *Critical Quarterly*, 3 (1961), 127–39.

Fraser, John. "*Othello* and Honour." *Critical Review* (Melbourne), 8 (1965), 59–70.

Garner, S. N. "Shakespeare's Desdemona." *Shakespeare Studies*, 9 (1976), 233–52.

Greene, Gayle. "'This That You Call Love': Sexual and Social Tragedy in *Othello*." *Journal of Women's Studies in Literature*, 1 (1979), 16–32.

Hodgson, John A. "Desdemona's Handkerchief as an Emblem of her Reputation." *Texas Studies in Language and Literature*, 19 (1977), 313–22.

Kirsch, Arthur. "The Polarization of Erotic Love in 'Othello.'" *Modern Language Review*, 73 (1978), 721–40.

Klene, Jean, C.S.C. "*Othello*: A fixed figure of the time of scorn." *Shakespeare Quarterly*, 26 (1975), 139–50.

Ranald, Margaret Loftus. "The Indiscretions of Desdemona." *Shakespeare Quarterly*, 14 (1963), 127–39.

Reid, Stephen. "Desdemona's Guilt." *American Imago*, 27 (1970), 245–62.

Smith, Fred Manning. See above, *Merchant of Venice*.

Snyder, Susan. "*Othello* and the Conventions of Romantic Comedy." *Renaissance Drama*, NS 5 (1972). Ed. S. Schoenbaum and Alan C. Dessen. Evanston, Ill.: Northwestern University Press (1974), 123–41.

Stockholder, Katherine S. "Egregiously an Ass: Chance and Accident in *Othello*." *Studies in English Literature*, 13 (1973), 256–72.

Wiley, Elizabeth. "The Tragedy of Underestimation: The Status of Women in *Othello*." *Susquehanna University Studies*, 7 (1964), 133–49.

Pericles: Prince of Tyre

Barber, C. L. "'Thou that beget'st him that did thee beget': Transformation in 'Pericles' and 'The Winter's Tale.'" *Shakespeare Survey*, 22 (1969), 59–67.

Flower, Annette C. "Disguise and Identity in *Pericles, Prince of Tyre*." *Shakespeare Quarterly*, 26 (1975), 30–41.

Melchior, Barbara. See above, *King Lear*.

The Rape of Lucrece

Allen, P. C. "Some Observations on *The Rape of Lucrece*." *Shakespeare Survey*, 15 (1962), 89–98.

Hulse, S. Clark. "'A Piece of Skilful Painting' in Shakespeare's 'Lucrece.'" *Shakespeare Survey*, 31 (1978), 13–22.

Kahn, Coppélia. "The Rape of Shakespeare's *Lucrece*." *Shakespeare Studies*, 9 (1976), 45–72.

Richard III

Tanner, Stephen L. "Richard III versus Elizabeth: An Interpretation." *Shakespeare Quarterly*, 24 (1973), 468–72.

Romeo and Juliet

Diverres, A. H. "The Pyramus and Thisbe Story and Its Contribution to the Romeo and Juliet Legend." *The Classical Tradition in French Literature: Essays Presented to R. C. Knight*. Ed. H. T. Barnwell et al. London: Grant and Cutler, 1977, pp. 9–22.

Everett, Barbara. "*Romeo and Juliet*: The Nurse's Story." *Critical Quarterly*, 14 (1972), 129–39.

Fliess, Elenore Stratton, and Robert Fliess. "Shakespeare's Juliet and Her Nurse." *American Imago*, 33 (1976), 244–60.

Nardo, Anna K. "Romeo and Juliet Up Against the Wall." *Paunch*, 48/49 (1977), 126–32.

Stevens, Martin. "Juliet's Nurse: Love's Herald." *Papers on Language and Literature*, 2 (1966), 195–206.

Sonnets

Fiedler, Leslie A. "Some Contexts of Shakespeare's Sonnets." *The Riddle of Shakespeare's Sonnets*. Ed. Edward Hubler. New York: Basic Books, 1962, pp. 55–90.

Mahood, M. M. "Love's Confined Doom." *Shakespeare Survey*, 15 (1962), 50–61.

Martin, Philip J. *Shakespeare's Sonnets: Self, Love, and Art*. Cambridge, Eng.: Cambridge University Press, 1972.

Neely, Carol Thomas. "The Structure of English Renaissance Sonnet Sequences." *ELH*, 45 (1978), 359–89.

Wheeler, Richard P. "Poetry and Fantasy in Shakespeare's Sonnets 88–96." *Literature and Psychology*, 22 (1972), 151–62.

Warren, Roger. See above, *All's Well That Ends Well*.

The Taming of the Shrew

Bergeron, David M. "The Wife of Bath and Shakespeare's *The Taming of the Shrew*." *University Review*, 35 (1969), 279–86.

Heilman, Robert B. "The *Taming* Untamed, or, The Return of the Shrew." *Modern Language Quarterly*, 27 (1966), 147–61.

Henze, Richard. "Role Playing in *The Taming of the Shrew*." *Southern Humanities Review*, 4 (1970), 231–40.

Hibbard, George R. "*The Taming of the Shrew*: A Social Comedy." *Shakespearean Essays*. Ed. Alwin Thaler and Norman Sanders. Special No. 2 of *Tennessee Studies in Literature*. Knoxville: University of Tennessee Press, 1964, pp. 15–28.

Jayne, Sears. "The Dreaming of *The Shrew*." *Shakespeare Quarterly*, 17 (1966), 41–56.

Kahn, Coppélia. "*The Taming of the Shrew*: Shakespeare's Mirror of Marriage." *Modern Language Studies*, 5 (1975), 88–102; rpt. in *The Authority of Experience: Essays in Feminist Criticism*, ed. Arlyn Diamond and Lee R. Edwards, Amherst: University of Massachusetts Press, 1977, pp. 84–100.

Novy, Marianne. "Patriarchy and Play in *The Taming of the Shrew*." *English Literary Renaissance*, 9 (1979), 264–80.

Pedersen, Lise. "Shakespeare *The Taming of the Shrew* vs. Shaw's *Pygmalion*: Male Chauvinism vs. Women's Lib." *Fabian Feminist: Bernard Shaw and Women*. Ed. Rodelle Weintraub. University Park: Pennsylvania State University Press, 1977, 14–22.

Ranald, Margaret Loftus. "The Manning of the Haggard; or *The Taming of the Shrew*." *Essays in Literature* (Western Illinois University), 1 (1974), 149–65.

Schleiner, Winfried. "Deromanticizing the Shrew: Notes on Teaching Shakespeare in a 'Women in Literature' Course." *Teaching Shakespeare*. Ed. Walter Edens et al. Princeton, N.J.: Princeton University Press, 1977, pp. 79–82.

The Tempest

Berger, Harry, Jr. "Miraculous Harp: A Reading of Shakespeare's *Tempest*." *Shakespeare Studies*, 5 (1969), 253–83.

Melchior, Barbara. See above, *King Lear*.

Sturgiss, Marie H. "Shakespeare's Miranda." *Shakespeare Association Bulletin*, 10 (1935), 36–44.

Titus Andronicus

Willbern, David. "Rape and Revenge in *Titus Andronicus.*" *English Literary Renaissance,* 8 (1978), 159–82.

Troilus and Cressida

Asp, Carolyn. "In Defense of Cressida." *Studies in Philology,* 74 (1977), 406–17.

de Almeida, Barbara Heliodora C. de M. F. "*Troilus and Cressida:* Romantic Love Revisited." *Shakespeare Quarterly,* 15 (1964), 327–32.

Lyons, Clifford P. "The Trysting Scenes in *Troilus and Cressida.*" *Shakespearean Essays.* Ed. Alwin Thaler and Norman Sanders. Special No. 2 of *Tennessee Studies in Literature.* Knoxville: University of Tennessee Press, 1964, pp. 105–20.

Newlin, Jeanne T. "The Darkened Stage: J. P. Kemble and *Troilus and Cressida.*" *The Triple Bond: Plays Mainly Shakespearean in Performance.* Ed. Joseph G. Price. University Park: Pennsylvania State University Press, 1975, pp. 190–202.

Roy, Emil. "War and Manliness in Shakespeare's *Troilus and Cressida.*" *Comparative Drama,* 7 (1973), 107–20.

Shaw, George Bernard. "Shaw's 1884 Lecture on *Troilus and Cressida.*" Ed. Louis Crompton and Hilayne Cavanaugh. *The Shaw Review,* 14 (1971), 48–67.

Voth, Grant L., and Oliver H. Evans. "Cressida and the World of the Play." *Shakespeare Studies,* 8 (1975), 231–39.

Yoder, R. A. "'Sons and Daughters of the Game': An Essay on Shakespeare's 'Troilus and Cressida.'" *Shakespeare Survey,* 25 (1972), 11–25.

Twelfth Night

Draper, John W. "The Wooing of Olivia." *Neophilologus,* 23 (1937), 37–46.

Fortin, René E. "*Twelfth Night:* Shakespeare's Drama of Initiation." *Papers on Language and Literature,* 8 (1972), 135–46.

Huston, J. Dennis. "'When I Came to Man's Estate': *Twelfth Night* and Problems of Identity." *Modern Language Quarterly,* 33 (1972), 274–88.

Moglen, Helene. "Disguise and Development: The Self and Society in *Twelfth Night.*" *Literature and Psychology,* 23 (1973), 13–19.

Taylor, Anthony Brian. "Shakespeare and Golding: Viola's Interview with Olivia and Echo and Narcissus." *English Language Notes,* 15 (1977), 103–6.

Two Gentlemen of Verona

Ewbank, Inga-Stina. "'Were man but constant, he were perfect': Constancy and Consistency in *The Two Gentlemen of Verona*." *Shakespearen Comedy*. Ed. Malcolm Bradbury and David Palmer. *Stratford-upon-Avon Studies*, 14. New York: Crane, Russak, 1972.

Stephenson, William E. "The Adolescent Dream-World of *The Two Gentlemen of Verona*." *Shakespeare Quarterly*, 17 (1966), 165–68.

Venus and Adonis

Asals, Heather. "*Venus and Adonis*: The Education of a Goddess." *Studies in English Literature*, 13 (1973), 31–51.

Bradbrook, Muriel C. "Beasts and Gods: Greene's *Groats-worth of Witte* and the Social Purpose of *Venus and Adonis*." *Shakespeare Survey*, 15 (1962), 62–72.

Kahn, Coppélia. "Self and Eros in *Venus and Adonis*." *The Centennial Review*, 20 (1976), 351–71.

Rabkin, Norman. "*Venus and Adonis* and the Myth of Love." *Pacific Coast Studies in Shakespeare*. Ed. Waldo F. McNeir and Thelma N. Greenfield. Eugene: University of Oregon Books, 1966, pp. 20–31.

Rebhorn, Wayne, A. "Mother Venus: Temptation in Shakespeare's *Venus and Adonis*." *Shakespeare Studies*, 11 (1978), 1–19.

The Winter's Tale

Asp, Carolyn. "Shakespeare's Paulina and the *Consolatio* Tradition." *Shakespeare Studies*, 11 (1978), 145–58.

Barber, C. L. See above, *Pericles: Prince of Tyre*.

Estrin, Barbara L. "The Foundling Plot: Stories in *The Winter's Tale*." *Modern Language Studies*, 7 (1977), 27–38.

Frey, Charles. *Shakespeare's Vast Romance: A Study of the Winter's Tale*. Columbia: University of Missouri Press, 1980.

———. "Tragic Structure in *The Winter's Tale*: The Affective Dimension." *Shakespeare's Romances Reconsidered*. Ed. Carol McGinnis Kay and Henry E. Jacobs. Lincoln: University of Nebraska Press, 1978, pp. 113–24.

Gourlay, Patricia Southard. "'O my most sacred lady.' Female Metaphor in *The Winter's Tale*." *English Literary Renaissance*, 5 (1975), 375–95.

Jamieson, Michael. See above, *General*.

Kiessling, Nicolas K. "*The Winter's Tale*, II, iii, 103–7: An Allusion to the Hag-Incubus." *Shakespeare Quarterly*, 28 (1977), 93–95.

Lindenbaum, Peter. "Time, Sexual Love, and the Uses of Pastoral in *The Winter's Tale*." *Modern Language Quarterly*, 33 (1972), 3–22.

Melchior, Barbara. See above, *King Lear*.

Neely, Carol Thomas. *"The Winter's Tale*: The Triumph of Speech." *Studies in English Literature*, 15 (1975), 321–38.

———. "Women and Issue in *The Winter's Tale*." *Philological Quarterly*, 57 (1978), 181–94.

Schwartz, Murray M. "Leontes' Jealousy in *The Winter's Tale*." *American Imago*, 30 (1973), 250–73.

———. *"The Winter's Tale*: Loss and Transformation." *American Imago*, 32 (1975), 145–99.

Contributors

JOHN C. BEAN received a B.A. from Stanford University in 1965 and a Ph.D. from the University of Washington in 1972, and is currently an Associate Professor of English at Montana State University, Bozeman. He has examined extensively the relationships between rational and daimonic forms of love in Shakespeare's comedies and in Spenser's *Faerie Queene* in articles for *Wascana Review*, *Studies in English Literature*, and *Modern Language Quarterly*. He has also published articles on Shelley and John Barth. In 1977 he was co-chairperson with Coppélia Kahn of the MLA Special Session on "Marriage and the Family in Shakespeare."

PAULA S. BERGGREN, educated at Barnard College and Yale University, is currently Assistant Professor of English at Baruch College of the City University of New York. She has published articles on Elizabethan and Jacobean drama in various periodicals, including *Studies in English Literature* and the *International Journal of Women's Studies*, and is working on a study of the English dramatic heroine in male disguise.

IRENE G. DASH has an M.A. in Modern Drama and a Ph.D. in Shakespeare and Literature from Columbia University. She currently teaches English and women's studies at Hunter College, CUNY. Her articles have appeared in *Shakespeare Quarterly* and *Shakespeare Studies*, in *The Lost Tradition: Mothers and Daughters in Literature*, and elsewhere, and she has given talks on women's studies and Shakespeare at conferences. She is completing a book on women in Shakespeare.

CHARLES FREY received a J.D. from Harvard University and a Ph.D. from Yale University and is Associate Professor of English at the University of Washington. He has published articles on Shakespeare, *Beowulf*, medieval lyric, and children's literature in *Shakespeare Studies*, *Shakespeare Quarterly*, *ELH*, *English Studies*, and other journals. His book, *Shakespeare's Vast Romance: A Study of the Winter's Tale*, was published by the University of Missouri Press in 1980.

MADELON GOHLKE was educated at Bryn Mawr College, where she received her A.B. in 1964, and at Yale University from which she received her Ph.D in 1972. She has taught at Middlebury College and is now Associate Professor of English at the University of Minnesota. She has published articles on Lyly, Spenser, and Nashe and is currently writing a book on femininity in Shakespeare.

GAYLE GREENE, educated at the University of California at Berkeley and at Columbia University, where she received her Ph.D., is currently Associate Professor of English at Scripps College, Claremont, California. She has articles on Shakespeare published or forthcoming in various periodicals, including *Journal of Women's Studies in Literature*, *Studia Neophilologica*, *Renaissance Drama*, and *Studies in English Literature*, and is currently working on Doris Lessing and on feminist and Marxist criticism.

JANICE HAYS entered the University of California at Berkeley as an adult student and received her B.A. in 1968 and her Ph.D. in 1978. She has taught at San Francisco State and is currently an Assistant Professor of English at Skidmore College. She has given papers on Shakespeare, women's drama, and composition at conferences, and her book of poems, *New House—A Book of Women*, was published by San Marco Press in 1972.

COPPÉLIA KAHN received her Ph.D. from the University of California at Berkeley and teaches English at Wesleyan University. She has published articles on *Venus and Adonis*, *Lucrece*, and *The Taming of the Shrew*, and her book, *Man's Estate: Masculine Identity in Shakespeare*, will be published by the University of California Press in 1980. She also edited, with Murray Schwartz, *Representing Shakespeare*, an anthology of psychoanalytic criticism of Shakespeare published by Johns Hopkins University Press in 1980.

JOAN LARSEN KLEIN received her A.B. from the University of Michigan and her Ph.D. from Harvard University. She is presently an Associate Professor of English at the University of Illinois at Urbana-Champaign. She has published several articles on *Hamlet* and *The Faerie Queene*.

LORIE JERRELL LEININGER received her Ph.D. from the University of Massachusetts at Amherst and has taught there and at American International College, the University of Kansas City, the University of California at Berkeley, and Bucknell University. Her publications include short stories and an article, "Cracking the Code of *The Tempest*," in the *Bucknell Review*. She is currently working on a life of Elizabeth Stuart, on a monograph on Frances Howard, the seventeenth-century "lustful murderess," and on a study of the political contexts of witchcraft in sixteenth-century Scotland.

CAROLYN RUTH SWIFT LENZ received her doctorate from Brown University. She is a Professor at Rhode Island College and has published articles about the teaching of drama, Thomas Tallis, Martin Luther, and John Lyly. She initiated the MLA Special Session, "Feminist Criticism of Shakespeare," has given talks on this topic, and is currently writing a book about the plays of John Lyly.

CAROLE MCKEWIN received her doctorate in English from the University of Maryland in 1977 after several years of teaching for Maryland's University College in the United States, England, and Germany. She has lectured and published on women in Renaissance drama, and recently conducted an interdisciplinary seminar in Wiesbaden, Germany on filmic images of women. The teaching of Shakespeare's contemporaries in production, and a study of the women in Ben Jonson's comedies, are her current projects at the University of Delaware. Her review article on feminist criticism of Shakespeare appeared in *Mosaic X*.

MADONNE MINER, a Woodburn fellow at SUNY-Buffalo, is working toward a doctoral degree in English with women's studies as a supporting—and ever informing—field of interest. While engaged in the usual round of graduate seminars, she also has participated in the difficult birth of a student-initiated course on feminist critical theory.

CAROL THOMAS NEELY received her Ph.D. from Yale University, and is an Associate Professor of English at Illinois State University. Her articles on Shakespeare's plays and sonnets and on Elizabethan sonnet sequences have appeared in *Shakespeare Studies*, *PMLA*, *ELH*, and other journals. She chaired the 1978 MLA Special Session, "Marriage and the Family in Shakespeare," has given talks at a number of conferences, and is at work on a study of women and marriage in Shakespeare.

MARIANNE NOVY is an Associate Professor of English at the University of Pittsburgh and also teaches in the women's studies program there. She received her Ph.D. from Yale in 1973 with a dissertation on Shakespeare's comedies. Her articles dealing with sex roles in Shakespeare have been published in *Philological Quarterly*, *English Literary Renaissance*, and *Southern Humanities Review*. She initiated the MLA special session on "Marriage and the Family in Shakespeare" and is interested in the relationships between Elizabethan family patterns, their psychological consequences, and Shakespeare's plays.

CLARA CLAIBORNE PARK was educated at Radcliffe and the University of Michigan and currently teaches at Williams College, where she received an honorary degree in 1976. She is the author of *The Siege: The First Eight Years of an Autistic Child* and *You are Not Alone: Understanding and Dealing with Mental Illness*, and has published articles on Trollope and the uses of literature in the community college. She writes reviews for the *Washington Post*, the *Nation*, and *Saturday Review*.

REBECCA SMITH received her M.A. from the University of Arkansas, Fayetteville, and her Ph.D. in 1975 from the University of Alberta. She has taught at the University of Prince Edward Island and is currently teaching at the University of Arkansas, Little Rock. She has written on Canadian theater history and women's literature, is a reviewer for *Branching Out*, a Canadian women's magazine, and is on the advisory board for *Atlantis*, an interdisciplinary women's magazine.

THE WOMAN'S PART

CATHARINE R. STIMPSON, the founding editor of *SIGNS: A Journal of Women in Culture and Society* and author of non-fiction and fiction, is Professor of English at Douglass College/Rutgers University. Her latest book is *Class Notes*, a novel (1979).

Index